Count Albert de Mun

Paladin of the Third Republic

Count Albert de Mun

Paladin of the Third Republic

Benjamin F. Martin

For Mamma and Daddy
Ben

Winston-Salem
Christmas Day, 1978

THE UNIVERSITY OF NORTH CAROLINA PRESS CHAPEL HILL

Manufactured in the United States of America
ISBN 0-8078-1325-7
Library of Congress Catalog Card Number 78-1739

Library of Congress Cataloging in Publication Data

Martin, Benjamin F., 1947–
Count Albert de Mun, paladin of the Third Republic.

Bibliography: p.
Includes index.
1. Mun, Albert, comte de, 1841–1914. 2. France—Politics and government—1870–1940. 3. Politicians—France—Biography. 4. Church and social problems—France. I. Title.
DC342.8.M8M34 320.9'44'081 [B] 78-1739
ISBN 0-8078-1325-7

For Those Who Are More Than Just Good Friends

Contents

Preface

My indebtedness to many people and organizations for their acts of kindness and assistance during the research and writing of this book is very great, and it is a delight finally to be able to thank them in print. I am particularly grateful to Prince Louis Murat, Madame Cl. Charles Duval, and Madame Delorme-Jules-Simon, who generously opened to my examination private papers in their possession. The Rev. Joseph Dehergne, S.J., of the Archives de la Société de Jésus, Province de Paris, and the Rev. Sauvage, S.J., of the Archives de l'Action Populaire in Vanves, and the staffs of the Archives Nationales, the Bibliothèque Nationale, and the Archives de la Préfecture de Police, Paris, greatly eased my tasks by allowing me extraordinarily untrammeled access to the documentary treasures in their charge. Their patience and endurance in dealing with an often impatient researcher will always be appreciated.

My pursuit of Albert de Mun would have been less stimulating and agreeable without the opportunity to discuss this project with the Rev. Guillaume de Bertier de Sauvigny, Abbé Charles Molette, Madame Gailhard-Bancel-Widerspach, Philippe Audollent, Jean Marie Mayeur, Philippe Levillain, George V. Taylor, Marvin L. Brown, Jr., Joan W. Scott, Norman M. Johnson, and John Raymond Walser. Joseph N. Moody and Eugen Weber graciously read an early manuscript of this biography and suggested important revisions. Lamar Cecil, who directed this study originally as a doctoral dissertation at the University of North Carolina, has patiently and closely examined every draft of it. His astute criticism and remarkable comprehension of the craft of biography have aided me in purging many flaws. Any that remain are, of course, entirely my own.

Matthew Hodgson, Lewis Bateman, Gwen Duffey, and Trudie Calvert of The University of North Carolina Press made the process of publishing my first book much less harrowing than I was prepared to believe. My research assistants at West Virginia Wesleyan College, Frances Rapking Piesbergen, Bonnie Lynn Gashlin, and particularly Debbie Grace King, greatly lightened the chores and brought order out of the chaos of typing and proofreading the manuscript and compiling an index. Worries about the financial difficulties involved in research abroad were largely dispelled by liberal fellowships from the Trustees of the John Motley Morehead and Georges Lurcy foundations. Grants from the Faculty Development Fund of West Virginia Wesleyan College underwrote the cost of preparing the final manuscript and contributed to defraying the expenses of publication.

My greatest debt is to my family and friends, whose encouragement made it possible for me to undertake this work and eventually to finish it.

Benjamin F. Martin
WEST VIRGINIA WESLEYAN COLLEGE
BUCKHANNON, WEST VIRGINIA

Acknowledgments

I am grateful to the following for permission to adapt and reprint material I first published with them: to the Society for French Historical Studies for "The Creation of the Action Libérale Populaire: An Example of Party Formation in Third Republic France," *French Historical Studies* 9 (Fall 1976): 660–89; to the Western Society for French History for "Albert de Mun, Charette, and the Appeal of Contre-Révolution," *Proceedings of the Western Society for French History* 4 (1977): 360–67; and to the Catholic University of America Press for "A Letter of Albert de Mun on the Papal Condemnation of the Sillon," *The Catholic Historical Review* 64 (January 1978): 47–50. I am indebted to Editions Bernard Grasset of 61, Rue des Saints-Pères, Paris, France, for permission to quote from Fernand Payen, *Raymond Poincaré: L'Homme, le parlementaire, l'avocat*, 6th ed. (Paris, 1936) and to Editions Beauchesne, 72, Rue des Saints-Pères, Paris, France, for permission to quote from Charles Molette, *Albert de Mun, 1872–1890: Exigence doctrinale et préoccupations sociales chez un laic catholique* (Paris, 1970).

Abbreviations

ACJF	Association Catholique de la Jeunesse Française
ACM	Archives Cercle Maurice Maignen
ALP	Action Libérale Populaire
AN	Archives Nationales
APP	Archives de la Préfecture de Police, Paris
ARD	Alliance Républicaine Démocratique
ASJ	Archives de la Société de Jésus, Paris Region
BN Naf	Bibliothèque Nationale, Nouvelles acquisitions françaises
CGT	Confédération Générale du Travail
JOAN	*Journal Officiel, Assemblée Nationale*
JOC	*Journal Officiel, Chambre des Députés, Débats Parlementaires*
JOCD	*Journal Officiel, Chambre des Députés, Documents Parlementaires*

Mise en Scène

The private chapels of the French châteaus are the most characteristic relics of an ancient code of honor, for it was within their walls that the nobility bore witness to a simultaneous worship of God and France. The floors are paved with stones on which square-limbed letters record forever the gallant death in battle of noble forebears. Here *Te Deums* were sung alike for the birth of heirs, the salvation of souls, and the triumph of French arms. Before Louis XIV converted many peers into frivolous ornaments of the monarchy at Versailles, the French nobility had been a warrior class, and since the time of the Albigensian crusade in the early thirteenth century it had tended to identify this profession of arms with service to God. Louis IX's martyr-death on the Seventh Crusade and his immediate canonization thereafter increased this sentiment, and it culminated in what appeared to be God's special instrument in French history, Jeanne d'Arc.

A nation's political elite determines the content of its ideology, and the blessing of God upon the endeavors of the French was institutionalized along with other ancien régime principles. Despite their frequent objections to the encroachments of royal power, the church anointed and crowned His Most Christian Majesty while the nobility fought under his banner. In turn the sovereign tempered his absolutism through the recognition of feudal and ecclesiastical privilege. The 1789 Revolution overturned these three pillars, and although the Restoration set them upright once more, the events of the preceding quarter century had seriously undermined the foundations upon which they rested. The Revolution acted as a catalyst to crystallize the latent spirit of egalitarianism that existed among large segments of the French people and opposed the monopoly of authority of nobility, clergy, and king. The nineteenth century witnessed an inexorable erosion of the political power of the old elites together with the concomitant ascent of various echelons of the former Third Estate, tenuously united in their efforts to demolish the traditional order.

The ideals and principles of this new elite, who were non-noble, nonroyal, and nonclerical, were in conscious opposition to those that had served as the base of the ancien régime. The destiny of France was now freed from the hand of God and rendered identical to that of the "people," whose will in turn was invested with a sanctity previously reserved for the deity. The modernization of warfare had long made a warrior nobility anachronistic, but France's new bourgeois masters despised while at the same time envying the honor of the past implicit in an aristocracy of birth. The new deification of the populace damned the church as the agent of oppression and belittled its role in the evolution of the nation. The firm establishment of the Third Republic by the 1880s made these principles the basis of government. Anticlericalism became a staple of republican rule, and membership in the nobility, unless disavowed, was an almost insurmountable obstacle in the pursuit of administrative position or parliamentary leadership. After 1830 the nobility generally ceased to play an important part in French politics. They acquiesced in their own overthrow by becoming *émigrés de l'intérieur*, retreating to their châteaus and salons to retain in the provincial and social world the eminence to which they could no longer aspire in the political. In the faubourg Saint-Germain and in ancestral demesnes, the nobility created an artificial world, the hauteur and exclusivity of which concealed their discomfiture at being impotent to guide the destiny of the nation. Barred from political leadership, the nobility rooted themselves in a sublime vision of past glories. They would have to wait in exile until such time as the sovereign people came to realize that France could regain its ancient glory only through a revival of the principles that had in happier times brought it to the pinnacle of power and civilization. While awaiting this summons, the nobility could do nothing more than fight desperate rear-guard actions to maintain their limited position.

The church, however, believed that it could not sit by and watch its traditional influence be destroyed, for its mission was divine and its authority therefore immune to the vagaries of political change. But French Catholics did not agree as to how the enemy might best be challenged and eventually defeated. The Roman curia and the papacy were inflexible in their militant reaffirmation of the church's attachment to the old order, and within France this uncompromising attitude was championed by the religious congregations and such Catholic publicists as the acerbic Louis Veuillot, whose *L'Univers* was the source of dogma to ultramontanes. Other French Catholics believed that intransigence would lead only to more reductions of the church's position. Despite major differences, Félicité de Lamennais, Charles de Montalembert, Alfred de Falloux, and the early social Catholics Armand de Melun and Frédéric Ozanam held that the church had no future unless it was prepared to seek an accommodation with the new order of society. Lamennais and Montalembert shared a conviction that kingship was not divinely ordained, and they reminded their clerical opponents that Old Testament kings had sorely tried the patience of the Lord and that Christ had declared that God and Caesar were not to be paid in the same coin. Instead of so radical a transformation of the church's tradition, Falloux sought a truce with France's new rulers. To this end he sponsored and achieved the passage of the Falloux law of 1850, which legitimized the church's preponderant role in primary and secondary education, in return for clerical support of the state. Melun and Ozanam disdained politics to concentrate on the plight of the poor. These two pioneers of Christian socialism argued that the church could not fulfill its mission if it continued to disregard the problems of the lower classes and merely contented itself with promising that the Christian reward for earthly suffering would be life everlasting in the world to come. At first these comparatively "liberal" tendencies were rejected by the dominant powers of the church. Pope Gregory XVI silenced Lamennais and sternly rebuked Montalembert. He also discouraged the social work of Melun and Ozanam although he did not condemn their solitary efforts. His successor, Pius IX, damned all who dreamed of reconciling the irreconcilables, the church and the modern world. His proclamation of the *Syllabus of Errors* in 1864 proved that the Vatican had neither learned nor forgotten anything. Only after the ascension of Leo XIII in 1878 did the ideas of the liberals receive a favorable hearing at the Holy See.

The general intransigence of the church and the nobility had consequences in France's government since the survivors of the old order, often in some combination of monarchism, formed the political Right. As power slipped relentlessly from them, their obduracy increased, and they refused to evolve into a responsible and loyal opposition. Instead, they engaged in unremitting antagonism toward every regime against which they were pitted. Ultras carped at Louis XVIII and even Charles X; Legitimists sniped at Louis Philippe; Orleanists and Bourbonites denounced Louis Napoleon; and after 1870 Bonapartists joined with the royalists to damn the Third Republic. These tactics were foolhardy, especially after the firm establishment of the Republic in 1879. The Right, Center, and Left commanded an approximately equal number of adherents, and because a union of the extremes was impossible, whichever group allied itself with the Center would become part of the governing majority. The defense of property and fiscal conservatism were issues on which the Right and Center could agree, but the refusal of right-wing leaders to attempt any reconciliation with the Republic compelled the Center to ally with the Left. To maintain this alliance, they were forced to make concessions to leftist demands, especially in the form of anticlericalism, which made the Republic still more repugnant to the Right.

This obtuseness revealed how politically unrealistic, even how fatuous, most members of the Right were. Many nursed their hatred of what France had become, and they preferred to defend hopeless principles, clericalism and monarchism, rather than seek an intelligent accommodation with reality, a free church in a conservative Republic. Their inability to compromise with the Center was paralleled by an inability to unite with each other, and throughout the nineteenth century the conservatives remained fragmented and faction-ridden, both a cause and an effect of poor leadership. Between the founding of the Third Republic and World War I the quality of this leadership dropped to its nadir as the capacity of the conservatives for self-delusion reached new depths. Those men of some ability and insight whom the Right did produce found their tasks insuperable because they faced the impossible duty of trying to lead a resolutely anachronous constituency of Catholic elitists in a world increasingly egalitarian and secular. It is the measure of the lack of capable rightist leaders that Count Albert de Mun would be the outstanding figure in the conservative ranks during this period. Visionary, emotional, always ready to take his hopes for reality, he would dream ceaselessly of "victory" but taste only defeat. His career was a tissue of bizarre contradictions, of political behavior that was occasionally so unrealistic that it can only be described as manifestly peculiar. He was an aristocrat who sought to build a popular party based on the masses, a fervid Catholic who would be undermined by his church, an idealist who did not scruple at illegal conspiracies, a patriot whose nation would reject his counsel until just before his death. He was untimely, even in comparison with some of his followers, and quixotic, perpetually tilting at windmills, almost quaint, hardly a man equipped to become a political leader. Yet such was the state of disarray among the conservatives that de Mun became their dominant force for almost forty years, summing up over the course of his life a period of profound political and social transformation for them. In the land of the sightless, even the purblind like de Mun have to lead.

Count Albert de Mun

Paladin of the Third Republic

I

Knight of the *Syllabus*

The village of Lumigny is located to the east of Paris, near the cathedral town of Meaux, in the flat plain of the Ile de France. Like their ancestors for countless centuries, the Lumignais still grow lettuce and shallots in the rich, moist earth, and the uncleared hardwood forests and tortuous roads testify that little has changed in the region besides the introduction of electricity and sewage. Beyond the northern fields there is a ruined castle that still betrays something of the grandeur of its prime more than a century ago. The Château de Mun was originally built for Louis XIV's minister Jean Baptiste Colbert in the seventeenth century and for two hundred years was expanded with additions. Some effort was made to emulate the Savoyard pleasure domes, and the wall moldings and variegated stone and brick show a definite Italianate influence. But the castle is unmistakably French, with a mansard roof, round spiked towers, and the air of Azay-le-Rideau. It stands unpretentiously in a grove of trees at the head of extensive grounds, and before fire and disuse in the twentieth century reduced it to a mere remnant, the château announced modestly but forcefully the high station of its possessor, the Marquis Adrien de Mun. Here on 28 February 1841, surrounded by midwives, priests, servants, and family, the marquise gave birth to her second son, Adrien Albert Marie. His father ordered a *Te Deum* sung immediately in the castle chapel.

Albert, as the child was called, was born a member of the *gratin*, the so-called crust of French society. His father's proud line emerged in the misty origins of the nobility with an Austor de Mun, who rode into Damietta alongside Louis IX in 1248 on the Seventh Crusade. But even before that time the family had acquired stature in the Bigorre region of Gascony at the foot of the Pyrenees, where their name came from a dialect usage of the word *moun*, a reference to the commanding position of the village in which they resided. The family rose to prominence through military exploits in the service of the king and celebrated their elevation to the dignity and position of count through the adoption of the motto *Servir* and the erection of a feudal castle and chapel in the twelfth century. Their dominance did not remain uncontested. Both buildings were destroyed in the bloody Gascon wars of religion in which many nobles exploited Protestantism to make the region a center of resistance to royal control. As partisans of king and church, the de Muns did not fare well. At the conclusion of the struggle, when the power of the throne was firmly established, the family raised a new castle and chapel on the ruins of the old and continued their traditional mode of existence. They resisted the Siren call of Versailles and remained in the provinces at their base of power. As they had done for centuries, they were content to develop their lands while sending sons to fight in His Most Christian Majesty's wars and daughters to pray in Our Lord's convents.

This life of isolation changed abruptly under Albert de Mun's great-grandfather, Alexandre-François de Mun. After winning rank and fame in the Seven Years' War, he took up residence at Versailles and in 1772 contracted a lucrative marriage with a daughter of the wealthy philosophe Helvétius, Elizabeth Charlotte, whose dowry was the demesne of Lumigny. The acquisition of an additional estate posed a difficult question for Alexandre-François, whether or not to make permanent his separation from the family's original lands. His own taste, and that of his new bride, made it almost inevitable that he would choose to settle at Lumigny. His branch of the family would henceforth forsake the south to move near Paris, where they might take a vastly expanded part in society and politics. This possibility was fulfilled in the single heir of the marriage, Claude Adrien, born in 1773. An émigré though a liberal in 1789, a lover of Madame de Staël in 1792, Claude Adrien managed to charm all, including Bonaparte, who granted him privileges and a position in the Napoleonic nobility, culminating in the Legion of Honor in 1811. So adroit was his political footwork that the Restoration caused him no discomfiture. In 1815, Louis XVIII created him marquis and hereditary peer and reconfirmed him in the Legion of Honor. Until his death in 1843 he sat in the Chamber of Peers.

His own son, Adrien, was the antithesis of this Enlightenment father. Born in 1817, he shared the romanticism of many others of his generation. Where the elder de Mun was urbane, superficial, politically promiscuous, and skeptical in religion, Adrien was an intense Legitimist and an ultramontane Catholic. His character seems to have been molded by his mother, the Duchess Emilie d'Ursel, a very distant descendant of Mary Stuart, closely related to some of the most ancient houses of France, and decidedly against her son's reproducing his father's image. In 1838 Adrien married Eugénie de La Ferronnays, who like himself was intensely devout. It was a love match in the Romantic tradition that captivated Adrien throughout his life, but also an advantageous one. The La Ferronnays family, Breton nobility whose prowess in arms and devotion in religion were legendary, like the de Muns had furnished officers to the king. But while the latter had provided captains and colonels, the La Ferronnays had always sent generals. Eugénie's father, Count Pierre Louis de La Ferronnays, sat in the Chamber of Peers and had been ambassador to St. Petersburg under Louis XVIII and later served as the foreign minister of Charles X. Within three years Eugénie bore Adrien two sons, Robert and Albert, but her health failed rapidly. Despite all precautions and a desperate trip to the warmer air of Italy, she died in Palermo of tuberculosis in the spring of 1842.

Hardly more than infants when their mother died, the two brothers never knew or perhaps even missed her. Their early lives were little different from those of other aristocratic youth, with frequent visits back and forth to neighboring estates, particularly that of Count Etienne de Biron at Fontenay, who had married their father's sister Antoinette. Little of this life was changed in 1848 when Adrien remarried, taking as his second wife Claire de Ludre, twenty years his junior. Their young stepmother shared with the boys her interest in art and music, but she had very little influence on them. Their real education was supervised by M. Esbelin, who had been their father's tutor. He drilled them in the classics, especially Latin. He found Robert a willing and interested pupil, Albert considerably less eager. The younger brother's mind wandered, and he far preferred his horses and games to books. Adrien determined that both boys should fulfill the martial tradition of the line, and in their midteens they were sent to the Jesuit Collège de l'Avenue de la Reine in Versailles to prepare for Saint Cyr. At such expensive and elitist schools the sons of the aristocrats were taught the mathematics and science necessary to pass the entrance examinations for the military academy and formed the friendships that made the French officer corps such a self-satisfied, closely bonded group. Robert did well academically there and at Saint Cyr, also making the contacts that later led him to be a favorite of the Count of Chambord, the Bourbon pretender. Albert was less successful, at least as a scholar. His work at the Jesuit school was mediocre, and he was unable to complete the *baccalauréat ès lettres*, being compelled at his graduation in 1860 to take the less distinguished *baccalauréat ès sciences*. Only with difficulty did he manage to enter Saint Cyr, where his undistinguished record placed him two years later 200th in a class of 249. Like his brother before him, he was gazetted to the Third Regiment of the Chasseurs d'Afrique in Algeria.[1]

At the age of twenty-one, Albert de Mun had acquired the trappings of his role as a proud cavalry officer. He was tall, imperially slim, growing a bluff mustache, and combing his curly brown hair back to reveal a high forehead. His upbringing had so formed his character for the part that he found its gestures automatic, and he remained a military man by temperament throughout his life. From his family he inherited a martial vocation and a tradition of royalism and ultramontanism. He was bred an aristocrat from top to bottom and had naturally affected the ennui and anti-intellectualism of his class. The elitism and snobbism of the Collège de l'Avenue de la Reine and Saint Cyr could only have intensified these feelings. With other aristocrats of the nineteenth century, de Mun shared an intense devotion to the church, but in him this sentiment sprang less from a worship of the old order and a desire that clerics retain their role as the moral policemen of the lower classes than from sincere religious feeling. His father had early insisted upon daily devotions, and mass was an integral part of life at Lumigny. The influence of the Jesuits at Versailles was also crucial: they boasted that a child entrusted to them was theirs forever. Albert was one of their successes in this regard because all his life he would champion the order and turn to one of its priests as his personal confessor. The Jesuits were also active at Saint Cyr, where they served as unofficial advisers to many students whose earlier education had been influenced by their brethren. Parades and maneuvers at the academy were often preceded by the sacraments and concluded with prayers. This military activity helped to complete the young de Mun's character. He had played at being a soldier from his boyhood, and he reveled in the actuality of leading troops. For it was the cachet of being an officer, of exercising leadership, that excited him and appealed to his aristocratic sensibilities.

De Mun's experience in Algeria heightened these character traits. He left home at the age of twenty-one to what he anticipated as "a purely military existence." He carried with him only three books, the Bible, the *Imitatio Christi*, and Sainte-Beuve's literary criticism, the *Causeries du Lundi*, all recommended by the Jesuits. Except for furloughs, he would remain in Africa for five years, and his home became the officer corps. Algerian service was coveted by French officers because it combined the delights of Moslem hedonism in the coastal cities with the opportunity for rapid advancement through combat with the Bedouin in the interior. De Mun recalled that he arrived in the French colony "bursting with an animation that increased the allure of an unknown country and the experience of an adventurous career." The danger was indeed not slight. There were five native uprisings in Algeria during de Mun's tour, and once his unit found itself surrounded and attacked by the Arabs at night and had to fight fiercely for their lives until dawn. Such experience in the field bred in de Mun the illusion, common to young officers, of an intimate kinship between leaders and men. This closeness did not survive into garrison duty. Officers were feted by the rich in the North African cities and spent evenings of conviviality in socially closed groups. Robert de Mun made certain that his brother was introduced to those who might one day further his career. One of these in particular was the Marquis René de La Tour du Pin, a close friend of Robert, who had emerged from the campaigns in the Crimea and Italy with decorations and promotions. He seemed surely destined to exchange his swagger stick for a marshal's baton in the tradition of his forebears, fifteen of whom had been generals or marshals during the ancien régime.

In 1867, de Mun was transferred back to France, to a unit of the Chasseurs at the dreary camp near Clermont-Ferrand. His departure was tinged with regret, but although he left "his twenty-year-old heart" in Algeria, he had much to look forward to in

France. His new posting enabled him to marry his pretty nineteen-year-old cousin, Simone d'Andlau, the scion of an old and august Catholic family from the Orne. He had courted her during his furloughs, and their wedding took place in early November 1867. The couple moved into the relaxed aristocratic suburb of Chamalières and quickly became part of the social whirl initiated by officers to lighten the monotony of provincial garrison duty. Within a year Simone produced an heir, Antonin. She also began to have a profound effect upon de Mun's habits, interesting him in literature, particularly Balzac and Shakespeare, but, more important, urging him to devote some of his spare time to Catholic charitable works, one of her favorite causes. Anxious to please his bride, de Mun began to visit the Oeuvre Catholique Ouvrière, an organization established by the lay brothers of St. Vincent de Paul in the early 1850s for the benefit of the working class. This activity gave him his first real acquaintance with the lives and problems of the poor. To his surprise he discovered that he enjoyed these visits, surely an outgrowth of his fervent Catholicism combined with the noblesse oblige tradition of the aristocracy and this variety of paternalism.

In August 1869 the regiment was sent on maneuvers to Châlons sur Saone, and here de Mun received his brevet of promotion from the hands of the thirteen-year-old Prince Imperial himself. From Châlons the Chasseurs were posted to Versailles, a billeting more in keeping with the status of its officers, and called into Paris twice in 1870 as a reliable unit to repress popular demonstrations. When the Franco-Prussian War broke out in July 1870, de Mun was aide-de-camp to General Philippe de Clérembault, commander of the Third Corps of the Army of Metz. The appointment was almost purely a social one, and de Mun had done little to justify his new position other than appear at ceremonies and arrange receptions. He discovered his own remissness and the general state of French military preparedness only when he was unable to find any maps for his commander's use. Because of his experience in the field de Mun was quickly transferred from his staff position to a line post. He displayed great heroism, leading charges on the Avron plain and at Gravelotte, where he was awarded the Cross of the Legion of Merit. To a great degree French officers tried to make up in panache what they lacked in organization. At

Rezonville on 16 August de Mun found himself riding beside La Tour du Pin, who was now on the staff of General Paul de Ladmirault. As they spurred into battle, La Tour du Pin recognized his friend and cried, "Charge! There will be great days for France!"

La Tour du Pin's judgment unfortunately did not equal his enthusiasm. The Prussian assault and the incompetence of Marshal Achille Bazaine, the commander of the Army of Metz, forced the French into ignominious retreat. By the first of September the army was huddled within the walls of the city it was supposed to defend. And here it remained until 31 October. There were a few attempts to break the encirclement, and in one of them de Mun was again decorated for valor. None of these forays was serious, for Bazaine and many other officers were persuaded that the war was lost and that the Army of Metz should not be sacrificed on the altar of national honor. Rather, it should remain in existence to face internal disturbances, and by this term they meant the republic declared in Paris on 4 September. This defeatism was less prevalent among junior officers like de Mun, but with their seniors they scorned the *levée en masse* decreed by the republicans and spoke with wrath of those who had revolted against the established government in time of war.

To save his army for the future domestic struggle, Bazaine, against the advice of his staff, surrendered it to the Prussians on 31 October without even attempting a face-saving battle. His officers and men were led to internment camps by the enemy, who had to protect the French troops from their own countrymen as they passed through Nancy. De Mun later recalled that during this humiliating ordeal he walked "head down, with tears in his eyes." He had not fully reckoned the shame of dishonor, of bloodless defeat, in refusing to fight to death for France. The contorted faces of the crowds at Nancy, bitter at the conduct of their soldiers, sacrificed to the Prussians for the political beliefs of the officer corps, forced de Mun to alter his perspective on the war and defeat. His anger at the republicans in Paris waned, and in its place came an insistent, gnawing desire to understand how the catastrophe of 1870 had befallen France. As a prisoner of war until mid-March 1871 he had ample time for reflection.[2]

The officers were interned at Aix-la-Chapelle and accorded exceptionally lenient treatment. They could receive visits from their families and had the run of the city, being required only to remain within its confines and not to appear in uniform. Here de Mun again met La Tour du Pin and found that he, too, sought an answer to the French collapse. In an almost automatic response formed by his background, de Mun led his friend to the city's Jesuit community to seek the guidance of the church. The request for counsel was the first of a series of chance happenings that would reorient de Mun's life. Among the Jesuits in Aix was Father Gustave Eck, a middle-aged intellectual in the order, who gave de Mun and La Tour du Pin a copy of *L'Encyclique du 8 décembre et les principes de 1789* by Emile Keller, a royalist deputy from Alsace, and urged that they read it as they pondered their country's rout. This essay was the most significant contribution by ultramontane Catholics, who had been writing eagerly since 1864 to contrast the *Syllabus of Errors* with the ideas of the French Revolution. In it Keller argued that the *liberté, égalité, fraternité* of 1789 was the heresy of man's complete autonomy, freed from the restraints of family, king, and God. In proclaiming that each man can decide his destiny alone, the revolutionaries had surely justified their name. One of their first acts had been to cast off the ancien régime's corporate guild structure to embrace an extreme individualism with the credo of every man for himself. This individualism broke down the community that had existed between master and apprentice and, with the growth of large-scale industry, had led to a cleft between social classes. Factory owners felt no responsibility for the workers they employed and treated them with contempt, forcing them to work long hours for low wages. The church's rejoinder was Pius IX's *Syllabus of Errors* of 1864. The pope insisted that the church's guidance was necessary in every human endeavor and opposed the spirit of economic individualism by proclaiming that men were not solitary beasts condemned to a life of unending struggle one against another, but brothers united in the fellowship of Christ. Keller predicted that if France did not embrace the precepts of the *Syllabus*, it would collapse from a moral decay directly traceable to the principles of the Revolution.

De Mun and La Tour du Pin read the book with wide-eyed amazement. Keller had written in 1865; by 1870 he seemed a prophet. Their background and the disasters of the preceding

lished and praised this manifesto. The publicity attracted a few anonymous contributions, and with these and their own money, the nine formed the Committee for the Oeuvre des Cercles Catholiques d'Ouvriers. Within it the two de Muns and La Tour du Pin assumed the burden of responsibility. From a corner in Robert de Mun's apartment at 51, Avenue de l'Alma in the elegant eighth district of Paris, La Tour du Pin directed propaganda, Albert de Mun organization, and Robert finances. Their military duties made it difficult for them to spare more than a few hours a day for the *cercles*, but what they lacked in time was more than compensated for by their devotion to a cause well-suited to their romantic idealism. For throughout their lives these three were to display an almost obsessive dedication to their cause. With the foundation of the *cercles*, Albert de Mun began a forty-three-year career on behalf of the established church and social reform, during which he would suffer great hardships but never fail to face them. In 1865, Robert de Mun had seen his bride of less than a year die suddenly. For the next six years he found nothing to requite his sorrow until his brother converted him to the *cercles*. Until his own unexpected death in 1887 he was their treasurer and tireless administrator. It was perhaps also in compensation for an impossible love that La Tour du Pin made the *cercles* and the evolution of Catholic social policy his life. At an early age he had fallen in love with a cousin only to learn that she was promised to another. He chose not to marry, waiting instead until her husband died forty years later to claim the love of his youth.[7]

De Mun and his compatriots realized that in order to win back the masses the church would have to adopt a more active social policy, and for their ideas they looked to the work of Armand de Melun and Frédéric Ozanam, the founders of social Catholicism in France. Their basic argument had been that mere charity was not sufficient to alleviate the poverty of the new industrial proletariat. For too long the church had been content to promise the lower classes that their pain on earth would be assuaged in heaven. The church had no organized social program, and charitable works, well-meaning but inadequate, were a holdover from the Middle Ages. Charity was dispensed in piddling amounts through small parish funds and the religious congregations. By the first years of the July Monarchy nascent industrialism had greatly increased the numbers of the urban poor in France's major cities, and when Melun and Ozanam investigated the wretched lives of these people in the 1830s, they discovered emotions toward the church ranging from indifference to outright hatred. Their findings persuaded them that for the lower classes the church was the instrument of the oppressive factory owners. It provided enough charity to keep the poor alive and working, while preaching that to revolt against their betters was evil. To win back the lower classes, Melun and Ozanam believed, the church would have to establish an active social policy designed to improve the lives of the workers and to cease acting as the agent of the rich in preaching against the organization of labor. Pope Gregory XVI was unreceptive to these ideas, but Ozanam and Melun found support from the Society of St. Vincent de Paul and the brothers of the Christian Schools. Through these orders *cercles d'ouvriers*, workers' clubs, were founded where laborers could come to seek charity, counsel, and relaxation away from the crowded and crime-ridden slums. The brothers hoped that the first members would bring others and that eventually a large segment of the working class would associate the church with these good deeds, but their success was limited. The *cercles* were opposed by a coalition of bishops and factory owners, the bishops fearing that the clubs would be independent of their control, the owners that they were a form of unionization. Most workers distrusted clerics and avoided the *cercles* as they avoided the churches. Despite these obstacles, scattered clubs did exist by 1870 in France's major industrial centers, Paris, Lyons, Toulouse, Clermont-Ferrand, and Lille.[8]

As de Mun and La Tour du Pin conceived their version of the *cercles*, the church would not merely distribute alms to the poor but would actively arrange ways for workers and employers to meet other than on opposite sides of a strike line. These gatherings would take place within the *cercles*, and blue blouse and owner could come to understand each other's problems through mutual discussion. To put the rich in touch with the poor was a laudable ambition, but the aristocratic men of good will could not escape their past nor the hierarchical conception of the church. The basis of the Oeuvre des Cercles was to be "the devotion of the directing class to the working class." Each *cercle* would have a committee of the "directing class" that would provide a club for the workers and rule it through the supervisors and Jesuit chaplain it appointed. Although the workers were to be assured a game room for billiards and gymnastics, concerts and tours, schooling for the illiterates, some free meals, and even a bank to issue loans and hold savings, and although the upper-class sponsors were to come to the club regularly to hold discussions with them, there was to be no question of an equal partnership. Paternalism would be the chief characteristic of the *cercles*. De Mun also insisted that a religious requirement be imposed on the membership to deter all who might want to exploit the benefits of the *cercles* but not share their goals. He insisted that every member wear the medal proclaiming the Immaculate Conception of the Virgin, say daily a series of prayers for the *cercles*, and attend each year two special masses for the working class.[9]

De Mun's idealism was strikingly rewarded when he found support in both the upper and the lower classes for this rigidly defined, almost military, program. In the shadow of the events of 1870 and 1871, both sides were willing to experiment with anything that might prevent a repetition of the horrors just witnessed. De Mun's committee decided that their first effort to found a club should be in Belleville, part of northwestern Paris, the center of the worst excesses of the Commune by both sides, because a success here would be dramatic and would generate momentum. Following three months of long preparations, during which the officers spent nearly all of their spare time canvassing every street in the quarter for sponsors, members, and a suitable location, all was ready. On 7 April 1872, a service of consecration was held at the new club. The workers stood self-consciously among the aristocrats, factory owners, and military officers, but there were handshakes all around and the promise of new understanding. De Mun stood on a chair to make a brief speech, touching all with the hope in his voice. It was a glorious portent of future progress, and de Mun and La Tour du Pin left "drunk with victory."[10]

In June 1871 a second club opened in Montmartre in the shadow of the framework of Sacré-Coeur, and a third followed soon after in the quarter of Vaugirard, in southern Paris. In August a group of like-minded men in Lyons asked help in forming a *cercle* there. The movement was expanding far more quickly than de Mun had anticipated. He and La Tour du Pin continued to dream their dreams, but now they had to worry more about technical matters. They could obviously no longer supervise every *cercle* themselves; a plan of national organization was necessary. In early 1872, at La Tour du Pin's behest, de Mun assumed the post of secretary-general and by fall produced a constitution for the Oeuvre des Cercles. It embodied in the main the principles of the clubs in Paris, the paternalism and the religious requirement, and confirmed the original nine founders as the central governing committee. To complement the *cercles*, de Mun established a women's auxiliary, the Dames Patronnesses, which would take as its concern the welfare of the many women workers in the country. A specific provision called for Jesuits as chaplains, perhaps an outgrowth of de Mun's personal experience but more probably because the order, commanded directly by the pope, was particularly free from episcopal control. This requirement revealed a shrewd appreciation of the realities of ecclesiastical politics on the part of the leaders of the *cercles*. They had very early placed the association under the tutelage of the church and had attracted the attention of Pius IX with their specific praise of the *Syllabus* in their first appeal. The pontiff in turn had blessed the *cercles* in a note to de Mun in January 1872. This approbation forestalled the episcopal disfavor that had handicapped earlier social Catholic efforts and was vital to the success of the *cercles*. Joseph Guibert, cardinal-archbishop of Paris, and Félix Dupanloup, bishop of Orléans and the most distinguished French cleric, had both opposed de Mun's scheme when he had approached them about it in December 1871. Like the bishops who combated Melun and Ozanam, these two worthies feared the program's lay control and independence from the local hierarchy.[11]

As de Mun drew up the pattern of administration, La Tour du Pin organized a study group to determine what social policies were permissible within the limits of Catholic dogma. Headed by Count Félix de Roquefeuil, an intellectual lawyer-economist, this group was christened the Conseil de Jésus-Ouvrier. If the *cercles* were to retain the favor of the Holy See, their leaders had to tread a narrow doctrinal line. They felt that the sufferings endured by the working class should call forth not only feelings of benevolence but the sense that such a plight was unjust. Yet to enlarge the sphere of justice was to diminish that of charity, an essential means, the church taught, to good works. From the point of view of the church, a factory owner who paid his workers a just wage but gave no alms ranked below his counterpart who paid subsistence wages but was magnanimous with his charity. There was also a second problem for the *cercles*. If they supported changes in social conditions that were contrary to the theory of economic liberalism, they risked trespassing into the heresy of socialism. While respecting private property, de Mun and La Tour du Pin would increasingly feel that the *cercles* needed the support of the state to help end labor abuses, that the state had an obligation to end the misery caused by untrammeled capitalism and unrepentant employers by establishing minimum standards for hours, wages, and working conditions. Such legislation would infringe upon the rights of private property, which Rome held sanctified. It was the task of the study group to walk the tightrope, to find some way of fulfilling the aims of the *cercles* without allowing them to lapse into heterodoxy.[12]

Between 1872 and 1875 the *cercles* enjoyed spectacular growth, particularly in the northern industrial sections of France and in conservative areas like the Vendée and Brittany, increasing to 150 clubs nationwide with 18,000 members.[13] De Mun's military superiors took no exception to his extracurricular activity, the goals of which they did not understand but the basic clericalism of which they endorsed, and allowed him time off from his duties to travel about the country addressing the clubs. His visits produced packed meeting halls, and not only because of the curiosity of an officer in dress-blues embracing the urban poor or because de Mun was secretary-general of the *cercles*. For he had become, to his own astonishment and the delight of his friends, a brilliant orator. Many who came to hear him were won to the movement by his eloquence. Tall and broad-shouldered in his uniform and sword, he was impressive in appearance at the tribune. He still sported the mustache and combed his hair back, but the youthful handsome face had become more rugged and crinkled, the high cheekbones more pronounced, the chin heavier, and the broad forehead much higher now that his brown hair was receding rapidly. He bore himself martially, but not stiffly, and in conversation his large, gentle eyes belied the sternness of his face. But when he spoke from the rostrum it was with passion and incomparable authority, and his eyes flashed with zeal. His words reflected conviction, hope, and a conscious architecture of phrase, and he used his voice as an instrument on which to play these qualities, now sonorous, rich, and vibrant, now hushed, almost breaking, and dramatic. The effect was electric. After he concluded an emotional appeal at Bordeaux in 1873, a young worker approached him, trembling, "Mon capitaine, you are the honor of your uniform" and threw his arms about him. Much later de Mun wrote, "I was quivering with emotion. After thirty-five years I believe that I can still feel on my cheek the burning mark of that worker's kiss." Many in a France seeking the answers to the war and Commune found de Mun's words intoxicating. Some greeted the message of social understanding with tears of gratitude, as did the laborer at Bordeaux. Others, carried away with his military imagery and fervent appeals to revitalize France, responded with frantic cheering.[14]

De Mun began his rounds of speaking in 1872 and expanded them in 1873 and 1874, when he seemed to spend every free moment with the *cercles*. His eldest son Antonin had died suddenly of diphtheria in April 1873, and de Mun sought to overcome his grief by making the *cercles* a surrogate child. Often leaving Simone in the care of his brother, he set out across the country to rear his new child, for on the day Antonin died, he resolved to dedicate the work of the *cercles* to his memory and that "my dear son will be our guardian angel." For the next two years he undertook a seemingly endless series of speeches for the clubs and led them on the pilgrimages the church used to revive the fervor of the faithful. During the August 1873 pilgrimage to Notre Dame de Liesse near Laon, de Mun's group of twenty-five hundred workers and owners was abruptly disturbed by an uninvited delegation complete with band led by Léon Harmel, a successful spinning factory owner from Val-des-Bois in the Ardennes. Harmel had already established savings banks, medical aid, and a *syndicat mixte*, a joint union of workers and managers, for his men. When the massive plebeian-looking Harmel read of de Mun's *cercles*, he realized that he had been a social Catholic in spirit without knowing it and hurried to give de Mun the benefit of his practical experience. From the date of the pilgrimage there began a close consultation between the two men on social policy.[15]

De Mun formed two other important friendships when he

spoke in March 1874 at the Ecole de la Rue des Postes, a Jesuit preparatory school for Saint Cyr and the Ecole Polytechnique, known popularly as Sainte Geneviève. Its rector, Father Stanislas du Lac, asked him to address an assembly of the school's recent graduates. A week afterward, four of these young cadets from Saint Cyr led by Hubert Lyautey rang at de Mun's door and offered to put their lives at his disposal. De Mun was astonished and could think of nothing to say. Afraid that they might not be sincere, he asked them to come back in another week while he considered their proposal. When they rang at the door a second time, de Mun asked them to form a small study group at the academy for the analysis of religious and social action. Other cadets from the Ecole Polytechnique did the same later. Lyautey was so deeply impressed by de Mun that when he moved on to the Ecole de l'Etat-Major in Paris, he devoted his leisure hours to working at the *cercle* in Montmartre. Reports of de Mun's extraordinary influence reached du Lac, who in consequence persuaded him to sit on the board of governors of Sainte Geneviève. Their relationship came to be one of deep mutual respect, and in the 1880s du Lac became de Mun's confessor and de Mun sent his sons to study under du Lac's guidance. The papacy also kept abreast of de Mun's success, finding it one of the most hopeful auguries in a misbegotten century. By 1873 Pius IX was so elated at the progress of the *cercles* that he made a gift to them of two thousand francs and awarded his special medallion to de Mun, his brother, and La Tour du Pin.[16]

The highly conservative government of the National Assembly smiled benignly at first on de Mun's endeavor. The elections of 1871, conducted during an armistice in the war, had produced a heavy majority for the partisans of king and church. Rarely running under the banner of royalism, they had instead called for an immediate peace with the Prussians, a trump card against bitter-end republicans in a war-weary, dejected nation. These social conservatives had little conception of de Mun's hopes for reform but approved any effort to win back the working class to clerical control. The leaders of the *cercles* came from the aristocracy and the army, and that alone sufficed for many conservative deputies. As premier, the Orleanist Duke Albert de Broglie named as his minister of agriculture Joseph La Bouillerie, a leading member of the *cercles*. But the majority of 1871 was rapidly becoming a minority as Frenchmen in by-elections rejected their now overt monarchism for the republicans, who were considerably less pleased by the progress of the *cercles* and dubious of the kind of revival for France planned by an organization led by such men of royalist heritage as de Mun and La Tour du Pin. At worst de Mun might be training the shock troops of a future royalist coup d'état; at best he would forge the working class into a constituency that the republicans themselves hoped to control.

As the voting in the nation turned against them, and the Bourbon pretender, Henri, Count of Chambord, frustrated every effort to make him king while refusing to allow his followers to transfer their allegiance to another candidate, some royalist and Catholic leaders thought to use de Mun as a new political resource. Baron General Athanase de Charette sought to win de Mun to active conspiracy. He had distinguished himself as a leader of the Papal Zouaves, French soldiers who defended the pope's control of Rome against the encroachments of the new Italian state, and now reportedly had more than six thousand men in the Vendée ready to bear arms for Chambord if the pretender would but give the word. Charette saw in the ranks of the *cercles* new recruits for insurrection and began to seek contacts with their leader. Although de Mun shared the Legitimism of his family and particularly admired Chambord's pronouncements on social reform, he did not belong to any royalist faction and wanted to keep the *cercles* out of politics, especially of the dangerous variety proposed by Charette. De Mun was much more open to the entreaty of Louis Veuillot, who couched his appeal on the plane of the church, not the throne. The strident editor of the ultramontane *L'Univers* wanted de Mun to go beyond his positive program of church and social reform to attack what *L'Univers* termed the elements in French society that poison morality and religion. On 15 February 1874, Veuillot wrote de Mun a letter in praise of his speeches, but advised that he should never spare his enemies or those of the church. His conclusion was pointed: "In the speech of an orator in uniform, there should always be a saber or at least a scabbard. . . . There must always be exterminating angels!" Enormously flattered by Veuillot's attention, de Mun was also quite open to the suggestion. The republicans had been increasing the virulence of their anticlerical slogans, and de Mun felt it just to respond in kind. In two speaking tours that summer he altered his style to accommodate Veuillot's direction. At Lille in June and throughout Brittany in August, he linked the republicans to the Commune and the Commune to the Terror of 1793. Almost as if he were quoting from Keller's writings, he damned the principles of the Revolution as the source of the nation's decay and weakness. Such language could only provoke a reaction from the republicans.[17]

On 3 September, François de Mahy, a republican deputy from Réunion, charged that "an officer [de Mun] has publicly uttered words at Sables d'Olonne designed to incite hatred among the citizenry." An inquest held on 1 October by the standing executive committee of the National Assembly cleared de Mun of any misconduct by establishing that Mahy had built his case on falsifications and quotations taken out of context. Nevertheless, as a result of the controversy, the army, which hoped to appear nonpolitical in spite of the antirepublican sentiment of the officer corps, decreed that henceforth, before addressing any gathering, an officer had to secure specific authorization from his commander. Soon all Paris-based officers were forbidden to speak before any but official military assemblies.[18]

The army's prohibition of speechmaking finally forced de Mun to choose between his two careers. The military had been his life for fifteen years, and more than that it was his livelihood. His father was still alive, and even after his death, as the younger son, Albert would receive only a limited patrimony. Like many noble families in France, the de Muns had more status than wealth. De Mun had some outside investments, but they could not allow him to live as he had on the income of a cavalry captain. Yet de Mun had pinned his fondest dreams on the *cercles*, and he would have to give them up if he did not break his sword. He pondered the decision for almost a year, wondering at his alternatives. In 1873 a representation from a constituency in Marseilles had petitioned him to run in a by-election as its deputy to the National Assembly. He had refused because he had no reason then to believe that he could not continue to combine his military and social Catholic activities. When committees of voters from Lille, Toulouse, and Pontivy (Morbihan) made similar offers in the spring of 1875 for the elections of 1876, his situation had changed. If he remained in the military, others would have to assume the burden of spreading the message of the *cercles*. But if he resigned to carry on the *cercles* himself, any success he might obtain as a private citizen could be magnified many times by a similar effort launched from the tribune of the National Assembly. A triumphant political campaign by the leader of the *cercles* would focus publicity and prestige on them, and after he had taken his seat among the deputies, he could sponsor the legislative program of social Catholicism. He decided at last in early May 1875 to seek election in Pontivy, the Breton homeland of his mother's family.[19]

Even with the decision made, he waited until 27 October 1875 to execute the painful task of resigning his commission. On the following day he wrote to his associate Félix de Roquefeuil, "I have no other flag now than our banner," but he concluded, "Pray for me, dear friend, I traverse a solemn phase in my life." The wound was opened again in December when the military bureaucracy forwarded to him its final acceptance of the resignation. More than thirty years later de Mun wrote of his feelings on that day:

> At thirty-seven, I had behind me fifteen years of military service, full of memories, some joyous, some grievous. All of my youth was in them. The war [of 1870] had marked my life forever; I emerged from it more attached to the army than I had been before, overwhelmed by the passionate hope for revanche. When I resigned from the army, I left behind a piece of my heart. Before me opened a new career, the way to which was obscure and uncertain, the difficulties and fatigues of which I could guess already. I was sad but resolute. I remember placing the letter from the ministry on my prie-dieu and renewing in the sacrifice it made irrevocable the offer of my strength to the cause of God.[20]

Morbihan, south-central Brittany, was royalist, clerical, and backward. Its provincial capitals, Pontivy, where de Mun would stand for election, and Vannes, were centers of commercial farming and fishing, respectively, as they remain today. The inhabitants are Breton to the core, still poor but proud, religious in many instances to the point of superstition, and fiercely independent. There were few great landowners in Moribihan; medium-sized estates belonging to the lesser nobility were far more common. Land tenure was about equally divided between those who worked small parcels of their own and those who were tenants of the lords. By tradition

Morbihan was Legitimist, but Bonapartism made deep inroads during the Second Empire, especially among the peasants, who found it a useful foil to the Legitimism of the landlords. By the last quarter of the nineteenth century the power of the landed nobility started to wane, and a new egalitarianism, partly a legacy of Bonapartism, appeared among the peasants and fishermen. By this time the power of the church here was also declining, although it had never been as great in Morbihan as in some other sections of Brittany. Nevertheless, despite slowly changing conditions, if properly mobilized and managed, the support of the clergy and the great estates was sufficient to guarantee victory at the ballot box.[21]

De Mun's decision to seek election here was in one respect bizarre. The seat was counted a relatively safe one for the Right, but the area was hardly suited to de Mun's reputation as a reformer. In this regard either Lille or Toulouse, although riskier chances for election, would have been a better choice. These two urban centers had welcomed the *cercles*, and de Mun could have run there as a social Catholic. Despite some initial success in the larger towns, what did the *cercles* have to do with the rural environment of Morbihan? De Mun surely chose the relative security of Pontivy to ensure that his resignation had not been in vain and that social Catholicism would have a voice in the Assembly, whether or not that voice was representative of its consituents. Having chosen Morbihan, he would have to stand as the advocate of either the church or the monarchy or of some combination of the two. Soon after his decision, he was approached by Count Edouard de Monti, a representative of Legitimist forces in the area. De Mun replied as he had earlier to Charette that he did not want to become too closely linked to active royalism since such involvement by him would inevitably politicize the *cercles*. Instead, he hoped to solicit the clerical vote by presenting himself as the champion of the church. Monti suggested that he would also need royalist votes for election and that some supporters of the throne might be dubious of backing him if he did not run clearly beneath their banner. De Mun demurred, confident that his relation to the La Ferronnays and his religious stance would lead many royalists to vote for him anyway. Indeed, that is exactly what happened in January 1876, when the Comité Royaliste of Morbihan met to consider de Mun's candidacy. Some of the landlords were in favor of boycotting the election since there was no simon-pure royalist in the field. A majority disagreed and endorsed de Mun. They had good reason to consider him one of their own. On 10 May 1875, the Count of Chambord had written to de Mun asking the honor of being named the godfather of the child Simone expected in August. Taken wholly by surprise but delighted, de Mun accepted the tribute, which was offered because Chambord shared de Mun's social reform goals. Since the act did not involve de Mun in royalist politics, it would not affect the *cercles*. But it clearly made him *persona gratissima* among Legitimists. De Mun reciprocated by naming the child, his third son, Henri, in honor of Chambord.[22]

Although de Mun had hoped for a relatively easy victory at Pontivy, the seat proved to be closely contested. When the campaigning began in late December 1875 for the 20 February 1876 election, he found he had two serious opponents, the perennial republican offering, Dr. Louis Le Maguet, and a Bonapartist, the Abbé Eugène Cadoret, a former navy chaplain and now canon of Saint Denis. The republicans did not yet have sufficient strength to elect Le Maguet, and he might be disregarded. Cadoret was another matter. Campaigning in his cassock, the abbé, who called for the enthronement of the Prince Imperial, threatened to steal much of the clerical vote from de Mun. The votes he won through his status as a priest could be combined with Bonapartist support to give him the victory. Facing such serious competition, de Mun sought powerful allies. On 28 January 1876, he wrote to Louis Veuillot to seek the endorsement of *L'Univers*, which was widely distributed in Brittany and considered the organ of the church. He concluded this appeal with a postscript that he would ask the bishop of Vannes, Jean Marie Bécel, for a formal disavowal of the abbé's candidacy. While bringing these big guns to bear on his opponent, de Mun bolstered his own image as the leader of the Catholic cause by posting this circular about the district: "Convinced that in the social order as well as in the political the Catholic faith is the necessary base of all laws and institutions, that it alone can bring a remedy to the revolutionary evil, destroy its effects, and assure the salvation of France, I have the firm resolution that upon whatever ground God calls me to serve, I shall devote myself without reserve to the defense of the principles of the Catholic faith."[23]

Delighted with this language, Veuillot replied on 14 February to assure de Mun the support of the paper and to praise his uncompromising tone. "Better a defeat on such a steed than a success won groveling. Such a defeat would only serve the cause, such a success only harm it." He published similar remarks on 20 February in the election-day edition of *L'Univers*. The bishop of Vannes responded with a letter on 15 February, condemning Cadoret and praising de Mun in glowing terms. "Your failure," he wrote, "would be a public misfortune. I would blush for my country." The bishop's endorsement was given in confidence because French law forbade the interference of the church in elections. But parish priests could be easily alerted to Bécel's preference and could work their influence, in private, on the faithful. With this backing, de Mun's confidence increased. On 19 February he wrote to Veuillot that on election eve "I await the vote with confidence . . . I believe that I shall be elected, perhaps on the first ballot."[24]

Between 1871 and 1914, with the significant exception of the years 1885 to 1889, elections to the lower house of the French legislature were carried out under the system of *scrutin d'arrondissement*, single-member constituencies. Any number of candidates could stand for election to the Chamber of Deputies, which with the upper house, the Senate, replaced the National Assembly by the constitutional laws of 1875. If one of the candidates won an absolute majority in the voting, he was declared elected. More often, no one received a majority, and two weeks after the first ballot, or *premier tour*, a second ballot, the so-called *ballottage*, took place. In the *ballottage* the candidate with the greatest plurality was declared elected, but in practice the *ballottage* rarely involved more than two serious opponents, the others having withdrawn, usually after having come to some agreement with one of the two leaders. In Pontivy after the first ballot de Mun led with 7,608 votes, Cadoret followed closely at 7,087, and Le Maguet trailed with 4,768. Le Maguet withdrew from the contest but refused to endorse either of his opponents, seeing little in their clericalism or monarchism to recommend to his followers. But there was whispered speculation that Le Maguet's republicans would be more likely to turn to a Bonapartist than to a Legitimist. Bécel heard the rumors and panicked. Desperately trying to prevent a victory by Cadoret, the bishop sent Veuillot a copy of the letter he had written to de Mun. Veuillot was then either sufficiently bold or sufficiently stupid to publish it in *L'Univers* on 5 March, the date of the *ballottage*. This flagrant violation of the election statutes made de Mun the official candidate of the church, and with this endorsement he defeated Cadoret 10,725 to 8,754. Since almost exactly the same number of votes were cast in each round, Cadoret must have lost some of his original supporters to de Mun because the abbé must surely have gained the bulk of the republican vote. The letter of the bishop was very likely decisive. In the Catholic press there was loud acclaim for de Mun's victory and a title that stuck, the Knight of the *Syllabus*. Veuillot wrote to Simone to declare that her husband "has within him the makings of a Catholic leader far superior to Montalembert." The republicans cried foul, and they had the votes to invalidate de Mun's election if they so chose because the balloting had followed the pattern of the by-elections and given them a majority in the new Chamber of Deputies.[25]

When the Chamber convened in March 1876, anticlerical republicans led by Léon Gambetta and Henri Brisson pressed for de Mun's ejection on the grounds of clerical interference in his election. They leveled the standard charges of the Left against Catholic candidates, alleging that priests tore down the posters of republicans and threatened to withhold the sacraments from those who failed to support the candidate most favorable to the church. But the telling point was the publication of the bishop's letter. In his defense de Mun made a poor maiden appearance before the Chamber. He attempted to justify Bécel's action on grounds of a bishop's responsibility to guide and admonish priests and laity and ended weakly by denying the letter's impact since it appeared so late in the campaign. This argument had no appeal to the republicans, who wished to lessen the power of the church, and Brisson added in a sarcastic retort that the publication of the episcopal denunciation as the electors trooped to the polls only heightened its effect. Badly outmaneuvered, de Mun stood flustered for a moment at the rostrum. Then he cried out angrily, "The challenge has been extended, and Catholics have accepted! That is the meaning of my election!" Startled by this outburst and unsure why their leaders would seem to prefer Cadoret's election to that of de Mun, many of the new republicans were confused. Rather than seat or invalidate de Mun, they provided a majority in favor of a further inquest.[26]

While a longer report was being prepared on his election, de Mun was allowed to take his seat provisionally. He actively intervened in debate and quickly demonstrated why republican leaders had sought his ouster. As he gained poise at the rostrum, his reputation for oratory spread far beyond the columns and red velvet of the hemicycle within the Palais Bourbon, where the Chamber sat, to the aristocratic faubourgs of Paris. In June and July the galleries were packed with richly dressed nobles and clerics when the impeccable de Mun debated the great, leonine Gambetta on the place of Catholic schools in the French educational system. They were at opposite ends of the spectrum, anticlerical against clerical, republican against Legitimist, but each had a vision of a new France, and each was young enough—de Mun but thirty-five and Gambetta only thirty-eight—to believe that he would see his dream a reality.[27]

De Mun had clearly made himself a marked man by the time the inquest on his election was completed. For many republicans he was that phenomenon most to be feared, a young man of great promise on the Right. Attractive, well-bred noble scions with exquisite manners were common in clerical and monarchist circles. Usually they were also empty-headed, vain, and incompetent. De Mun was different because he combined birth and breeding with oratory of fiery brilliance, the capacity to raise men from their seats with a single phrase—a Gambetta of the Right. He was the leader of the *cercles*, whose avowed enemy was the principles of 1789 and whose expanded reputation in five years had been rapid enough to create fear on the Left. At the tribune of the Chamber, with the nation as his audience, such a man could be more dangerous still. Because the burden of guilt was clearly on de Mun for the manner in which he won election, the republicans could rid themselves of this foe with relief even as they uttered expressions of pious rectitude for the sanctity of the voting procedure. De Mun could only protest his personal innocence in the publication of the letter as, on 13 July, the Chamber, by a vote of 297 to 171, ratified the recommendation of the inquest that he be invalidated.[28]

Back before his Breton constituents, de Mun called on them to defend their rights by reelecting him. His posters this time were more clarion calls than discussions of issues. "Stand up, children of the land of granite! Stand up for the honor of Brittany, for the safeguard of your faith and the vindication of your most sacred rights!" Despite his narrow defeat, the Abbé Cadoret failed to enter the lists a third time, and de Mun faced only Le Maguet. In the 27 August by-election he defeated the republican 9,789 to 9,466, a surprisingly close vote that suggested the limits of both royalist and clerical influence, even in Brittany. Le Maguet filed the usual accusations of interference by the church, but this time there was no evidence against de Mun. The Chamber validated his election on 15 December 1876, and de Mun triumphantly took his seat on the far right.[29]

2
Gambetta of the Right

By 1876 the political battle lines were drawn between the royalists and the church on one side and republicans of all stripes on the other. The by-elections of 1871 to 1875 had been skirmishes, the general election of 1876 the first significant action. The victory of the republicans meant that the royalists would have to counterattack to survive, and combatants of both sides began building their breastworks for the forthcoming engagement.[1]

The Right had dominated the National Assembly in 1871 and chosen Marshal Patrice de MacMahon chief of state in 1873. Their support in the country was deeply rooted and strong, many Frenchmen holding as an article of faith the belief that only a king could prevent anarchy, but they were weakened by their divisions. Some were Legitimists, followers of the Count of Chambord, who was the grandchild of Charles X and the only direct heir to the Bourbon inheritance. Others were Orleanists, seeking the reestablishment of the cadet line of Louis Philippe in the person of the Count of Paris. Still a few kept the faith of Bonaparte. When Chambord refused to accept the tricolor flag of a postrevolutionary France, negating the efforts of his champions between 1871 and 1873, and the Legitimists declined to follow the Count of Paris while the childless Chambord remained alive, the royalists failed in their most imperative objective—to agree on a candidate for the throne. A third Bonaparte was impossible until the Prince Imperial attained his majority, and with Thiers increasingly leaning toward the republicans, the monarchists turned to MacMahon. As a suitable stand-in, he could be elected to a seven-year term in the hope that in its course Chambord might die, the Legitimist and Orleanist ranks would be united, and the Count of Paris could take the throne. MacMahon would humbly step aside for his king, after having the Chamber of Deputies and Senate ratify the restoration. The Bonapartists acquiesced in this plan, while plotting that Napoleon IV and not Philippe of Orleans would ultimately be the beneficiary.[2]

The ally of the monarchists during the nineteenth century, the Catholic church had in turn blessed all three political varieties. It sought the protection of a monarch in part because of tradition but more because it remembered the excesses committed against the church during the 1789 Revolution. To its supreme head, Pope Pius IX, *liberté, égalité, fraternité* was an unholy trinity and all republican governments the work of Beelzebub. Many of his French bishops, reared under the Restoration on similar notions, shared his conceptions, if to a lesser degree. To the church of Pio Nono any king was preferable to a republic, and this sentiment was deeply inculcated in all who attended the church's schools. In France almost one-half of the children were educated by the clergy, giving the church tremendous influence. Through this hold on French education the church meant to buttress its position because the Jesuits were not alone among the teaching orders in boasting that their students were the vanguard of the faithful.[3]

Opposing the forces of throne and altar were the republicans. Lineal descendants of the men of both 1789 and 1793, they were neither the monolithic mob seen by Pius IX nor the howling anarchists feared by the conservatives. They were united by the ideal of a republic, but differed bitterly over its character. Thiers, conqueror of the Commune and first chief of state of the National Assembly, moved from constitutional monarchism to become the leader of the moderate wing of the republicans. Many of his followers favored a republic because, as Thiers expressed it, this would be the form of government that would divide Frenchmen the least. Thiers muted the demands of all republicans to convince the country that a republic could be sane, responsible, and unlikely to provoke chaos. His program was pragmatic, but conservatively so, what would later be termed "opportunism." The radical republicans were a different breed. Their leader was the flamboyant lawyer Léon Gambetta, who had floated out of Paris in a balloon over the besieging Prussian troops to direct the *levée en masse* of 1870. Gambetta's Radical party subscribed to his Belleville program of 1869 that called for the separation of church and state, liberty of press and assembly, free and compulsory lay public education, and the removal of laws against trade unions. These followers were particularly vehement in their opposition to "clericalism," which they seemed to define as every activity of the church, especially its role in education. Along with the positivist-scientific outlook, the ideology of extreme individualism, of total self-autonomy, most nearly defines the philosophy of the Radical position. To feel the need of the church for anything—salvation, marriage, education—was to submit to its authority and therefore could not be allowed.[4]

The elections of 1876 were a disaster for the conservatives. In the defunct National Assembly they had held a divided majority, but in the new Chamber of Deputies their numbers were reduced to 193, while the republicans held 340 seats. Clearly the nation had repudiated them. The republicans were triumphant, and, sensing the destruction of the conservative position, the Radicals called for the resignation of MacMahon, whom they saw as a symbol of royalism. Anticlericalism became a rallying cry, and when such defenders of the church as de Mun rose to vindicate it, they were shouted down. If the Right accepted a Chamber ruled by a republican majority, they would have to abandon any hope of achieving a restoration in the foreseeable future. There was but one ploy left. As provided by the constitutional laws of 1875, MacMahon, as president of the Republic, with the consent of the Senate, could dissolve the Chamber of Deputies. On 16 May 1877, he did just this and called for new elections. The conservatives intended to "make" these elections by bringing to bear upon the voters all manner of administrative pressure. Local officials whose loyalty to the conservatives was suspect were removed, and there was a wholesale replacement of doubtful prefects. It was to no avail. In the October 1877 balloting Frenchmen returned a Chamber of 326 republicans and only 207 monarchists. The results saved the Republic because few conservatives, especially MacMahon, had the stomach for a coup de force and because they demonstrated that the country no longer feared the republican creed. The masses of rural France repudiated the authority of clergy and old notables and voted for the new notables of the Left. The vindicated majority of the Chamber was sure to remember its enemies, and friends of monarchy and church prepared for a new onslaught.[5]

De Mun shared the apprehensions of his fellow conservatives and cast about with them to find ways to counter the republican threat. His first efforts, tentative and circumspect, were also remarkably obtuse. In January 1877 he wrote to Louis Veuillot to propose that *L'Univers* celebrate 21 January in honor of the martyr-death of Louis XVI, seeing the date as a counter to the republican Bastille Day. Even Veuillot dismissed this suggestion. In the Chamber, de Mun often took the rostrum to defend the church against scurrilous attacks in Radical newspapers, but he presented a justification of the need for clerical interference in all phases of life so like Pius IX's *Syllabus* and so wholly unappealing to the republican deputies that Gambetta's single rejoinder, "Cléricalisme, voilà l'ennemi!" delivered sarcastically from his seat, was once sufficient rebuttal to de Mun's hour-long speech. Unlike many of his more experienced colleagues of the Right, however, de Mun realized that MacMahon's dissolution and call for new elections was a mistake. The conservatives had very little to win and much to lose. Still split into three factions, the Right would be unable to agree on fundamental changes in the regime even if they did carry the voting. A loss would mean double repudiation by the nation and a serious undermining of MacMahon's influence.[6]

Once the decision was made to hazard all on new elections, many of the conservatives, including de Mun, became much less cautious in their words and deeds. The usually staid Legitimist Charles Chesnelong adopted language more characteristic of de Mun, and the immoderate Bonapartist Paul Granier de Cassagnac became more so. The republican attack on "clericalism" led de Mun to urge the members of the *cercles* to campaign for all "Catholic candidates." By inviting the royalist extremist Charette to address the general assembly of the Oeuvre des Cercles in Paris on 30 May 1877, de Mun ensured that his definition of "Catholic" was a broad one. Charette was wildly applauded by the workers for his belligerent sentiments toward the republicans, and at the conclusion of the address de Mun kept the audience on their feet by warning, "It is necessary to redouble activity, because the respite of today will not last, and you must then risk your lives for the defense of Catholicism!" His appearance with Charette seemed to indicate that de Mun might openly join the royalists, but when he eulogized Chambord at another meeting of the *cercles*, the members became restive. Fearing that the workers might not follow him any closer to Legitimism, de Mun then withdrew from the national campaign of the conservatives, pleading the need to concentrate on his district in Morbihan.[7]

Once in Brittany, de Mun could not be readily recalled to Paris, and to ensure that he would not be, he wrote letters to Veuillot and others exaggerating the strength of his opponents. Actually, his competition was weak, the republican Le Maguet and a maverick former Bonapartist prefect Lefèvre, and they were undermined by the government's administrative pressure in de Mun's behalf. He was delighted to be back in Pontivy, where he could accept royalist support without openly acknowledging it or compromising the *cercles*. His brief stint in the Chamber had solidified his position among the partisans of monarchy and church in Morbihan, and their confidence in him was reflected in a resounding first-ballot victory on 14 October, 12,920 to Le Maguet's 6,817 and Lefèvre's feeble 1,678. But despite this large margin of victory, it was almost inevitable that the republicans would once again challenge the legality of his election. De Mun was a potentially dangerous opponent, whose flirtation with Charette was ominous, and the republicans were in a mood to settle old scores. The invalidation of the Knight of the *Syllabus*, on whatever pretext, would be fine revenge against the church. De Mun understood these considerations, and when in May 1878 his victory was disputed on the grounds of clerical interference, he charged, "It is not the man you wish to invalidate but the cause; it is not an election but Catholicism itself that you wish to submit to inquest." Georges Clemenceau then retorted from the Radical benches, "M. de Mun is then the candidate of the pope?" and the republican majority voted an examination of the charges of interference.[8]

During the long summer parliamentary recess, as he awaited the completion of the inquest, de Mun attempted to evolve a systematic and coherent statement of his political philosophy. He had begun reading the articulate and influential figures of continental conservatism, Joseph de Maistre, Juan Donoso Cortès, and Louis de Bonald, and he wanted to distill their ideas and those of the *Syllabus* into a pithy credo, in his own words, for himself and the *cercles*. Convinced that it was the ideas of the Revolution that he opposed, he termed his formulation *contre-révolution*, "counter-revolution," a word not then widely used.

To oppose to the Declaration of the Rights of Man, which has served as the basis of the Revolution, the proclamation of the Rights of God, which must be the foundation of the Counterrevolution, and the ignorance of which is the true cause of the evil that leads our society to ruin. To aspire to an absolute obedience to the principles of the Catholic church and to the infallible teaching of the pope, and to carry through all the consequences that naturally are the result in the social order of the full exercise of the law of God on societies. To propagate by a public and indefatigable apostolate the doctrine thus established. To train men determined to adopt this as the rule of their public lives as well as of their private lives, and to show the application of these consequences in the work of the Oeuvre des Cercles itself through the devotion of the propertied classes for the working class. To work without cease to make these principles and doctrines part of our customs and to create an organized force capable of making them find expression in the laws and social institutions of the nation. This must be the spirit and goal of our association in order that it may respond to the program it drew up at its origin, when, by the Appeal to Men of Good Will of 25 December 1871, it declared war on the Revolution.[9]

On 8 September 1878, de Mun addressed a meeting at Chartres of all the *cercles* of the Paris region, speaking as usual of his goals for social reform. He denounced economic liberalism and socialism as philosophies inevitably heightening class conflict by assuming that employer and worker were antagonists. In their stead he praised the conception of the *cercles*, that of social justice determined jointly between classes. In his peroration, however, he turned to a vision of the *cercles* leading a martial crusade against the influence of the Revolution, concluding, "We are the irreconcilable Counterrevolution!"[10]

As a figure of speech, "Counterrevolution" was laden with ambiguities. It naturally provoked criticism from the Left, which labeled de Mun the eponym of reaction. Less expectedly, it also aroused sharp censure from the Right, in the person of Count Alfred de Falloux, the author of the 1850 law allowing the church a vastly expanded freedom to establish schools and increase the number of students under its control. Although retired from politics by 1878, Falloux was still a figure of enormous importance in royalist and clerical circles. In the 20 September *L'Union de l'Ouest*, the largest daily newspaper in Brittany, he addressed de Mun an open letter making clear his disapproval of the term: "I think that there could hardly be a symbol less 'true' or more poorly chosen.

. . . It is besides a word badly defined and perhaps indefinable, pregnant with prejudices, misunderstandings, and in consequence, tempests. . . . The church . . . cannot compromise itself or allow itself to be compromised by such contestable theses that could not withstand an hour of contradictory and serious discussion." Falloux continued his attack in the Catholic biweekly *Le Correspondant* of 25 October, concluding: "God in education, the pope at the head of the church, the church at the head of civilization. This was the program I traced in my short political career. I avow today that it is still sufficient and that 'counterrevolution,' which can add nothing to it, could greatly impede its success."[11] Falloux was afraid of the inflammatory potential of the term and worried that some who might support the legitimate demands of the church would be deterred by its implications. The difference between Falloux and de Mun was that between a man seeking only operating room for the church and one dreaming of overturning the history of nearly a hundred years. De Mun stubbornly refused Falloux's advice and instead made counterrevolution the focus of his most important parliamentary speech yet, the defense of his 1877 election.

The report of the inquest presented before the Chamber of Deputies on 16 November 1878 recommended de Mun's invalidation on the grounds that the chaplains of the *cercles* had campaigned in his behalf. The charge was ridiculous on its face because there were only a few *cercles* in Morbihan, and had Jesuits in fact been imported from outside, according to the charge, they would have been so obvious as to invite invalidation. In his reply de Mun disdained even to answer such fabricated evidence, convinced now that he would be deprived of his seat even if he disproved the charges. He chose instead to define as sharply as possible the chasm between himself and the Left. "You are the Revolution!" he began, "That is sufficient to explain why we are the Counterrevolution! What was this Revolution of yours? . . . the overthrow of kings, the unchaining of popular passions and bloody riots, a doctrine . . . that pretends to found society not on the will of God but on that of man." Yet de Mun did not want a return to the ancien régime, for he saw the seeds of the Revolution in the materialist Enlightenment, the usurpation by kings of the rights of the church, and the widening gap between rich and poor. "The Revolution was already present in the Old Regime. . . . We want neither;

we want a 'Christian society.'" The Revolution, he charged, had led inexorably to Napoleon, the Second Republic to a second Bonaparte, and the Third Republic would lead to yet a third dictatorship. The Chamber was strangely silent as its majority heard this denunciation in words of dramatic intensity. There were none of the usual raucous interruptions as de Mun, dignified in dress and composure, hurled fire from the rostrum. "I leave this tribune," he concluded, "as in a moment I shall leave the Chamber, without bowing my head to your decree, sure of my right and certain of finding in the public conscience the justice I can no longer ask of you." There was a hush, followed by general applause. His opponents could envy his undaunted pride even as they invalidated him. They could appreciate his quaint idealism even when it was combined with an anachronous policy of reaction.[12]

Four days later in the royalist press the Count of Chambord published a long letter to de Mun in praise of his speech before the Chamber. Elated by this recognition, de Mun wrote his colleague Roquefeuil, "The king has just taken the lead of the Catholic movement and this enraptures me." But he did not travel to the pretender's castle in his Austrian exile at Frohsdorff to do obeisance before him personally nor did he request his guidance. Instead he would lament the "sterile immobility" of the Bourbons, so many words followed by so few deeds. Unlike the royalism of his brother Robert, who had retired from the army and attended Chambord several months of the year as well as working for the *cercles*, de Mun's was based less on hopes of a restoration than on family tradition and his belief that counterrevolution was possible only under a "Christian king." Because Chambord shared his fervent Catholic faith and a paternalistic brand of social reform, he felt an allegiance to him that he could never feel for the Orleanist princes, whose skepticism and economic liberalism he found distasteful. Although written twenty-nine years later, the note he composed on 24 August 1907 expressed his sentiments in 1878.

It has been twenty-four years today since the Count of Chambord died, an event that staggered me. Not because of the hope of a restoration (since 1873 I no longer believed that this was possible nor that its hopes rested on reality), not even because of monarchist faith (mine, however intense, held more to the idea of a *Catholic* royalty than to the royalty itself), but because of the practical conception of the *Christian Counter-*

revolution, incarnated in a man who represented at one time all tradition. Since that time, I have attached myself *exclusively* to the church. The rest of my life I have had an ardent Catholic faith and a social doctrine. I no longer have a political faith; I have sought only expedients.[13]

At the beginning of 1879, de Mun returned to Pontivy to begin his fourth campaign for the Chamber in two years. Republican groups in Paris focused national attention on the effort to defeat de Mun and sent money to support his opponent, the inevitable Le Maguet. There was no quarter at the hustings, and each side accused the other of election fraud. De Mun's partisans charged that the newly republicanized local administration padded voting lists and stuffed ballot boxes, while Le Maguet's replied that landowners had threatened to evict and the clergy to withhold the sacraments from any with the temerity to vote republican. When the ballots were counted at the close of the 2 February voting, de Mun had lost his first election, 10,392 to 9,872. Le Maguet's total had increased 3,500 votes from 1877, de Mun's decreased over 3,000. The 1,150 voters who remained at home this time would have been sufficient to give him victory. He was almost surely a victim of the same variety of official pressure that had guaranteed him such a large majority eighteen months earlier. In a circular issued the following day, de Mun thanked those who had remained faithful to him and rejected calls to file a protest, declaring that an appeal to the republican majority of the Chamber would be futile.[14]

No longer a deputy and with the next general election two years away in 1881, de Mun had more time for the social leisure of his class. In 1876, following his resignation from the army and election to the Chamber, he had installed Simone and his sons Bertrand and Henri in a commodious apartment in the newly refurbished *hôtel* at 38 Rue François I. Two more children were born here to the couple, Marguerite in 1877 and Fernand three years later. With four children under the age of ten, Simone increasingly preoccupied herself with their rearing and at the age of thirty-two began to adopt a genteel frumpiness, a surrender to bearing five children in thirteen years of marriage. She slowly discarded the colorful, airy frocks and crinolines of her youth for the flowered hats, rolled parasols, and drab, heavy, all-encompassing skirts of the Belle Epoque's variety of Victorian and Biedermeier fashion. She furnished their home as she dressed. Throughout the apartment were the heavy brocade chairs, mahogany tables, baroque brass candlesticks and clocks, ruffled lamp shades, cut glass and mirrors, and everywhere pictures, photograph miniatures in etched gold frames and oil portraits in gilt, all of the paraphernalia that overcrowded and cluttered the houses of the wellborn and wealthy during the last half of the century.[15]

The de Muns lived in the stylish eighth district, hardly two blocks from the Champs Elysées, a smart "new" quarter of Paris to which many of the younger members of the upper classes were moving. By birth and breeding their world was directly across the convenient Pont de l'Alma and the Seine, in the faubourg Saint-Germain, where the grandest Parisian mansions and the most ancient Legitimist aristocracy combined to create an atmosphere of almost incredible hauteur. What was regarded here as de Mun's rather excessive sympathy for the downtrodden was forgiven in light of his impeccable social credentials, a Jesuit education, graduation from Saint Cyr, service as an officer, and a thousand-year-old name. He could clearly be considered part of the *gratin*, and the thrill of one of their number as an oratorical master in the Chamber drew noble gentlemen and their ladies to the galleries whenever he spoke. Particularly after his defeat in 1879, de Mun adopted the Parisian nobility's Anglophile habit of spending their afternoons at "clubs," which in Paris were hardly more than salons with a permanent guest list. He was quickly asked to join the group of clubmen who met each day in frock coat and wing collar at the home of the Countess Laure de Chévigné, whose husband Count Adhéaume was gentleman-in-waiting to Chambord. She attracted a following of ultras, among them Counts Costa de Beauregard, Louis de Turenne, and Henri de Breteuil, the last a close friend of the Prince of Wales. They gathered to dissect politics, deride the Republic, and honor the "king."[16]

Evenings were for more formal gatherings, often at the salons of Countesses Jeanne de Loynes and Anne de Noailles, where the literati of the Right were the central attraction. At these soirées de Mun and Simone made the acquaintance of the stellar lights, both present and future, of French conservative belles-lettres, Ferdinand Brunetière, Viscount Eugène Melchior de Vogüé, and Paul Bourget, whom they liked, Germain Bapst and Georges de Porto-Riche, with whom they were friendly, and Count Robert de Montesquiou, whom they despised. Simone encouraged her husband to cultivate Brunetière and Vogüé, reasoning that literary contacts might broaden his interests and eventually contribute to his political success. This world of glitter, ease, and exclusivity did not ensnare de Mun. He remained true to his basic instincts. One grande dame gossiped that a beautiful Madame de X . . . , finding him without Simone for the evening, offered to ride him home in her carriage and made him advances. "You can see that I am tempted," he replied, "but I never deceive my wife." Hostesses complained that his religious sentiments were genuine but his piety a little ostentatious. De Mun did feel out of place in Saint-Germain despite his background. Although lionized for his political promise, he resented the almost ossified rigidity of their prejudices and disdain for the lower classes. He was offended by the dandiness of some of the belles-lettrists like Montesquiou. A symbol of reaction in the Chamber, de Mun was a liberal among those whom one British observer described as "arrested in intelligence, [hating] . . . the present, the past two centuries, the Government, the future." He also lacked the wealth to match the splendor of their opulence. In reaction, he and Simone entertained little themselves and practiced in their private lives a self-denial that would culminate in 1903 with their taking the vows of the Third Order of Saint Francis.[17]

Some of the utter hatred of the Republic by the *gratin* resulted from a new desperation that set in between 1878 and 1880. The death of Pius IX in 1878 was a possibly decisive loss since his successor Leo XIII was rumored to be far less intransigent. The continued success of the republicans was a further blow. Discredited and repudiated by the elections of 1877, MacMahon had still clung to office. When the senatorial elections of January 1879 turned out a number of monarchists and gave moderate republicans a majority there also, he felt that he must surrender the presidency. To follow him at the Elysée palace, the Chamber and Senate chose Jules Grévy, touted as the successor to Thiers, who had died in the midst of the 1877 campaign. A man of 1848 grown respectable, Grévy was old, drab, and reassuringly moderate. With the Chamber, Senate, and presidency all in their hands, the republicans could begin to enact their program.[18]

On 5 March 1879, the minister of education, Jules Ferry, presented a bill designed drastically to reduce the church's grip on

French education. By the Falloux law of 1850, anyone with minimum credentials could open or direct a school for elementary- or secondary-grade students. During the twenty-nine years that followed, the church used the new freedom to create a large number of schools and attract to them about half of all French children. Radicals found this situation intolerable; monks and nuns, the "multicolored militia without a fatherland," as Gambetta described them, were wrenching the souls of youth from the Republic. Moderate republicans recognized in this attitude a useful tool, viewing an attack on clerical education as a means of preoccupying the Radicals and deflecting their demands for social and economic change. At the same time that this flank attack on the church united the republicans, it would be safer than a frontal assault on religion, which might provoke a backlash. Beyond these political considerations, idealists like Ferry among both Radicals and moderates felt that this legislation would release children from the obscurantist tutelage of the church and make possible a new education that would form ideal citizens for the Republic, enlightened, tolerant, and free-thinking. To this end Article Seven of Ferry's proposal would undo the effects of the Falloux law. It took advantage of the distinction, dating from the "Organic Articles" that Napoleon had unilaterally attached to the 1801 Concordat between the church and the French state, of "authorized" and "unauthorized" religious congregations. The former had formally applied for and been granted corporate status under French law; the latter existed only on sufferance of the government. Among the unauthorized orders were the Jesuits, Marists, Dominicans, Augustinians, and Franciscans, as indeed were all but five of the men's congregations. Ferry proposed to ban all members of unauthorized orders from teaching in any school, public or private, on the tenuous grounds that they were agents of a "foreign power," the pope. By concentrating his attack on the Jesuits in particular, Ferry hoped to awaken the latent hostility among the poor to an order that was frequently identified with the rich and powerful. He also endeavored to exploit the apathy of those Catholics who felt that the congregations were an appendage of little use to the church.[19]

While republicans whispered hoary tales about the Jesuits and claimed that the congregations taught hatred of the Republic, the conservatives retorted that the Radicals were attempting to create "schools without God" and that by denying the congregations the right to teach, Article Seven would end freedom of education. The effect of the law would be to close many Catholic schools, forcing parents to send their children to the state schools, where, by yet another provision of Ferry's bill, the religious instruction previously permitted would be forbidden. For fervent Catholics the issue was not merely political but intensely spiritual. They considered the failure to teach religion in the schools closely akin to endorsing atheism: laic instruction removed God as the central focus, denying his primacy and ultimately his importance. Catholics feared, and rightly, that it would be impossible for a laic schoolmaster to refrain from commenting on religious matters, to maintain what Ferry called "neutrality" on such sensitive issues as the life of Jeanne d'Arc. If he insisted that Jeanne followed the words of God, he would foster religion; if he dismissed the "voices" as her imagination, he would defame church teaching. Conservatives interpreted Ferry's proposals as a first, but a giant, step along a road that if followed would lead inexorably to the collapse of the church's influence in France.

The Chamber quickly approved Ferry's bill, but in the Senate, Jules Simon, one of the moderate leaders, shamed his fellow republicans by pointing out that Article Seven violated the very conception of liberty that the Republic had vowed to defend, and in the Senate that provision and the proscription of religious instruction were eliminated by a sizable majority in February 1880. Ferry and Premier Charles de Freycinet then pressed Grévy to ban the unauthorized congregations by executive order. The president was loath to invoke a power the precedent for which, Napoleon's tenure as first consul, ill-befitted a Republic, but he remembered to whom he owed his new dignity and issued two decrees on 29 March 1880. The first singled out the Jesuits for special treatment, ordering the dissolution of their houses and their departure from France within three months. The second granted all unauthorized congregations of men the same length of time in which to apply for authorization or leave. After receiving assurance that their classes could be assumed by nuns or local priests, almost all preferred to follow the Jesuits into exile rather than submit to the government. Altogether, between nine and ten thousand monks, from 216 houses, departed. The Jesuit schools were closed, although the more famous of them, like Sainte Geneviève, continued under other direction. Such men as du Lac moved to schools outside France, like the military academy at Cantorbéry on the channel island of Jersey. Although many of the monks and priests, including some Jesuits, did filter back into France and gather together again after several years, with a more lenient government ignoring them, the republicans had demonstrated their power. More important for the conservatives, there had been little outcry by a nominally Catholic nation against this repression. Following this first victory the anticlericals pressed their attack harder. The Ferry legislation had denied Catholic faculties the right to confer higher degrees or call themselves universities. In 1882 all religious instruction in state primary schools was banned, and the laicization of these schools was guaranteed in 1886 by a law forbidding the further recruitment of "authorized" monks and nuns as teachers. In 1884 divorce, illegal since 1816, was restored to the Civil Code. More drastic schemes to suppress all religious orders and confiscate their property, to recall the ambassador to the Vatican, and to abrogate the 1801 Concordat failed only by narrow margins. Many Catholics felt that their church was under siege and took these proposals of the republicans for harbingers of worse to follow.[20]

In this atmosphere of crisis, conservative leaders began feverish new activity in 1879 and 1880. They sought additional support from among the workers and within the military, and for success with either group, the participation of de Mun, with his control of the *cercles* and contacts like Lyautey among the officer corps, seemed essential. Legitimist Georges Berry took charge of sponsoring political banquets for members of the *cercles* and their friends at which they could eat, drink, denounce the Republic and its antireligious policy, toast the church and often Chambord. Although some royalists considered these extravaganzas useless—one saying, "I have a sword and a pen; I fight with both; but the fork is an arm which I refuse . . . [as] . . . ridiculous"—Berry and Charette were delighted when de Mun endorsed the program, blessed the role of his followers in it, and addressed the largest of the banquets, a four-thousand-man gathering at the Cirque d'Hiver in Paris on 10 July 1879. He also agreed to assume overall direction of the ephemeral Cercles Catholiques Militaires, which were formed at various forts by junior officers, mostly graduates of

Jesuit schools. Often idealistic like Lyautey and attracted by de Mun's charisma, these young lieutenants and captains were also unhappy with a government that persecuted their religion. De Mun saw his efforts as "Catholic above all" and had no plans for subverting the army, but he was in the company of increasingly dangerous royalists who wanted to use his talents and organization. The republican government had cause to worry because the plans of Charette, Berry, and fellow Vendéen Armand Baudry d'Asson did not stop at armed insurrection, and they had violent new allies in such Bonapartists as Paul Granier de Cassagnac, who, after the death of the Prince Imperial fighting Zulus in South Africa in 1879, turned toward the Legitimist camp rather than hail the anticlerical Prince Jérôme Bonaparte.[21]

The task of converting de Mun to their plans did not appear absolutely impossible because, under the influence of Saint-Germain and bitter at the treatment of the church, he had become more openly royalist. In 1877 at Goritz he had been briefly presented to Chambord, and in November 1880 he finally joined his brother at Frohsdorff to consult the pretender on the crisis in France. In de Mun's state of mind this visit worked magic on him. He knew that the Bourbon cause was without hope, that when the childless Chambord died the line would be extinct. Yet he felt compelled to make a symbolic protest, an act of conscience, against the godless Republic in favor of this "Christian king," whose piety and exquisite manners charmed him now and who appeared to incarnate "Counterrevolution." In disregard of his previous careful avoidance of undisguised participation in royalist politics, de Mun impulsively accepted Chambord's invitation to address a rally of the pretender's supporters at the Legitimist stronghold of Vannes in March of the following year.[22]

De Mun had already been telling the *cercles* that he did not doubt that they would "follow him in the struggle," but he clearly meant a moral one. As he began to form closer contacts with Charette in late 1880 and early 1881 after his return from Frohsdorff, the right-wing extremists began to hope that he would come to advocate a physical conflict against the Republic. His position would be decisive. If he could carry the *cercles* with him, the royalists might rally more than fifty thousand workers in an insurrection, more than enough, strategically placed, for a successful coup. De Mun's speech at Vannes on 8 March did not discourage them. He eulogized Chambord and distinctly called for a restoration of the Bourbons to replace the Republic that had inflicted so many economic, social, and religious woes upon the country. The monarchy, he declared, would respect the church, restore France's position in world affairs, and heal internal dissensions.[23]

This profession of royalist faith delighted Charette and Berry and thoroughly alarmed the republicans, who immediately increased the surveillance of the *cercles*. The head of the Sûreté Générale at this time, Emile Schnerb, particularly feared the *cercles*, urging in 1883 their dissolution as a violent counterrevolutionary group. Both sides, however, overestimated de Mun's commitment to royalism and his willingness to pledge the *cercles* to the cause of Chambord. They were ignorant of a memorandum he had circulated on 15 February 1881 to the members of the central committee of the Oeuvre des Cercles in which he declared that he was making the speech at Vannes in his name only and that his intention was to continue to withhold the *cercles* from royalist politics. To the disappointment of the extremists, de Mun later made this position public in his address to the general assembly of the *cercles* in May 1881 by emphasizing that the association "has never varied in its principles or its goals . . . it will remain constant in its form and affirmations." He continued to insist, as he had as early as 1878 in a letter to Roquefeuil, that the *cercles* were not to be a religious sect, an economic school, or a political party. They were not to be at the personal service of La Tour du Pin, Maignen, Harmel, himself, or anyone else. Instead they were to be the spirit of the counterrevolution, the example of the "Christian society" in action.[24]

In his blackest moments of hatred toward the Republic, de Mun may have been tempted to join the extremists, but he would not endanger the *cercles* in what was a highly risky endeavor at best. In 1881 there were more than 550 *cercles* comprising over 50,000 members. Their conspicuous success had come when throughout Europe the Catholic church was on the defensive, and it made de Mun a particular favorite of the Vatican. Some French bishops might resent the independence and lay control of the *cercles*, but their grumbling was muted because in the 1870s Pius IX had given the association his blessing four times. When Pius died in 1878 and

Gioacchino Vincenzo Cardinal Pecci was elected his successor as Leo XIII, de Mun led a delegation from the *cercles* to the Holy See for the enthronement. The new pontiff renewed Pius's blessings and received de Mun in a private audience that lasted over an hour, during which he lauded his social work. Yet despite Leo's praise and the fears of the republicans, the expansion of the *cercles* had slowed, and disputes over policy and politics racked the headquarters. La Tour du Pin was increasingly interested in corporatist theory and failed to maintain an understanding of the practical needs of the *cercles*. Harmel, never comfortable with the extreme paternalism of the movement, wanted to organize the worker members into self-governing unions, undercutting the very basis of the original conception. De Mun seemed increasingly preoccupied with the royalism of his brother and tempted to use the *cercles* for intrigue.[25] He had acquired his worker following before he had a political program, and when he developed one it turned out to be reactionary. How long would the workers remain behind him? For the moment de Mun imposed his will as secretary-general, but to maintain it he needed the authority of political success.

In the general election of August 1881, de Mun again presented himself as a candidate at Pontivy. Le Maguet, who had defeated him in a close race in 1879, sought an easier opponent and shifted to another district in Morbihan, and the republicans could field only a mystery candidate, M. Le Fur, who billed himself as a "peasant republican from the canton of Géméné." Little had been heard of him before the election and nothing would be afterward. Since Le Fur had not gained the following of Le Maguet, the race was not difficult, and with de Mun an obvious victor many voters stayed home. The margin was still impressive, 4,467 to 3,550, and even more so since the conservatives suffered crushing losses in the voting, winning only 88 seats to the 459 of the republicans. Ernest Constans, the minister of the interior, had skillfully wielded the weapon of administrative pressure and had carefully scheduled the elections at the height of the harvest season, when many conservative peasants would be tempted to abstain. The conservatives contributed to their rout by presenting a generally lackluster performance, with no new ideas, only old hatreds. They were particularly distressed that the election could be interpreted as an endorsement of anticlericalism since the gains of the Left were made principally by the Radicals, who now held 40 percent of the seats. This dramatic repudiation by the country ended the intrigues of the royalist extremists, whose plans had already been crippled by de Mun's refusal to provide their needed shock troops.[26]

To republicans of all varieties these election results seemed to portend four fat years. Instead there were four lean ones. The sweetness of the economic revival that had followed the war of 1870–71 turned sour in 1882. Phylloxera infected the vineyards, harvests proved barren, and the financial climate was upset by the spectacular failure in February 1882 of the Union Générale, a so-called Catholic bank established to oppose the Rothschilds. Business throughout Europe suffered from a general depression, which in France spawned labor unrest.[27] In the midst of the growing crisis, Gambetta died in December 1882 at the age of forty-four. With him disappeared much that was fresh and innovative in the Republic. His followers rallied about Jules Ferry, the man of Article Seven. Ferry had grand schemes for France, but in the general atmosphere of disquiet he felt it more expedient to preach reform than to seek its immediate enactment. This attitude won for him and his followers the admirable designation "Opportunists," republicans who in their hearts believed in fundamental reforms but who felt that these should not be put through until the time was opportune, which it seldom was. Because solutions to questions as complex as the "social problem" were divisive of republican ranks, the Opportunists tacitly agreed to concentrate on issues such as anticlericalism that united them. The Protestant free-thinking Ferry made it his practice to divert the country with attacks on clerical power and added a colonial policy the bravura of which might distract those beset by economic distress. French expansion in Africa and Asia eased European tensions by pleasing Bismarck, who knew that infantry stationed abroad could not be used for revanche along the Vosges.

During most of these four years the conservatives were in full retreat. The sense of dejection and failure instilled by the elections of 1881 was only deepened, at least among the Legitimists, by the unexpected death of the Count of Chambord on 24 August 1883. No scheme or insurrection now could redeem the cause of the Bourbons and all that the Legitimist monarchy implied for French tradition. De Mun's reaction was typical of Chambord's followers: "A king is still possible, *the* king no longer so." With Charette and

La Tour du Pin he traveled to Frohsdorff for the week of obsequies, and he recorded his impressions in a private journal. At the sight of Chambord's casket he felt "crushed, . . . the past, the hopes of the future all fleeting." He had never cared for the Orleanist princes, whom Chambord had designated his successors, particularly disliking the new pretender, the Count of Paris, whose relative modernity did not fit his image of a "Christian prince." He was further offended when the Orleanists refused to attend the interment at Goritz on 3 September because the Spanish Bourbons, closer to Chambord in blood, would be given the place of highest honor in the funeral procession. In hailing the Count of Paris as Philippe VII, de Mun sent only the laconic telegram, "The king is dead! Long live the king!" He criticized the new pretender's absence from Goritz in an interview printed in the Orleanist *Le Gaulois* and published a letter in which his lack of enthusiasm for the line of Louis Philippe was only thinly veiled: "Whatever our fear and grief, we do not have the right to despair or to withdraw in a culpable indifference. We shall continue to serve the cause of monarchy openly and without reservation." His friends knew of his hesitations. When Lyautey asked whether or not to embrace the Orleanists, de Mun replied by describing his visit to the pretender's castle at Eu. "He certainly made us very welcome . . . [and] spoke to us of social questions and the workers in our movement as one who has studied them. . . . But it is not the same thing . . . he shakes your hand . . . you dine in black tie." At Frohsdorff no one had approached Chambord without kissing his hand; dinner had always been in white tie. De Mun also emphasized that for himself, the church and the *cercles* would always continue to come before royalism. "We must unite ourselves behind Philippe in loyal and sincere service," he urged, "but also remain what we are, Catholics vigorously united about the task of giving value to the social and economic ideas that we believe to be the best foundation of a good government."[28]

The reluctance of some Legitimists to rally to the Count of Paris meant that bitterness remained between them and the Orleanists, and no true fusion of the two groups was possible. De Mun's attitude was particularly resented, and he was publicly accused of fainthearted royalism. The union of conservatives was further complicated by the refusal of the Bonapartists to give up their last hopes and by the acrimonious splits among their movement. Agents for

Prince Jérôme continued to stir the embers of imperial sentiment, and Bonapartist candidates often contested those of the royalists in elections. Legitimists, Orleanists, and Bonapartists were united in their distaste for the Republic but in little else. Competition among them destroyed any chance they had of overturning it. As de Mun rode the train back to Paris in September 1883 following the burial of Chambord, he encountered the Marquis Gaston de Gallifet, one of the few republicans in the army high command but hated by the Left as the "Butcher of the Commune." Gallifet asked him, "Well, when do you intend to restore the monarchy now?" De Mun replied jokingly, "Whenever you like!" Gallifet was more serious. "In this country," he counseled, "impressions pass rapidly. If you do not act within six months, no one will again take royalism seriously." He had accurately defined the penalty for delay.[29]

The same dissensions among the conservatives made it impossible for them to act as a group in the Chamber. In 1881 they organized themselves into a parliamentary faction, the Union des Droites, with the tough realist Baron Armand de Mackau, a Bonapartist turned Orleanist, as its president. The meetings of the union only demonstrated the irreconcilable differences of the various conservative divisions. Mackau hoped to initiate a "politics of interests," exploiting the issues of empty stomachs and pocketbooks, while reducing dependence on the religious and dynastic appeals that had been so ineffective in 1881. Idealists like de Mun and Cassagnac found this approach an affront to their exalted view of the French people, whom they felt would eventually rise up to defend their religion and cast off the Republic. Even when conservatives agreed with Mackau's overall strategy, they disagreed over tactics, which issues to exploit, and even which side of an issue to defend.[30]

Mackau therefore quickly found it impossible to unite the Union on any issue. He began by proposing that they stand as a bloc against the budget, but even on this basic element of opposition tactics he was unable to obtain unanimity because some conservatives wanted to vote in favor of appropriations they approved or wanted to reward republican fiscal responsibility. There was even less chance of agreement on an issue as complex as Ferry's imperialism. Those like de Mun who had commanded colonial units were pleased at the extension of French empire but jealous that it was the

Left planting the flag. Although they supported successful operations, they carped at every reverse and were outraged at the dabbling of republican politicians in the conduct of military operations. The majority of conservatives opposed any colonial expansion on the grounds that it took France's eyes from the blue line of the Vosges and the prospect of revanche in Alsace-Lorraine. The divisions were still sharper over social policy. De Mun and about twenty other deputies in the Union favored the inauguration of a program of industrial reform legislation based on social Catholic principles. To the remainder of the Right these ideas smacked of socialism. Mackau was unable to impose discipline on the Union des Droites, and it united only to oppose the anticlerical legislation and the constitutional amendments enacted in August 1884 forbidding modification of the republican form of government, revising the election procedure for senators, and prohibiting public prayers at the convocation of the Chamber and Senate. On issues where there was some disagreement between Opportunists and Radicals, a unified Right might have wielded influence. Against anticlericalism and the amendments, the eighty-eight negative votes of the conservatives could make no conceivable difference. It was a sorry performance.[31]

For de Mun his first full term in the Chamber was frustrating and ineffective. He had regained some political authority with his election victory, but his unconsummated flirtation with Charette and Berry had rendered him suspect among both extremists and moderates of the Right. He was at odds with many of the conservatives over social policy and with Mackau over the defense of the church. Although de Mun's eloquence and the promising capacity he had demonstrated in developing the *cercles* marked him as a future candidate for leadership, he found himself partly isolated from those with whom he sat. Mackau did call upon him to denounce the conduct of the republicans at the joint session of Chamber and Senate enacting the constitutional amendments, and de Mun responded with a speech laden with expressions of vitriol. "We have seen the meeting hall of the National Assembly transformed into a jousting list," he derided scornfully, "the rostrum taken by siege, and the representation of the nation compromised by scenes of violence." He also spoke for the colonialists among the conservatives, lecturing the Ferry ministry on military tactics, and when French hopes were at their nadir in Tunisia in late 1881, charging that a republic was incapable of maintaining the honor of France. These words provoked enthusiastic cheering from the Right, torrents of abuse from the Left, and near censure from the chair.[32]

De Mun also continued to mount the tribune as the avenging sword of the church, and he did so far too often for Mackau's taste, and, significantly, that of the Vatican. Pope Leo XIII was already at work on the encyclical published in 1885 as *Immortale Dei*, in which he would underscore the church's indifference to a state's form of government, a significant shift from the overt royalism of Pius IX. Mackau's policy was to relegate religious defense to the status of one among other concerns in his politics of interests, rejecting the identity between throne and altar that had been characteristic of royalism under Chambord for the simple reason that this identification facilitated republican attacks on the church and cost the royalists potential support in anticlerical but conservative regions. The dovetailing tactics of the Holy See and the leader of the Union des Droites required that royalist deputies be less conspicuous in their vindication of the church, that they cease to seem the exclusive defenders of religion in France. The subtleties of this artifice were lost on de Mun, who characteristically reacted with outrage whenever the privileges of the church were called into question. He flatly rejected Mackau's counsel that since the conservatives had no means of blocking the anticlerical program they should confine their opposition to brief, reasoned argument. Instead de Mun cried forth his witness emotionally, frequently, and at length, even carrying the fight outside the Chamber to mass meetings of Catholics, where, with the eloquence of passion, he violently denounced the new laws governing the schools and urged disobedience of them.[33]

He was not alone among the deputies to defy Mackau, who had not the means to silence them, nor among Catholics to disregard the hints of the Vatican, when the pope had not yet spoken. In *L'Univers*, Eugène Veuillot replaced his deceased brother Louis in 1883 with no change in tone, and Monsignor Charles Freppel, the epithet-hurling bishop of Angers and deputy from Brest, outdid even de Mun in bitter polemics. These outbursts had almost unlimited potential for placing new weapons in the hands of the republicans, who could pontificate on the immoderation of French churchmen lay and clerical and the extremism of royalists and Catholics in alliance. The Radicals in particular took delight in goading the conscience of the fervent. When Victor Hugo died in May 1885, they proposed that to honor the rebel who had been the incarnation of all that was unfettered and who after the coup d'état of December 1851 had exiled himself to the channel island Jersey until with the overthrow of *Napoléon le petit* liberty should again become the bride of France, the Republic should surpass the obsequies of the first Napoleon in 1840. The symbolic value of such republican sacerdotalism was evident to the Opportunists, and Hugo's remains were placed in a mammoth urn to lie in state beneath the Arc de Triomphe. Following a pretentious processional across the Seine, he was entombed, to the horror of Catholics, after a civil ceremony of brass bands and speeches, in the Panthéon, which was secularized for the occasion.[34]

Social policy confronted de Mun with his most perplexing dilemma. As he and the Oeuvre des Cercles came to advocate some government sponsorship and guarantee of reforms, he found his position closer to the Left than the Right. The very social Catholicism of the *cercles* that had carried him to prominence among the conservatives now created tension between him and their majority. Yet as he was a royalist Catholic, his seat could only be with the Right, among those whom he bitterly assailed as "insipid bourgeois, who have only scorn, disdain, or wrath for the aspirations of social reform." When the Opportunists decided in 1883 that it would be expedient to seek the legalization of trade unions, de Mun provoked an open split in the Union des Droites by leading the social Catholics among them to support the proposal to overturn the 1791 Le Chapelier law, which had forbidden associations of workers. During the nineteenth century a number of unions were tolerated, especially if the owner approved, as in the case of Harmel's mixed union at Val des Bois, but most employers emphatically disapproved, refusing to deal with them and ruthlessly crushing the strikes they called. Yet the idea of the union survived because workingmen instinctively realized that only in unity could they hope to secure their demands. The Left saw trade unions as the adversaries of employers; de Mun advocated rather the mixed union as closer to the conception of the *cercles*. He asked preference for them in the legislation, but when the republicans refused, he proclaimed his intention to support any bill extending the right to form unions of whatever type. This gracious concession grew out of Harmel's new conviction and warning that workers often feared that the presence of the owner in the union would mute demands or lead to reprisals against militants. De Mun also recognized that even the *cercles* were unprepared for mixed unions. A survey of the owners among their membership in February and March 1883 revealed that while all accepted their responsibility to undertake the "devotion of the directing class," only 20 percent would agree to meet the workers on an equal basis.[35]

These "ideas of M. de Mun" that were heard discussed in the corridors of the Chamber and this attack on laissez-faire branded him a maverick. Some of the conservatives were frankly offended. De Mun found himself completely unable to convert the Right to his brand of social reform, and he acquired the habit of looking beyond them for support of his proposals. It could not be to the Left except in brief instances, for although a number of them admitted the sincerity of his concern and admired him as a man, this admiration did not temper their anticlericalism. There were the *cercles*, although their expansion had slowed, and perhaps more young men like Lyautey at the universities. De Mun experimented with lectures in 1885 to students in Belgium at Louvain and in Switzerland at Fribourg and was inspired by the enthusiasm and receptivity of his audiences. Assistance might also come from the Vatican, where Leo XIII had taken an interest in his social work and approved it in the encyclical *Humanum genus* of 20 April 1884, although only in a vague manner. When told by Harmel that conservative critics taxed the *cercles* with breeding socialism, the pope replied with agitation, "No! It is not socialism by Christianity!" and charged Archbishop Benoît Langénieux to be the cardinal-protector of social Catholicism in France.[36]

But in spite of de Mun's notability, he had proved to be a striking failure as a politician. He was forty-four in 1885, the same age as Gambetta when he died but very much less effective than the Great Tribune had been. He was headstrong and at odds with the conservatives over strategy and tactics. There were few who would follow his lead, yet he would not willingly follow anyone else. The Left had at first thought him a danger but now recognized his isolation. He sat with the Right, which became more ineffectual each year, watching as the republicans enacted whatever legislation they deemed opportune. Did not Gambetta's influence even after death surpass his own? The church was besieged; a restoration had never been less possible. If de Mun were not to remain a political cypher, he would have to develop the talent for organization he had shown in the *cercles*, exploit the power of his oratory, and gain a capacity for political maneuver and compromise. He had depended too much on his instincts, passions, and prejudices. He had shown the bloodlines of a paladin, not a politician.

3
The Catholic Party and Boulangism

As the elections of 1885 approached, it became evident that the four lean years since 1881 had worked a hardship on the country. The tactics of Opportunism followed by Ferry and the remnant of Gambetta's legions had failed. The clericals were on the run, but the blood and treasure expended on colonial schemes made Ferry's foreign adventures increasingly detested among the republicans. Moreover, the economic malaise had deepened into a depression, and the premier's inability to move the economy out of its doldrums split the ruling majority. Most of the old Radicals, led by Georges Clemenceau and Camille Pelletan, found him too cautious and unwilling to experiment with new policies. The remainder of Ferry's followers, the so-called Opportunists, stood by his methods but were afraid to face the electorate while burdened by the government's numerous failures and difficulties. They were so sensitive that they forbade the use of the phrase "Pontius Pilote était opportuniste" in the church catechism.[1] Both Radicals and Opportunists agreed that Ferry must not be the republican standard-bearer for the elections and sought to dissociate themselves from him. When March 1885 brought reports of French reverses in Indochina, his majority deserted him and joined his enemies in the Chamber to drive him from office, pursued by cries of "Ferry-Tonkin!"

The republicans could not solve their differences by merely chasing Ferry offstage, and his sudden exit further complicated their dilemma by leaving them bereft of a leader capable of appealing to both factions. Almost in desperation they then tried to evoke the ghost of Gambetta, on 24 March resurrecting his scheme to conduct elections under the system of *scrutin de liste*, by which voters chose an entire slate of candidates for each department, and abandoning the single-member constituencies of *scrutin d'arron-*

dissement, which had been in effect since 1871. Royalists as well as republicans were willing to experiment with the election procedure, and the proposal passed with almost no debate.[2] The decision was a serious mistake for the republicans. *Scrutin de liste* allowed great waves of public opinion to sweep away local issues and local men, and by the summer of 1885 public opinion was running against the Opportunists and Radicals. They were still beset by sharp divisions and unable to agree on a single list of candidates for each department. In over half of the departments each group submitted different lists, thereby splitting the republican vote. Leaderless, saddled with failure, and rent by dissension, the ruling majority was ill-prepared to wage the unified national campaign required by the new election procedure.

While the Left bickered and divided, the Right showed its first signs of unity in years. By July 1885 the various factions of the Union des Droites had agreed to avoid talk of a restoration in their campaign propaganda and to "hide their flags" by concentrating instead on an attack of the record of the Opportunists. In September, Mackau released a preelection appeal, the "Déclaration des Droites," which reflected these tactics and sought support from the victims of the lean years: "Persecuted Catholics, hard-pressed taxpayers, humiliated heads of families, peasants crushed by taxes and high interest, businessmen hard hit by [foreign] competition, shopkeepers affected by recessions, Royalists, Bonapartists, Imperialists, Solutionists, and honest disillusioned Republicans! Vote for the Conservative list—that is, against waste, against faraway expeditions, against violence, against infamy, against Republican turpitude! Vote for God, for Order, for *La Patrie*!" The conservatives were not agreed on how to govern the Republic, if republic it was to remain. They were agreed on a single opposition list to oppose the two republican lists.[3]

When France went to the polls for the first ballot on 4 October 1885, the Right made a remarkable advance, capturing 3.5 million votes, 1.6 million more than in 1881. Protests against the majority's performance during the past four years and a split of the republican vote produced 177 seats for the conservatives and only 127 for the Opportunists and Radicals. Terrified that the Right might regain the control of the Chamber that it had lost in 1876, the republicans closed ranks, and for the second ballot on 18 October they settled on a single list. The conservatives in the meantime failed to play their hand wisely. Some of them misread the initial success as a mandate for a restoration and predicted that a king would ascend the throne by the end of the year. As soon as the ballots of 4 October were counted, *Le Gaulois*, as the spokesman for the Count of Paris, erected an illuminated sign above its Paris headquarters reading, "*Le Gaulois*—177 Monarchist Deputies—Vive la France!" Shortly afterward Paul Granier de Cassagnac published an editorial in another monarchist newspaper claiming that the nation had begun to vomit the Republic. The flags were no longer hidden. Although other conservatives realized that these tactics were fatal and that their gains had come more from dissatisfaction with republican policies than from disaffection with the Republic itself, their warning did little good. The country was alarmed at the renewed threat to the regime as the grimly united republicans sounded the tocsin. In the *ballottage* of 18 October the conservatives won only 26 more seats out of the 281 contested. The final tally of the elections showed the republicans holding a very substantial majority in the Chamber, 381 to 203. Nevertheless, the Right had doubled its representation and attracted 44 percent of the 8 million votes cast, less than a million behind the republicans. If they could capture only 500,000 more votes in the future, victory might be theirs.[4]

As on all other issues, the conservatives were divided on how best to seek the additional votes. Mackau favored his politics of interests, the creation of a conservative appeal through which the monarchists could attract votes far beyond the constituency of throne and altar solidly enlisted in their ranks in the elections of 1885. He was handicapped, however, by the inability of the Right to formulate any positive program of social and economic goals, and the "Déclaration des Droites" revealed their essentially negative thinking. Others rejected this subterfuge, continuing to believe that deep reserves of faith in church or king lay untapped. De Mun was within this group, but he separated himself from those who wanted to mount a new campaign in favor of Philippe VII. The appeal of the restored monarchy had been tried and found wanting. It was time, he was persuaded, to emulate the Catholics of Belgium, Austria, and Germany, who had banded into confessional parties and achieved striking political success. He saw himself as a French Ludwig Windthorst, leading a nationwide, societywide Catholic movement, a Catholic party, in which he could move the focus of conservative politics from the restoration of the throne to defense of the church and the enactment of a social Catholic reform program. His Catholic party would draw support from monarchists and republicans, from all who were true to the best interests of their religion. It was a vast potential membership, but in its political diversity lay an extreme difficulty. Monarchist Catholics opposed not simply a series of anticlerical measures but the Republic itself; republican Catholics might resent the laic laws but would not desert the regime. The crucial question would be whether the bonds of religious confession would be strong enough to contain both groups.[5]

De Mun first broached the idea of a Catholic party in a letter to Mackau in July 1885, writing to complain that the "Déclaration des Droites" merely papered over the divisions of the conservatives and proposing his idea as an alternative. Not unexpectedly, Mackau rejected his suggestion out of hand. De Mun then began a series of maladroit maneuvers to launch a Catholic party on his own. He first sought impressive backing for a program of "religious defense" by persuading Mackau, Keller, Chesnelong, and nine other conservative leaders to join him in issuing an "appeal to Catholic voters" in August 1885. Although the twelve considered the document just another piece of campaign propaganda, de Mun had carefully drafted it to laud the church but omit all reference to royalism. On 8 September, a month before the first ballot, he revealed his true intention by sending an open letter to Admiral August Gicquel des Touches, a signer of the August appeal and a former minister of the navy under MacMahon, proposing that Catholics organize themselves into a confessional party to defend the church and promote social Catholic reforms. There was no mention of opposition to the Republic and no prior consultation of Mackau or other conservative leaders. Finally, on 19 September, de Mun announced that he had begun actively to recruit members for a Catholic party.[6]

De Mun's campaign produced immediate opposition. Many Frenchmen—and not all of them conservatives—saw his initiative as a blatant attempt to seize the leadership of the Right. *Le Temps*, as spokesman for the Opportunists, derided him as a "former paladin become miserable politico." Mackau and such other leading monarchists as Falloux were angered by his audacity, by his ambition, and by what they considered his calculated betrayal of their cause. The opposition of men of their stature, who wielded vast power among the traditionalists of the Right by virtue of their long years of leadership and an ingrown sense of hierarchy, made the costs of joining de Mun very high, even for those who found his position congenial. Because he seemed in contempt of the conservative leadership, de Mun could attract only 14 of the 203 deputies of the Right elected with him to the Chamber. No republican even considered joining him. This failure among the deputies forced him to turn elsewhere for support, and his only option was the *cercles*. On 28 October he sought the approval of their central committee for a plan to use the *cercles* as the organizational base of a Catholic party. Accustomed to following his leadership, the committee acquiesced, but Robert de Mun abstained on the vote rather than openly oppose his brother's dubious scheme. More than Albert, who was emotionally committed to his idea, Robert de Mun saw that any plan for a Catholic party had been doomed by the refusal of leading conservatives to endorse it and that basing the movement on the *cercles* would turn it into an essentially working-class phenomenon rather than a universalist confessional party. It would also have the unfortunate effect of politicizing the *cercles*, something always previously avoided at his brother's insistence.[7]

Albert de Mun was not quite ready to admit defeat. Hoping to win added support if he clarified his goals, he published a second open letter, this one on 3 November to Viscount Louis de Bélizal, one of his meager number of recruits. In it he outlined an ambitious religious and social program. The state would guarantee to uphold the 1801 Concordat in letter and spirit, granting the congregations freedom to exist in France, revoking the divorce statute, returning to the Falloux law in education, and requiring religious instruction in the public schools. Comprehensive social reforms would be enacted, providing for cessation of work on Sundays, elimination of night work for women, reduction of working hours for women and children, and institution of insurance against industrial accidents, sickness, and unemployment. But even as de Mun edited his text for publication, letters were in transit that would decisively rout his project. Monsignor Freppel wrote to deny that a party could function in the Chamber without taking a stand on the question of the regime. Emile Keller lectured him that all France was not so militantly Catholic as his Breton electors and concluded, "You must not judge France by your voters alone; you would do well to listen to impressions coming from less privileged departments." Mackau was nearly as sharp, declaring that a Catholic party would only further fragment the conservatives. Even Adrien de Mun wrote to criticize his son as rash and assertive. All hope of persevering disappeared when the papal nuncio delivered a letter to de Mun from Leo XIII condemning the venture as inopportune. Like the leaders of the Union des Droites, the pope did not feel that a confessional party could be successful if its members had not achieved consensus on the status of the Republic. De Mun received the papal admonition on 8 November and on the following day he announced through *L'Univers* that he had abandoned his plan to form a Catholic party.[8]

De Mun's idea had been utterly crushed; it was, he said, a "rude blow!" There had been almost no one, even among his family, to follow his leadership. His isolation had never seemed greater. He immediately tried to repair relations with Mackau, writing him, "My dear friend, I hold no grudge in having had to give up my project." Mackau, who saw de Mun as one of the prima donnas with whom he had to deal in the Union des Droites, accepted this apology. Others were less ready to forgive. Falloux in particular was incensed at de Mun, as he had been in 1878 over "counterrevolution." He considered him inexperienced, incapable, and far too ambitious, and he quoted the usually even-tempered Chesnelong's description of de Mun as a "ravager." This wrath overflowed in a letter to Mackau as Falloux called

> de Mun's behavior toward M. Chesnelong and M. Keller unspeakable. . . . de Mun moreover has two great faults, but he can neither repent of nor correct them because he does not even suspect their existence. Through his undisciplined speeches he gives the enemy all the pretexts it needs to act, and he insists on playing the role of leader, a role that does not belong to him and for which he possesses not even the elementary qualities. . . . He has the most ungenerous nature I have ever known. His character is all calculation and pretension, and here is his incorrigible fault, he wants at any price to be chief. He has incontestable and brilliant qualities as a soldier orator, but outside of that, he is incapable . . . very egotistical, and personally divorced from the ideas and men he tries to use.

The same Leo XIII who had consistently supported the work of the *cercles* and earlier in 1885 awarded de Mun the Cross of St. Gregory the Great now disowned the Catholic party. In the eyes of all, de

Mun stood condemned of overreaching ambition or at best political immaturity.[9]

De Mun did not fully recognize what a critical question he had raised for the conservatives, what a decisive juncture they had been forced to confront in his plan for a confessional party. De Mun's own royalism had never been perfervid, and the death of Chambord had destroyed what ardor there was by severing any possible link between it and the social and religious philosophy of the *cercles*. No one could mistake the Count of Paris for an advocate of counterrevolution. The church meant far more to de Mun than did the monarchy, and his conception of a Catholic party omitted the traditional royalist frame of reference. It was this critical departure from the past that excited the most vehement objections from royalist leaders. In it there was the sense, not yet clearly perceived even by de Mun and those other conservatives who were frustrated by royalism's failures, that it was possible to be conservative but not monarchist, in opposition to republican laws but not to the Republic. Such a position for the Right, the foundation of the Ralliement in the 1890s, was still impossible in 1885 because conservative deputies, de Mun himself among them, clung grimly to the faith of monarchism although a restoration was now almost beyond political reality. Royalism was their link to the past and tradition; to betray it was to desert the faith of their forefathers. The conservative leadership comprehended the instincts of their troops far better than did de Mun, who reflected bitterly and most unrealistically that the cause of the church had been sacrificed to monarchist politics.

The only consolation he could claim was a first-ballot victory in Morbihan because even with the *cercles* his touch seemed to fail. Their expansion had slowed in the early 1880s, and this slowness threatened to become stagnation. New *cercles* were founded but most of them did not prosper, and some of the weaker older ones collapsed. Because the total membership hovered around sixty thousand, de Mun had to question whether or not he had attracted all of those workers susceptible to the appeal of social Catholicism. Ominously, Marxian socialism seemed a more vibrant force than his own. Young workers found paternalism much less tolerable than their older brothers had only ten or fifteen years earlier. Although the reality of class solidarity remained a myth among the workers, the idea was immensely appealing in its assertion of independence from the owner, and anticlericalism soon became de rigueur for social rebels. The *cercles*, with their stuffy "devotion of the directing class," were unsuited to the changed environment. De Mun could have sought new support from the army as he had in the past, but even junior officers were unlikely to break down the sense of hierarchy and formality that were now burdens to the *cercles*. For an infusion of new talent and blood de Mun therefore looked to the young men of the universities, organizing many into a new movement allied to the *cercles*, the Association Catholique de la Jeunesse Française (ACJF), which he founded in 1886. These young students, who fortified their religious fervor in annual retreats, monthly corporate communions, and organized study groups on the Christian's duty to society, might eventually revitalize the *cercles* through their youthful enthusiasm and prove that the church could still appeal to the working class.[10]

While waiting for the ACJF to reanimate the *cercles* de Mun grew discouraged at harassment from within Catholic ranks. In February 1886, *L'Association Catholique*, the monthly de Mun and La Tour du Pin founded in December 1876 to promote the study of social Catholic theory, carried an article by an Austrian economist, Jean Loesevitz, whose proposals came very close to socialism. De Mun, who had never served on the editorial board and had not seen the article prior to its publication, was compelled to disavow it because of the journal's close links to the *cercles*. Despite this repudiation, the bishop of Nancy, Monsignor Charles Turinaz, violently denounced de Mun and his followers as opponents of private property. The attack was so furious that de Mun sought the support of Cardinal Guibert of Paris, who, after consulting with the Vatican, assured him that Leo XIII continued to approve of the work of the *cercles*. But while de Mun eagerly grasped these words of encouragement from the pope, no encyclical came forth placing the papal imprimatur on social Catholicism. Lacking it, de Mun found the *cercles* opposed in several dioceses by bishops who, like Turinaz, believed his movement to be dangerously independent of episcopal control and possibly close to heretical socialism. The power of the prelates was considerable and compelled him to act cautiously. "To be prudent!" he wrote to du Lac, who in 1885 had become his confessor. "Oh yes, I know how necessary it is. But how difficult!" By September 1886 he had reached a nadir in frustration, and he asked du Lac, "When I combat economic liberalism, when I propose corporatism and insist on the duty of the state [to intervene], what proves to me that I do the will of God? I believe that I am right, but there are many Catholics who do not. And the bishops . . . and the pope? Do you not think that they would prefer me to keep silent? Witness the affair of the Catholic party!" When his brother Robert died suddenly in February 1887, de Mun felt more alone than ever before. For three months he and his family withdrew from Paris to Lumigny in a mourning that for de Mun was also an escape from responsibilities. He returned in May to deliver his address to the annual general assembly of the *cercles* and to take up his duties again in the Chamber. His zest and vigor revived at new political developments, but he could not escape his depression until he led a pilgrimage of *cercle* members to the Vatican in October. Leo XIII twice called him to private audiences, and with a thrill of vindication de Mun heard him ask for documents and ideas from the experience of the *cercles* as a basis for the curia to prepare an encyclical on the social question.[11]

The new political developments of May 1887 held almost as much potential for de Mun as did the proposed encyclical. Mackau had seemed to march the conservatives a crucial step away from monarchism and toward significant influence in the Chamber by seducing the Opportunists to his politics of interests. The maneuver was possible because the elections of 1885 had left the republican deputies almost evenly divided between the Opportunists and the Radicals, and it quickly became apparent that they had difficulty working in the same harness. One of their differences was timing—the Opportunists being willing to delay reforms, the Radicals demanding them immediately—because increasingly they represented different constituencies. The Opportunists had become "moderates," supported by a middle class that voted, according to the aphorism, with their hearts on the Left but their pocketbooks on the Right. They were *arrivistes*, repelled by the hauteur of the royalists and happy to find a home in a "respectable" Republic. The Radical voters also had their hearts on the Left but sometimes carried no pocketbooks at all. They were the lower middle class and small shopkeepers, who resented the prosperity of their economic superiors, and landless farm workers and urban poor, who with very little to lose even leaned toward socialism. As a group they generated shudders among the self-satisfied Opportunist supporters. The Radicals also sponsored a vicious anticlericalism based less on a fear of church power, the motive of the Opportunists, than on a vindictive glee at the discomfiture of authority and the impotent rage of the wealthy faithful. In spite of their tensions, the votes of both groups were necessary to command a republican majority in the Chamber, and for eighteen months after the elections they maintained an uneasy alliance based on their lowest common denominator, opposition to the Right. Since the foundation of the coalition was negative, as soon as the republicans exhausted their latest projects attacking the conservatives, it was subjected to increasing, and finally unbearable, strains.

The republicans found unity most easily in anticlericalism, and Ferry's successor as premier, Opportunist Charles de Freycinet, began the parliamentary session by insisting that all private chapels be "authorized," much as monastic orders were to be. He directed the police to begin closing noncomplying chapels, and during one of these sorties in April 1886 a worshiper resisted and was accidentally killed. When the cabinet contented itself with merely expressing its regret for the "unfortunate incident" and declared its intention to continue the closures, Mackau encouraged de Mun to make one of his immoderate denunciations. When he responded by proclaiming that "between you and us there is a broken cross" and threatening that "it will not be forgotten and it will end in your atonement," the Radicals bothered only to laugh and fling catcalls. The Opportunists proceeded with their sedulous pruning of clerical influence in education, introducing a bill in October 1886 to deny all monks and nuns the right to teach in the primary public schools. Republicans also solidly supported a law to exile the male members of the former regnant families. The Radicals had long demanded this banishment, and the Opportunists were galled by the soirée given in the capital by the Count of Paris in May 1886 in honor of the marriage of his daughter Amélie to the Duke of Braganza, heir-apparent to the throne of Portugal. There had been toasts of "Vive le Roi!" to the father of the bride, and the royalist daily *Le Figaro* declared the reception a symbol of the strength of monarchist sentiment. Alarmists among the Opportunists whispered the dangers of a coup d'état because Philippe VII was residing in Paris, and Clemenceau's bile had been stirred by a long delay when his carriage was caught in the traffic jam created by the party. Protests by conservatives, de Mun among them, that the proposal was a contradiction of the *liberté*, *égalite*, *fraternité* of the Republic were useless. The bill easily cleared the Chamber and Senate in June, and the Orleanist and Bonapartist princes boarded trains for exile. Little public sympathy followed them.[12]

The abject failure of the conservatives to prevent the banishing of their figureheads shocked them into reconsidering their strategy. In November 1886, as the Radicals pressed for graduated income and inheritance taxes, Bonapartist Edgar Raoul-Duval called upon his colleagues of the Right to forsake their traditions in order to defend their treasure. He reminded them that they shared opposition to the proposed taxes with the Opportunists and suggested that the two groups form a Center-Right government to exclude the Radicals. This proposal was not very far in advance of what some conservative leaders were considering. In the summer of 1886, Cassagnac cautiously advanced the possibility of conservative endorsement for specific republican policies, if sufficiently authoritarian, and the royalist *Le Soleil* proposed that the Right support an Opportunist cabinet that adopted an "acceptable" attitude toward the church, meaning a liberal enforcement of the existing anticlerical strictures. In September the Count of Paris extended his blessing to this offer in a private communiqué to his supporters and reiterated it publicly through the monarchist press, counseling the conservatives to cease their systematic opposition to the regime and to take their stand on "conservative issues." The conciliatory effort of the Right had great strategic potential. Within the Chamber it might drive a wedge between the quarreling republican forces. For the nation at large it might have far greater impact, convincing the half million additional voters whom the Right needed to become a majority that the conservatives were responsible and could be trusted.[13]

The Opportunists were wary of glib conservative promises and sought deeds to back up words. When none were forthcoming, they remained tenuously allied to the Radicals. Bickering between the two factions on taxation policy brought down Freycinet's ministry in early December 1886, but the Opportunists, not trusting the conservatives, had no choice except to patch up an agreement with their traditional partner. The new cabinet of René Goblet was therefore only a repetition of the old, and its conduct showed that it would inherit the problems of Freycinet. On 17 May 1887, it was toppled from within by a budgetary dispute. Goblet moved too far toward the Radical position and was disowned by the Opportunists, who then joined with the conservatives to overthrow him. The premier's fall was also determined by the conduct of his war minister, General Georges Boulanger, a holdover from the Freycinet cabinet and the darling of the Radicals. His foolhardy and reckless policy toward Germany had fomented such serious border incidents that Bismarck threatened war. With France totally unprepared to face Germany in battle and the Radicals unwilling to disavow Boulanger, conservatives and Opportunists joined to remove this menace from power.[14]

In the two weeks that followed, political maneuver produced a realignment. The Radicals insisted on Boulanger's inclusion in any new government as a prerequisite of their support, a demand unacceptable to the Opportunists. At the same time the conservatives renewed their conciliatory gestures. Acting in the name of the Union des Droites, Mackau met twice with President Grévy at the Elysée palace on 20 and 25 May, offering to guarantee at least 160 votes to an Opportunist ministry that would enforce the anticlerical legislation liberally. The agreement would be an armistice, not a capitulation. The conservatives would neither participate in nor be clearly allied to the new ministry; they would merely make possible the functioning of government. Grévy passed this information to Opportunist leaders who, after some hesitation, carefully constructed a cabinet with the moderate financial expert Maurice Rouvier at its head and the conciliatory Jacques Spuller at the sensitive ministry of public worship. When Rouvier presented this ministry to the Chamber on 30 May, it won approval by a majority composed of Opportunists and conservatives, the first instance since 1877 that the Right had voted confidence in a cabinet.[15]

The conservatives were quickly able to judge the value of their new alliance. In June a Radical-sponsored military-recruitment bill came up for consideration, calling for the reduction of required service from five years to three and the elimination of exemptions for seminary students, the creation of the so-called *curé sac au dos* about which they cackled with malice. The Radicals viewed the army as the preserve of the conservatives, if not royalists —lionizing Boulanger so excessively because he was that rarity, a republican general—and considered that the less time French youth spent under its influence the better. Seminarians, a lost cause for the republicans, might remain under the colors forever. Mackau's obvious choice to speak against the bill for the conservatives was de Mun, his finest orator and a former cavalry adjutant, who would reflect the prejudice of the officer corps that only long service could create in a trooper instant obedience in the face of death. "An officer," de Mun began, "who turns to his men, revealing to them in his glance their probable death in duty accomplished and glory won, must read in their faces an abnegation ready for any sacrifice." He explained that he comprehended the Radical ideal of a more democratic army, but he insisted that the question for France had to be not what were the social effects of military service but what made an effective fighting force. With the ease of long familiarity, he explored technical aspects of recruitment and training, but then he paused. His voice choking with emotion, he evoked the defeat of 1870, the shame of the loss of Alsace and Lorraine. Deputies throughout the Chamber were hushed by his fervor as through almost clenched teeth he pledged that if the army were made strong it would not fail again, that there would be a reckoning with Germany. His voice then rose as he defiantly recalled the passion of French bravery, "that charge at Sedan which wrenched from the Prussian king a cry like that of William of Orange at Neerwinden, 'Oh! les braves gens!' as the other had raged 'L'insolente nation!'" Transports of applause cut the heavily charged tension of the Chamber like the crack of a whip as the deputies, no longer Radicals, Opportunists, or conservatives, now only Frenchmen, were torn from their seats by this image, cheering, shouting "Bravo!" some with tears in their eyes in an emotion that far transcended party. He had spoken with the adoration of an apostle and the fire of a champion, and for the first time in his parliamentary career his thrilling words carried the day as the Opportunists and even some Radicals joined the conservatives in defeating the proposal.[16] The coalition had held. A few months earlier the Opportunists would have felt it necessary to approve this bill as a gage for Radical support.

The new coalition was in existence only for the month of June and part of July before the parliamentary summer recess sent all the deputies home to consider its implications. Some of the conservative constituency thought that their representatives had received little from the bargain since provincial civil servants did not slake their anticlerical zeal. Mackau had hoped for a direct order from Spuller restraining his underlings, and in August he made a special trip to Paris to warn the ministry that "we want nothing more than to support [you], but you must not make it impossible for us." Second thoughts particularly plagued the Count of Paris in his London exile. He began to fear that the conservatives might become habituated to parliamentarianism. The magic of personal devotion to a king had been the property of the Legitimists, and as the example of de Mun indicated, they did not transfer it to the Orleanist pretender. If the conservatives won enough concessions from the Opportunists, they might find the Republic preferable to a never-ending quest for a restoration. This thought led the Count of Paris to revise his tactics once more and in September 1887 to astound royalists and republicans alike by betraying the parliamentary traditions of his house and calling for a plebiscite to restore the monarchy. This reversal had little immediate impact on the conservative-Opportunist coalition. Mackau wanted to test the arrangement longer, and most of his followers shared de Mun's unreadiness to trade their new limited gains for the uncertainties of another anticonstitutional campaign. The effect of the manifesto was also diminished by its publication when the Chamber was out of session.[17]

Yet two months later, in November, the coalition partners were enemies, separated not by the pretender's instructions but by their inability to overcome the complications caused by the scandal of Daniel Wilson, the son-in-law of President Grévy. Himself a deputy, Wilson had discovered a unique method of peddling his influence, carrying on a brisk trade in the sale of Legion of Honor insignia and other decorations from an office in the Elysée palace and not even scrupling to use the presidential letterhead to solicit business. Grévy became implicated when he ordered the police to destroy the evidence against Wilson, and, when their bungling led to a revelation of his intervention, a merely sordid scandal became a presidential crisis. On 5 November the Radicals moved the creation of a commission to investigate the affair. The Opportunists, who recognized Grévy as one of their own, and Rouvier, who after all had to assume responsibility for the police action, were opposed.

The conservatives were caught in a dilemma. If they continued to support the premier, they would also assume the onus of defending Grévy and his son-in-law. If they voted against him and for the investigation, his ministry might fall, ending the attempt at cooperation. Rouvier temporarily solved their predicament by declining to make the motion a question of confidence, freeing the conservatives to vote for establishing the commission. They returned the favor immediately by supporting him on a Radical-sponsored resolution of no confidence in his general conduct of government. As the month progressed, however, this balancing act became impossible to maintain because local royalist committees pressured them to show outrage at republican malfeasance and to demand Grévy's removal from office. Within the Union des Droites the less pragmatic deputies like de Mun were very restive at the equivocal position of the conservatives. When Rouvier continued to defend the president, Mackau reluctantly withdrew the support of the Right from him, and on 19 November the conservatives joined with the Radicals to overturn his ministry and withhold backing for any new cabinet as long as Grévy remained at the Elysée. With no ministry capable of attracting a majority in the Chamber, the president was faced with a governmental impasse and tendered his resignation on 2 December.[18]

It is difficult to overemphasize the political consequences of the conservative desertion of Rouvier. Although the Radicals laid plans to restore republican union, the Opportunists were aloof, feeling betrayed by all sides. They mistrusted the Radicals and resented having to sacrifice Grévy to them, but the animus was tempered by a tradition of cooperation. Their most bitter recriminations were for the conservatives, to whom they had offered an opportunity to redeem their monarchist past and who in return had recklessly renounced their first effort at parliamentarianism. The conservatives were hardly happier than the Opportunists since there was now little chance of renewing the coalition and once more their 203 votes would be useless against the reunited republicans. This state of political disorganization was clearly demonstrated when the Chamber and Senate met in joint session at Versailles on 3 December to choose Grévy's successor. With all parliamentary alliances in disarray, the Radicals opposed the election of the Opportunist candidate Jules Ferry, while the Opportunists in turn blocked that of Freycinet and Charles Floquet, the favorites of the Radicals. Mackau had recognized that neither side would approach the outcast conservatives, and he abandoned his cautious strategy of the previous months to return to conspiracy. On the night of 29 November he met secretly with General Boulanger, who, since his fall from office, had been commander of the 13th Army Corps at Clermont-Ferrand, and proposed that he approach his Radical friends and promise to deliver enough votes, those of the conservatives, to elect one of their candidates president in return for a pledge to return him to the war ministry in the next cabinet. Once back in office Boulanger would betray the Republic for the Count of Paris and receive command of the royal armies as a reward. Although Boulanger was ambitious and politically promiscuous, the plan was chimerical and highly dangerous, and it fell apart at Versailles. Freycinet and Floquet refused to deal with Boulanger, and most of the conservatives, especially former army officers including de Mun, disavowed Mackau's negotiations because they did not trust the conversion of the Radical general. With no candidate of their own, the conservatives then abstained while the republicans wrangled for two days before settling on a compromise choice, a lackluster former finance minister with a famous republican name, François Sadi-Carnot. The Radicals were not altogether pleased with the peace they had made because Carnot's choice for premier, Pierre Tirard, assembled an all-Opportunist cabinet, and their dissatisfaction meant that the government was weak and indecisive, always unable to count on a working majority.[19]

The Wilson scandal and the subsequent presidential election revealed how shallow the roots had been of the conservative-Opportunist coalition of May 1887. Conservative leaders were frustrated; they had tried to practice parliamentarianism, but they felt that they had had no choice but to withdraw their support of Rouvier when he would not withdraw his of Grévy. Much of the legacy of bad feelings between the erstwhile partners could have been avoided if the conservatives had had the sense to vote for Ferry at Versailles, but their political instincts were so feeble and their sensibilities so tender that this alternative was never seriously considered. Not only did such archclericals as de Mun remember Ferry as the man of Article Seven, but the conservatives as a group resented the failure of the Opportunists to court their votes. By the beginning of

1888 they realized that for the present they had absolutely no opportunity to exert meaningful influence in the Chamber and returned to their previous low opinion of parliamentarianism. At best, progress in the Chamber would be slow, and some conservatives were impatient for a quick success: Mackau was involved in conspiracy within days of the fall of Rouvier. Their alternatives now seemed limited to the plebiscitary appeal of the Count of Paris. When he had issued it in September 1887, the conservatives were placing their hopes on compromise with the Opportunists, and most of them ignored it. In early 1888, with the situation wholly transformed, a few began to embrace the idea. At this point General Boulanger decided to attempt a political recovery. As he had in the previous November, this former Radical would treat with the conservatives, and when he did, the banner of the plebiscite found a bearer, a man on horseback, and the tracks he left charging across France with that standard would be called Boulangism.

Boulanger had been named war minister as a sop to the Radicals when Freycinet formed his cabinet in January 1886. At forty-eight he was the youngest of the French generals and the protégé of Clemenceau. Although he came from a Catholic conservative background, he had learned to boast republican, even radical sentiments and soon became the darling of the Left. As war minister he shamelessly cultivated national attention in a series of flamboyant acts, ordering brass bands to meet recruits, transferring conservative officers to dismal garrison towns, and recommending the abolition of seniority as the basis for promotion. He proved his popularity with the masses on Bastille Day in a review at Longchamps, where Parisians cheered in frenzy as the blond-bearded general, mounted on his black charger Tunis, rode at the head of his troops. With little justification, he came to think of himself as the emblem of French military hope, but the crowds obliged his fancy by calling him "Général Revanche." The adulation went to his head, and in the spring of 1887 he provoked the series of border incidents with Germany that led both conservatives, who already stood aghast at his treatment of the officer corps, and Opportunists to regard him as a reckless menace.

The Rouvier ministry sent him off to distant Clermont-Ferrand, as he had sent others, and Clemenceau disowned him in the Chamber, finally recognizing, he said, the general's vacuity. Other

Radicals continued to adore him, but in his semiexile Boulanger looked for any means to regain the war ministry. Mackau was only the first conservative who thought to exploit Boulanger's charisma and ambition for his own use and to find with satisfaction that the general's political morality was plastic. At the end of December 1887 two Bonapartists, Georges Thiébaud and Count Arthur de Dillon, proposed to Boulanger that they place his name on the ballot in a number of parliamentary by-elections. If he attracted votes, his popularity would be proved, and he might be recalled to office. Boulanger agreed, and across France in February and March 1888, Thiébaud and Dillon unveiled a campaign that appealed to practically every group that was disenchanted with the political corruption and governmental immobility of the Republic. They portrayed Boulanger as the patriot who had stood up to Bismarck, the "man of the people" who had ordered soldiers sent to control a strike to share their rations with the workers, the leader for the future who could give the Republic dash and color by rescuing it from the impotent and cowardly. In each of eight by-elections he amassed an impressive quantity of votes, each of them an embarrassment to the government, which found its only response in dismissing him from the army.[20]

The conservatives were the ones who relished Boulanger's success, particularly after he called in March for a revision of the constitution to allow a plebiscite on government reform, a platform sufficiently vague to permit it to be used for purposes other than Boulanger's personal ambition. *Le Gaulois* now found him far less distasteful and claimed that he might be "the microbe that will transmit the mortal illness to the Republic." The general told Thiébaud and Dillon of his contacts with Mackau, and, quick to grasp that their program might have broad appeal to the monarchists, they solicited contributions from the royalist wealthy with promises that Boulanger would restore the throne. Mackau and the Marquis Ludovic de Beauvoir, the principal private secretary of the Count of Paris, similarly concluded that Boulanger's rampant popularity could provide the vehicle for their own campaign of revision and plebiscite, but they expected to displace Thiébaud and Dillon as the masterminds of "Boulangism" through their control of royalist funds. The strategy would be to open these coffers to "Général Revanche," who in return would avoid any detailed description of his program. Mackau and Beauvoir would organize an electoral "parallel march," actively exploiting the success of Boulanger for a plebiscite, after which he might be safely discarded. To bring this ambitious plan to fruition, they would have to choose their confederates with care, and this task was made more difficult by the aversion, well known to Mackau by his failure of the previous December, of many conservatives to Boulanger as an individual.[21]

At the beginning of April, Mackau approached de Mun on the floor of the Chamber to recruit him for the new cause. Although de Mun still considered Boulanger a renegade general and a disgrace to the officer corps, Mackau was determined to persuade him. The experience of the Union des Droites had made him suspect that de Mun's reputation as the uncompromising Knight of the *Syllabus* might attract many Catholics to Boulanger and all but certain that de Mun considered his own political creed so worthy that he could justify even tainted means to bring it to power. Mackau began therefore by reminding him that "God helps those who help themselves" and that, while "Boulangism is not perhaps the best entrance to power, as there are no doors, far better to jump in by this window than to remain outside." He added that older conservative leaders, Falloux, Chesnelong, and Keller, were unwilling to take risks and that it was up to younger men, such as de Mun, to seize the opportunity offered in Boulanger. This appeal was clever since it had been those older men, and, of course, Mackau himself, who had so completely deflated de Mun's scheme for a confessional party. De Mun remained dubious but apparently deluded himself that Boulangism would benefit the church by turning out the scoundrels who had voted the anticlerical laws. With characteristic impulsiveness he agreed to join with Beauvoir and Mackau's four other recruits, Cassagnac, the Marquis de Breteuil from de Mun's "club," Count Edmond de Martimprey, and Jacques Piou, in attempting to persuade the Count of Paris to support the intrigue. There was deep irony in this decision. In Boulanger Mackau seemed to offer the means through which de Mun might fulfill his dreams, but Boulanger himself was repugnant to a man with a deep and passionate regard for the discipline of the army. The tension in de Mun's attitude can be discerned in a letter he wrote that night to Colonel Fernand de Parseval, a friend from Algerian service and as preceptor to the Duke d'Orleans, eldest son of the pretender, his sole close link to the Orleanist royal house. Almost as if to convince himself, de Mun fantasized that on Boulanger "the will of God seems to rest."[22]

From that moment de Mun immersed himself in the conspiracy. Two weeks later, on 16 April, Mackau led most of his recruits, bolstered by the addition of Arthur Meyer, the editor of *Le Gaulois*, to meet the Count of Paris in his London exile and try to convince him to commit the Orleanist fortune and political machinery to Boulanger. Like many of his followers, the pretender clearly did not trust the general and was not enthusiastic about the plan of his lieutenants. But when he inquired whether it would not be safer to remain aloof, de Mun replied almost brutally that the Count of Paris should not deceive himself as to the strength of royalist sentiment in France, for he would be gravely mistaken if he believed that universal suffrage would restore the monarchy. Boulanger in contrast commanded an extraordinary following, and his campaign for a plebiscite was similar to that of the pretender. With Orleanist money Boulanger might win victories that could later be converted to monarchist ones. The Count of Paris considered de Mun's words in light of Boulanger's latest success in the Nord, where he received nearly 70 percent of the vote, converting an Opportunist majority of twenty thousand in 1885 into a Boulangist one of one hundred thousand. No one since Louis Napoleon had won such triumphs. Mackau then cautioned the pretender that such wealthy royalists as the Duchess Marie d'Uzès were already giving Boulanger immense sums of money and warned that to avoid losing control of his own movement he was compelled to embrace the general. Reluctant to tie his cause to this military adventurer, the Count of Paris was nonetheless impressed by the urgency of the situation as well as by its possibilities. He also found himself reassured by the presence of de Mun, never previously interested in an Orleanist restoration, declaring later that "when I saw a Christian of the eminence of Count de Mun . . . point the way, I thought my duty lay there, and I never shirk my duty." Resisting no longer, he agreed to prepare a new declaration, published in *Le Gaulois* on 25 April, repeating his plebiscitary instructions of the preceding September and calling on Frenchmen to support "the current campaign of constitutional revision." Boulanger was not mentioned by name, but the implication was obvious: conservatives should vote for "Général Revanche."[23]

This decision freed the conservatives to treat with Boulanger, and on 1 May Mackau and his coconspirators held their first meeting with Thiébaud and Dillon to plot strategy. They planned to organize the conservative campaign and fundraising through a Ligue de la Consultation Nationale, which would include conservative deputies and voters and be headed by a committee of twelve, the Douze, composed of the original seven less Beauvoir, who maintained liaison in London, and conservatives Armand de Maillé, Léon Chevreau, Eugène Berger, Sosthène de La Rochefoucauld, Jules Delafosse, and Eugène Jolibois. The Ligue met in plenary session on 25 May in Paris at the Hotel Continental to pledge initial funds and hear de Mun celebrate the chances of a "consecrating plebiscite." Several Catholic papers objected to these sentiments, especially in their similarity to Boulanger's campaign, but at de Mun's request they began to see praiseworthy aspects to revision and plebiscite. Mackau was delighted at de Mun's initiative and influence, and he planned to ensure his continued participation by involving him even more deeply in conspiracy. As early as March, Boulanger had been patronized by the enormously wealthy, still youthful, and widowed Duchess d'Uzès, who had become completely infatuated with him and delighted in hearing his grandiose plans even when he brought along his aristocratic mistress Madame Marguerite de Bonnemains. The duchess met the Count of Paris at Koblenz in late June and promised to add three million francs to the million she had already spent on her protégé. The pretender himself pledged up to five million francs from the Orleanist fortune. On Mackau's counsel both requested de Mun's presence on the subcommittee of the Douze that would disburse these monies, a charge de Mun assumed cheerfully.[24]

Yet even as he took these actions, de Mun began to have doubts about Boulanger. Since his discharge from the army the general had sat as a deputy for the Nord, and in the Chamber on 4 June he made an imperious demand for constitutional revision. With his huge election margins behind him and the conservative deputies shouting encouragement, he posed as a new Bonaparte, but Floquet, who had replaced Tirard as premier in April, punctured his vanity by deriding, "At your age, General, Napoleon was dead!" Boulanger renewed the debate on 12 July, and, when he found no additional support, foolishly resigned his seat. Before he left the floor, he exchanged insults with Floquet, and both arranged for seconds. Two days later they parried sword thrusts until Boulanger, woefully unfamiliar with the foil, could contain his impatience no longer and rushed at his opponent, impaling himself on the elderly lawyer's blade. He lay critically wounded for several days, and although thereafter he made a rapid recovery, his reputation as a dashing warrior did not. On 22 July he was defeated in a by-election in the Ardèche trying to regain a seat.[25]

Even Boulanger's new conservative allies were now afraid that he was badly discredited. The Count of Paris disgustedly resolved to break relations with him, and Beauvoir had to intervene skillfully to calm the pretender's mercurial temper. De Mun wrote Mackau ridiculing the "brav' général" in contemptuous terms and expressed his dismay to Parseval, condemning Boulanger for lacking "strength of character, purpose, or even political skill" and concluding that "neither his character, his intelligence, nor his thought reveals a single serious quality." But whatever his opinion now in July, de Mun did not feel able to afford the luxury of abruptly sundering his ties to Boulangism. He had become deeply implicated in the plot because he had guilelessly trusted Mackau, accepting his contention that the triumph of Boulanger would also be that of the church. This impetuous misapprehension, rash even for de Mun, had been strong enough to overcome his antipathy to the Count of Paris and to join him to the camp followers of a soldier of fortune. The measure of de Mun's naiveté can be taken from two letters he wrote at the end of April, soon after the Count of Paris agreed to commit the royalist machinery to battle. He sanguinely confided to Félix de Roquefeuil that "this is the best occasion that the Catholics have had in fifteen years to take charge of the [conservative] movement." Still obsessed with the conception of confessionalism, he also wrote excitedly to Mackau of uniting all Catholics in a "party of action" to propel Boulanger to victory. Even in midsummer he continued to see the general as a means, somewhat less than ideal, but one that might be tolerated. Or perhaps not, since de Mun's personal attitude toward Boulanger was extraordinarily volatile, and he was dubious of using such a man to advance the cause of the church. Should the general fail, as he surely would if the pretender withdrew his support, the sacrifice of principles would have been in vain. Conquering his disgust, in late July de Mun wrote a long memorandum in the general's behalf to the Count of Paris, this intervention and the efforts of Beauvoir sufficing to prevent a breaking off of Orleanist backing.[26]

Because many of the doubts of de Mun and other conservatives in June and July grew largely out of Boulanger's failure to live up to his reputation, they were also largely dispelled by the abrupt resurgence of the general's popularity. On 19 August he won three departmental by-elections by wide margins in the Nord, Somme, and Charente-Inférieure. Using half a million francs from the Duchess d'Uzès alone, the monarchists mounted a saturating campaign of publicity. Boulanger had completely recovered from his wound by 10 August and whistle-stopped his final series of speeches. It was as if his popularity had never suffered a reversal, and on hearing the news de Mun felt so reassured that he wrote to Mackau proclaiming that Boulangism was "the one grand and serious effort in the past fifteen years to make progress in the mire."[27]

But despite these words, he found himself increasingly anomalous among the conspirators about the pretender. His old suspicions and grievances against the Orleanists haunted him more and more, forcing him to question whether it was worth the effort to topple the Republic of the Opportunists to found the monarchy of Philippe VII. Almost alone among the chief Boulangists, he was outraged by the general's abortive attempt in October to divorce his wife and marry his mistress, almost alone considering the negligible difference between those who enacted a divorce statute and those who would seek its advantages. He also found no escape from his dilemma in the advocacy of social reform. In March and May he had eloquently defended proposals to provide compulsory accident insurance to miners and industrial workers, and in June, amid the planning for the financial support of Boulanger, he called for a broad series of reforms during a speech condemning the daily abuses suffered by women and children in unregulated employment. His words and sincerity won him votes and even grudging praise from the Radical seats, but most of the conservatives stonily rejected his pleas and the Opportunists found them interesting but untimely. The Opportunists were the enemy whose opposition was expected; the conservatives drew de Mun's bitterness. Their attitude, he despaired, was "deadly, sterile reaction, a backward march! . . . Such men may be elected, but to govern, to change the country, to inspire confidence, never!"[28]

He found the most satisfying outlet for this political ambivalence in the countercentenaries of the Revolution planned by the conservatives in competition with the celebrations proposed by the republicans. At a general meeting of the *cercles* in June he requested a serious study of how the Revolution had betrayed the high ideals and promises of 1789, an endorsement of its beginnings that few other conservatives would countenance. He also declared his intention that the *cercles* participate fully in the most important of the countercentenaries, that planned for November at Romans in the Drôme. It would commemorate the protests of the Dauphiné Estates against edicts of the king in the prerevolutionary period, protests de Mun naively believed might have led, if heeded, to reform rather than revolution. As he planned his appearance at Romans, he came to see the gathering as an opportunity to declare once more his own "counterrevolution," to condemn the present Republic but advocate more than the Orleanist monarchy. There was still the necessity of working with Boulanger—what else could bring on the transformation—but the general had behaved himself since October, disavowing divorce and gathering momentum throughout the nation. It was therefore with a measure of confidence and little embarrassment that de Mun endorsed Boulangism, although not by name, to the thousands of conservatives attracted to the countercentenary, claiming that "the people are tired of the perpetual internal wranglings of the republicans. . . . To this legislature, which has taken for its motto the partisan slogan, 'clericalism the enemy!' a weary and disabused nation calls back in a menacing echo, 'parliamentarianism the enemy!' " But Mackau and the Count of Paris could not take complete comfort in his words. The greater part of the speech was addressed to the issue of social reform and to the necessity of repairing the position of the church. There were murmurs against de Mun from the crowd when he spoke of social justice rather than of mere duties, and he felt compelled to confront his detractors directly. "You have reproached me," he said heatedly afterward in a discussion, "for being in accord with the Radicals, a charge of guilt I am happy, even proud, to accept. In spite of the divisions that separate us, Radical deputies and I have been able to discover a ground where we may join hands, where our hearts may beat in unison, in a common sentiment of humanity, of love for the people. And if on this basis an alliance of the moment may be made that gives the worker a little joy, peace, or happiness, who are you to complain of it?" This language left the majority of conservatives feeling uncomfortable about de Mun's politics—even as he himself was uneasy about his position among the conservatives—but there was no need or effort to diminish his role in the conspiracy. Some of Boulanger's constituency were dissident workers, and this tone could be retailed to them. De Mun would also continue to perform the important, even crucial, function of providing Boulangism with a cachet of respectability for arch-Catholics, to whom the cause of the plebiscite and the Count of Paris meant little.[29]

The climax of Boulanger's success came in January 1889. There was finally a vacancy in the representation for Paris, and Boulanger eagerly accepted the challenge to prove that he could triumph in the capital, for a century the epicenter of republicanism. The Opportunists and Radicals could find no candidate of stature to oppose him, and on 27 January Boulanger won by an astonishingly large margin, polling almost one hundred thousand more votes than his lackluster adversary out of only four hundred thousand cast. A legend has taken root that this victory night was a *coup manqué* for the general, that he could have marched with cheering followers to the Elysée and seized power. Indeed, the regime would have been hard pressed to resist a determined challenge. Actually, Boulanger and his conservative allies intended, as they had all along, to win what they could within the limits of legality if possible. Expecting to be swept into power by the voters in the general elections set for the fall and with Boulanger's popularity at its zenith, they would have been fools to stake all on a coup d'état.[30]

For their part the republicans were frightened by Boulanger's victory in Paris, and Opportunists and Radicals cast off their apathy and complacency to work together against the menace. Because *scrutin de liste* allowed one man to head an electoral list and carry a whole department with him, it was a cornerstone of Boulangist strategy and success. Votes for the general would drag dozens of his followers into office on his coattails, and through multiple candidacies Boulanger's popularity could be exploited on every departmental list. Grasping this implication at last, Premier Floquet rallied a majority of republicans on 11 February for a return to the single-member districts of *scrutin d'arrondissement* and to propose that candidates be limited to filing for a single seat. But the weak Floquet was not up to taking the measures needed to quash the Boulangist conspiracy. Three days later he resigned, succeeded by Tirard again, who took as his minister of the interior Ernest Constans, an expert at devious stratagems. Constans let it be known that he intended to charge Boulanger with plotting against the state and that, because a jury would likely acquit the immensely popular general, he would convoke the heavily Opportunist Senate to sit as a high court. Taking this threat for reality, Boulanger fled Paris for Brussels on 1 April. The conservatives bravely refused to allow his flight to make them seem abandoned, and Cassagnac congratulated him for playing a good trick on the government by placing himself beyond the range of any republican attempts at assassination. Some of the general's supporters—such as the Duchess d'Uzès, who temporarily halted her contributions—worried privately at the stigma of cowardice, but most felt that the damage could be made right if Boulanger returned in time for the elections in the fall. They were dismayed, however, by the changes in the election law, especially by the proposed elimination of multiple candidacies, finally voted in July, since all of the leading conservatives, as well as Boulanger, had planned to run in several constituencies. Suddenly there was a dire need for additional strong candidates to represent the Boulangist cause.[31]

The Opportunists hoped that with Boulanger's flight the conservatives would give up their flirtation with this new Caesarism, and in June they made a generous offer of peace, Ferry himself declaring before the Chamber that anticlericalism should be pressed no further. Far from accepting the offer, the conservatives countered with a sensational and deadly reply by de Mun. "It is too late! . . ." he cried sternly, "There are men from whom we could accept advances—from you never! Everything done against us was done by the moderates. . . . The Radicals gave the orders, the Opportunists carried them out. Religious war has been the cement of your union . . . it is on you like the poisoned shirt of Nessus, you cannot escape from it, it is burning you, it will destroy you!" Through this diatribe the conservatives proclaimed that despite some minor discouragement in April they now had regained their confidence and were once again prepared to wager their future on Boulangism. There remained significant discontent in the nation to mobilize against the republicans, and Boulanger's popularity had not disappeared after his flight. By midsummer they were back in their electoral districts campaigning hard to take advantage of it, with a leading Boulangist assigned to each geographic area to coordinate political activity and disburse funds. In Paris, Constans applied his considerable power and ingenuity to foiling them, implementing the means of administrative pressure at his command to win the elections for the republicans. In no voting since 1877 had the preservation of the regime seemed more in doubt.[32]

As overall campaign manager for the conservatives, Mackau deputized de Mun to oversee the Boulangist effort in Brittany, and throughout July, August, and September he received detailed reports from his lieutenant on political developments. At first de Mun found reason to support the optimism of the conservatives: the Bretons were eager to hear denunciations of the government, and the Boulangist candidates seemed to gain strength in all areas. The local elections at the end of July were especially encouraging because several incumbent republicans lost their seats. Elsewhere, however, this voting for the departmental councils was the first test of Constans's administrative apparatus and resulted in setbacks for the conservatives. By August even distant Brittany began to feel the effects of this policy, and de Mun's reports grew more pessimistic as the government used the civil service and prefectoral bureaucracy to bully voters and to disrupt the rallies of the conservatives. But in spite of this obstruction and its implications for further mischief when voters cast their ballots and those ballots were counted, de Mun continued until the 22 September voting to predict a narrow majority in the new Chamber for his side. Other Boulangists, from areas less conservative in temper than Brittany, were gravely worried. They felt the necessity of a dramatic flourish to end the campaign, a finale that would reawaken public interest in the plebiscite, and this could only be the return of Boulanger to France. The conservatives sent a delegation for him, but he refused their pleadings. By September the general's appearance alone could have offset, through his personal appeal, the handicaps faced by Boulangism in the revised election laws and severe administrative pressure. In his absence only those as naive and misinformed as de Mun were surprised that on the first ballot the Boulangists won only 128 seats against the 203 of the republicans. Their minority was assured before the 6 October *ballottage* made the final tally 358 to 210. The conservatives had maintained the 45 percent of the popular vote that they had rallied in 1885, and Mackau pointed out that the voting had actually been closer than the seat totals indicated: in eighty-seven instances the republican margin of victory was less than a thousand votes, while all of the conservative margins were wide. Yet the conclusion was inescapable that in four years of constant political activity, the expenditure of enormous sums, and the staining of the reputation of the royal house of Orleans through its association with a military adventurer who first sold himself to the highest bidder and then proved a coward, the Right had not improved its position.[33]

The votes of the first ballot had hardly been counted before the conservatives began scrambling to justify their roles in the debacle. In an apologia on 24 September to the Count of Paris, Mackau claimed that Boulanger's appeal might have won the conservatives those half million votes they lacked for a majority in 1885 and that although the gamble had failed, without it they would have been reduced to the level of 1881. He added an attack on the sloth of those conservatives who, through timidity or foresight, had failed to embrace Boulangism: "One must pay for them, think for them, act for them." Piou and Cassagnac joined him in qualifying the results of the election as a "relative success" that should not be scorned. The Count of Paris insisted upon accepting full responsibility for the decision to ally with Boulanger and even defended it as the only sound one. But because the gambit had failed, at a meeting of his closest advisers in late September he required that Orleanism sever all links to the general. A terse note in the 8 October *Le Gaulois* announced this decision.[34]

De Mun was not present at the pretender's strategy session. Although he had contributed to the heavy Catholic vote for Boulangist candidates, he had never belonged to the coterie around the Count of Paris, and he was not invited now that his usefulness to them was finished. In retreat with his family at Lumigny, de Mun came to conclusions of his own. Boulangism had been a mistake, and the cause of royalism was not much more practical since the dynastic issue could never command a majority of Frenchmen. With the retrograde social views of the pretender and his chief supporters it could no longer hold the allegiance even of a traditionalist like himself. But if he rejected the political faith of his fathers, he risked the most utter isolation. Temporary cooperation with the Opportunists or Radicals on certain issues was possible, but he could not countenance joining with them and thereby endorsing the persecution of the church, which he felt was an integral part of the regime.

His compass had led him to a cul-de-sac, to remain the orator of lost causes.

As always, however, he was convinced that his solution to the problems of the conservatives was the only correct one and that his colleagues on the Right would do well to follow him smartly. On 1 October he wrote to Mackau to urge that the Union des Droites be led away from dynasticism, officiously counseling, "In acute circumstances and moments of crisis such as these, I believe that we should, as much as possible, await developments and not announce our positions in advance. . . . I think that you will do well to carry the battle on grounds other than the dynastic but to ignore the disposition to rally to the Republic." This language sounded vaguely like Mackau's own politics of interests without the essential allegiance to the throne as rationale for the strategy. How different it was became clear two weeks later. Receiving no reply from Mackau, de Mun wrote to him again, this time to announce that he had granted an interview to Wickham Steed, editor of the *Pall Mall Gazette*, and that Mackau would find it interesting. When the text appeared in *L'Univers* on 13 and 14 October, his words were read not only with interest but with extreme consternation by most conservatives.

> Boulanger has been beaten it seems, but the force of Boulangism should not be misunderstood or underestimated. Its origin and strength are a popular reaction against the power of untrammeled finance, less a protest against the Republic than a rising against the power of mammon. . . . In order to assume the command of such a movement, conservatives must free themselves of all dynastic complications and remain independent of all [current] political parties. I can assure you that regardless of my personal preference for another form of government, I shall be the first to give the example of a peaceful acceptance of the present regime in order to devote myself to religious, social, and economic interests if this government can become stable, honest, respectful of religion and consciences, devoted to the interests of the people, and truly open to all. But where is such a government in the Republic?[35]

De Mun seemed to be returning to his idea of a confessional party, a political faction that, while not accepting the Republic as its preferred regime, could work within it for religious and social goals. Monarchism would have no place. He expanded his argument in another letter, to the Marquis Antoine de Castellane, who had just published *La Politique conservatrice en 1889* calling for a conservative program of tax equalization, religious pacification, and emancipation of the workers, a formula at least close to his own. De Mun felt that the Republic remained the antagonist of the church—"Between it and ourselves there are barriers we cannot clear"—but he could foresee the possibility of cooperation: "I shall be the first . . . to accept the established order if this government ceases to be exploited by a sect for the profit of antireligious passions and becomes truly national, free, and open to all. . . . I feel that we must renounce combat on the grounds, and with the cadres, of monarchism and instead turn our effort to those social questions that call men of good will, regardless of origin, to work with courage and devotion to convince the people of our sincerity, that we will put their needs, interests, and rights before the form of government."[36]

His reward for these words was a barrage of criticism. Following the publication of his interview with Steed, Meyer at *Le Gaulois* and Cassagnac at *L'Autorité* ridiculed his opinions and denounced him as a traitor. Mackau made no effort to restrain them, and de Mun wrote him defiantly, "I am stoned by the intransigent monarchist press . . . but I have a tough skin."[37] He stood firm because reflection on the performance of the conservatives since 1885 left him with a sense of disgust. In those four years he had learned firsthand the deceits of party maneuver and had sullied his own idealism. The experience had taught him finally that the morality of politics was amorality. In 1885 he had tried to separate the conservatives from dynasticism. The failure of his confessional party seemed to him to prove that the Catholic Right was more attached to the corpse of royalism than that of Jesus Christ. In 1887 the same men who had rejected his plan for a party to defend their church accepted an alliance with the Opportunists to defend their wealth. When the Wilson and Grévy scandals destroyed the coalition, the conservatives, with de Mun himself in the fore, caught the fever of Boulangism, joining a rebellious general in search of a God-fearing government. Here indeed was the ultimate casuistry, the end justifying the means. In grasping the vision of a right-wing triumph, the conservatives became the minions of a military poltroon. The failure of this meretricious adventure taught de Mun that his instincts of 1885 had been correct after all. But four years later in 1889 his goals of social reform and religious defense were no closer to realization, and, tarred with the pitch of conspiracy, he had no clear notion of what new direction to follow.

4
The Ralliement

The failure of Boulangism left the conservatives badly shaken and their alternatives severely limited. French voters had rejected a legal restoration, and no one seriously considered a coup de main. The legislature was now the only arena in which they could work, but operating room there was very cramped. Alone, the conservatives could not prevail against the republicans, at least as long as the Opportunists and Radicals remained united. Those ranks would have to be split, as in May 1887, when the conservatives and Opportunists had joined to sustain the brief ministry of Maurice Rouvier. It had been their common desire then to exclude General Boulanger from office and block the taxation proposals of the Radicals. Similar common ground would have to be surveyed and staked out to repeat the maneuver, but there was real question whether the moderate republicans would welcome any new conciliatory initiative. Practically every member of the Union des Droites had been compromised by Boulangism, and the Opportunists might require proof positive that the conservatives had given up their plotting. The gage could well be an open acceptance of the regime.[1]

De Mun's outspoken proposal in October 1889 that the conservatives cast off dynasticism to concentrate on religious and social issues provoked outrage among their leaders, and Mackau warned the Count of Paris to expect further desertions. No one else advanced to a position quite as excessive as de Mun's, but there was a general and rueful sense among the conservatives that the old ways had failed. When they gathered in Paris on 24 January 1890 to discuss the political situation, it was with little cheer and keen anticipation of future success. Before disbanding they held their own elections, for the Union des Droites, confirming Mackau as president again and choosing Duke Sosthène de La Rochefoucauld and Jacques Piou to be his assistants. The selections were indicative of their prevailing mood. Boulangism had finally made Mackau leery of conspiracy, and La Rochefoucauld, while a member of the Douze to plot with Boulanger, president of the snobbish Jockey Club, and bearer of the proud title duke de Doudeauville, was a social Catholic and disposed to make peace with the Republic. Piou, the third member of the triumvirate, was the most significant choice. Born in 1838 the son of a Toulouse barrister and local politician, he had made a name for himself practicing law first in his hometown and after 1870 in Paris. He returned to Toulouse to run on the monarchist list for Haute Garonne in 1885 and was elected. In the Chamber his talent for maneuver and oratory quickly made him a leader in the Union des Droites, and he was among the first to follow Mackau in the conspiracy with Boulanger. The ludicrous failure of the general convinced him that dynasticism was a dead weight on the conservatives, and he resolved to convert them into a party whose concentration on economic issues might attract the collaboration of the Opportunists.[2]

On 31 March 1890, Piou announced the formation of a Droite Indépendante, quickly rechristened the Droite Constitutionnelle, tenuously allied to the Union des Droites, with sixteen founders, all royalist deputies, and a detailed political program. The group declared its willingness to "accept" the Republic and called for fiscal responsibility—no new loans, taxes, or spending—repeal of the laws exiling the princes of the regnant families, reestablishment of religious instruction in schools requesting it, and exemption from military service for seminarians. This program could easily appeal to the Opportunists, hard pressed as they frequently were on fiscal matters by the Radicals, especially as it would mean only moderating the enforcement of, not actually repealing, the anticlerical laws already on the books. Piou hoped to win the majority of the Union des Droites to his party by emphasizing that although it would "accept" the Republic as the lawful government, it would not "adhere" to it. In the political language of this period the distinction between these two terms was quite clear. "Acceptance" did not bind the conservatives to support the Republic if ever there were a strong possibility of a restoration; "adherence" committed them to its defense under any circumstances.[3]

But instead of gathering strength, Piou's new faction wandered in undefined murkiness. Did he mean to seek active collaboration with the Opportunists or would he keep the party lurking in a hinterland between Philippe VII and Marianne? Was he really abandoning royalism or merely omitting it from public reference? These questions were most often posed by the conservatives, who found themselves somewhat annoyed at the tactics of their supposed assistant leader and declined to join him. Their attitude was orchestrated by Mackau, who feared that Piou might stray too far from royalism. Too much direct pressure might force the Droite Constitutionnelle to bolt the Union des Droites completely, and Mackau preferred that Piou's initiative collapse from internal contradictions. In contrast to this discouragement from his own ranks, the Opportunists fostered his tentative steps toward the Republic. In January 1890 they ensured that for the first time in half a decade the conservatives would have seats on the Budget Committee, the Chamber's only standing committee. They also displayed a remarkable tolerance for the conspiracy of the previous year. From August to October 1890 a series of articles entitled "Les Coulisses du boulangisme" appeared in *Le Figaro*, signed only "X," recounting the most intimate secrets of monarchist participation. Until then, the republicans had only suspected the depth to which de Mun, Mackau, and Piou had been involved. As minister of the interior Constans now had sufficient cause to charge all three with plotting the overthrow of the state, but ignoring the vindictive cries of the Radicals, he refrained in hope of winning them to the Republic.[4]

While willing to facilitate the conservatives' acceptance of the Republic, the Opportunists waited for them to make the first move toward reconciliation. Without wider support within the Union des Droites, Piou could not do so. At this impasse Pope Leo XIII decided to intervene in French politics. He had long felt frustration at the sterility of French royalism and decided that the church must escape its fatal relationship with the throne. The disgraceful failure of Boulangism had reinforced his opinion and gave him hope that French Catholics could be led to forsake monarchism for the Republic. His Holiness was not given to the illusions of Pius IX and was not afflicted by the rigidity and intolerance of his predecessor. Yet however different Leo's methods of diplomacy, patience, and long-suffering might be, the aspirations of the two pontiffs were essentially identical, and it was in pursuit of two of these goals that Leo formulated his new strategy for France. He considered that as a direct result of a rallying of Catholics to the Republic the church might be spared the harshest of the existing anticlerical strictures. He also dreamed, hopelessly, of enlisting French aid in restoring at least some of the territorial possessions lost to the new Italian kingdom by the Holy See, a vision hardly conjurable as long as the church was the enemy of the Republic.

The pope had laid the groundwork for his planning much earlier. In the encyclical *Immortale Dei* of 1 November 1885, he had demonstrated that the constitution of a state is unimportant to the church as long as its authority is based on the law of God. This vague pronunciamento meant that the Republic was morally acceptable in France, and this was the acceptance the pontiff now desired of Catholics. In the fall of 1890 he called Charles Cardinal Lavigerie, primate of North Africa and archbishop of Algiers, to Rome and asked him to seek a propitious moment to call for a rallying of French Catholics to the Republic, feeling that all would recognize the hand of the Vatican in his proclamation. Lavigerie was an excellent choice for this assignment, a former Bonapartist who had become disgusted at the incompetence of the monarchists. As founder of the White Fathers and leader of the campaign against the African slave trade he was also known and respected far outside the circles of the faithful. His endorsement of the Republic would be dramatic and substantial. Lavigerie found his opportunity in Algiers on 12 November 1890, when as host of a dinner in honor of the French Mediterranean Fleet he raised his glass in toast to declare that "when the will of a people has been clearly expressed, when, as the pope has recently declared, the form of government has nothing in itself contrary to the sole principles by which Christians and civilized nations can live, since only *adherence without reservation* can save the country from the horrors that threaten it, the time has come to put an end to our divisions, to sacrifice all that conscience and honor allow. . . . In saying this I am certain that I shall not be contradicted by *any* ecclesiastical authority." The officers were astounded, and the guest of honor, Vice-Admiral Victor Duperré, a Bonapartist, had to be prompted to reply, "I drink to his Eminence the Cardinal and to the clergy of Algeria."[5]

When the cardinal's words reached France some Catholics and conservatives professed to believe that Lavigerie had spoken only in his own name and not that of the Vatican. Diehard monarchists saw the only alternative to this desperate hope in a repudiation of Leo's right to intervene. They countered in a speech on 8 February 1891 at Nîmes by Count Othenin d'Haussonville, who, since the failure of Boulangism, had replaced Beauvoir as the chief representative of the Count of Paris in France. He lashed out at both the toast of Lavigerie and Piou's formation of the Droite Constitutionnelle, terming one an unwarranted interference in French internal affairs and a breach of Gallican tradition if sponsored by the pope, the other a sordid begging of favors from the Republic. Cassagnac had also denied the right of the pope to dictate politics, if that indeed was the wish of His Holiness, and addressed Piou, "I know you; I have seen your kind before under the Empire. Then your name was Emile Ollivier!" Others, principally much of the episcopacy, grasped the implications of Lavigerie's words and were willing to compromise with the Republic, if someone else would lead the way. The attitude of the bishops had always been one of respect for the civil authority of the Republic, and they opposed it only when religious interests were menaced. By far the most popular reaction was a middle ground, the formation in May 1891 of the Union de la France Chrétienne. Ignoring the explicit language of Lavigerie's call to embrace the Republic without reservation, the sponsors of the union, François Cardinal Richard of Paris, Mackau, Breteuil, and de Mun, inaccurately interpreted the toast of Algiers to mean that the pope preferred that Catholics organize themselves into a party dedicated to religious defense, which could cooperate with republicans but not necessarily be republican. In essence they foresaw a group similar to Piou's Droite Constitutionnelle but emphasizing different issues. Misinterpreting Lavigerie's meaning was an elaborate self-deception by the Unionistes, for they found it extraordinarily difficult to cut the last ties binding them to royalism. They traced their lineage from families that for generations had considered it the highest honor to die for their king. Their social circle referred to the Republic contemptuously as *la gueuse*, the slut, and were not at home to republicans. The regime seemed more than merely a form of government; it was rather a doctrine fundamentally opposed to the Catholic religion. The members of the union would treat the Republic as they would an influential *arriviste*, using him to make money even as they cut him dead socially.[6]

De Mun's appearance among the sponsors of the union ended his withdrawal from conservative politics dating from the fall of

1889 when he had aroused such ire with his outspoken rejection of dynasticism. He had ignored Piou's blandishments because the Droite Constitutionnelle had no social policy and had retreated to nurse his wounded pride instead, complaining that "in 1878 Falloux treated me like a Don Quixote and the economic liberals called me a madman; in 1885 the royalists and Catholics conspired to denounce me as a disrupter to the point of having the pope himself silence me; and in 1889 they damned me as a renegade and accused me of perverse socialism. I have lost count of the times I have been accused of ignorance and pretension, of being the courtesan of the people." In defiance and sulk he had proclaimed his independence of all political posturing and maneuver and his intention to concentrate exclusively on social reforms. He began by daring to side with the Radicals in November 1889 in supporting the principle of a minimum wage. In the summer of 1890, after meeting earlier with republican reformers, he pledged the votes of the few social Catholics for new proposals by the Opportunists to forbid the employment of children below the age of thirteen, to limit to ten hours the length of the workday for women and minors, to reduce to eight hours the workdays preceding holidays, and to provide convalescent leave to pregnant women. The acclaim of the reformers and the consternation of opponents on the Right provided him with vengeful satisfaction that combined with a sense of righteousness to make him continue. Early in 1891, armed with precise information gathered by the network of the *cercles*, he made his appearances at the tribune unmatched in force and pathos as he evoked tears at the tragedy of the little flower girl who died because she had to return to work the same day her child was born, at the *veillée*, the vicious system in the factories of the couturiers during the fashion season compelling women to work all night without previous warning, at long hours for women, who described their labor and absence from the home as the "destroyer of children." He even defended striking mine workers at Fourmies, mortifying the conservatives and drawing a remarkable reply and tribute by Clemenceau from the Radical benches, who recalled de Mun's conversion to social reform as a soldier twenty years before when "so much did the desperation of the Communards affect their enemy that he who shot them has become their defender. I say this as much to the glory of the Communards as to the honor of our colleague." But for de Mun the true honor came just a few days later on 15 May, when Leo XIII at last issued his promised encyclical giving papal endorsement to social Catholicism. *Rerum novarum* renewed the anathema on socialism but labeled as unchristian many of the abuses of labor current in the late nineteenth century, denouncing child labor in purple prose as "forcing young buds to blossom before their day." Only the church, Leo counseled, by inculcating in the entrepreneur and the government a spirit of charity, could provide a complete solution to the social problem. Owners and workers could make a beginning themselves by forming Christian associations, like the *cercles*, "whether composed of workers alone or mixed." Some official regulation of working conditions would be necessary, especially to build impetus for reform, and here government intervention, as de Mun had proposed, would be crucial.[7]

The encyclical was the vindication of the *cercles*, but it came too late, when their momentum and spirit came from the inertia of coasting downhill. Friction with the bishops, competition from the socialists, and an anomalous position within royalism had sapped their vitality by dividing their ranks. The strongest cohesion became the long effort to bring social Catholicism under the protection of church doctrine, and when the basic principles of de Mun's program appeared in *Rerum novarum* even that disappeared. The leadership of the old guard was badly missed. Despite other commitments as a deputy, de Mun had maintained control of his creation through his brother. After Robert's death in 1887 and de Mun's own intense involvement in Boulangism this dominance lapsed. Harmel was busy with his factory in Val-des-Bois, leaving only La Tour du Pin among the founders with the time to supervise the *cercles* closely. He was ill-equipped for the role. His long study of corporatism had made him too much the intellectual, too theoretical to solve the malaise of the *cercles*, too prone to fill the pages of *L'Association Catholique* with complicated and controversial notions about "family salaries" and profit-sharing that increased dissension. Late in 1890 de Mun dealt with this difficulty summarily by separating the journal from the *cercles*, an extreme step, but one he justified by complaining that "we are dying of theory . . . philosophical speculations have made the *cercles* lose sight of their true line of action." But even de Mun's renewed attentions and short-lived determination to refound his politics on social reforms could not reverse the decline of his original conception. The ACJF had already begun to flourish, even as the first *cercles* had, but its young men had minds of their own and politely declined to risk their success by trying to save the *cercles*. De Mun kept them alive—even until his death in 1914—but the corrosion of the 1880s had so weakened them that the controversy of the Ralliement, which would shake the conservatives during the next years, would complete their ruin.[8]

The popularity of the Union de la France Chrétienne derived from its ability to claim conformity to the direction of the Holy See, if indeed that was the agent behind Lavigerie's toast, yet not to go so far as to embrace the Republic. Of course, this balancing act could be maintained only as long as Leo kept silent. De Mun welcomed the union as an expression of his call for a transformation of the Right, but most of its members had no urge to be transformed and sought only a plausible compromise between the demands of their king and their pope. For the memories of old feuds kept returning. In early October 1891, as a group of pilgrims from the ACJF visited Rome, one of the bravos wrote, "Vive le pape" in the visitor's book at the tomb of Victor Emmanuel. In succession the highly sensitive Italian government protested; the French minister of public worship banned further pilgrimages; the archbishop of Aix, Xavier Gouthe-Soulard, objected and was fined by the courts; and *L'Univers* and *Le Figaro* paid the fine through a public subscription. By the beginning of 1892 it was apparent that only the pontiff's personal intervention could prevent the policy of the Ralliement from being stillborn. Leo acted on 16 February, issuing the encyclical *Inter innumeras*, complete with an official French translation to avoid multiple "free" renderings, which confirmed Lavigerie's admonition and placed upon it the papal imprimatur. Catholics were henceforth to distinguish between "constitution" and "legislation," pledging the regime "adhésion sans arrière pensée," while laboring ceaselessly to alter noxious statutes by all legal means. To dramatize the new sacrifice demanded of French royalists, Leo also granted an unprecedented newspaper interview to Ernest Judet, editor of *Le Petit Journal*, a Parisian daily of large circulation, during which he forcefully confirmed the language of the encyclical. Those who had previously denied that open adherence to the Republic was necessary were now compelled to decide whether or not to defy the Vatican, and the choices split and embittered the conservatives. Emile Keller and Mackau of the union attempted to maintain its ambiguous position by issuing a statement claiming that by their words they had already heeded the papal teaching. Because Leo's encyclical clearly belied this declaration, Eugène Veuillot of *L'Univers*, de Mun, Cardinal Richard, and other ultramontanes resigned. Their defection shattered the union, which dissolved itself three months later in May as some of its prominent members, led by Keller, placed throne before altar and retired from active politics rather than renounce their king. Other intransigents felt more combative, formally disputing Leo's authority outside the realm of the spiritual. The slow attrition of the royalist ranks so incensed them that in June they drafted a manifesto of their "obligations as Catholics and citizens" that was so insulting to the Vatican that none dared sign it. When the Panama Canal scandal broke in September their behavior seemed justified, and Cassagnac gloated at the Republic of the Ralliés, "Elle est belle, leur fiancée."[9]

De Mun had been among the first to encourage the Right to disavow dynastic politics, and this heresy alone had led to his denunciation by the intransigents. Whether or not he fully comprehended the papal role in Lavigerie's toast, he was unwilling to suffer more until the pope himself required it. Instead he helped to form the Union de la France Chrétienne and continued to talk of seeking religious and social gains through a confessional party. When the encyclical demanding a Ralliement appeared, he hesitated. His conscience demanded prompt and complete obedience no matter what the cost, but despite Leo's distinction between constitution and legislation, de Mun identified the Republic too closely with anticlericalism. Two days afterward he had to speak against a republican bill to dissolve the "authorized" congregations, and once again Clemenceau answered him, this time addressing the Opportunists to damn any rapprochement with the church. "You say a hand is held out to yours?" he warned, "Put yours in it. It will be so firmly grasped that you cannot escape. You can, you will, be captives of the church, for it will never be in your power." This hostility made de Mun hedge any adherence to the Republic, even as he moved closer to a clear break with royalism. On 9 March he urged the members of the ACJF to "unite in a 'constitutional' party" but declined to join them there. Even this small amount of maneuvering room was denied him by a pastoral letter from Leo on 3 May expressing his gratitude to the French episcopacy for joining the Ralliés. The message excluded further equivocation. As the new nuncio Dominique Ferrata expressed it, French Catholics had been warned thrice; they now had either to accept or to declare themselves rebels. De Mun could resist no longer. Telling his wife Simone that the future could hold only "cruel tests," he traveled to the Vatican, there in a dramatic audience to inform Leo personally of his decision to rally. The aged pontiff threw his arms about de Mun and implored him to become the emblem of the Ralliement, even as he was of social Catholicism. Inspired by this charge, he returned to France seeking only an appropriate moment for his profession and finding it at the ACJF congress at Grenoble on 23 May. Here he pronounced the irrevocable formula, "In order to conform to the wishes of the Holy Father, I shall henceforth conduct my political action within the limits of the constitutional order."[10]

De Mun realized that to rally meant to break many old friendships, to sadden and disappoint others, to seem to desert royalism in its time of defeat. Political preferences, social situations, personal prestige, old and dear affections, all demanded that he remain a royalist, but he obeyed the pope. The Vatican secretary of state, Mariano Cardinal Rampolla, published a letter praising his words at Grenoble, but those words also began the cruel tests he had foreseen and dreaded. La Tour du Pin, already upset by the treatment accorded *L'Association Catholique*, publicly separated himself from his friend of a quarter century and resigned from the Oeuvre des Cercles. The salons that had beckoned him now closed their doors, and even his relatives denied him their support. Old friends turned their backs as he approached and refused to shake his hand. Simone was treated as meanly as her husband, and their apartment near the Champs Elysées became a place of refuge and exile, in which they seldom received guests and from which they were rarely invited. Although flinching under this strain, they still bore themselves nobly and with grace, seeing in these trials a testing of their faith in themselves and in the church. They retreated to a new self-sufficiency and began the study and denials that would prepare them to assume the vows of the Third Order of Saint Francis in 1903.[11]

As the Ralliement created bitter cleavages among the conservatives, the republicans disputed how to judge their new brethren. For most of the Radicals the decision was easy. Like Clemenceau they warned that the new papal policy was a Trojan horse from the belly of which would eventually spill enemies of the Republic if Marianne's defenders did not mistrust clericals bearing gifts. Radical leaders played the part of Laocoön, Léon Bourgeois snapping, "You say you rally to the Republic? So be it, but do you rally to the Revolution?" The Opportunists did not dismiss the Ralliement out of hand, although Ferry reminded Catholics that the Republic had "got along for twenty years without you and against you." They saw the Ralliés as reluctant republicans, *résignés*, who would have to prove by deeds their hesitant words of affirmation. Some of the Opportunists were already worried by the presence of twelve thoroughgoing socialists in the 1889 Chamber and an increase in anarchism, and they blessed the pope for supplying the established regime with new friends to oppose potentially dangerous enemies. Even so, only the most right-wing of the republican moderates, Etienne Lamy and Gaston David, were ready immediately to clasp the hands of the postulants.[12]

David was the brother-in-law of President Carnot and thus potentially influential. Lamy, a former deputy turned writer, thought himself already so. Lamy was a sincere Catholic, and his republican credentials were nonetheless impeccable since he had been among the famous 363 deputies in May 1877 to oppose MacMahon. Defeated in 1881 because his republican constituency would not tolerate his opposition to the laic laws, he had discovered that in French politics it was impossible to practice both republicanism and Catholicism. When the Ralliement altered the fixed constellations, Lamy was able to pose as the sole leading republican Catholic not compromised by Boulangism, and he joined with David to create a conservative party of Ralliés and republican moderates. In March 1892 the two announced the formation of a Ligue Populaire pour la Revendication des Libertés and sought to attract members to its program of "adherence" to the Republic, decentralization, fiscal restraint, and modification of the anticlerical laws where they conflicted with the rights of families to educate their children as they saw fit. David looked for support among the Opportunists, trying to allay their basic mistrust by whispering warnings of socialist gains. Lamy courted the conservatives with appeals to their sense of duty, urging that they abandon the monarchy, which they could not save, to reprieve the social order, which they had not the right to let perish. David and Lamy felt that they had to act swiftly for fear that many conservatives would lapse into political indifference after disavowing royalism for the pope and, after May, for fear that de Mun's conversion might preempt Lamy's role. David cautioned that while de Mun was the natural leader of the new Ralliés, his Boulangist past would deny him a similar position in the general republican Right. Lamy would have to convince him to have no ambitions higher than those of lieutenant.[13]

Negotiations began in mid-June among Lamy, Piou, and de Mun but quickly broke down over what should be the essence of the Ralliement. Lamy and Piou agreed that economic conservatism would best cement the Opportunists to the Ralliés and planned a merger in all but name of the Droite Constitutionnelle and Ligue Populaire, with Piou deferring to Lamy's leadership as more acceptable to the moderate republicans. De Mun refused to join them, unwilling to barter social reform even for favors to the church. Lamy then transferred the contest for dominance to public opinion, opening this second round with a carefully planned appearance at Bordeaux to celebrate the republican feast of Bastille Day. Addressing the holiday crowd, he posed as the leader of the loyal opposition in a speech touted "Un Programme de Gouvernement," which called for decentralization, a formal bill of rights, fairer treatment of the church, and vigilance against socialism. His tactic was to draw a sharp distinction between himself and de Mun, who was mistrusted now not only for his brand of Christian socialism but for his part in the Boulangist conspiracy. In contrast, as Lamy flattered the provincial republicans, the mainstay of the Opportunists, he soothed their fears of the Ralliement through the example of his past and the presentation of a program to which they could hardly take serious exception. De Mun did not immediately respond, but his interventions within the Chamber indicated that he envisioned the Ralliement as an opportunity for social reformers to work together unhindered by the labels of royalist and republican. He was particularly encouraged when the Chamber gave final approval on 2 November 1892 to France's first major piece of industrial legislation, a law limiting the workday for women and children to eleven hours and imposing even more stringent restrictions on their labor at night. Exactly six years had elapsed between the bill's introduction and enactment. Throughout, de Mun had found himself working for its passage in conjunction with the Radicals and against most of the conservatives and Opportunists. Although a few of this opposition had finally joined the reformers, he did not view with eagerness helping to stabilize a Republic of laissez-faire industrialists. When he did reply to Lamy on 18 December, he chose not a commercial capital like Bordeaux but the industrial center of Saint-Etienne. After setting the repeal of the anticlerical laws affecting education as the price of Rallié votes for the government, he insisted that the Ralliement be a social movement, that the ideal of the new Catholic republicans be to renew society. If it were not, the "natural heir of pagan capitalism would be revolutionary socialism."[14]

Between de Mun's carrot of reforms and Lamy's stick of repression there was little room for accommodation in the Ralliement's attitude toward the increasingly socialist working class. Lamy had the larger constituency, but by early 1893 this contest of ideology and personal dominance paled before a seeming threat to the whole papal experiment. In August 1892 the progress of the Ralliement had appeared so irresistible that even the cynical Mackau made a virtue of loyalty to the Vatican in professing himself a Rallié. Cassagnac was too intransigent to follow, but he understood his friend's motive of avoiding isolation. In the months that followed, the revelations of the Panama Canal scandal grew seamier and the stain of corruption ever broader within the republican ranks. Some of the *résignés* among the new converts brought out their old royalist colors and declared that the Republic should perish if not founded on integrity. Less reluctant Ralliés desperately sought reassurance that the form of government was above the fen of corruption. Lamy, Piou, and de Mun had avoided commenting on this republican dirty linen because they felt to do so would only antagonize the Opportunists. Now it became essential for them to denounce the scandal while simultaneously insisting that reforms take place within the bounds of the Republic. It was an opportunity to prove that the "constitutional" Right could act responsibly and would defend their new flag. At the end of January 1893, Lamy called on "all who support the regime," from Radicals to Ralliés, to clear away the corruption and senseless persecution of religion that had characterized it at its worst. They should return, he urged, to the original conception of the Republic, one shared by men as disparate as Thiers and Gambetta, the creation of a truly liberal and open government of which all Frenchmen could be proud. The evocation of the anticlerical Gambetta by a self-proclaimed leader of the Catholics was sensational, but hardly more so than Piou's forthright pledge to the Chamber on 16 February, when he vowed that "the Republic of M. Clemenceau will never be ours," but that the Ralliés would help form the majority of a ministry that promised to enforce the laic laws "justly." Lamy made the assurance more unequivocal ten days later at Lyons by denying that the current scandal could be "cured" by royalism, Bonapartism, socialism, or any remedy outside the republican tradition. De Mun added his voice in March by declaring before the deputies that whatever the revelations of misconduct, there was no question among the Ralliés of returning to monarchism, only of finding for the Republic "men who govern for France and not for the interests of a clique."[15]

This united oratory in combination with vigorous lobbying by the three Rallié leaders recovered the resolution of their followers and impressed the Opportunists, but it did nothing to settle the differences over social policy. De Mun was not disposed to compromise, as he quickly proved in April at Toulouse and Arras. Proclaiming that the church must not be the gendarme of bourgeois society, he called for its alliance with the lower classes and for Catholics to seek laws protecting workers as much as capital. There were horrified charges from economic conservatives that once again he had gone too far, that he was now preaching almost a form of class war. He brushed them aside, and on 10 June at the general assembly of the *cercles* stunned even his colleagues in social Catholicism by insisting that it was time to reduce the patronage of the directing class to allow the workers to stand for themselves. Harmel had long favored this evolution, and he was supported by the young men of the ACJF. De Mun found that the transformation did not fit ill with the legislation to emancipate labor that he had supported in the Chamber. He had also seen the failure of the patronage of the Oeuvre des Cercles and was willing to experiment with change, not only to rejuvenate it, but to conform more closely to the thinking of the republican reformers with whom he hoped to have closer contact. Politically, this intransigent emphasis on the social question even in Piou's home district of Toulouse put Lamy on notice that under no circumstances would de Mun accept the economic program of the Ligue Populaire and Droite Constitutionnelle. Lamy and Piou had begun to consider de Mun the reformer a dubious asset, but he did command the allegiance of thirty social Catholic Ralliés, almost half as many as their own sixty-five followers. They needed de Mun's ranks even to pose as a major party. With the elections only two months away in mid-August they had no more time to outmaneuver de Mun and had to treat with him to derive a platform on which all the Ralliés could stand as a group. The result was hardly satisfying to either wing because, with no agreement on social policy, the issue was omitted and the platform seemed remarkably sparse, limited to a pledge of unconditional adherence to the Republic and a demand for liberalizing amendments to the laic laws. Nevertheless, when it was presented to the public at a fund-raising dinner on 21 June, it had to be heralded as the first bold step of an important new party. There were nearly two hundred banqueters, the ninety-odd parliamentary members of the three factions and a larger number of well-wishers and the press, and it was held in the very room of the Hotel Continental on the Rue de Castiglione in Paris where five years earlier the Boulangist conspirators, de Mun and Piou among them, had toasted the Count of Paris. This time the excitement of intrigue and sense of imminent success were missing. Instead, despite the surface conviviality, there was the tension of fundamental disagreement and personal clash as well as anxiety about the course of the elections with a hastily contrived union.[16]

The apprehension was well-founded. The conciliatory words of the Rallié leaders during the past twelve months had revealed how eager they were to cooperate with various republican groups. In early 1893 there did seem a genuine change in the attitude of the Opportunists as Premier Charles Dupuy led them to oppose the Radicals on the questions of retaining the ambassador to the Vatican and supporting the maintenance, through government concordatory funds, of canons at several provincial cathedrals. Anticlerical laws seemed to be enforced with unusual laxity. After May, Dupuy reversed this policy because the surprisingly prescient Opportunist leadership determined that they could win the elections without the aid of an alliance with the constitutional Right and saw no further need to curry its favor. This abrupt shift caught the Ralliés in a whipsaw. In Brittany and the West they found themselves denounced as traitors by unrepentant monarchists, and everywhere they faced strong competition from Opportunists and Radicals. Their strategy was to help Opportunists in the *ballottage* if their own candidate appeared unlikely to succeed, but the Opportunists rarely returned the favor. Dupuy frankly conceded that the Ralliés had more to gain from his faction's victories than from Radical ones and saw no need to reward them. Attacked from all sides, the ninety-four Rallié candidates had little hope of success. Only thirty-six of them were elected, and all three of their leaders were defeated. Many right-wing voters simply stayed away from the polls in despair, and the "old" republican groups raised their share of the total vote from 55 percent to 82 percent. It was an electoral disaster for the conservatives because even lumping the Ralliés with the monarchists, they had lost almost half of their two hundred seats. The great gainers from this debacle were the Opportunists, as they had foreseen. With more than three hundred deputies, they supposed that they would not need to ally with either Left or Right.[17]

The losses of de Mun, Piou, and Lamy had all resulted from facing a strong Opportunist candidate, while losing the votes of traditional conservatives. Rather than vote for a republican or a "traitor," intransigents abstained. This attitude was especially apparent in de Mun's defeat. From Paris the editors of the royalist *Gazette de France* conducted a shrill daily campaign against him and arranged for their paper to be distributed throughout Morbihan to give the denunciations a wide audience. To make his republicanism suspect, they pretended that he had kept up his dues to the local royalist committee; to alienate his Catholic support they insisted that the Rallié program of compromise on the laic laws betrayed the interests of the church. In utter scorn and blatant falsehood, they finally labeled him a *minimiste*, in favor of a minimum program of demands, and insisted that the former Knight of the *Syllabus* was passing slowly to the side of the anticlericals. De Mun's protestations were hopelessly inadequate to counter this skillful offensive because many of the conservatives in Morbihan were now prepared to believe any libel against their turncoat deputy, and they watched with grim satisfaction as he lost on the first ballot to Albert Le Clec'h, a moderate Opportunist. De Mun nevertheless hid his bitterness and put a brave face on the loss, writing to his young friend Charles Geoffroy de Grandmaison of the *cercles*, "I am in no way troubled or discouraged. The church will not make the leap to democracy without effort, struggle, and sacrifice. It is up to us to trace the route even if the effort destroys us. I have begun. I will go all the way. There are many ways in which to offer our lives; we should gaily accept the one open to us. We will fall, perish perhaps. Many will denounce, scoff at, and reject us. What does it matter if the church succeeds? This is the true meaning of the Ralliement." Such equanimity was evidence of his commitment to Leo's plea that he make the Ralliement a part of his life, even as he had social Catholicism, and also the measure of self-control he had acquired after months of constant abuse in the royalist press and from former social acquaintances. It was another example of the profound devotion to the church that had always characterized his life and had led him often in the past to suffer in its name. Only a month after he had seen his political career of almost twenty years disintegrate at the ballot boxes of Pontivy, he seemed almost indifferent to the defeat, announcing that he would now seek to revive the *cercles* by resuming the personal proselytizing he had left to others since 1876. He began by courageously confronting the intransigents of Brittany, first at Landerneau in late October and then at Saint Brieuc in early November. He demanded that they not sacrifice the *cercles* on the pyre of Rallié-royalist strife, that the social mission of the church must not be the victim of political pique. Churchmen applauded, along with many peasants and workers, but the royalist nobility did not disarm. Although these ultras had encouraged the *cercles* before 1890 as potential royalist cells, the very identification of social Catholicism with de Mun and the encyclicals of a casuistic republican pope made them stand haughtily aloof now. Even so, de Mun had planned a new campaign for the *cercles* through the provinces when the death of one of the social Catholic Ralliés who had survived the voting presented him with an opportunity to recoup his political fortunes. Belying his former resignation, he grasped at the chance, canceling his planned speeches and immediately filing for the by-election. "It is up to us," he had written, "to trace the route . . . I have begun. I will go all the way."[18]

It was the Viscount Emile de Kermenguy, deputy from Morlaix in Finistère, who, for de Mun's purposes, had died so conveniently. To a noticeable degree his politics had been a mirror of de Mun's. He had been a convinced social Catholic, one of the fourteen to subscribe to the Catholic party, and an early if not enthusiastic Rallié. Because Morlaix, and much of Finistère, were politically atypical of the remainder of Brittany, his death created a vacancy in one of the few districts where de Mun could have reasonable prospects for electoral success. As in Morbihan, most of the constituents were fishers of crab and lobster or commercial farmers growing cauliflower, artichokes, and onions. The important difference was in the social structure. Around Pontivy the great noble landowners, while few, wielded enormous economic and political power, and the clergy deferred to them. Their wrath at de Mun had been sufficient to defeat him. Conversely, in Finistère, and particularly in the region about Morlaix known as Léon, there were no great estates, and the nobility had always been the traditionally impoverished country squires with limited influence. The parish clergy were recruited largely from a peasant stock who had little awe for the landlords and less fervor for a royalism the nobility had not the power to impose. Instead, they welcomed the Ralliement as an opportunity to free the church from its crippling identification with monarchy. This dichotomy appeared clearly when priests and nobles met at Plouvon in early January 1894 to endorse a single candidate for the by-election to replace Kermenguy, but found themselves hopelessly split, the nobility for the royalist Count de Kerdrel, the more numerous clergy for de Mun. Enraged, the landlords refused to be bound by the result of the caucus and retired to their manors to sit out the election, a subprefect from Morlaix reporting to Paris that "a spirit of revulsion against de Mun is manifested by the nobility here." Knowing that he could not convert the royalists, de Mun ignored them and directed his appeals entirely to the Catholic and peasant vote, promising to enact agricultural reforms and to curb anticlericalism as the Ralliés created a "good Republic." The clergy ensured that he was recognized as the favorite of the church, and in the 25 January 1894 voting, he easily defeated a local republican, Yves Cahill, by 8,154 to 5,885.[19]

After two years the Ralliement had to be counted a failure. Only a portion of the conservatives had heeded Leo XIII's call, and in the new Chamber there were only 37 Ralliés, counting de Mun and nearly 70 intransigent monarchists. Besides splitting the ranks of the Right, the Ralliement had not convinced the Opportunists to trust the new conservative republicans as allies. Instead, the moderates had labored as diligently to defeat Rallié candidates as royalist or Radical ones. And in the elections they had been very successful. The Ralliés and Radicals lost their top leadership; Piou, de Mun, Clemenceau, and Floquet all were defeated; and the Opportunists emerged with 310 seats, a clear majority by themselves. As their new premier Jean Casimir-Périer presented his government on 4 December 1893, the only flaw in his party's triumph was the increase of Socialist representation from 12 seats to 48. Five days later the calm of the Chamber and the self-satisfaction of the Opportunists were shattered, and they turned to Ralliés as new bulwarks of the social order. What de Mun, Piou, and Lamy had failed to do in twelve months of oratory, a bomb thrown into a session of the deputies by anarchist Auguste Vaillant did in a matter of seconds. Although there was more smoke than explosive in the crudely made projectile and only one deputy was injured, the attack terrified the Opportunists, who now personally experienced the terrorist outrages that had wreaked havoc in much of the rest of Europe. In their panic they concluded that the sharp increase in socialist votes and deputies presaged imminent class war and revolution. The danger on the Left made the moderate Right, the Ralliés few as they were, seem much more attractive.[20]

The new attitude of the Opportunists became apparent during a debate on 3 March 1894 about government policy toward the church, when the minister of public worship, Eugène Spuller, a close associate of Gambetta during the early years of the Republic, created a sensation by denouncing the "sectarian spirit" that had fomented such animosity between the Republic and Catholics. He promised in its stead a "new spirit" under the Casimir-Périer cabinet. The Radicals sharply attacked the declaration as "clerical" and damned it in a resolution that failed 291 to 197, supported only by the Radicals and Socialists. A large number of Opportunists, opposing the motion, abstained for fear that Spuller and Casimir-Périer would offer too many concessions to the conservatives. Among them was Louis Barthou, one of the leading members of their younger generation. Following the defeat of the Radical resolution, he offered one of his own, recognizing the "new spirit" but calling for the maintenance, at least formally, of the laic laws. Spuller endorsed this formulation in the name of the ministry, and it passed easily, 280 to 120, but again with many abstentions. This time it was the conservatives, especially the Ralliés, who queried the meaning of the proposal. De Mun voiced their dilemma. They wished to demonstrate their support for Spuller's sentiments but not enough to conquer their scruples about a public acceptance of the anticlerical laws. Their solution was a refusal to vote either way. They were also taken unaware and disconcerted by such attention, since they were so few, and, until de Mun's by-election was validated on 12 February, absolutely leaderless. Prior to the 3 March debate their only noticeable act had been to adopt the name "Independent Republicans," yet because they remained divided over social policy they could not even claim the unity a single designation implied. The elections had left only about twenty of the thirty-seven holding to the traditional conservative opposition to unionization and industrial reform. The remainder inclined in greater or lesser degree to the reformism of de Mun. If the Ralliés were to make their votes count for much in the intrigues of the Chamber, these votes would have to be delivered in a bloc because the Opportunists would not likely tolerate an unreliable ally for long.[21]

As a wealthy director of the Anzin mining company, Casimir-Périer was acutely familiar with labor unrest and worried more than most of his following about the dangers of socialism. He had turned for additional support to the Ralliés, but he quickly discovered that their divisions on social reform disastrously hindered their ability to support a ministry of moderate republicans united by economic conservatism. On 30 April, Jean Jaurès, the tribune of the forty-eight Socialists, tried to disrupt any incipient Rallié-Opportunist collaboration by claiming that social Catholics were as great a threat as the Socialists to the established capitalist order. These words required a rejoinder from de Mun, who had no difficulty dismantling Jaurès's faulty reasoning. He was cheered enthusiastically by Opportunists, Ralliés, and royalists as he went on to denounce socialism as a "permanent peril" hardly to be distinguished from anarchism in its dream of violent revolution. This response encouraged Casimir-Périer to believe that he could govern with the support of the Ralliés on a program of relaxed enforcement of the laic laws and repression of socialism or any hints of labor radicalism. His grand scheme lasted only three weeks. On 22 May he forbade participation in a trade union congress by employees of the national railway system on the grounds that unionization of the workers would enable them to threaten a nationwide railroad strike. As patrons of the workers, the *cheminots*, the Radicals responded with a resolution of no confidence in the ministry and thereby created a new dilemma for the Ralliés and many Opportunists. Both groups disliked the prospect of the premier's fall, but many of them considered that on this occasion he had made a serious error of judgment since there was no law prohibiting the organization of state employees. He should have proposed legislation, not fiat, to solve the problem. De Mun had led the social Catholics to believe that the Ralliement could bring both tolerance for the church and social reform. For the first time they discovered that these objectives might be in conflict. They split their seventeen votes, nine abstaining, eight, including de Mun, voting against the ministry. About eighty Opportunists joined in abandoning the premier, and almost as many more abstained. This disaffection combined with the solid opposition of the Radicals and Socialists to overthrow the government by a vote of 265 to 225.[22]

The brief dalliance of Casimir-Périer with the Ralliés produced within de Mun an intense ambivalence. As so often previously in his political career, he felt compelled to reexamine the course he had followed, and once again he found that he had compromised his idealism in the very attempt to implement it. He had practiced casuistry, the paladin as politician. Could success be worthwhile at such a price? As a faithful soldier in the papal army he had adopted the Ralliement, and in what was a contest of ideology as much as personal political power, he had blocked the effort of Piou and Lamy to convert the Ralliés into an auxiliary of the right-wing Opportunists. The Ralliés had to be more, he insisted, more than a few extra votes to preserve the bourgeois paradise of the Third Republic. The pope of the Ralliement was, after all, the pope of social Catholicism. But political reality denied this role to the Ralliés. Most of them had no taste for reform—although many of these had been defeated in the elections—and, more critically, neither did the Opportunists. For while the Radicals welcomed the company of de Mun and his followers on social legislation, they absolutely refused any accommodation with the church; the Opportunists would compromise the lay Republic, but only to ensure a profitable one. When the predicament was finally clear to de Mun, the clarity of his understanding almost staggered him. What a burden he had borne, and had forced his family to bear, for a cul-de-sac, from which the church could emerge unshackled only by resuming the position of society's gendarme. In early June de Mun began to suffer from tic douloureux, and the spasmodic neuralgia so contorted the left side of his face that it became a torment even to speak. He withdrew from Paris with his family to Lumigny for more than a year, returning only rarely to the Chamber for crucial votes. This affliction, often psychosomatic, typified the breakdown of self-control he experienced now after having carried on stoically through almost two years of vituperation. It was a reaction as close to despair as any he had ever known.[23]

The experience of the Ralliés during his absence could not cheer him or lighten his gloom. Returning to succeed Casimir-Périer was Charles Dupuy, who had scorned compromise with the Ralliés during the 1893 elections. He did so now although anarchist outrages reached their height in France at Lyons, when on 24 June 1894, Santo Caserio, an Italian baker's apprentice obsessed with the idea of violence, struck down President Sadi-Carnot. Remembered for his harsh attitude toward socialism, Casimir-Périer was overwhelmingly elected to succeed him. The votes for him by the Ralliés were wholly unnecessary, and, as in the elections a year earlier, Dupuy felt under no obligation to reward what had been given freely. As premier he managed to avoid all difficult issues by the simple expedient of postponing them, until finally in January 1895 internal bickering among the Opportunists cost him his majority. He never asked for Rallié assistance, and not surprisingly he never got it. His resignation came at almost the same time as that of Casimir-Périer from the presidency. The former premier had hoped to strengthen the largely ceremonial office, but failing, he quit in disgust. With both top offices vacant, the Ralliés had an excellent opportunity to deal with some faction of the squabbling Opportunists by offering to throw their votes one way or another. Piou would have been well suited for these negotiations, but he was no longer a deputy and could not speak with authority. De Mun had all but exiled himself from the Chamber for the past six months and could not be considered for the task. Of the remainder, only Mackau had the requisite experience, but it was his very experience to which the

Opportunists objected. They regarded him as the chief author of Boulangism and his conversion to the Republic as utterly cynical, and for them he was persona non grata. Lacking a diplomat, the Ralliés failed to engage in negotiations with any republicans and found themselves isolated, scorned by the royalists and ignored by the Opportunists. As a result they had no effect on the 18 January election of Félix Faure as the new president, although they voted for him, typically enough because his wife was a practicing Catholic. They also had no stake in the new ministry formed by Alexandre Ribot on 28 January.[24]

This cabinet was an attempt to lure at least some of the Radicals back to a coalition with the Opportunists before they became too friendly with the Socialists. Because Ribot would not accede to the principal economic demand of the Radicals, an income tax, he thought to cement the reunion by endorsing their latest anticlerical scheme, a tax on the religious congregations, and won its passage by late April. This tax was not stiff enough to ruin the congregations, but for the Catholics there was the question of principle to be fought. Ribot's policy seemed to indicate how little the Ralliement had accomplished for the church, and the furious attacks on the new law by various prelates and the clerical press, particularly *L'Univers* and *La Croix*, a new daily published by the Assumptionist order, seemed a reversion to the days before Lavigerie's toast. Even Leo XIII did not reprove the assaults. Five months later, in October, Ribot nevertheless managed to offend his Radical patrons and a good portion of the Opportunists by his inept handling of the bloody glassworkers' strike at Carmaux, and on 28 October, his ministry was defeated 269 to 187, the Right, royalist and Rallié, voting unhesitatingly against him.[25]

Because the Radicals had been instrumental in overthrowing Ribot, President Faure bowed to parliamentary custom by offering them a chance to govern, calling their leader Léon Bourgeois to form a cabinet. It was a challenge that most Opportunists hoped the Radicals could not meet, but Bourgeois surprised them. On 1 November he presented the Chamber with its first all-Radical ministry, his majority resting upon a shaky coalition of Socialists, Radicals, and the left wing of the Opportunists, those who were loath to forsake the republican tradition of "no enemies to the left," even at the price of a tentative embrace of the Socialists. The cabinet was consciously opposed to the Ralliés, whose policy the Radicals blamed for drawing the Opportunists to the Right. In his ministerial declaration Bourgeois assailed "those who have affirmed the formula of our institutions without accepting the spirit and social consequences of them." His virulently anticlerical minister of public worship Emile Combes went further, purposely antagonizing Catholics by claiming that Freemasonry was a religion more moral than Christianity, and threatened the abrogation of the 1801 Concordat as well as severe new laws against the church. Bourgeois's majority swallowed these words, but his attempt to ram through a progressive income tax bill and his complete reliance upon the votes of the Socialists to remain in office turned his Opportunist supporters against him, and their desertion led directly to his fall in April 1896. This interlude of Radical rule was of the utmost importance to the evolution of the Ralliement. The threat of truly harsh new anticlerical strictures made de Mun and the social Catholics more eager to seek a renewal of the new spirit, fully realizing that any alliance with the moderates would restrain their freedom to press for social legislation. One horn of the dilemma had proved sharper than the other. More important, the income tax issue aroused the fear of all economic conservatives. It convinced the Ralliés that they would have to work with the Opportunists and led even many of the royalists to relax their hostility to conservative republicans. It served to persuade the right-wing Opportunists, led by Jules Méline and Raymond Poincaré, that there was a need for a broad conservative majority to defend property and that this majority should include the Ralliés. With these thoughts in mind, Faure turned to Méline as Bourgeois's successor.[26]

The new premier was from the Vosges and had taken as his chief interest the protection of agriculture from foreign imports. It was in connection with his tariff proposals that he had come to meet Ralliés and royalists, many of whom were landowners attracted to protectionism, and to find with them broad areas of agreement. His cabinet of moderates was an invitation to the conservatives to continue that cooperation, since at the crucial ministries of public worship and education, foreign affairs, and the interior he placed, respectively, Alfred Rambaud, Gabriel Hanotaux, and Louis Barthou, all favorable to the Ralliement. He promised the Chamber that with these associates he planned a balanced budget, appeasement of religious hatreds, and no fiscal adventures, the political shorthand for economy, tolerance, and no income tax. He could not win for this program the left wing of the Opportunists, about eighty deputies who had already proved their independence by often supporting the Bourgeois cabinet. He managed nevertheless to produce a majority of 278 to 244 when he presented his ministry on 24 April by combining the votes of the Ralliés, and indeed of a few royalists, with those of the remaining 230 Opportunists. "The Right is not voting with us," Méline explained to the republicans who questioned his reliance on "reactionary" deputies, "it is voting against a social revolution."[27] But if the Ralliés, tugging the royalists behind them this time, enabled Méline to survive his debut before the Chamber, for some of them it was to do more than pull the country out of the "antechamber of communism," as the *bien-pensants* called Bourgeois's proposals, and into the boardroom of capitalism. The obvious spokesman for this position would be de Mun, and in May 1896 he was finally ready to assume his role.

During the first months of the year, as the Bourgeois ministry neared its denouement, de Mun recovered from his tic douloureux even as he decided that the social Catholics would have to risk sterility in allying with the Opportunists, if only to preserve the church from an alarming fate at the hands of Radicals like Combes. He felt his first certitude in months, and he celebrated this sensation by moving his family from the Rue François Ier to a new apartment, in an *hôtel* recently erected a few blocks away on the Rue de l'Alma. It was something of a fresh start, out of the rooms that had become an exile, away from the titled neighbors who snubbed him, and, in much the same sense, out of a kind of Ralliement that had failed. He also regained his crusading ardor; there were battles to be won in which perhaps only he could lead the charge. If the Ralliés were compelled by raison d'état to enter into an unequal alliance with the Opportunists, there would surely remain moments for increasing their influence and making crucial what little weight they carried. De Mun began by delivering his first speech in almost two years, choosing to address a celebration at Reims on 14 May 1896 of the fourteenth centenary of the baptism of Clovis. Exploiting the historical parallel, he called on Catholics to baptize the Republic as the church had the barbarian king of the Franks. In June he made a carefully planned return to the tribune of the Chamber, replying to

Socialist leader Jules Guesde's accusation that a society of private property could never grant justice to its laboring classes. De Mun attacked the Marxian basis of this argument, denying that the lot of workers was becoming increasingly bad. Already the advance of social Catholicism, unionization, and a few industrial reforms had proved Guesde wrong. It was rather socialism that would bring suffering to all through bloody revolution. Méline's Opportunists warmly applauded his words and deeply appreciated his rebuttal, but not so much as they did the votes of Ralliés and royalists that provided a narrow margin of twenty-nine a few weeks later, on 7 July, when the conservative majority defeated another proposal by the Radicals to establish an income tax.[28]

In his turn Méline quickly demonstrated a willingness to defend the church from anticlericalism. He continued the republican practice of rigorously prosecuting clerics who interfered in elections, but he did eliminate many minor irritants, such as the prohibition of religious processions. More tangibly for the Ralliés, Barthou at the ministry of the interior began to overlook the return of several unauthorized congregations of men, who, banned in 1880, had filtered back in small numbers and reopened a few of their schools. Barthou's enforcement of the decrees against the monks was so lenient that by 1898 there were more of them in France, with more schoolchildren in their charge, than had been the case eighteen years earlier. Although the Radicals often questioned the government about its unusual tolerance toward the church, Méline beat back their attacks with his solid majority. He could appreciate the church's appetite for prestige and recognition, and as his confidence in the Ralliés increased, he took care to cater to it. In early October 1896 Tsar Nicholas II and the Tsarina visited France personally to crown the defensive alliance arranged between the two countries in 1894, ending for both the threat of a single-handed war with Germany. All of the negotiations from the French side had been handled by the Quai d'Orsay and the army general staff; the Chamber did not even have the task of ratifying the pact. All French leaders, with the exception of a few doctrinaire Socialists like Guesde, were nonetheless in favor of it. When the Russian royal family reached Paris, they reacted like many a sightseer in asking President Faure, their first official visitor, whether they might have the pleasure of touring Notre Dame. Quickly informed of the request, Méline arranged for Cardinal Richard on 7 October to precede him in the protocol of formal presentations and play the part of a personal and highly publicized guide for the Tsar and Tsarina at the cathedral. At the beginning of 1897 the premier gave further proof of his allegiance to the Ralliement by joining with de Mun in January to defeat a Radical-sponsored attempt to abrogate the law of July 1873 granting government appropriations and endorsement to the construction of Sacré-Coeur. He even took delight in exposing some of the cherished myths of the anticlericals, ordering at the same time the examination of the tombs of Voltaire and Rousseau to refute the widespread supposition that at the Restoration pious hands had robbed the vaults of the two bodies and flung them in a ditch. During the next three months his official support of the intercession by French Catholics with the Ottoman Empire for the rights of their coreligionists in Armenia and Crete brought his reputation among conservatives to a zenith. Foreign minister Hanotaux made representations at Constantinople, and such noted republican intellectuals as the historian Ernest Lavisse joined with de Mun in protesting the treatment of subject Christians by the Turks.[29]

The first serious breach in this policy and coalition came in the wake of the Charity Bazaar fire of 4 May 1897, in which over a hundred people perished. Most of the victims were wives and daughters of business leaders and the high nobility, who for more than a decade had organized an annual social and benevolent extravaganza in a rambling wood and canvas firetrap off the Champs Elysées, and in Paris there was mourning throughout the aristocratic quarters. The Dames Patronnesses of the *cercles* lost four members and sixteen associates, and de Mun's wife and daughter, who found in the Dames Patronnesses an escape from social ostracism, had barely made it to safety from the inferno. A Requiem Mass was celebrated for the dead at Notre Dame on 8 May, and in a gesture of reconciliation Méline and Faure agreed to attend, the first time since 1879 that a premier or president of the formally lay Republic had been present officially at religious services. The occasion would have been a manifestation of the reality and success of the Ralliement but for the homily delivered by an intransigent Dominican, Father Marie Joseph Ollivier, who, to the literal horror of the congregation, called the fire a divine punishment for France's apostasy. It was a gratuitous insult to the republican tradition, and to Faure and Méline in particular, and they were barely persuaded not to stalk out. When the Radicals gleefully questioned the ministry about the incident, the premier felt constrained to use harsh words in reference to the arrogance of "certain clerics." De Mun followed Méline at the rostrum and managed to make the tenor of the premier's remarks less offensive to the conservatives, who conceded that the expression of Ollivier's prejudices had been ill-advised and highly unsuited to a Requiem Mass. The internal relations of the coalition were nevertheless strained for a few weeks until another effort by the Radicals to pass an income tax bill helped to heal the running sore. Instead of splitting the allies even further apart, as the Radicals had bizarrely hoped, the ploy only revived their cooperation, with Méline relying on fifty-two votes from the Right, including many royalists, for his thirty-three-vote margin in defeating the proposal.[30]

Although de Mun and the Ralliés had won concessions for the church through their timely support of Méline, the policy of economic conservatism that bound together the coalition of Opportunists and Right seemed at first sight to preclude any significant social legislation. Such a negative view imposed, nevertheless, too rigid a boundary on the political options open to Méline and failed to take account of the diverse nature of his majority. The premier himself recognized that the Ralliement might not conform forever to political reality, and there were other moderate Opportunists who shared this attitude. They found it not unwise to temper the antagonism of the Radicals by endorsing one of their more "opportune" reform proposals. At the same time they would be providing an inexpensive pourboire for de Mun and the social Catholics in return for their crucial backing. Méline quickly settled upon an acceptable reform, accident compensation for industrial and transport workers, which de Mun had proposed as long ago as 1886 and which the Radicals had quickly picked up. The plan had been "seasoned" in the smokehouse of Opportunist committees for about a decade and by the mid-1890s was hardly opposed by most factory owners. Indeed, it actually appeared quite mild in light of the systems of social security already enacted in other parts of Europe. Méline sampled the political breeze in early 1897 and had been about to adopt the accident insurance bill for his own when the Charity Bazaar fire disrupted the Chamber for two months. It was only in late summer that he could arrange a suitable setting again, and when he did, he guaranteed the proposal's almost unanimous approval, 518 to 12, on 28 October.[31]

From the moment that he pledged the support of the social Catholics to Méline, de Mun had known that retrograde social views would predominate within the ministry. The church had been the winner for his tactics, and during most of 1896 he tolerated the absolute lack of progress on reform almost meekly. But the silver anniversary of the *cercles* on 27 December had to be an exception. At a gala banquet held in the Cercle Sainte Geneviève in Paris, de Mun reviewed the bases of the Oeuvre des Cercles and its progress in twenty-five years. There was a touch of magic in this retrospective, as he evoked the idealism of the Men of Good Will and their successors, but the emotion that tinged his words and lingered about his audience came from a recognition that no remedy had been found for the increasing debilitation affecting the clubs. De Mun could bring these dedicated social Catholics to their feet with a new promise to pursue their goals within the Chamber, but he grasped the hollowness of his words. In deference to Méline he had not mentioned social reform in the Chamber since April, and it was only here outside that he broke his silence. His first glimmer that the premier might make even a minor concession came with the receipt of a letter from Paul Deschanel, an aspiring young moderate close to Méline, complimenting his address to the *cercles*. De Mun replied cordially, and diplomatically, that he hoped that their union in sentiment could lead to union in action, but he heard no more until Méline's declaration in late summer. Then, to ministerial acclaim, he could praise the accident insurance plan and even suggest improvements, which the premier graciously agreed to take under advisement for the future. The passage of this bill did not whet the reforming zeal of the social Catholics. Rather, it seemed to allow them more easily to succumb to the comfortable illusion that the majority that slaked the leash on the church was also relatively liberal toward the working class. Half a year later, in June 1898, when the Radicals and Socialists formally questioned Méline about his ministry's failure to support reforms, the social Catholics loudly supported the premier and supplied his victory margin, 294 to 271.[32]

By the fall of 1897 there seemed no real difficulties for the

Méline cabinet except the effort by a small group of Jews and Radical politicians to reverse the court-martial of a convicted traitor, a Jewish captain named Alfred Dreyfus. Although the evidence against him was slim and contradictory, in late 1894 Dreyfus had been judged guilty of selling French military secrets to the Germans and condemned to Devil's Island for life. In 1895 Colonel Georges Picquart stumbled upon new evidence indicating that a Major Walsin Esterhazy was the true culprit, but he was told by his superiors that the case could not be reopened, that the honor of the army would be at stake if it could be proved that the court-martial had erred on such a grave matter. To prevent him from revealing his speculations, the army transferred him to Tunis. A year later, however, Mathieu Dreyfus, brother of the condemned man, independently arrived at the same conclusions and demanded a new trial for his brother and the arrest of Esterhazy. He was supported by a group of Radical and Socialist leaders, Georges Clemenceau, Jean Jaurès, and Auguste Scheurer-Kestner. As the first bitter winter winds bore down on Paris, these "Dreyfusards," all enemies of Méline, began a blustery campaign of condemnation against the army and the ministry for sheltering a guilty traitor and permitting an innocent man to rot on Devil's Island.[33]

The leftist leaders had not been the first choice of Mathieu Dreyfus to fight for the rehabilitation of his brother. These men were not in control of the government; Clemenceau was no longer even a deputy. In search of a powerful ally, Dreyfus had gone first to de Mun, hoping that his reputation as a champion of the oppressed would lead him to exert his influence in favor of a new trial. But Dreyfus had not reckoned on de Mun's unquestioning loyalty to the decisions of the high command, built up during fifteen years of military service and founded upon an aristocratic warrior heritage. Although he had resigned his commission twenty years ago, his sense of duty remained undiminished. To proclaim Dreyfus innocent was to declare the army guilty. He would not besmirch the honor of its officers. It was as if he had been asked to curse the church or spit on the workers of the *cercles*. When Mathieu Dreyfus called at the Avenue de l'Alma in May 1897 to enlist his aid, de Mun received him coldly, his sense of mercy lacking altogether, replying, "I have nothing to say to you on this subject," and left his valet to show Dreyfus out.[34]

By the end of the year, the allies that were recruited instead had mounted such a campaign in the press that the Dreyfus "case" had become an "affair." The public asked why the government did not act either to silence its critics or to reopen the trial, and slowly the deputies began to grow anxious. Within the Chamber there was confusion and uncertainty about the increasing controversy and little evidence except the fact of Dreyfus's conviction. With Dreyfusard attacks on the army and the government building to a crescendo, on 4 December some of Méline's supporters finally asked his reassurance that the accusations were false. The premier himself was impatient to lay to rest lingering doubts about the trial. He had inherited it from his predecessors and was unwilling that the court-martial of a traitor, accomplished long before he took office, should shake his ministry. He replied with characteristic candor that he took his stand on the *res judica*, that a judgment had been rendered and that until conclusive evidence could be produced, the verdict would have to stand. He could not have been more forceful in declaring fatefully, "Let me make what will be the decisive statement on this matter: there is no Dreyfus affair. There can be no Dreyfus affair."[35]

For many deputies this categorical denial sufficed. For de Mun, outraged by the recent scurrilous attacks on the high command, and particularly on General Raoul Boisdeffre, chief of the general staff for whom Father du Lac also served as confessor, it did not. He followed Méline in addressing the deputies and, to the premier's surprise, demanded that the minister of war, General Jean Baptiste Billot, personally reply to the imputations lodged against the army and vindicate its leaders. His voice soaring with passion, he pounded on the rostrum as he excoriated the Dreyfusards as partisans of treason. Then, looking directly at their parliamentary champion, Joseph Reinach, he first suggested that there was a Jewish conspiracy, a "Syndicate," behind the agitation and insisted that the deputies "must know whether there is a mysterious occult power [of Jews] strong enough to disrupt the entire nation as it has for the past two weeks, to cast doubt and suspicion on those who command the army, on those who may one day have to lead the country against the enemy. This cannot be a question of politics. Here we are neither friends nor adversaries of the government, here only Frenchmen, anxious to preserve their most precious possession, that which rests above all our struggles and party conflicts, the common ground of our invincible hope [of revenge], the honor of the army!"

Much of the Chamber was on its feet as one man. The deputies had applauded from de Mun's first words, but now the walls resounded with the thunder of the "Bravos!" and clapping. Reinach remembered later that he felt on his head at that moment the hatred of three hundred hypnotized fanatics. All that had been required to allay their doubts about Dreyfus was confident leadership, which Méline and de Mun had just supplied in excess. The applause had hardly died when Billot climbed the stairs to the rostrum to declare unequivocally, "For me, in my soul and conscience, as a soldier and chief of the army, I consider the judgment sound and Dreyfus guilty. In the name of the army I ask the Chamber to halt this campaign of accusations as quickly as possible." From his seat de Mun formulated a resolution reflecting Billot's charge, and after Méline adopted it as the ministry's, it passed by a lopsided 372 to 126 vote. The margin was remarkable, more than a hundred deputies above Méline's normal working majority, and it not only revealed the sentiment of the Chamber at this point on the affair but quite interestingly suggested that de Mun wielded considerable power among the deputies, at least on this issue. The subject was not clearly within his bailiwick, but he had delivered stirring speeches on the army before, and his brand of oratory, frothy and white-hot, was particularly effective on emotional questions, as the affair had become. Somewhat surprisingly, the usually cautious Méline had allowed him his head this time and ended by staking the ministry on de Mun's resolution. He was dangerously close to granting de Mun a tacit authority to commit the government on this issue, and by failing to curb him in December 1897, Méline unwittingly prepared the sensational debate six weeks later in which through de Mun the government and the Ralliement would become inextricably entangled with the unyielding opposition to the Dreyfusards and their cause.[36]

In an effort to quiet the agitation, the army brought Esterhazy to trial on 11 January 1898, but triumphantly acquitted him the following day. On the morning of 13 January, in Clemenceau's daily *L'Aurore*, the Dreyfusards responded dramatically with novelist Emile Zola's "J'Accuse!" an open letter to President Faure charging the army and the government with a plot to maintain the conviction of Dreyfus in the face of conclusive evidence to the contrary. That afternoon in the Chamber, de Mun began the session with a stirring demand to know what action the ministry planned against Zola. Another deputy suggested that the question be set aside, since neither Méline nor Billot was present, but de Mun replied imperiously, and to immediate acclamation, "The army cannot wait!" Obediently, the deputies filed out as the session was suspended for nearly an hour, while the premier and the war minister were called. They had hoped that in their absence the Chamber would leave the question of Zola alone, since to bring him to trial would only give the Dreyfusards extended free publicity and provide their first cross-examination of the army. This argument was lost on de Mun, if indeed it was ever presented to him. Forever the paladin, in his wrath he demanded revenge. Reinach found de Mun's authority proving that the Ralliement had led to the dominance of the Right over the deputies and the government. "To be obeyed de Mun had only to speak, or even to threaten to do so. The government submitted to him immediately rather than risk the address that would have affirmed so brutally the dominant position of the Catholic orator." When Méline did arrive, he carefully refrained from commiting the government to prosecution and instead declaimed vaguely about the "legitimate emotion and indignation within the Chamber." He was loudly applauded for this tactically low profile, but the wildest cheers were again for de Mun. Denouncing "J'Accuse!" as a "deadly affront" to the army, he swept the Chamber with him in another passionate harangue, and the deputies overwhelmingly voted with him when he moved that Zola be imprisoned for treasonous libel.[37]

Undeniably, he spoke for a large number of deputies, who, although more circumspect and cautious in their denunciations—in case they should ever have to retract them—made up the ranks of the "anti-Dreyfusards." It was their attitude, a mixture of prejudice, complacency, and conservatism, that de Mun reflected in its most extreme fashion at the rostrum. He also gave it a classic formulation in his reply to the doubts of one of his literary acquaintances, the medievalist Gaston Paris. Referring to that first debate in December 1897, de Mun wrote,

> When I intervened at the tribune to demand that the minister of war vindicate the chiefs of the army, I felt certain of fulfilling my duty. This sentiment, far from being shaken, has been fortified during the past two months. It comes not only because I view certain actions with the wrath of an old soldier but also because I believe that all of the facts of the case have been explored. The judgment freely rendered by men worthy of respect and confirmed by their highest superiors suffices for my conscience. If a verdict cannot be accepted by citizens except on the condition that it may be revised in all of its elements by public opinion at the pleasure of whoever would put it in doubt, it would be the end of all justice, civil or military. My conviction would have been weakened only if a decisive proof could be opposed to the verdict. No one has been able to do this after six months of agitation, and I do not pardon those, who on vague presumptions, have disturbed the country so profoundly and opened the door to a torrent of insults against the leaders of the army.[38]

Trapped by de Mun's resolution, the government promptly tried Zola, sentencing him to a year's imprisonment, which he avoided by leaving abruptly for England while his case was under appeal. During the trial anyone in France who could read had taken a side in the affair. There were frequent clashes in the streets, a revival of dueling, and deep divisions even within families. In the most famous Caran d'Ache cartoon of the period, a large family sits down to dinner to the father's injunction, "No one is to speak of it!" The next panel shows utter confusion, tables and chairs overturned and silverware flying, entitled, "They spoke of it!" Most of all, the intellectuals were split, following Zola into the fray, divided roughly by whether they assigned first priority to justice or fatherland. After Zola's flight in February 1898, these intellectuals alone sustained the acrimony, because without sensational new revelations, which the government naturally did not want and the Dreyfusards could not produce at will, the affair could not, and did not, maintain the interest of a France too susceptible to ennui.

By March, Méline considered that he had restored the calm and stability that had enabled him to rule for almost two years, a record no previous ministry of the Third Republic could approach. This success was a testament to the Ralliement, moderate Opportunists governing in union with the Right. Neither partner could be totally satisfied, but thus far each had feared that the alternative, a return to Radical participation, would be worse. The alliance was a marriage of convenience, and Méline worried about its vulnerability to complacency as well as to disruptive issues like the Dreyfus affair. It was wise, he felt, for the two groups to remind themselves and one another how much they had accomplished together, and he encouraged the periodic exchange of encomia. De Mun's entrance into the Académie Française on 10 March 1898 provided just such an occasion.

This elevation of de Mun to the realm of the forty Green Cardinals—so called because of their regalia and status as arbiters of the French language—was in itself a symbol of the Ralliement. He had been elected on 16 April 1897 to fill the seat vacated by the death of Jules Simon ten months earlier. It was one of the traditionally "political seats" among the forty and ordinarily would have gone to a distinguished member of the Opportunists, most probably a moderate, since the Académiciens were a fairly conservative body. Simon himself had been a "radical" republican under the Second Empire, but after 1873 he had been one of Thiers's successors. Now that the Ralliés had become part of the government, some of the conservative republicans and de Mun's friends within the Académie, the freshly converted Catholic Ferdinand Brunetière, editor of the *Revue des Deux Mondes*, and Gaston Paris, the gentle historian at the Sorbonne, thought to solidify the alliance Méline had constructed by rewarding de Mun for the sufferings he had undergone between 1892 and 1896. It would be a signal honor, although one for which de Mun was perhaps not the best recipient, since he had only his oratory to recommend him as an intellectual. But he was naturally loath to disavow the efforts in his behalf, and Simone felt, with much justification, that she had prepared the way by introducing her husband to literary lights at many soirées for many years and that it would be a partial recompense for their long isolation. He would never have been considered before 1896, nor after 1898, when he would be on the ultimately losing side in the Dreyfus affair. The circumstances of his election laid on him a debt he repaid at his installation in March 1898. By custom a new member of the Académie makes his entrance by eulogizing his predecessor, although on rare occasions these eulogies have been sharply critical. De Mun had been the antagonist of Jules Simon throughout two decades of anticlericalism, but, impeccably attired in white tie and tails under his new green regalia, he celebrated Simon as a tragic figure forced by political circumstances to attack the church.

In supremely elegant language, he recounted how Simon's personal quest for certainty and salvation had been crippled by the spirit of rationalism and natural religion into which his republican politics had cast him. The implication was obvious; the Ralliement had healed wounds on all sides. This generous attitude in treating one of the gods within the republican pantheon drew the warm praise of Méline's Opportunists, who recognized that it was not easy for an arch-Catholic so lightly to excuse Simon's anticlericalism. The Radicals found de Mun arrogantly patronizing, and two days later they again formally accused Méline of endorsing clericalism by allying his ministry to the Right. The premier returned de Mun's favor by answering coldly, "Anticlericalism for you is just a machine of war against moderate republican ministries. It is a platform, an electoral program, and if anticlericalism did not exist, you would invent it."[39]

Méline and de Mun were both anxious to maintain good relations in early 1898 because general elections for the Chamber were set for May. They hoped to translate a parliamentary alliance into an electoral one, concentrating on the defeat of the Socialists and the Radicals. By late March the two leaders agreed that the Right would not challenge Opportunist candidates, the Opportunists returning the favor, and that it would be best completely to avoid raising the issue of the laic laws. The premier was prepared to promise in confidence a continued liberal enforcement of the strictures, but he could not agree to repeal them, at least not until he had further prepared the Opportunists for such a compromise. In theory, these tactics seemed to ensure that the conservative-moderate majority would sweep the elections, but in practice they could be effective only if de Mun and Méline had control of their followers, parliamentarians and local voters. There were here two separate problems. The political algebra and bargains of Paris often meant little against the hatreds and prejudices of local French politics, an inevitable feature of *scrutin d'arrondissement*. Deputies were somewhat easier to control, although in the absence of truly organized political parties, not entirely so. The Opportunists were an amorphous faction, but they were accustomed to following a leader, who, for the present, was Méline. The premier could also mobilize the prefectoral machinery to help enforce his promise if necessary. Although he became increasingly the spokesman for the entire Right in the alliance with Méline, de Mun's situation was much less satisfactory. His leadership seemed somehow the result of default—Piou and Lamy not having won election—and de Mun had no real power other than persuasion to enforce his commands. Some of the royalists resisted following him at all, most of the conservatives rejected his stand on social issues, and many felt nagging doubts about their support of the Republic in the absence of a definite commitment not just to ignore the laic laws but actually to repeal some of them.[40]

De Mun did not have to rally the conservatives behind Méline by himself. Supporting him now was Piou, who after his election defeat in 1893 had returned to his estates in the Gironde but retained his political contacts in the Chamber. In June 1897 he published an important article with Brunetière in the *Revue des Deux Mondes*, praising de Mun and the conservatives for their alliance with the Opportunists. Claiming that it was chimerical for the royalists to think that they could stem the democratic tide that had swept over much of Europe since 1789, he urged them instead to create out of France's Republic a free, open, Christian society. "The hour has come," he warned, "to think more of your children than of your ancestors." De Mun was relieved to have the endorsement of Piou, and their relations began to improve despite continued differences over social reform. This change made him feel more confident facing the fulminations of d'Haussonville and the remaining clique of the Count of Paris. Whether intransigent or resigned, their *politique du pire* was exemplified by Emile Keller, who damned democracy as a sign of decadence and a prelude to despotism, while calling for "Better one more Radical than a tepid Catholic capable of any capitulation." With royalist faithful now largely confined to a few areas in Brittany and the Vendée, de Mun could ignore their threats. What undercut him was the reappearance of Etienne Lamy, claiming that Leo XIII had designated him, and him alone, to lead the Catholics to victory in 1898.[41]

Since the death of Ercole Cardinal Consalvi in 1824, the Vatican had not boasted a single diplomat of stature, with the result that Roman pontiffs often acted from ignorance when dealing with other countries. Although an aristocrat with some experience in foreign affairs, Leo XIII suffered as had his predecessors from a dearth of precise and informed reports from nuncios, and his cardinal secretary of state was the well-meaning but hardly astute Mariano Rampolla. In consequence, he seriously misread the situation of the Ralliement in France when, in January 1896 at the height of the Bourgeois ministry, he concluded that Rallié leaders like de Mun were too compromised by their past to entice the moderate republicans into an alliance. In an effort to emphasize a tradition of republican Catholicism antedating 1892, he thereupon called Lamy to Rome and charged him to lead the Catholic election effort in 1898.[42]

The choice was a very poor one. Lamy had been out of the Chamber since 1881 and had hardly displayed consummate political acumen in the direction of the Ligue Populaire in 1892 and 1893. He also bore an animus toward de Mun, who had won the position of influence in a right-of-center coalition that Lamy had coveted for himself. Lamy's selection completed the poisoning of relations between the two by seeming to indicate papal disfavor with de Mun and reducing his role to that of parliamentary spokesman. It also sparked jealousy from Piou, who quickly discovered that Lamy did not intend to share his mandate with anyone. Piou tried for a few months to revise Lamy's plans, but, failing, cast his lot with de Mun in June 1897 through the *Revue des Deux Mondes*. Lamy also rejected the cautious strategy of his rivals. De Mun had recognized how difficult it would be to arrange an accord on issues, and in his negotiations with Méline he had concentrated on a list of names each side would support, or at least not oppose. Anxious to achieve a striking success that would elevate him immediately to national prominence, Lamy hoped instead to mobilize all of the Catholic vote, creating an electoral federation so strong that he could demand concessions on the repeal of the laic laws in return for the votes of the faithful. Leo XIII supported his plan by sending two French monks, Dom Sébastien Wiart, abbot general of the Cistercians, and Father François Picard of the Assumptionists, around to the bishops in August 1897 with a pastoral letter directing them to assist Lamy, for his scheme would require the utmost assistance. He proposed to league under his general direction the efforts of Catholics across the political spectrum: his own moderate, economically conservative Ligue Populaire now rechristened the Politique Nouvelle; the social Catholics of de Mun's ACJF and an allied group under Léon Harmel, the Union Fraternelle du Commerce et de l'Industrie; the right-wing Justice-Egalité and Congrès Nationaux Catholiques, made up of wary churchmen suspicious of too many concessions to the Opportunists; and the left-wing Union Nationale and Christian Democrats, who had already elected two deputies, Jules Lemire and Hippolyte Gayraud, and wanted drastically to liberalize the image of the church. Under extreme pressure from the episcopacy, and behind it Rome, all seven groups agreed to form Lamy's Fédération Electorale, allowing him to proclaim it triumphantly in December 1897. But while it seemed imposing, in reality the goals of the individual members remained in many instances self-evidently contradictory, and Lamy lacked the political savoir faire to make it operational. He had to make too many concessions to particularist sentiment, with the result that the platform of the Fédération consisted of only three vague points: loyal adherence to the Republic, reform of all laws contrary to common law and liberty, and entente with all who desired a reign of peace in liberty and justice. There was no general agreement on the delegation to a central committee of the vitals, regulation of campaign funds and endorsement of candidates. Lamy, largely a self-proclaimed chief, held the office in name only.[43]

Nevertheless, he proclaimed himself pleased with his creation. Those who were left outside of it were not. De Mun was disturbed by Lamy's inclusion of the Christian Democrats and the consequent necessity for the ACJF to associate with them. He found them altogether too liberal and even dangerous, especially in their social program, which seemed to him to ape the Socialists in pitting workers against owners in bitter antagonism. He asked what could possibly be Catholic about such a portrayal of the social problem; it directly contravened the teaching of *Rerum novarum*. In the spring of 1897, when they obtusely sought his blessing, he twice scolded them publicly, using "too much politics" and "poorly conceived" as euphemisms for the severe condemnation he expressed privately. Lamy recognized his hostility and even the abyss between the conceptions of the Christian Democrats and the ACJF, but he insisted that he needed both within the Fédération if he were to win votes from the constituencies to which each appealed. He foresaw the ACJF attracting votes from a middle class convinced that it would eventually have to come to terms with a social revolution and resigned to seek the best terms it could; the Christian Democrats could win votes from the Socialists. This blithe optimism disturbed de Mun, who with Piou was kept at arm's length from the Fédération because he did not believe that Lamy was confronting the political situation with candor. If Lamy tried to impose a national policy on issues about which there was such wide disagreement, the vaunted Fédération would collapse in disarray and mutual recrimination. If he intended to allow local strengths to dictate tactics in each election district, why establish an unwieldy federation that would only highlight the differences in the Catholic ranks? For de Mun the only realistic strategy was to work out an agreement with Méline, with whom he had managed after all to deal quite effectively for the past two years, by which Catholics would support Opportunist candidates where Opportunists were strong and vice versa. Hoping to circumvent Lamy, de Mun conducted amicable, and what he considered final, parleys with the premier in March 1898 to adopt this strategy.[44]

But Lamy would not be outmaneuvered. Instead, on 3 April he attempted his own negotiations with Méline, ignoring those already completed by de Mun. Under pressure from the members of the Justice-Egalité to force explicit concessions from the premier, he demanded that Opportunists who expected Catholic votes would have to promise the repeal of the laic laws. When Méline replied that the most he could promise was that both sides maintain a discreet silence on the issue, Lamy terminated the interview. He convinced himself now that the only way to hold the Fédération together was to challenge the premier publicly, calling on Catholic voters to carry the election themselves without Opportunist help. It was a counsel of weakness, the threats and braggadocio of a general whose troops quarrel, melt away, dispute his leadership, and do anything but guarantee victory. On 18 April, less than a month before the voting, Lamy held a giant rally for the Fédération in the Salle Wagram in Paris, where he repeated his demands to Méline and called his attitude toward the church—perhaps rightly but certainly inappropriately—one of appeasement, not true cooperation. "We are ready," he perorated, "for alliances between equals; anything less is capitulation." In the audience de Mun turned wearily and disgustedly away to quote Jean François Cardinal de Retz that it is far easier to fight one's enemies than to get on with one's friends. Even so, Lamy's inept and abrupt tactics had only seriously damaged, not destroyed, the chances for a Catholic-Opportunist entente in the voting. Fearing the fall of his ministry should the partnership fail, Méline did what he could to save it. In a speech in his home district at Remiremont on the same day that Lamy preached intransigence in Paris, Méline stressed compromise between the two groups. He also recognized that de Mun and Piou, not Lamy, more accurately represented the thinking of the rightist members of his majority, and he sent foreign minister Hanotaux to them, offering optional religious instruction after class in public primary schools and the proposal that seminary students serve their army duty in the medical corps during peacetime. These concrete concessions, while to some extent proving Lamy's point that the premier could offer the Catholics more, were insufficient to overcome the attitude among provincial churchmen created by him during the previous two years. The efforts of de Mun and Piou were at the ministerial level. Lamy was the only Catholic leader to organize the local groups, and he had led them to expect a substantial requital for their votes. Accustomed to being swindled in the corridors of the Palais Bourbon, they put their faith in the color of deeds, not vague promises. When Opportunist candidates experienced hostility from Catholic voters, they encouraged the same from their supporters toward the Catholics. The obstinacy of local politicians and election districts became a major difficulty for both sides. De Mun and Piou could not give effective orders to Catholic voters in the provinces, and Méline did not fare much better with his followers because Barthou at the interior ministry, insulted by Lamy's tactics, pursued the application of administrative pressure unenthusiastically.[45]

Normally in a general election the incumbent ministry could expect to maintain or expand its majority because of its control of debate in the chambers and the influence it could bring to bear. Méline had the right to expect a favorable outcome. The two years of his cabinet's rule had been prosperous for France, marred only by the ghost of Dreyfus, and at election time even this specter had been laid to rest for the moment. Yet the bickering and mistrust created by Lamy among local Opportunists and Catholics threatened to cost the election. On the 8 May first ballot the Radicals and Socialists made considerable gains, largely at the expense of the Opportunists, and a grim-faced premier closeted himself with de Mun and Piou, both of whom had won easy election. Lamy now retired into the background. His ambitions were shattered by the voting totals that even denied him a seat, and he would soon be disavowed by the Vatican. The three reached an agreement on a list of names to be supported in the *ballottage*. Internecine bouts that could redound to the profit of the opposition were to be avoided completely. They secured the withdrawal of many competing candidates, but some of those sponsored by the royalists or the Justice-Egalité refused, with the result that their partisans wasted their votes on an obviously losing Catholic and cost the Opportunists almost sixty seats.[46]

This intransigence, dogmatism, or just familiar right-wing obtuseness therefore produced a swing of more than a hundred seats to Méline's detriment. On 22 May, when the final results were tallied, there were 32 royalists, 74 Ralliés, 215 Opportunists, 200 Radicals, and 64 Socialists. Méline's moderates among the Opportunists had suffered a sharp setback, and the advance of the Ralliés did not suffice to offset it. The premier was far from convinced that he could continue in office. He had de Mun's assurance that the Ralliés would support him absolutely, and he had often previously picked up votes from among the royalists. His worries came from his own party. Even before the election there had been a left wing of the Opportunists who chafed at cooperation with the Ralliés. During the campaign some of them actually deserted the party and adopted the Radical label. Méline worried that those who remained might fail to back him in a crisis. When the Chamber reconvened on 13 June, the Radicals and Socialists tested his majority immediately by questioning his conduct of policy for the preceding two years. They reserved their harshest words for his alignment with the "clericals," "the reluctant republicans," the Ralliés. The debate continued into the following day, with Méline considering that he had won when he was able to rally a majority, 295 to 272, in favor of a resolution by one of his supporters calling for approval of the premier's self-justification. Undeterred, the Radicals responded with a resolution of their own, this one demanding that the ministry rely upon a majority "exclusively republican." Had Méline endorsed the resolution and called upon the Ralliés to vote for its adoption, he would have survived the day with a majority approaching unanimity. Instead, his political instincts failed him as he felt compelled to oppose it because the Ralliés seemed clearly excluded by the Radical definition of "republican." To the left-wing Opportunists this decision proved that Méline was completely in the thrall of the Right, and they deserted him. When the vote went against the ministry 295 to 246, the premier and his cabinet picked up their portfolios and immediately recessed the Chamber to the cheers of the Radicals and prepared to submit their resignations. As he left the hemicycle, Méline turned to de Mun, who was still startled by the sudden shift in the vote, and bitterly recalled how the intemperate demands of Lamy and his confederates had cost the election. Then he concluded acidly, weighing every word, "Remember this day well! It will haunt you."[47]

5
In Opposition

The fall of Jules Méline's cabinet on 14 June 1898 put an end to the Center-Right coalition that had governed France for more than two years. For a successor President Faure turned by tradition to the faction that had unseated the incumbent majority, the Radicals, and called Henri Brisson to form a cabinet. This Radical chieftain constructed a ministry carefully composed of Radicals and left-wing Opportunists in hope of reviving the traditional alliance of republican concentration. Since the conviction of Zola in February there had been no further developments in the Dreyfus affair, and the premier, on taking office, cautiously made no mention of it, not wanting to precipitate a controversy that might disrupt his peacemaking on the Left. Godefroy Cavaignac, his ambitious minister of war, did not share this prudence, proclaiming in August that there was irrefutable proof of Dreyfus's guilt. His boast was immediately put to the test by the Dreyfusards, and when the proof was revealed a forgery and its author, Colonel Hubert-Joseph Henry, committed suicide rather than face examination, Cavaignac resigned in disgrace. General Thomas Zurlinden, who succeeded him, failed to agree with Brisson on the treatment of the new revelations and also resigned. By October, threatened by Reinach and other Dreyfusards among the Radicals, the premier decided to order Dreyfus home from Devil's Island for a new trial, but his third war minister, General Charles Chanoine, balked at this and departed as had his predecessors. On 25 October Brisson's majority also deserted him, convinced that the premier could no longer govern.

Faure now turned to a veteran Opportunist, Charles Dupuy, whose previous ministries had rested on Center-Left support. He did not renounce his past, and on 31 October he assembled a cabinet that commanded the backing of the 200 Radicals and two-thirds of the 215 Opportunists. The Socialists refused him their votes, although they had supported Brisson. The Ralliés, the royalists, and

Méline's closest followers among the Opportunists were offended by Dupuy's promise to reinstitute a policy of anticlericalism and formed the opposition on the Right. The new premier realized that the Dreyfus affair was now political nitroglycerin, and because he wanted to be rid of its responsibility, he immediately dispatched the case to the highest French court, the Cour de Cassation.[1] Quickly thereafter, the climax of the Fashoda crisis overshadowed that of Dreyfus, threatening war between France and Great Britain over possession of the White Nile and solving one problem for the premier by saddling him with another that was much more grievous. When the outcry over French withdrawal in the face of British threats subsided in mid-November, Dupuy found himself with a vastly increased field of maneuver. To maintain it he hoped to hold together the Radical-Opportunist alliance with the traditional cement of anticlericalism, which to many Radicals had never seemed more necessary.

During Méline's ministry the church had recouped many of its losses of the 1880s, and in particular, the congregations had returned in force to regain their pupils. This alone would have been enough to excite the passion of the Radicals against the church, but now they had its link to the campaign against Dreyfus. The great sinners here were the noisy and foolish priests of the Assumptionist order, who, lacking the prestige and wisdom of the Jesuits and Dominicans, had tried to offset their novelty by the thunder of fulminations in their newspaper *La Croix*, through whose provincial editions they commanded a vast audience across France. They began as less than loyal defenders of the Ralliement, but found their voice only with the Dreyfus affair. Ignoring the warning of more prudent clerics to hold the church aloof from so violent a quarrel, the Assumptionist fathers zealously attacked the defenders of Dreyfus and created the mistaken impression that every good Catholic was an anti-Dreyfusard. The conclusion was false, but readily credible when three hundred priests joined more than a thousand right-wing army officers, among them fifty-two generals, in contributing to a memorial to the suicide Henry, or when *La Croix* sought to outdo even the abominable Edouard Drumont and his *Libre Parole* in execrating the Jews and the "traitorous Dreyfus." The clergy and laity who were revolted by this antisemitism in a paper bearing the symbol of the crucifix and believed that even Jews deserved justice, or who could not see what the "honor of the army" had to do with lying and forgery, did not widely publicize their views because the cause of Dreyfus was championed principally by those who were enemies of the church.[2]

The Assumptionists were such a conspicuous target that Dupuy decided to concentrate his anticlerical proposals on the regulation of the congregations and particularly on their role in education. The control of the regular clergy and their orders from Rome and the consequent immunity from episcopal authority was an old grievance to the French state, and rulers from Philip the Fair in 1300 to Jules Ferry in 1879 had preceded Dupuy in trying to take their measure. The Radicals agreed with Voltaire that monasteries were places "within which men swear to God to live at the expense of others and to be useless," and damned them as the refuge of superstition, reaction, intolerance, and antidemocracy. It was loathsome enough that they should be allowed to exist in France at all, but far worse to be teaching almost half of French children enrolled in elementary schools. Anticlerics charged that the religious had "used their unlimited power in education to produce the people we now have: ignorant, superstitious, brutal, a stranger to any rational notion of duty and a prey to all forms of intemperance." As their predecessors had for half a century, they repeated that the students of clerical schools felt an allegiance first to Rome and only secondarily to the Republic. As if to end this plaint, Dupuy in mid-November 1898 asked the Chamber's Education Committee to consider proposals to place the responsibility for all public instruction in state hands.[3]

The renewal of anticlericalism with ministerial backing served to emphasize the transfer of power within the Chamber; it was now the Left, not the Right, who would formulate policy, the Right, no longer the Left, who would have to react to it. De Mun learned the new lessons immediately after the elections. When the Radicals falsely accused the clerical professorate of the Ecole de la Rue des Postes, the famous Sainte Geneviève on the board of governors of which he had sat since the 1870s at the request of his confessor du Lac, of disclosing to their students in advance the questions on the examinations to enter Saint Cyr and the Ecole Polytechnique, de Mun sent an outraged letter to the war ministry in rebuttal. It arrived as Méline's government fell, and under Brisson's direction the rumors were not denied, although no formal charges were filed. So, too, de Mun found with the new revelations on the affair, despite his hastening Brisson's departure in October with his criticism of the rapid turnover of war ministers and with proposals on education. Both de Mun and Piou sat on the twenty-two-member parliamentary Education Committee and decided in a panic on the need for mobilizing as quickly as possible a broad campaign to blunt the danger to Catholic education. In this plan the ACJF, with its large membership and wide contacts within the universities, could provide the eager and committed shock troops of youth. De Mun felt ill at ease with Henry Reverdy, the current ACJF president, but close to Henri Bazire, the vice-president and favorite to succeed Reverdy at the quinquennial elections the following spring. He had begun a correspondence with his young friend in late 1897 and now cautiously broached a plan for the ACJF to lead a program of speeches and petitions against the proposals of the anticlericals, calling the effort "an excellent opportunity to extend the activity of the Association." Bazire objected that to act in haste might be to "aviver l'incendie," to fan the flames of anticlerical feeling, and to thrust the group undesirably into politics, but he agreed to pass the idea along to Reverdy. Within a week de Mun had recovered from his panic, when he found the committee, chaired by the relatively moderate Alexandre Ribot, disinclined to destroy the freedom of education that allowed Catholics to found their schools. He softened his proposal to Bazire, now asking that the ACJF merely hold itself ready for any sudden assault.[4]

Dupuy's recommendations did die in committee by the end of 1898, and as de Mun's attention shifted from the threat to the Catholic schools he turned back to the debate on the affair. The calm following the submission of the case to the Cour de Cassation was broken in December 1898 by the appearance of a diatribe in English, *The Dreyfus Case*, by Frederick C. Conybeare, which immediately swept the salons and clubs of Paris. Purporting to be a scholarly treatise, the book was instead the pseudonymous product of an Oxford don, Frederick Cornwallis, who was ideologically committed to the anticlerical position of the Radicals, to disestablishment, and to belief in the fiendishness of "Romish" plots. Like Reinach and several other Dreyfusards, Cornwallis claimed that a military and clerical dictatorship threatened to seize power from the Republic and that the conviction of Dreyfus was part of an anti-Semitic plot by the Jesuits, their students on the general staff, and the "Latin Church." De Mun was naturally incensed. He replied in a letter published in the London *Times* on 11 January 1898, refuting "Conybeare" almost page by page, demonstrating, for example, the absurdity of a "Jesuit conspiracy," when but a dozen of the 180 general staff officers had attended their schools. His anger persisted, increasing his bitterness against the Dreyfusards and even acting the part of their caricature. By mid-January he had impulsively sent a contribution of fifty francs, one of the largest from any politician, to the subscription opened by *Libre Parole* to erect a monument to Henry. He also wrote to Bazire asking him to obtain the adherence of the ACJF to the recently formed Ligue de la Patrie Française, a group of anti-Dreyfusard, anti-Semitic intellectuals led by the critic Jules Lemaître and novelist Maurice Barrès.[5]

De Mun's contribution to *Libre Parole* placed him among bad company, but the members of the Patrie Française frequented the same salons of the nobility to which he had entrée once again after his reputation among the conservatives had been resurrected during the Méline ministry. In particular, there was that of the Countess de Loynes, née Detourney, who had inherited a large amount of money, acquired her title from a short and unhappy marriage, become *maîtresse en titre* of Lemaître, and dedicated herself to putting all of Paris at her feet. She presided over the most important rightist salon of the period and, in addition to Lemaître, called her own such conservative literati as Barrès, Brunetière, François Coppée, and the cartoonist Jean-Louis Forain. The aristocracy had always held the Jews in distaste as "moneylenders" and "aliens," but the anti-Semitism that Jeanne de Loynes cultivated, and for which she found ready acceptance with her salon, was a product of the last fifteen years, and especially the last three. Drumont had made anti-Semitism a force with his *La France Juive* in 1886, running to 127 printings within two years. With the simple thesis that "when the Jew rises, France declines," he had connected his enemy to anticlericalism, revolution, scandal, divorce and the breakdown of the family, and the destruction of the traditional French economy and community through big department stores and the anonymous power of high finance. With Drumont as a model, many Catholics found the Jew a ready scapegoat for an entire century they despised, and *La Croix* openly proclaimed itself "the most anti-Jewish newspaper in France, the one that bears Christ, a sign of horror to the Jews." Some social Catholics like La Tour du Pin tended to use Jewish examples of grasping, unconscionable employers. But for the affair, this kind of anti-Semitism would have been ephemeral, since by 1894 even Drumont had lost most of his subscribers. The arrest of Dreyfus and the subsequent revisionist movement by his family gave the prejudice new vigor and respect, for the attempt to vindicate a convicted traitor, and thus to sully the name of the army, soon came to be denounced as a "Jewish plot." The litany of Rothschild and the failure of the Union Générale and Cornélius Herz and the Panama Canal scandal was lengthened to include Reinach, Dreyfus, and the affair. Anti-Semitism came to take on a hysterical tone, as conservatives desperately defended the last of their precious traditional institutions "uncontaminated" by the Jews. De Mun's brush with anti-Semitism in January 1899 should best be viewed against this setting. Doubtless, he shared the old prejudices of his birth and breeding, and perhaps also, very quietly, the more repugnant and violent hatred of the late 1890s. Certainly he did so under the spell of Cornwallis's polemic. Yet he himself never joined the Patrie Française, and specific examples of anti-Semitism are not to be found in either his public utterances or his correspondence. After reading de Mun's letter to the *Times*, Lord Russell of Killowen, the lord chief justice of England, wrote to him deploring the attitude of French Catholics in the affair and particularly their calumniation of the Jews. In reply at the end of January, de Mun acknowledged the anti-Semitism of the army's defenders, but while he justified it, after a fashion, he emphasized that he personally had taken no part in it. If in so writing, de Mun overlooked his feelings of the previous fortnight, he might be excused. His temper was more passionate than long-lasting, and he was far too occupied with the defense of the army and the church to invest his time in the bitter recriminations of the Patrie Française. Consciously or unconsciously, he did realize that the cause of the Ralliés, especially if they hoped for any additional aid from the Opportunists, could not be furthered by the identification of their leader with anti-Semitism.[6]

The cause of army and church was not advanced by the foolish plans of Paul Déroulède, a professional patriot, who denounced all partisans of Dreyfus as traitors worthy of death. The sudden demise on 16 February of President Faure, of a stroke in the Salon d'Argent of the Elysée *en pleine action* in the arms of his mistress, provided Déroulède and a few of his rowdy Ligue des Patriotes an opportunity to reveal the depth of their vacuity. The Ralliés preferred Méline as Faure's successor, but, fearing defeat, he refused to be a candidate. Instead, the conservative opposition watched helplessly as Dupuy's majority elected a colorless left-wing Opportunist, Emile Loubet, the Panama premier, who had hushed up the scandal in 1894. Faure had been determined to prevent a new trial for Dreyfus, but Loubet seemed to favor the Dreyfusards. Resolved to prevent the president's accession, Déroulède attempted an almost single-handed coup d'état at Faure's state funeral on 23 February. The effect was comic, the result a farce, and its author carted off to jail. But the attempt gave substance to the baseless charges that the opponents of Dreyfus intended to use the agitation about the affair to overthrow the Republic.[7]

The more perspicacious of French Catholics now realized that the church had blundered into a position on the Dreyfus affair the possible political consequences of which might be analogous to its unfortunate previous links to royalism. Although the Vatican and the high French episcopacy had refrained from comment, their silence in conjunction with the outspoken zealotry of the Assumptionists and de Mun, both of whom often claimed to speak with the authentic voice of the church, had identified French Catholicism with the anti-Dreyfusard cause. In turn, this sponsorship was seen by the Radicals and some Opportunists as antirepublican. If the opponents of Dreyfus were to lose, the church would almost automatically be among those to suffer in consequence. De Mun seemed to have grasped this danger when, in his letter to the *Times*, he sought to dissociate the church from the affair by disputing the link of the Jesuits to the general staff. Following Déroulède's lunacy, the outcry in the Chamber by the Radicals against the "reactionaries" convinced him that Catholics should prepare for the worst. Sensing that the threat would come in a renewed attack on the Catholic schools, he turned for support and organization to the ACJF. Bazire had already laid initial preparations, and after his selection on 30 April to succeed Reverdy, he promised de Mun the wholehearted backing of the association. Gratified, de Mun called him "the right man in the right place," and the two organized a Comité pour la Défense de la Liberté d'Enseignement to raise opposition to new anticlerical proposals. De Mun assumed the presidency and prevailed upon Senator Emile de Marcère, an Opportunist of Méline's persuasion, to be a largely titular vice-president. ACJF members manned the active positions. In proclaiming the Comité at Lyons on 24 May, they explained that its members desired battle with no one, but de Mun added a warning, "If war is declared, we shall not want for combatants."[8]

The effort of the Catholics to gird themselves was timely. On 3 June 1899, the forty-six judges of the Cour de Cassation ordered a new trial for Dreyfus, and Clemenceau splashed the single word "Justice" across the front page of *L'Aurore*. His counterparts on the other side were enraged, the more hotheaded deciding on actions that would compromise all of them. President Loubet attended the Grand Steeplechase at Auteuil the following day, and while sitting placidly in his box, he was assaulted by the cane-waving Baron Fernand de Christiani. Loubet was uninjured, but in striking the president's top hat, Christiani and his band of well-dressed young rightists, who chanted in pounding rhythm "Dé-mis-sion Pa-na-ma!" struck the pride and dignity of the Republic. De Mun's eldest son, Bertrand, was among the demonstrators temporarily remanded to custody. For the Radicals and many of the Opportunists it seemed that the agitation had gone too far, that there was real danger to the regime. It was no longer a solitary fanatic like Déroulède plotting the overthrow of the Republic, but instead the children, the shock troops, of the "reactionaries." After shouting down efforts of conservatives, de Mun among them, to minimize the outrages against the president of the Republic, Dupuy's own majority bitterly attacked him for failing to guard Loubet more securely. By 12 June the premier could not find enough support to govern and had to resign.[9]

There was no obvious successor because the agitation surrounding the affair had wrought fundamental changes in the Opportunist faction of the Chamber. Before 1899 the group had constituted a fairly unified party of the Center that could form governing coalitions with the Left, its traditional ally, or the Right, Méline's choice in 1896. By June 1899 the Center had broken into three components. The left wing, about thirty to forty deputies, had already deserted Méline, and now, taking the violent activities of men like Déroulède seriously, cast their lot with the Radicals. There were about seventy to eighty deputies in the middle who had no desire to move left but who disapproved of Méline's variety of conservatism since his former allies now seemed in league with hooligans. Notable among them were such young stellar lights of Opportunism as Ribot, Poincaré, Barthou, and Eugène Etienne. They styled themselves "Independents" and broke away from the right wing of the faction, the approximately one hundred firm supporters of Méline and the alliance with the Ralliés. This most conservative faction of the Opportunists now called themselves "Progressives." Because the Center was asunder, any new ministry would have to be clearly Left or Right; the days of Center-Left or Center-Right conciliatory alliances were gone. Loubet was now convinced of Dreyfus's innocence, and he refused to offer any opponent of a second trial for the captain the chance to form a cabinet. For a week he canvassed politicians of the Left before his choice fell on René Waldeck-Rousseau, distinguished attorney, former protégé of Gambetta, and willing to assume the task of crushing the foes of the regime. To avoid any contamination from anti-Dreyfusards, he decided to seek a majority clearly on the Left. But to do so he would have to base his ministry on anticlericalism, the one issue on which Socialists, Radicals, and their new converts, the left-leaning Opportunists, could agree. From that point he was the prisoner of this majority and this program.[10]

When Waldeck-Rousseau presented his cabinet before the Chamber on 23 June, there was a howl from all sides. As his commerce minister he had chosen the Socialist Alexandre Millerand, their one member so hungry for office that he would defy the party's prohibition against serving in a bourgeois ministry. The Right and some sections of the Center hurled anathemas at the premier for admitting a revolutionary into the government. Their cries were paltry compared to the pandemonium created by the Left when the Marquis Gaston de Gallifet, the butcher of the Communards in 1871, was announced as the minister of war. When cries of "Assassin!" rang out at him, the bristling general barked back, "Présent!" Waldeck-Rousseau stood at the rostrum for over an hour trying to make himself heard over the din, but despite the chaos, his two unorthodox choices revealed his political skill and courage. Because

Jaurès had been defeated in the 1898 election, Millerand was considered the tribune of the Socialists and could come close to guaranteeing their cooperation. Those most offended by his elevation would not have voted for the cabinet had he been excluded. Gallifet, although detested by the Left, seemed the one man so respected by the army, yet also a Dreyfusard, that he could force its chiefs to accept the innocence of Dreyfus without goading them into open rebellion. Neither man was delighted to serve with the other, but the personal ambition of Millerand and the long friendship of Gallifet for the new premier enabled them to overcome their scruples. When the vote of confidence was finally taken, the Left was rallied by its leaders to stand firm against the violence of the anti-Dreyfusards and swallowed its hatred of Gallifet, giving Waldeck-Rousseau a narrow 262 to 237 victory. This margin seemed too thin to govern upon, but the ministry was spared further close votes by the Chamber's adjournment on 29 June until November.[11]

In the late summer during the recess, the Dreyfus affair reached its climax. On 8 August the new court-martial for Dreyfus convened at Rennes and a month later, on 9 September, rendered the ludicrous verdict of guilty, with extenuating circumstances. Waldeck-Rousseau and Gallifet were outraged, but finding the military unwilling to certify Dreyfus innocent, they could only convince Loubet to issue, and the twice-convicted prisoner to accept, a presidential pardon ten days later. Throughout this denouement *La Croix* and the Assumptionists led the conservatives in vituperation of the government, titling Loubet "Panama I." The Patrie Française sponsored passionate speeches and carried their argument to its ultimate conclusion, "innocent or not, Dreyfus must return to Devil's Island." These torrents finally decided Waldeck-Rousseau, who had hitherto shown remarkable forbearance toward this scurrility, to make examples. On 12 August he charged Déroulède and his few followers with treason and haled them before the Senate as a high court, where, for the ministry, the judgment would be assured. In September it was the turn of the Assumptionists, charged with constituting an "unauthorized" order. But for them, Waldeck-Rousseau had to rely on the same vague precedents from the First Empire that had been referred to for Grévy's decrees of March 1880. This unsatisfactory resurrection of the past for underpinning offended the premier's Cartesian legalism and made him feel acutely the need for a "republican" law clearly regulating the status of religious congregations in France. Yet the anticlericalism of this frigid and distant man was devoid of the usual leftist passion and was essentially political. He saw that the debates surrounding the passage of such a statute to control unruly monks and nuns would provide him with an opportunity to solidify his narrow majority.[12]

When the Chamber reconvened in early November 1899, Waldeck-Rousseau was ready with a proposal, the famous Associations bill. It had two parts, the first granting broader liberty to such groups as labor unions, learned societies, and political parties to organize themselves, a wider freedom long promised and expected. The second section dealt with the congregations, requiring that all "unauthorized" orders disband or seek state "authorization," formal consent, to remain in France. Once so authorized, a congregation would have to request further permission to create new branches. With all such warrants to be granted by the Council of State, an administrative body with some judicial functions dominated by the premier, the ministry could regulate the growth, even the existence, of the orders. Waldeck-Rousseau also provided for the dissolution of a congregation or any of its establishments, such as a school, by executive decree, thereby ensuring that the government would have tight control of them and could, by threat, compel their good behavior. Any congregation dispersed by decree would have its property confiscated by the state and sold for profit at auction. This draft legislation, carefully drawn by the premier to leave its enforcement in his hands, now escaped him. It was sent, in accordance with parliamentary procedure, to an ad hoc committee whose duty it was to study the proposal, examine possible amendments, and occasionally, as in this case, radically alter the original. In the committee the proposal would be strengthened or weakened, and when it emerged, in the hands of its reporter, it would be the committee's bill, no longer the premier's. Debate could begin only then, and with desperate fighting inevitable within the committee, the preliminaries were likely to last more than a year.[13]

Debate outside the Chamber began at once. The conservatives, particularly the Catholics, suddenly forgot the fate of Dreyfus in their haste to defend the church. De Mun called on Bazire to organize a purely lay opposition, to make it clear that clerics were not the sole proponents of the parochial schools. He had a special project in mind for himself, an extended commentary on the ministerial proposals, briefly stepping down from the tribune to make his first written foray. He planned a series of four essays in the form of open letters to Waldeck-Rousseau and arranged for their appearance in the widely read *Le Correspondant*. In them de Mun conducted a dispassionate, closely reasoned assault not only on the proposed Associations law but on the very basis of the new ministry, revealing a shrewd new appreciation of political reality that had been notably lacking in his career until his association with Méline. He began by accusing the Left of seeking revenge on the Right for their honestly held belief that Dreyfus was guilty. Because the leftists dared not touch the army, the nation's sole defense, they turned on the church, for anticlericalism was the only issue on which the partners of the Left could agree. Radicals and Socialists would find little common ground on economic questions. De Mun pointed out that the fruit of their alliance, the Associations proposal, made mock of leftist *égalité* by making monks and nuns second-class citizens, singling them out for special treatment. Waldeck-Rousseau, to be sure, had promised to apply the law fairly, but he was the prisoner of his majority. Too often when the anticlericals spoke of tolerance, it was argot for intolerance to Catholics. He concluded his last essay with an ironic discussion of the anti-Jesuit mania in France that blamed the society for Boulanger, Panama, Dreyfus, Méline, the fall of the Bourse, local famines, and all else from natural disasters to household accidents. Behind it all, he claimed, was the implacable "Jacobin" demand to control the system of education and the practice of religion. "The Revolution, in the name of tolerance and freedom, burned churches and guillotined priests. Its descendants have no such dark designs; they limit themselves to closing the convents and oppressing consciences." In reply, the Catholics could only, he promised in final summation, "lay on the harness of battle."[14]

Yet these battle arrays would be very few if de Mun could not rally support from beyond the Catholics and Ralliés, and particularly from within the ranks of the moderates. Emile de Marcère of the Progressives was already a recruit, and de Mun now charged him to organize resistance to the ministry in the Senate. The policies of the premier, he wrote, required the protestation not only of

Catholics but of all liberals, all who opposed the tyranny of a minority by an oppressive majority. De Mun bizarrely termed such men "liberals" because in favoring equal liberty for all, including a general freedom to teach, they would ostensibly oppose illiberal laws directed against the church and the congregations. In adopting this appellation, he ignored the identification of liberalism with anticlericalism throughout the remainder of Europe. Speaking for his Progressive colleagues in the Senate, de Marcère replied that they would join de Mun's band of liberals. That band quickly grew to include most of Méline's followers in the Chamber and, from outside of politics, influential conservatives like Brunetière. Some of the new conservatives now enrolled, including Count Ferri de Ludre and former general Armand de Jacquey, came bearing the insignia of the Ligue des Patriotes or Patrie Française, but de Mun could not afford to be overly selective since the appeal did not work well leftward of the Progressives. Thinking the Left the winner this time, Paul Deschanel, claiming to be an Independent and touted by all as a future leader, turned him down politely but firmly. This scampering for support laid a heavy burden on de Mun, which was eased somewhat by the reappearance of Jacques Piou, who, returned to the Chamber by the 1898 elections and eager to regain his role as a leader, lent his aid in a series of speeches against the ministry in the spring of 1900. His tactic was hyperbole, overemphasizing the threats of the ministry and appealing to emotion and prejudice. At Rennes, Arras, Toulouse, and Lyons he spoke to ever larger and more fervent crowds. Even the discredited Lamy joined the effort at de Ludre's urging, and an invitation in July to address the graduates of Sorèze, the famed Benedictine academy in the Tarn, drew from him a stirring appeal.[15]

Yet the valiant words were not deeds. The ministry and its majority could note with pleasure that on an issue tinderbox-ready for combustion the opposition had thus far created much more smoke than conflagration. Indeed, the government inflicted piquing defeats on their opponents during early 1900 even as de Mun vowed that his forces were pulling on their armor. After a trial lasting only two days, on 24 January the Ninth Correctional Chamber ordered the Assumptionists dispersed. An appeal carried to the Paris Court of Appeal by Reverdy and Bazire failed in March. At Easter time, in mid-April, Jean de Lanessan, the minister of the navy, suddenly commanded that the fleet might no longer lower the tricolor to half-staff for Good Friday. Waldeck-Rousseau remained serenely above the increasing din, allowing his lieutenants to reply to the "clericals." Their arguments did not touch him, and instead he welcomed them, since intemperate attacks on his policy drew his shaky coalition together. He entered the lists only on 28 October at Toulouse, on the eve of the Chamber's reassembling after its long summer recess, to utter words that his followers would repeat throughout the coming debates. There were, he charged, "two youths" in France, brought up in separate, hostile compartments, divided less by their social station than by their education. The condition was the result of unregulated growth of the congregations, which had now become a state within the state, with wealth under mortmain of perhaps a billion francs. The gasps from the audience revealed the use of milliard as a masterstroke. It was a round figure, but more so, it recalled the "milliard des émigrés," the sum given to the ancestors of the noble enemies of Dreyfus under the Restoration in compensation for their losses during the Revolution.[16]

The premier's proposal on associations was not reported out of committee until late December, but because of the changes it had undergone during the previous months it dominated all discussion from the beginning of the new session. Influenced by a strong Radical contingent, the committee considering the bill had heavily revised two sections of it, making the original draft very much harsher and far more dangerous to the Catholics. Jules Ferry's famous Article Seven of 1879 had been incorporated almost verbatim, forbidding members of unauthorized congregations to teach and providing for the closure of schools that employed them. The power to authorize had been removed from the Council of State, and thus by extension from the premier, and vested in the Chamber and Senate. With these two changes, the anticlericals would have the instrument, long desired, with which to close most Catholic schools. Either house could delay forever any authorizations—if indeed it did not deny them altogether—and in the interim the ministry could padlock the schools, nearly all of which employed at least one member of an order lacking authorization. The stakes for the Catholics had suddenly become very high.

When the Chamber opened its general discussion of the bill in January 1901, the division of forces quickly became apparent. It was de Mun's liberals who would be beaten. Since the preceding summer, Waldeck-Rousseau had actually gained a few votes from the Independents in the Center, but his support remained predominantly on the Left. To hold the Radicals he had to accept the modifications in the Associations bill as his own. The opposition, from the majority of the Independents to the extreme Right, took an intransigent position against the ministry and its proposed law. These opening debates took on undiminished the passions of the Dreyfus affair. Such Socialists as Alexandre Zévaès outdid even the Radicals in conjuring up hoary tales of priestly abuse. The opposition replied that the cabinet had embarked upon a policy of atheism and tyranny, the destination of which was the seizure of church property. It was, Piou claimed, the inevitable result, and that only the beginning, of admitting a Socialist to the governing circles. The polarity of politics post-Dreyfus encouraged this rhetoric of extremism and made mutual concessions impossible. When Abbé Jules Lemire, a member of the Christian Democrats, ventured that the premier might apply the law with moderation, de Mun harshly interrupted, "At such a moment, you should never speak in these terms!"[17]

More rational arguments extruded through the hot words when the specific provisions of the bill were debated in March, but there were few uncommitted votes to sway. It was very clear that the issue was not freedom of assembly or association; it was the general liberty to teach. The Independents were particularly sensitive to limitation of basic rights, and they made their most telling and unified contribution to the opposition cause in attacking the "tyranny" of the proposal. Liberties were intangible or not liberties at all. Stung by the accusation, the ministry and anticlericals bluntly and angrily replied that children, as a natural resource, belonged to the state and should be reared as the state declared best. This shocking arrogation of power closed one day's debate, but on the following day, de Mun, appalled by the undisguised brutality of the majority and certain that the parliamentary battle was lost, rebutted and issued a new warning. How, he asked, could any assembly, the majority of which could change from election to election, maintain that it should determine the education of all children? Was it not the ultimate tyranny to wrench the child from its parents, to educate it in opposition to the parents' ideals?

"If you require a man to abandon his most sacred beliefs and convictions to rear his child as you see fit, must you not believe that he will revolt?" For de Mun and his allies, this eloquence or bombast —one anticlerical later declared that their speeches were "one of the the most brilliant pages in our parliamentary history"—was spent in vain. The Chamber's final vote on the bill on 29 March was cast along lines predictable since the previous summer, Waldeck-Rousseau winning 303 to 224. In the Senate, de Marcère could not delay the ministry's triumph, as the senators concurred in the Chamber's approval by a 169 to 95 vote on 22 June. Loubet promulgated the new law on 1 July 1901. To overthrow Waldeck-Rousseau the opposition could now look only to the national elections coming up in 1902. The contest promised to be dour.[18]

Goaded by the fear of failing to carry the country with them, the opposition began their campaigning a year early. When the Progressives and Independents complained of the attack upon all liberty implicit in the Associations law, their genuine concern for personal freedom was buttressed by a growing alarm at the increase of Socialist influence made strikingly apparent by the presence of Millerand in the cabinet. Hence Méline at Remiremont on 28 April 1901 berated the ministry for its illiberal policies and alliance with the extreme Left. Similarly, at Nancy on 12 May, Poincaré termed government confiscation of congregation property a tyranny and ominous precedent. Piou also realized the electoral capital to be gained from exploiting the pervasive fear of socialism among the bourgeoisie. He told bankers and lawyers that it was far easier to oppose the revolutionaries when they tried to take power by storm, as in the Commune, than when they did so insidiously, through parliamentary coalition. Today they commanded a seat on the ministerial bench, tomorrow perhaps the whole government! To shock and unsettle his audience further, he spoke in horrified terms of how "such offensive doctrines of German socialism as free love had found defenders even at the tribune of the Chamber" and said that conservatives would have to defend their daughters from violation.[19]

Even in the midst of this fustian, de Mun and Piou engaged in delicate negotiations with Progressive and Independent leaders about a close alliance with the Ralliés for the elections. They had no clear conception of how such a coalition would be organized but hoped that it would provide a unified campaign against the injustices meted out to the church under the Associations law and the seeming Socialist menace. Neither Mèline nor the Independents, who admitted no chief, would consider this proposal. They feared that the Ralliés remained too closely identified with clericalism and that a formal association of the three groups might drive away some Progressive and Independent voters. This constituency, like its deputies, did not favor the repeal of the laic legislation, only its liberal enforcement, an axiom sanctified by Mèline's two years as premier. Instead, they pointedly suggested that Piou and de Mun should first tighten their own ranks and join them in the traditional variety of loose electoral alliance in which each faction would campaign on its favorite issue, the Ralliés against anticlericalism, the Progressives and Independents against socialism. The decision was a disappointment for the Rallié leaders. They were aware that the Socialists had developed an embryonic party structure based on friendly labor unions and that the Radicals were attempting to emulate their current ally through the establishment of local election committees. If the Left succeeded in creating what France had lacked, organized political parties capable of enforcing national discipline down to the individual voter, it was incumbent upon the Right to forswear particularism and duplicate the feat or concede the political struggle.[20]

Piou and de Mun had not been so sanguine as to believe that their proposal would have been more than a first step, the unity of parliamentary representatives, in the formation of a conservative party. Yet because the individual deputies valued their autonomy, and because many of them could finance their own campaigns themselves in the small election districts and could thus resist dictation by a national office, this initial objective would have been difficult to achieve even with the unalloyed support of leaders like Méline. Piou and de Mun were only too familiar with the ragged fashion in which the Ralliés followed their commands, particularly in the 1898 election. To create out of them a disciplined army that would obey its marching orders now became a necessity if their leaders were to try to organize a national party. During April and May, de Mun and Piou contributed to this effort delicacy, flattery, endurance, patience, and a diplomatic papering over of basic differences among the deputies. Most helpful of all was a blunt and belated recognition by the Ralliés themselves of the dangers of continued disunity. On 11 June 1901, therefore, to some amazement within the other ranks of the opposition, Piou was able to announce the reorganization of nearly two-thirds of the Ralliés and a few other deputies from the Progressives and royalists as the Action Libérale, taking the name for this new conservative party from de Mun's unusual definition of the term "liberal." The group counted fifty-eight members, only 10 percent of the Chamber, but its leaders did not intend to do battle in the election without allies. To publicize the program of the Action Libérale, Piou addressed a crowd of twelve hundred people at the Salle des Agriculteurs in Paris. He emphasized that it was part of a general effort to overturn the power of the Left: "We have no thought of marching alone to combat. We are only one corps in a great electoral army." In apocalyptic terms, he warned his cheering audience, "Today, France is divided in two camps, on one side the savage Jacobins, the sectarians, and collectivists, on the other, the patriots, liberals, and conservatives. The time for hesitation is past! Each must choose a side!"[21]

Late in the spring of 1901, de Mun had begun to feel the first acute pain of angina and had to ask Piou to assume the presidency of the Action Libérale and the most active role in the party. It was not an easy decision for a man who had always previously grasped for leadership and whose vigor in the past had belied his middle age. Yet he considered his retrenchment temporary, and because of his excellent relations with Piou now, he had no doubt that his influence in the party, especially on strategy, would be capital even from the position of vice-president. Piou had therefore announced the formation of the party and sounded the clarion at the Salle des Agriculteurs, but these were only the most public manifestations of a determined effort planned by both men to establish the new party firmly. They had to secure money, members, and publicity to have any hope of success. The need for funds was the most pressing problem and had to be dealt with first. A Sûreté Générale report of 18 June 1901 cited "unimpeachable sources" claiming that the Action Libérale had been guaranteed financial support for at least ten years. The agent could not discover the origin of the funds but surmised the congregations or the high episcopacy, a suspicion that was most likely accurate. Because large sums were involved, it seems probable that the French church, realizing its danger and gratified by the certain support of the Action Libérale, secretly donated the money through an intermediary.[22]

The treasury partially filled, de Mun and Piou sought to augment the party's numbers and to establish a hierarchy by sending out letters to prospective deputies, especially those Rallíés who still held themselves apart, and cajoling several already enrolled to assume positions of leadership. As much as they needed additional members immediately, however, they could not afford to enlist without circumspection. It would have been easy enough to attract nearly all of the extreme right wing of the country, intransigents like Keller, who had just published a vicious diatribe against "free thinkers" in *Le Correspondant*, or Cassagnac, whose output in *L'Autorité* continued unchanged and undiminished, but such men would have compromised the party with allies on its left flank. As in the fight against the Associations law, recruits were taken from the Patrie Française in large numbers, but they made the transfer with the understanding that antisemitism was not to be included in their baggage. De Mun was particularly pleased by the ranks enrolled from the ACJF and when friends like Brunetière added their names and suggested those of others. The support of the pope was especially valuable in this mustering. As soon as Leo XIII heard of the enterprise, he informally urged all Catholics to rally round the party. To ensure sufficient publicity of such endorsements, de Mun and Piou arranged to establish a weekly propaganda journal with the Bonne Presse of Catholic publishing magnate Paul Féron-Vrau. Well known in the circles of the faithful for having purchased the bankrupt *La Croix* when Waldeck-Rousseau banished the Assumptionists, Féron-Vrau had already joined the party and made sizable contributions to its treasury. By 20 November 1901, he was able to produce a well-edited, slick-paper *Bulletin Action Libérale* for national distribution.[23]

After six months of intense organizing, a party of parliamentarians had been created, but on the local level the name of the Action Libérale was hardly known. Here it would have to rely on the efforts of parochial groups, the remnants of Lamy's Fédération Electorale, and former royalist committees that had endorsed the

Republic. Nationally the Action Libérale would set common policy for its members and attempt to make this platform known throughout the country by means of the *Bulletin* and a vigorous program of speeches by party leaders. The theme had already been set by de Mun, when, before the Chamber in June, he called Waldeck-Rousseau a captive of his majority, who would be compelled to join in its ever more extreme anticlericalism if he wished to maintain office. De Mun's words were resigned and tinged with disgust. By late fall the Action Libérale had adopted a tone much more shrill. On 17 November at Lille, a Catholic redoubt, Piou began a series of speeches by party leaders that would continue unabated until the elections in April and May 1902, with never less than five rallies a week throughout France. Before this mass meeting of six thousand, and surrounded by prelates, Piou unveiled an appeal of intimidation, decrying "the official organization of an atheist crusade" that would abrogate the Concordat, secularize Notre Dame, and demolish most of the churches. The expropriation of private property would not follow far behind. Galvanized by these terrors to their faith, the crowd stamped and cheered for many minutes when he proclaimed that the assaults of the "modern barbarians" might be repelled if Catholics trooped to the polls in rigid formation, uniting behind the Action Libérale in a "severe discipline and precise program."[24]

In these veritable orgies of rant, which replenished the desperate fears of Catholics about the Left, Piou was joined principally by Paul Lerolle, an eloquent Rallié, Hyacinthe de Gailhard-Bancel, a social Catholic first elected to the Chamber in 1899, and to a lesser extent de Mun, who had been warned by his physicians to limit his public speaking for a few months. But to saturate the country with rallies, the Action Libérale relied on a very large number of other orators, often nonpoliticians like ACJF leaders or local industrialists, who were thoroughly terrified of socialism. These tactics were not amenable to the elaboration of a positive program. Gailhard-Bancel and de Mun formulated a counterproposal to Millerand's idea to establish government-directed pension plans for industrial workers. They called instead for the decentralization of the program, for voluntary participation within it, and for each industry to design its own specific pension proposals to deal with its specific problems. A national standard retirement age of sixty-five, for example, would effectively deprive mine workers, who rarely lived that long, of ever receiving pensions. Yet, instead of exploiting the possible popularity of their variant among the workers, the Action Libérale never mentioned it either during the rallies or in the *Bulletin*, the pages of which denounced Millerand as a dangerous "collectivist." Even de Mun criticized the minister of commerce by name, although he knew that he was beginning his movement across the political lines of the Chamber, thus making him almost a conservative by 1914. In its essence the appeal of the Action Libérale was negative. Abbé Pierre Dabry, a member of the Christian Democrat movement, was hardly an unbiased observer of the party, but he was essentially accurate in condemning it for adopting as members elements hostile to the Republic, making religious demands the basis of its platform, and presenting itself basically as a "party of reaction." The "clerical specter," he feared, had reappeared, with all of its terrors for republicans. Like the Jesuit Father Coubé at Lourdes in 1901, the Action Libérale, by its actions, had proclaimed that in the elections there would be only two candidates, Barabbas and Jesus Christ.[25]

To defeat Barabbas and elect more dequties of its own, the party spent money lavishly. Reports to the Sûreté indicate that in hope of doubling its representation of fifty-eight, the Action Libérale supported the campaigns of nearly two hundred conservative candidates, allowing them five to ten thousand francs apiece for expenses. In less than eight months, Piou and de Mun disbursed between one and two million francs, a staggering total in relation to traditional French political spending of the day, and this amount excludes the cost of publishing the *Bulletin*. Boulanger, an extravagant man, spent less than five million francs in all of his campaigns for himself and his followers. Some of the Action Libérale money was raised by a subscription opened through the *Bulletin*, but this amounted to hardly more than half a million francs. Sûreté agents reported that de Mun arranged for Piou to pick up separate contributions of two hundred thousand francs in Lyons and Marseilles from wealthy right-wing sympathizers. Together these sources account for less than a million francs. The remainder, perhaps another million, came from the secret funds promised in June 1901, almost assuredly provided by the church through a lay representative, whose identity cannot now be discovered and who masked the provenance of the money he delivered to de Mun and Piou.[26]

The Progressives and Independents conducted more leisurely campaigns, spending less money, holding many fewer rallies, and engaging less in polemical and apocalyptic rhetoric. The impetus given the opposition effort by the Action Libérale nevertheless produced the impression that all antiministerial forces would register substantial gains. In response, the ministry used every time-tested device and pressure to win the elections, warning prefects that gains by the Action Libérale in their departments would cost them their positions. The premier himself took pains to distinguish between his policy of anticlericalism and what the opposition termed "anti-Catholicism." Emile Combes, minister of public worship in the Léon Bourgeois cabinet of 1895, was sent out to damn the Progressives and Independents for having failed to "refrain from all equivocal collaboration" and having "speculated upon reactionary support." The cabinet's fears were based less on news of growing opposition support than on nervousness that the loose electoral alliance of the three factions would enable them for once to concentrate their fury against the Radicals and Socialists and not against each other, as so often in the past. Because the voting was a straight fight on the Associations law and cooptation with socialism, uncomplicated by other issues, the alliance, as translated on the local level, was largely successful in this aim. Out of the 585 constituencies, there were only 108, 18 percent, in which candidates from the three groups competed in the first round of voting. Such competition could have caused the election of a ministerial candidate in only ten of these cases. Not once did opposition candidates contest one another in a *ballottage*. In several instances where more than one opposition candidate competed, the seat was so firmly in the control of either a ministerial or an opposition incumbent deputy that the contest took on the nature of a trial run for future elections.[27]

The importance of the voting attracted about 80 percent of the electorate to the polls, and when their some seven million ballots were tallied, Frenchmen were found to be almost equally divided, the ministerial parties winning 51 percent, the opposition 49 percent. Because of inequities in the population of electoral districts, the relative strength of each faction within the Chamber was slightly different, the ministry controlling 321 seats, 55 percent, to the opposition's 264, 45 percent. The net effect for the opposition was no gain, for while the Action Libérale increased its deputation by 20, from 58 to 78, the Progressives lost an equal number to drop from 100 to 80. The Independents did no more than hold their own at 75. The remaining 13 seats of the opposition were held by the extreme Right, with whom the Independents and most of the Progressives would have little to do. As always, the victories of the Progressives and Independents were scattered throughout mostly northern France, reflecting the normal strength of the former right-wing and moderate Opportunists. The triumphs and gains for the Action Libérale came in traditional bastions of conservatism and Catholicism, the West, particularly Brittany and the Vendée, the Nord, the North-East around Lorraine, and the South-West near the Pyrenees. The party's candidates used variations on the national platform in these four corners of the country. In the Nord the tradition of paternalism and social Catholicism among employers retained the votes of many workers, while defense of the church won the support of the middle class in this strongly Catholic region. The platform of antisocialism and clericalism also easily captured the West and South-West, former royalist strongholds still powerfully controlled by aristocratic elements. In the North-East, however, where the sentiment of revanche remained strongest, the party won seats by claiming that the anticlerical program would divide the nation and undermine the capacity to face Germany. The Action Libérale was able slightly to expand the areas previously controlled by the Ralliés by couching its appeal to fit differing circumstances. Nevertheless, it was rare for a candidate to go far beyond the issues of anticlericalism and socialism.[28]

The elections were a victory for the Left. The country had vindicated the policy of governing solely with their backing and had ratified the major work of the ministry, the Associations law. The Radicals and Socialists could claim a mandate to push for harsher strictures against the church, and with their majority, slender but firm, pass such legislation. "There are too many," Waldeck-Rousseau had replied when told of his victory. As much as the opposition, he realized himself the prisoner of his majority, one that might now force him either to adopt a far harsher anticlerical position than he desired or to step down. Either would be ignominious. Pleading the decline of his health, he resigned before even facing the new Chamber. Loubet had no other dominant leader to whom he could turn, and he sought instead a man who would be easily accepted by the majority. At the recommendation of Waldeck-Rousseau, who apparently hoped to prove how moderate his ministry had been in comparison to that of a genuine fanatic, Loubet's choice fell on Combes. The virulent anticleric could surely command the confidence of the Radicals and Socialists, eager to continue the assault on the church.[29]

The result of the voting had a profound effect upon the bitterly disappointed opposition groups. The closeness of the popular ballot and its proof that their ideas found many adherents in the nation hardly compensated for the government's continued ascendancy in the Chamber. Waldeck-Rousseau's resignation meant only that they faced Combes, an implacable enemy of the church as determined as his predecessor had been to maintain the alliance with the Socialists. Méline felt badly discredited by this second failure in a row of the Progressives and ceded the group's leadership to the younger and more vigorous Paul Beauregard, who, as a close friend of Piou, might be expected to move the Progressives into a tighter alliance with the Action Libérale. But Piou had devoted so much time to the national campaign that he had severely neglected his own district and had failed to win reelection. Despite other gains, the leaders of the Action Libérale had fallen far short of their sanguine goal of 110 deputies and failed to develop any positive proposals for their platform. The Independents found themselves caught between the Radicals on the Left and the Progressives on the Right, unwilling to join the anticlerical majority yet apprehensive about remaining clearly among the opposition. For the moment they disappeared from all political councils, debating individually what course to follow, with some electing to form a loose group, the Alliance Républicaine Démocratique (ARD). The Action Libérale was the only one of the three to understand that election victories, especially for the opposition, require organization. As early as 30 April 1902, the *Bulletin* lamented that "despite the efforts of the Action Libérale, it is by the absence of organization that the opposition has sinned." In the ten months before the election de Mun and Piou had been able to make only slight progress in forming their grand conservative party. With four years before the next election, they vowed that by then the Action Libérale should become a truly organized political party, its network descending to the most humble villages and its membership on the local level extensive.[30]

On 17 May 1902, in accordance with the Associations law they had fought, de Mun and Piou presented a set of statutes forming the Action Libérale Populaire (ALP) to the magistrate at the Paris Prefecture of Police. The leadership of the old Action Libérale now established offices at 7, Rue Las Cases in the faubourg Saint-Germain, but the addition of "Populaire" to the name indicated that the party would no longer be solely a faction of deputies and a few others. De Mun insisted on the new name and suggested that the three words formed a positive platform in themselves: "It is called *Action* because it must be a center of life and activity. It is called *Libérale* because it wishes to maintain or restore in their integrity all public liberties, without refusing their benefits to anyone. It is called *Populaire* because it takes its strength through the number of its adherents and wants to defend above all the interests of laborers constantly betrayed by those who promise everything before the election but deliver nothing afterward." De Mun assumed the task of organizing the newly reinforced ALP ranks in the Chamber, while Piou resolved to use his enforced exile from parliament to create disciplined, serried cohorts of ALP adherents in every department of France. The election of 1906, both men pledged, would not be lost for want of organization. With only a few months of preparation in 1902, the Action Libérale had enlarged its representation from fifty-eight to seventy-eight, an increase of 35 percent. The ALP promised to do far better than that in 1906. In a report filed on 22 May 1902, an agent of the Sûreté outlined the plans of the new party and concluded: "I believe that special attention should be paid to this point, that organized throughout the country, this party will be highly dangerous to the present government."[31]

6
Organizing the Opposition

It was to Emile Combes and the strengthened leftist majority that de Mun and Piou hoped that their broad-based conservative party would prove the greatest danger. The successor to Waldeck-Rousseau had studied for the priesthood as a youth, but shortly before he was to assume minor orders, he was denounced as "proud" and encouraged to withdraw from seminary. Although Combes abruptly switched his interest to medicine and then to politics, he never forgave the church for spurning the ambition of his youth. In reaction he developed an anticlericalism that far surpassed a desire merely to reduce the church's influence in politics and society. He seemed rather to want to punish it for sins, real or imagined, against himself and France. With this attitude and his frock coat, white goatee, and stooped shoulders, he seemed the embodiment of Flaubert's caricature Homais. The comparison is ultimately unfair because Combes did recognize the church as the repository of what he would call "necessary spiritual values," although he would reduce them to a modern deism. As premier during a ministry of two and a half years, he would act as if the elections of 1902 had been a mandate for the ruthless anticlericalism that to him was an article of faith and as if his majority, victors in the popular ballot by only a quarter of a million votes, should punish the minority they had so narrowly defeated.[1] It would be intolerance in the most virulent form, and it would present the new Action Libérale Populaire with the opportunity, and the challenge, of leading the resistance.

Combes began his campaign with a fierce assault on Catholic schools, and in his ministerial circulars of 27 and 30 June 1902, he ordered the closure and sealing of approximately three thousand of them on the tenuous grounds that the presence of even one monk or nun sufficed for classification as an establishment of a congregation. In order to avoid debate in the Chamber on such an unreasonable interpretation, he had intended that this action be postponed until mid-July, when the legislature would have recessed. Although a premature disclosure revealed his plans, his majority had no difficulty beating back an attack by de Mun and Edouard Aynard on 11 July. The Progressive Aynard claimed, "This kind of repression is not French but a crime against liberty!" Combes replied placidly, "We will go all the way."[2] So apparently would the ALP.

By the middle of July, government informers, *mouchards*, determined that de Mun and Piou had decided to use the party to mount a campaign against the premier's orders. On 18 July, de Mun published a letter in *Le Figaro* and *Le Gaulois* calling on Parisians to form mammoth demonstrations against the enforcement of the ministry's decision. At the same time, ALP deputies were sent out like representatives on mission in 1793 to rouse the countryside, especially to such clerical areas as Brittany. The *Bulletin* carried banner headlines, "Citizens! Will you bow your heads to tyranny? Or will you act as free men? Unite for the safeguard of your liberties!" An article by Piou followed, denouncing Combes in libelous terms and inciting the nation to rise in protest.[3] It was quickly apparent that the issue of the school closures had excited considerable discontent against the ministry, particularly because children were involved. Piou and de Mun shrewdly exploited maternal fears by organizing a march by the "Mothers of Paris" on 27 July. Ten thousand of them were easily recruited to march behind Madame Piou and Countess de Mun down the Champs Elysées to seek an interview with Loubet at the presidential palace. Earlier in the week the two distaff leaders had sent a letter, presumably drafted by their husbands, to Madame Loubet, a devout Catholic, who was reportedly much disturbed at Combes's treatment of the church schools. They begged her to use her influence over her husband to force the countermanding of the premier's orders. On the day of the march Loubet barred the gates to the Elysée and departed abruptly for an extended holiday at Rambouillet. The following afternoon the ALP held an impressive rally near the busy shopping district of Strasbourg-Saint Denis, attracting another ten thousand demonstrators to hear Piou and his lieutenants, foremost Paul Lerolle and Amédée Reille, denounce the "government of tyrants." De Mun had left the previous evening to direct operations in Brittany, where the most strenuous opposition to Combes was expected. Piou began the rally by reading a speech de Mun had left behind, repeating the call for resistance but now emphasizing that it must be "a calm and proud manifestation of our right."[4]

In the provinces the ALP agitators attracted crowds of protesters, but except in Brittany the resistance they roused promised to remain as peaceful as that so far in Paris. Piou and de Mun were convinced that the party could convert resentment against Combes into commitment to his opponent. If the ALP-led demonstrations became violent, however, not only might the government have just cause to proceed against the new party, but those people whom Piou and de Mun hoped most to convert, apathetic Catholics and conservatives, might be frightened away. The situation in Brittany therefore held dangers for the ALP, and it was to calm his own bailiwick that de Mun departed so abruptly. Already there was grumbling within the party, with Mackau telling *Le Figaro*, "I am a man of order above all, and a *violent* resistance to a governmental decree, even one arbitrary and unjust, is not to my liking." De Mun's initial survey of Brittany convinced him of the danger and that his own Finistère was the most likely to erupt in violence, its prefect so fearful that he was awaiting the arrival of troops before proceeding to close schools. Once more forswearing violence publicly, de Mun dashed from village to village, heedless of his health, urging the Bretons to lay down the pitchforks and harpoons they carried as they sat in vigil around the schools. And during the tense first weeks of August he restrained the outraged peasants and fishermen. The most serious threat of bloodshed came on 12 August at Roscoff, where de Mun had just purchased a summer home. There was high drama behind the prefect's laconic notation, "Closure of Roscoff school accomplished this morning after long delay caused by the crowd; the sisters themselves opened the door." Telegraphed reports to the wire service Agence Fournier and the *Petit Parisien* by their correspondents in Finistère tell of the prefect's leading two companies of infantry and one hundred gendarmes to confront nearly three thousand Roscoffites before dawn near the school. The soldiers carried loaded rifles, the Bretons shotguns; intransigence might have combined with some hothead to produce a massacre. De Mun thrust himself between the opposing forces and convinced both sides to retreat a few critical yards, while he climbed over the wall of the barricaded school to persuade the nuns to leave peacefully.[5]

De Mun's success typified the ALP's masterful handling of the resistance, exploiting the indignation, while abstaining from violence. The party could now capitalize on the demonstrators' feeling of impotence by preaching that a strong conservative party might have stifled the anticlericals. During mid-August, ALP speakers tacked onto this course: at Vannes, Nancy, and Mende, and in many other towns throughout France, the party's orators shifted their appeal from the organization of demonstrations to that of a political party. The response to such a message was clear in Brittany on 18 August, when twenty thousand people endured a pouring rain at Quimper to hear de Mun. But Piou best expressed the call to arms: "For it is not sufficient merely to unite; we must have organization: not for an ephemeral demonstration, not for an election on its eve, but for a long, patient, and persevering struggle. From particles of dust, organization can create granite." The campaign of recruitment continued unabated throughout the late summer and early fall with significant success, and even as early as 20 August the *Bulletin* noted a rapid increase in the membership rolls. The greatest improvement came in conservative bastions that had provided the party's deputies, but now every region of the country seemed to produce new ALP stalwarts. De Mun, suffering often severely from angina again, made no further speeches after Quimper, but he did publish two long appeals in *Le Gaulois*, aimed at least partly at the Patrie Française, but urging all conservatives to concentrate their efforts within the ALP. When the Chamber reconvened in October, he disobeyed his doctors to address the deputies, joining his voice to those of Progressives, Independents, many of them members of the new ARD, and others from the ALP who denounced Combes's tactics. Striking the rostrum for emphasis, he concluded by warning the Left that in the elections of 1906 they would face a determined and organized opposition that would drive them from office.[6]

The gesture was costly. The strain of the speech, delivered over the catcalls of the Left, combined with de Mun's own disregard of his health and the constant tension of the preceding three months to rend him with crippling seizures of cardiac pain. By late

October friends commented on his weakness and panting voice. This time his doctors sent him to the warmth and provincial calm of Pau, and when they did allow him to return to Paris a few months later, it was with the counsel to moderate his activities and the stern warning that it would be tantamount to suicide ever again to attempt a major speech. De Mun chafed anew at this second period of political retirement, but he now felt so weak that he did not resist the pleas of his family to rest. He resolved to leave the direction of the ALP solely to Piou, at least until the following spring. In the meantime, he withdrew from public life. At Pau he sat for hours in the sunshine regaining his strength, while Simone read aloud his favorite Balzac. There were also trips to nearby Lourdes, where he restoked his religious passion in praying for a speedy return to the political bearpit. The enforced leisure also enabled him to make long visits to his children in their new homes. In spite of the austerity he and Simone continued in Paris, he had ensured great wealth for his scions through marriage alliances to the nobility. The de Mun name held the cachet of antiquity, and after 1896 the success of the conservative connection to Méline had reopened to its proud bearer many of the salon doors that had been closed to him immediately after the Ralliement. Bertrand, a reserve officer, had wed the only daughter of the Werlé family, possessors of the greatest vineyards in Champagne. Ashamed of embarrassing his father by cursing Loubet at Auteuil, this eldest son redeemed himself by assuming charge of ALP organization in Reims and in 1914 would be elected a deputy. Henri and Fernand, likewise reserve officers, would soon inherit châteaus in Normandy through their marriages to daughters of the noble lines of de Perquer and de Bourquenay. De Mun had just the previous June united his only daughter, his darling Marguerite, with Pierre d' Harcourt, heir to much of the Hennessey distillery fortune. When de Mun did return to Paris in the spring of 1903, he was hardly recovered fully, but he was very anxious to pick up the work he had laid down.[7]

Because both he and Piou were absent from the Chamber and because Combes's majority was firmly in control, there was little that the ALP could do to influence legislation for the moment. Rather, there was excellent reason to make a beginning on the manifold problems that had to be overcome before the party could be powerful enough to win the 1906 elections. As is usual in these undertakings, money was in the shortest supply. Piou solicited donations from all sides, but these generally small sums could cover only day-to-day expenses. Immense amounts would be necessary to carry on the program of rallies in the countryside, and Piou had additional ambitions of purchasing provincial newspapers. To finance the campaign of the previous summer, Piou and de Mun had asked wealthy members to contribute 500 francs apiece, the appeal netting 131,000 francs in all. They hoped that the effort would attract the much-needed monetary support, and they were not disappointed. At the beginning of 1903, highly placed clerics, who to this day remain anonymous, covertly approached both leaders, offering to open to them the treasure chests of the congregations as a reward for the ALP's unstinting opposition to anticlericalism. Although de Mun and Piou may have suspected that the secret funds donated in June 1901 came from the French church, they, like the Sûreté, were unsure of their provenance. This time they were well aware that clerical money would support their party, specifically that of the now exiled congregations. To accept the proposed initial donation of six million francs from them would expose de Mun and Piou to grave risk. Legally, the contribution would fall under the statute interdicting the participation of the church in elections and make the funds liable for confiscation. Revelation of the donation would also be embarrassing politically. Piou and de Mun did not want the ALP to be solely the party of Catholics but the nucleus of a large conservative opposition. The only way the ALP could hope to attract large numbers of Progressives and Independents was to avoid the stigma of clericalism. Yet they accepted the offer of the clerics along with the risks. To conceal the new wealth, they arranged to deposit the money, and subsequent amounts, with the London banking house of Coutts, well known for its discretion, with the understanding that interest on bonds purchased with it should not be transferred to the ALP or its directors except by subterfuge. The interest or withdrawals from principal would be sent in small amounts to designated individuals, who would either turn it over to the party or divide it among still more ALP members. These in turn would finally contribute it to the party. Thus would be created the myth of many small donations, an indication of broad support. In the parlance of the 1970s, the funds were "laundered." Agents of the Sûreté quickly suspected the truth of these arrangements and reported that "the strong boxes [of the congregations], long closed, are now wide open," but they were never able to secure evidence to substantiate the charge.[8]

With such amounts of money, all, or at least many things were possible. Piou was pleased with the *Bulletin*, but he wanted to control a network of provincial papers whose relationship to the party would be more veiled. To this end he allied himself further with Féron-Vrau, who saw in Piou's ambition gain for the Bonne Presse as well as for the ALP. Between 1903 and 1908 he and Piou combined their resources to purchase fourteen clearly republican provincial journals. Féron-Vrau also committed *La Croix* and its regional editions to the ALP, giving the party a propaganda instrument capable of saturating much of the nation.[9] The *Bulletin*, expanded in February 1903 to become almost a weekly review, took as its task the clarification of the party position on political and social issues. To edit it and to care for the administrative apparatus at the Rue Las Cases, Piou and de Mun recruited a number of vigorous young assistants, most notably Louis Laya, Auguste Cavalier, and Antoine Salvetti, hired for a reputation of ruthless efficiency in organization, despite their previous unsavory connections to the Justice Egalité of the Assumptionists and Déroulède's Patriotes. Under their direction, each issue of the *Bulletin* ran a lead editorial by one of the party's deputies discussing current topics, the rationale being to create a platform broader than "religious defense" on which the party could campaign. Readers of the new editorials quickly learned that in addition to preservation of the rights of the established church, the ALP stood for fiscal restraint, industrial reform legislation of the social Catholic variety, and a return to *scrutin de liste* voting. By forcing candidates to campaign throughout an entire department and not merely a single district, and to appear on a party list, the change in the election procedure would make them more dependent on the "national office" of their party for funds and would put a premium on the organization that the ALP intended to achieve. The social planks were partly a concession to de Mun's past, but much more an effort to attract the lower-class vote, which the party had virtually ignored in 1902. The *Bulletin* prominently displayed the Gailhard-Bancel plan for retirement pensions and called for free medical and legal aid to the indigent.[10]

All of this money and publicity were, however, only the means to the ALP's end, the organization of a party claiming a large national membership. The seventy-eight ALP deputies in the Chamber and the five in the Senate naturally formed the leadership. In common with the great majority of every parliamentary group, including even the Socialists, they were almost entirely aristocratic landowners, former military officers, industrial capitalists, lawyers and professional men, and a few litterateurs. Almost half of the delegation had no previous legislative experience, handicapping tactics but allowing Piou to boast that he had brought new men into politics to replace the tired and defeated. The party militants, the *populaire* of the ALP, came from all classes. The well-to-do entered as sustaining members, *membres sociétaires*, paying twenty-five francs a year in dues, but the ranks were filled principally by ordinary members, *membres adhérents*, whose yearly subscription came to but one franc apiece, well within the budget of the working class. The imposition of dues in such trifling amounts was hardly to fill the treasury. Instead, by exacting an annual payment, the party excluded indifferent followers from its membership, voluntarily keeping it far below its voting strength. The faithful gathered in local committees, seven hundred by 1904 at the first party congress, comprising some 160,000 members. By way of comparison, the Socialists counted only 35,000 members in 1905. A party principle was decentralization in nominal matters, and Piou granted large autonomy in organization, recruitment, and propaganda. For guidance on crucial concerns, local leaders could turn to the reams of tracts, pamphlets, and the *Bulletin* sent out from the Rue Las Cases or ask for an appearance by one of the deputies at a rally. In Paris there were also archives, the Section d'Etudes, for research into difficult questions of law, especially as the anticlericals tried to apply it. Soon there would be a youth corps, the Jeunesse Libérale, and a women's auxiliary, the Ligue Patriotique des Françaises, even a banner and an anthem. Piou and de Mun suggested that local committees follow the lead of the national office in Paris by founding placement bureaus and *secrétariats populaires*, which provided not only the free medical and legal assistance recommended by the the *Bulletin* but also low-interest loans. Although often little more than gimmicks in some localities, they still enticed an interested working class to the party.[11]

Undeniably, there had been an excellent beginning, and in early 1903 Piou wanted to concentrate his efforts on developing and consolidating for the future these early gains in recruitment and propaganda. Instead, he found himself facing an immediate crisis that threatened first the credibility and then even the existence of the party as the leader of the opposition. The threat came initially from Combes, when the premier audaciously announced his plan to deny authorization to all congregations of men except for five contemplative or missionary orders. The silent Trappists were spared because they could not corrupt the minds of children, the White Fathers and the others involved in missions because they were a boon to French imperialism in North Africa: even Gambetta had denied that anticlericalism was an export product. To facilitate the legislature's action, he lumped all of the requests for authorization into three groups, preaching, teaching, and selling, the last a special derisory category for the Chartreux. Since the requests required the confirmation of both houses, defeat in one meant disapproval, with the less anticlerical Senate unable to block the excesses of the Chamber. Between 18 and 26 March, in three easy votes, the deputies disbanded 400 congregations. Another 215, including the most prominent, Jesuits, Dominicans, and Franciscans, had expected the worst and did not bother to apply for authorization. The speeches by the ALP and Progressive representatives were useless, and even protests by Independents like Ribot were worth nothing. The congregations of women suffered a similar fate in June. In between, the ministry seemed to sponsor the interruption of church services by rowdies—Apaches, the Catholics called them—or at least made no effort to protect priests and worshipers. The Abbé Hippolyte Gayraud, who left the Christian Democrats for the ALP, warned the cabinet that "last year I considered it my duty to intervene to stop possible violence between the [Catholic] population and their oppressors, but if you pursue these policies, I shall never do so again!" Such impotence to blunt the government's program, although unavoidable, was discrediting to the ALP. The party's initial success had excited some jealousy among other opposition groups, and this envy was mixed with fear on the extreme Right. The few unrepentant royalists were afraid that if de Mun and Piou were successful in creating a powerful republican party, the monarchist movement would meet its long-overdue extinction. In the wake of the spring repression, royalists Emile Keller, the old stalwart, and Denys Cochin, the glib new spokesman, laid grandiose and unrealizable plans for a vast confessional party, the Comité Catholique, which would be larger than the ALP since it would ostensibly include all French Catholics, royalists as well as republicans. Keller and Cochin fantasized that they would be able to secure the blessing of Leo XIII for their enterprise and eventually force the ALP to amalgamate with the Comité Catholique, in which it would be outvoted and overwhelmed.[12]

This project was utterly divorced from reality, but it held a danger for the ALP. Although de Mun and Piou recognized that the plans of the royalists were illusions, they also saw that this endeavor had to be aborted in order to maintain at least a tenuous unity in the Catholic conservative ranks. Piou was prepared to admit the party's current weakness. In November 1902, in a major speech at Lille, he had reminded his audience that the Right had not won an election in twenty-five years and that the ALP deserved a chance to break the spell in 1906. In March 1903 he had repeated this counsel in an article for *Le Correspondant*, adding an attack on the royalists, whose lack of organization and program, he charged, had crippled the conservatives for so long. "The moment has come to change tactics, to see that politics, like the war it is, requires organization, method, even science." The *Bulletin* set upon the defeat of Maurice Barrès in a Paris by-election in April as an example of intransigent stupidity. By refusing to court the Progressive vote with an affirmation of republicanism, the novelist had cost himself the race. Also in April, the party clearly demonstrated its nationwide organization, on a single day placarding every department with a series of antigovernment posters. This kind of ammunition and preparation gave de Mun and Piou confidence when Keller and Cochin actually announced their plans formally in mid-April and solicited support.[13]

Back in Paris, de Mun wrote Piou emphatically: "We must cut short this stillborn enterprise, which can only divide, trouble, and turn money away from the Action Libérale Populaire . . . I consider this initiative of Keller very regrettable, to say nothing harsher. The ALP must be the sole organized force. It should be sufficient for any battle we face. As long as [the conservatives] cannot understand this idea, or do not want to understand it, we shall continue to be beaten." Piou snapped at Keller, "Our place is not within an organization founded to supplant us!" De Mun nevertheless drafted the party's official reply to the Comité Catholique in moderate terms, hoping eventually to lure some of its proponents to the ALP:

> We regret that we are unable to give our adherence or encourage that of our friends. Here are our reasons. On the one hand we are persuaded that the multiplicity of parties, the dispersion of resources and of efforts that is the consequence, is one of the principal causes of the weakness of the conservatives. On the other hand we consider that no Catholic association, called to exercise a political action (which will necessarily be the case of the one you plan, religious questions being more than ever the basis of general politics today) can exercise power or receive the indispensable approbation of the pope if it is not republican. The Action Libérale Populaire, already strong and growing more powerful daily, better than any other organization is able to face the exigencies that confront Catholics today. It should form, as it has done already with success, the "Union of French Catholics." To create beside it another organization would necessarily weaken it morally and materially. The unity of command and cohesion of efforts are the essential needs of our cause.[14]

In large measure the idea of the Comité Catholique was a revival of the 1891 Union de la France Chrétienne, and, like its predecessor, as de Mun had predicted, it was stillborn. Keller and his ilk had learned nothing in a decade. One of the most powerful weapons of the ALP against them was the party's confidence of continued Vatican support. Through de Mun the ALP was the heir to social Catholicism and the Ralliement, the two policies by which Leo XIII had hoped to revive the French church, and the aged pontiff blessed the party and its members. This papal approbation was no mean asset among Catholics, and the ALP had utilized it effectively in their early organizing, especially in soliciting funds. It had been, therefore, with apprehension during 1902 and early 1903 that de Mun and Piou contemplated the pope's extraordinary age and increasing feebleness, and finally a blow, although long expected, when Leo died in mid-July 1903 at the age of ninety-three. French Catholics hoped for the election of Rampolla as a Leo XIV, but the white smoke from the consistory cleared to reveal the elevation of Giuseppe Sarto, the little-known Patriarch of Venice, who took the name, ominous to the liberals, of Pius X. To determine whether the new pope would continue Leo's support for the ALP, de Mun hastened to the Vatican in early August, there to find a startling change. In contrast to his cultured aristocratic predecessor, Pius was of peasant stock, the first pontiff in centuries to have known true poverty, narrow-minded, and woefully uninformed about the political situation in France. He had surrounded himself with like-minded advisers, not necessarily of such lowly birth, but of equally dogmatic temperament, the most typical being the new cardinal secretary of state, Rafael Merry del Val, an austere Spaniard. As a favorite of Leo, de Mun had for more than a decade been spared the elaborate ceremonial and protocol of the Vatican, the endless kneeling that formalized audiences and prohibited confidences. Now he was forced to observe them again. De Mun took this reduction in status as a warning that the intensely conservative Pius might disavow Leo's liberal work, especially since the French church was subject to such withering attack. On his return to Paris, de Mun decided that for the present the safest course to chart would be to link the ALP, the current symbol of the Ralliement, so tightly to social Catholicism that the Vatican could not forsake one without the other, a double repudiation of his predecessor that a new pope would not undertake lightly.[15]

De Mun was also brought to this decision by his sense that the ALP should adopt a much more affirmative stand for social legislation. Bazire had already chided him gently about the party's failure to press for new reforms, and indeed their progress during the past decade had been almost nil because their parliamentary champions, de Mun included, had neglected them in the partisan disputes of the Ralliement, the Dreyfus affair, and the new anticlerical struggle. An active social policy might broaden the party's appeal and be the attraction for the working class that "religious defense" could never be. There was already some progress to build upon, the *secrétariats populaires*, editorials in the *Bulletin*, and the Gailhard-Bancel pension plan. But to emphasize the issue, in the fall of 1903, de Mun and Piou staged a "Social Congress" for mid-October, holding it at Pau, where de Mun could combine attendance with rest after a hectic summer. One entire issue of the *Bulletin* was devoted to the promises of the congress, as Piou expressed it, "never to forget the misery, sufferings, and injustices." Besides such vague bombast, the congress formally called for a living wage, improved working conditions, shorter workdays, prohibition of work on Sundays, and old-age pensions in a program of sickness, accident, and unemployment insurance. Every effort was made to join the ACJF to the ALP through these proposals. The previous May, Piou had called upon its members to "broaden their action," that "wherever the enemy is, there the Jeunesse Catholique should be to combat it." In response Bazire had encouraged his followers to fan out through the countryside in June to refute the "lies of anticlericalism." With that the ACJF edged closer to active collaboration with the ALP, although within it there remained some reluctant troopers who felt that politics compromised their social efforts. To help hold the majority, de Mun broke a year's silence to speak very briefly before the ACJF national meeting at Besançon on 29 November. Condemning Combes for pursuing anticlericalism while delaying social reforms, he recalled that "in 1793 and 1794 the philosophes of the Convention spoke of humanity, fraternity, and compassion while the tumbrels left from the door of the assembly to begin their sinister journeys. Today only consciences are guillotined, but the accompaniment is the same." Piou culminated this new emphasis for the year in a speech of his own in Paris, the former economic liberal flatly warning industrialists that if they held themselves aloof from their workers and refused to make proper reforms in a Christian spirit, socialism would be the inevitable conqueror.[16]

De Mun also made one serious effort to rejuvenate the sadly neglected Oeuvre des Cercles and heal a split that had developed within social Catholicism. De Mun's creations had represented the conservative side of the movement, closely identified with the church and very careful to retain the approval of Rome if not always that of the local hierarchy. The many strains of Christian Democracy in the mid-1890s, with its militant priests meeting in defiance of the prohibitions of their bishops and a social policy that seemed to approach socialism, were located completely across the political spectrum to the Left. The Christian Democrats disintegrated quickly after 1900, extreme individualists to the end, but surviving them was an energetic social Catholic group, the Sillon of Marc Sangnier, which shared some of their social views and their lack of deference to the institutional church. Founded in 1894 by a group of young intellectuals who met in the crypt of the Collège Stanislas, the Sillon never numbered more than ten thousand members at its height and was held together less by an administrative structure than by the charismatic personality of its leader, a cult of youth, and a sense of comradeship. Sangnier encouraged an unabashedly lay character within the Sillon and sought to extend its appeal by insisting on only the vaguest "Christian" or spiritual inspiration as a condition of membership. This attitude caused alarm at Rome and among much of the episcopacy. Yet the Sillonistes gloried in their role as the new vanguard, advising Catholic youth, "If the Sillon scares you or your parents, you can safely enroll under the banner of the ACJF." De Mun was pained to see such discord among social Catholics, and while he clearly favored Bazire and the ACJF over the Sillon, he did not want to lose Sangnier's talents. The pudgy leader was a brilliant speaker, who had the capacity to excite intense devotion and who had already offered his voice to the ALP and served ably in the demonstrations of 1902. In late 1903, de Mun proposed a truce that contained the possibility of an accommodation. Bazire and Sangnier would both join the Oeuvre des Cercles and work jointly to revive it, each submerging his animosity and preferred tactics to provide a unified auxiliary for the ALP. Bazire was reluctant but finally agreed to the plan in early December. Sangnier would not do so, and in January 1904 de Mun sadly expressed his deep disappointment. He could not help but admire the fire, albeit misdirected, of the young man, and he could compare him to himself as an impatient youth in the 1870s. Sangnier would continue to speak for the ALP, but the Sillon was to be allowed its head, de Mun never publicly rebuking it.[17]

Personal rivalries like those that tore at social Catholicism also hampered the ALP in winning a unified political front. The party's initial gains were so impressive, nevertheless, that the ministry considered it a very serious danger. As early as the summer parliamentary recess of 1903, Combes singled it out for special calumny whenever he spoke, proclaiming, "l'Action Libérale Populaire, voilà l'ennemi!" Warning that it had "absorbed the old opposition and was in the process of assimilating the centrist republicans," he went on to deride "the new man of the Action Libérale, in whom all can recognize the old man of *action cléricale*." Piou only replied in scorn, "France has hardly made revolution after revolution in order to be a prey to such a regime, not toppled monarchy after monarchy to install in the Chamber and Senate five hundred little Caesars in waistcoats!" The anxiety of the leftist parties became so intense that at the Radical party congress at Toulouse in October 1904, Louis Bonnet, the party executive secretary, insisted that "the battle will be even hotter in 1906 than in 1902. We face especially the elements of the Right and Center which the ALP organizes with as much cleverness as hypocrisy. We have never before fought an organization so strong, so extensive, and so well-endowed." But if the majority parties actually believed their fears and exhortation, they seriously underestimated the difficulties of joining disparate groups into a harmonious unit and forgot the squabbles among themselves that made agreement on anything other than anticlericalism difficult. The organizational success of the ALP seemed impressive for future campaigns, but its chief effect by 1904 was to force its friends and allies to decide whether to submit to its direction or to remain independent and risk becoming isolated without influence. A Sûreté report of January 1904 identified vigorous ALP groups in sixty of the departments, and earlier ones had emphasized that the party seemed to have tapped an inexhaustible supply of funds, spending an average of twenty-five thousand francs a month and receiving pledges of new contributions totaling nearly seven million francs. Significantly, money that had formerly gone to other right-wing and centrist groups now flowed to the ALP, which had impressed contributors as well as Combes with its potential for overturning the Left. Piou and de Mun at first intended to exploit this position of economic dominance to gain the clear leadership of those opposed to the premier.[18]

Would money alone be sufficient? The opposition was severely fragmented, riven by its traditional cleavages, the "clerical line," social policy, and ambition. Piou and de Mun found themselves trying to solve an equation the right side of which equaled success but the left side of which contained too many variables. Some of the Progressives were tempted by the ALP wealth, most notably Eugène Motte, whose election machine controlled much of the vote in the Nord and who needed money to pay his debts, and Jules Roche, who sat on the Budget Committee and whose Ligue des Contribuables was attracted by the ALP's opposition to new taxes and by promises of financial assistance. Yet most of the Progressives and all of the Independents maintained a clear separation from the ALP. Their concerns were not primarily religious, and they were very leery of being identified too strongly with "Catholic" interests. As former Opportunists, they were divided from the leaders of the ALP by their outlook on the past as well as on the future. In June 1903, Waldeck-Rousseau startled the Senate with a bitter hour-long tirade against the way Combes had enforced the Associations law. The Progressives and Independents welcomed him back as a repentant sinner; the ALP still considered him a reprobate, de Mun calling "deplorable" the ready forgiveness. When Waldeck-Rousseau died hardly more than a year later in August 1904, de Mun had not softened his attitude. In the *Bulletin*, Cavalier asked whether the former premier "had been a great man?": only in comparison to Combes was the disdainful reply. The Independents and the Progressives were willing to consider confederation, an election alliance with the ALP in 1906 even tighter than that in 1902, but any dreams by Piou or de Mun of a grand conservative federation would remain dreams. The defense of religion that did not fall clearly under defense of individual liberty always caused slippage in the opposition's left-flank vote, and when in mid-1904 Combes broke diplomatic relations with the Vatican after a series of bitter incidents, the ALP would stand helplessly alone in the Chamber, "clericals" who put church before nation. Such a condemnation would have fallen on anyone who had the temerity to vote with them.[19]

Nor could social policy bring the opposition together. Piou preferred to interpret de Mun's ideas as allowing the ALP to promise something of a French "Tory democracy." He had quite readily joined with de Mun in 1903 to create a social program for the party, but some of the members grumbled quietly then and more openly later. Ferri de Ludre even defended an extreme form of economic liberalism in the *Bulletin*. Social Catholicism certainly would not attract the Progressives and Independents, who blanched at its very title, the stigma of Catholicism and socialism from which they shrank. There was even some question whether a prominent display of the famous ideas of de Mun would not drive away more votes than they would attract. True socialists could always outbid Christian socialists for the vote of the working class, while both tended to frighten the same timid, conservative constituency. Within the wealthiest Catholic ranks there was also the suspicion that *Rerum novarum*, like its author, might soon pass away, and with it those bands of idealistic youth following Sangnier or Bazire and his "absurd" dictum, "social because Catholic." De Mun himself shocked them with his conviction that the adjective "Catholic" "contained all doctrine, all social truth." These circles found hope in September 1904 when Pius, at an audience for Jeunesse Catholique pilgrims, seemed to hedge his approval of lay social action. De Mun recognized that his insistence on a social program had, as he told Piou, "resulted in a dualism [within the party], a division where there must be union at any price." But he did not mean "at any price," since he had no intention of disavowing social Catholicism.[20]

No one among the opposition seemed to have any intention of forswearing his traditions, but in the heat of political struggle differences were more easily overlooked. If true unity of command was impossible for Piou and de Mun, then their best alternative would be a continued close and tactful cooperation among allies. During the by-elections of January 1904, Piou and de Mun made remarkable concessions to the Progressives in order to close the gap between some of what de Mun termed these parallel actions. Especially in the Nord the opposition won new victories when Piou called upon all ALP supporters to vote for the Progressive in their district. At the same time the *Bulletin* treated Méline very gently when he found it necessary for local political security to endorse a Radical running for office in his home district of Remiremont. Piou and Paul Beauregard, the new leader of the Progressives, also appeared at some joint rallies, but at first only in very conservative areas like Bordeaux and the West, where the Progressives could risk such open association with Catholics. During the 1904 May municipal elections and August voting for departmental councillors, the alliance continued to hold even though the ARD declined to join. Just as the Progressives seemed to approach the ALP, the Independents moved further away as the whole question of church-state relations seemed about to be resolved against the Catholics. As was usual, those local elections suffered from a high rate of abstention—approaching 60 percent—making the outcomes subject to misinterpretation. Yet there were some significant gains for the ALP and Progressives on municipal councils and marginal ones among the departmental councillors. De Mun and Piou felt that their alliance with the Progressives had to hold. The church had faced more terrors in 1904 than even in 1902, and with the destruction of the church's position, the Independents became less and less likely to vote with the opposition. There would have to be new allies, more dangerous ones, however, since they would come from the right flank. As Carlo Montagnini, secretary to the nuncio to France would write to Merry del Val, "In the face of the mounting evil, the Action Libérale never rests." Piou established new contacts with the fading Patrie Française, whose strength was confined to Paris, and even with the remnants of the Ligue des Patriotes, whose bully boys could be the party's "cossacks and enforcers." De Mun began to try to win back the participants in the Comité Catholique, concentrating on the urbane Denys Cochin, a friend of his daughter's husband Pierre d'Harcourt, and clever enough to hide the monarchism of those he might bring with him to the ALP.[21]

Because it lacked sufficient allies, the Catholic cause in early 1904 seemed to reach a new low. In March, Combes raced through the Chamber a bill requiring that monks and nuns from authorized orders close their schools as soon as the state public ones could be expanded to handle the influx of students, or in any case, within ten years. Once more the ALP, Progressives, and ARD deputies dusted off their traditional and occasionally impassioned pleas. A much-disturbed Ribot warned that "we seem in this country to be developing a taste for the use of force, especially when accompanied by brutality, to cherish the absolute right of a majority . . . an attitude that is the negation of the true republican spirit." There seemed, however, no discernible effect upon the ministry as it won by an easy margin among the deputies, 306 to 241, and likewise among the senators, 166 to 105, later, in July. De Mun had to sit enviously as his colleagues in turn climbed the steps of the rostrum, monotonously and with little éclat to proclaim their faith, to vindicate the congregations and their schools. His absence from the debate could not possibly have made a difference of more than a few votes, if any, in the final total. But although he had lost his voice, he now found his pen. Twice in *Le Gaulois* and once each in *Le Correspondant* and the *National Review* of London—which asked him, as a conservative congenial to its editorial policy, to explain the commotion in France—he belabored the ministry in print, the beginning of regular political columns he would write for the rest of his life and eventually publish in four major Parisian dailies. His written style did not yet have the luster of his oratory, seeming to lack passion and verve. But then nothing about the opposition's effort to block this laic teaching bill could be said to have sparkled. There would be little improvement during the six months after March.[22]

By early 1904, de Mun and Piou had become seriously worried about their position at the Vatican. As long as Rampolla remained in the chancellery, the Ralliement would have a proponent, but the new pope had been enthroned since August of the preceding year and as yet no new blessing had been extended to the ALP. In an attempt at personal diplomacy, de Mun traveled to Rome at the beginning of April to plead the ALP's case himself before Pius X. Unfortunately, the moment was not propitious. The Vatican was in dudgeon at the announcement of a forthcoming state visit by President Loubet to Victor Emmanuel at the Quirinal on 24 April, part of France's ultimately successful diplomatic effort to wean Italy from the Triple Alliance. Both the pope and Merry del Val were aware of the necessity for the Quai d'Orsay to detach Italy from Germany at a time when Russia was embroiled with Japan in the Far East and unable to assist its ally; they also knew that protocol demanded that the French return the Italian king's visit to Paris in October 1903. The French deputies and senators approved credits for the trip by lopsided votes, 502 to 10 and 258 to 2, with even the Catholic opposition disappearing except for de Mun and a handful of diehards. Nevertheless, since the Italian expropriation of Rome in 1870, no chief of state of a Catholic country had recognized this seizure by visiting the city. Loubet's trip was therefore a dramatic affront and supremely ironic because it had been to France that Leo XIII had looked, hoping the Ralliement would ultimately restore the temporal domains of the papacy. A few halfhearted proposals were made to mitigate the humiliation of the Vatican, but they came to nothing, and in this gathering crisis of papal prestige, the pontiff and his secretary of state told de Mun that they could make no promises regarding the French political situation.[23]

From this attitude de Mun could only conclude that to receive any papal endorsement, the ALP would have to support a fortiori whatever position the Holy See assumed on the Loubet visit, no matter how that might separate the party from its allies. In mid-May, Merry del Val drafted a formal protest to France that rivaled even the *Syllabus of Errors* in its untimeliness. Frenchmen were told that they should be proud of their large representation in the College of Cardinals—actually a miniscule seven in comparison to the forty of Italy—and that they should forswear any friendship with Italy in blithe disregard of the consequences. With consummate folly, Merry del Val circulated a copy to all European governments, and, as is common with hubris, retribution followed, the anticlerical Prince of Monaco sending his copy to Jaurès, who published it on 17 May in the Socialist mouthpiece *L'Humanité*. There was great indignation in France, especially when it became clear that the version circulated about Europe contained a sentence, omitted from the original directed to the Quai d'Orsay, that implied that the nuncio would remain in Paris only because the fall of the ministry could be expected. Combes had been conducting a running feud with the Vatican over episcopal appointments and the discipline of two bishops who had been blatant in their disregard of the injunction against sexual misconduct, and feelings were already raw. He saw an opportunity to exploit the resentment against the protest to place increased pressure on Merry del Val by recalling the French ambassador to the Vatican. On the very day that Jaurès printed the protest, the Chamber supported the premier's decision 427 to 95, leaving the ALP and a few royalists an isolated minority. When the disputes were not resolved quickly, Combes decided to break off relations entirely on 29 July. Throughout, a despondent ALP publicly attempted to justify the Vatican position. In *La Croix* and *Le Gaulois* de Mun assailed Loubet, Combes, and foreign minister Théophile Delcassé for their parts in the "tragedy of rupture." He claimed that the countryside would disavow it, that "the ministers are not France; they are only her masters for a day. The majority that supports them is not France;

it is only a party, less than that, a political coterie." Yet privately there was deep despair. Instead of coalescing the opposition as had been its effect in 1901 and 1902, defense of the church now seemed to be dividing it completely. And the abnegation of the ALP did not even impress the Vatican. In mid-July, Merry del Val sent Piou a letter commending his party for its "fidélité," but this was hardly the public endorsement for which de Mun had hoped and for which the ALP had broken ranks with its allies.[24]

Worse seemed in the offing in September, when Combes began to talk openly of crowning his anticlerical program with "Separation," the abrogation of the 1801 Concordat binding church and state. He may have merely wanted to threaten the Vatican anew, since he had often called the Concordat an effective instrument of control, but on 22 October the Chamber voted 318 to 230 in favor of the principle of Separation, coming close to forcing Combes's hand. Like Waldeck-Rousseau before him, he could also become the prisoner of his majority. Six days later, before this could happen, Jean Guyot de Villeneuve of the Patrie Française mounted the rostrum to read a series of index cards, fiches, containing reports on the private lives of French military officers. On his assumption of power Combes had promised the rewards of patronage only to those of his own political species, not an unusual policy for the generally pork-barrel Republic. His minister of the army, General Jean André, had greatly expanded the system, deciding that in keeping with the tone of the cabinet he should block the promotion of any officer so reactionary as to attend mass, allow his family to do so, or send his children to a Catholic school. To compile his dossiers André sought unverified reports from an officer's subordinates and from the Freemasons, who often were associated with anticlericalism, within the military or living near its installations. It was the worst sort of talebearing. There had been rumors earlier in the year about André's methods, but only when the parliamentary leader of the Patrie Française, Gabriel Syveton, through what was essentially a bribe, obtained from a Mason some of the fiches on which the reports were submitted, could an effective attack be mounted on André, and behind him Combes. Even some of the premier's majority flinched at Guyot de Villeneuve's disclosures and further ones by Syveton on 4 November, but the ministry was spared disaster when Syveton struck the abject army minister, an older man, after hearing André baldly deny all knowledge of the fiches. This brutal act by a man already of low repute—he would commit suicide a month later to escape prosecution for embezzlement of funds from his party and the seduction of his daughter-in-law—led to a counterrevulsion and saved Combes from immediate defeat. But the premier's control over the Chamber had been clearly weakened. There were some acts, apparently, that even the majority could not condone.[25]

Suddenly, the condition of the army seemed to become a potential political issue, and the offices of the ALP literally overflowed with mail from the provinces denouncing the system of promotion by denunciation. Progressives and Independents were also outraged, rekindling the sense of a unified opposition that had been lost during Loubet's Roman holiday. The revelations of profound mistrust and division within the military awakened fears about its readiness for war, especially when Russian aid was uncertain. In keeping with the Radical preference for a short-term enlistment and as part of the revanche of Dreyfus, the Left had proposed the reduction of required military service from three years to two. Each fall France called to the colors the so-called "class," all of the twenty-one-year-olds. Under the proposed change the classes with three and two years service would be released together and only the latter replaced by the new class. The nation's men under arms would thus be reduced by approximately a third, after allowing for those recruits normally released after only one year because of a complicated series of deferments for education and dependents. During the summer de Mun had attacked in *Le Gaulois* what he called "antimilitarism" among the deputies, and privately he spoke of the Chamber's most "horrific achievement, the lamentable disorganization of our army." This reaction was extreme even after the revelation of the fiches, probably characteristic of all former cavalrymen. But a sense of disquiet began to pervade the entire opposition and even part of the majority, although it would be short-lived without a definite international crisis to convert it into a panic.[26]

In the midst of this period of ambiguous unity among the opposition groups, de Mun and Piou had scheduled the first ALP party congress to meet in Paris. They had planned as early as the previous January to test the party's increasing organization and demonstrate its formidable strength, de Mun telling Piou that "the ALP must prove that it is ready for the campaigns for which it was constituted by reaffirming the principles upon which it was founded and by demonstrating the extent of its organization. This manifestation must reveal the ALP powerful and self-sufficient enough to convince all that it is not a transitory phenomenon formed purely for the elections but a durable party, in complete control of all of its membership and ready not only for the struggles of today but for the eventualities of tomorrow." Piou emphasized these points in a speech at Arras in May and by an article in an October issue of *Le Correspondant*: "To act methodically and with patience, to discover or excite devotion, to extend throughout . . . the network of an organization that combines discipline with decentralization, to have committees and trusted men everywhere, and to do it all without cease or weakness . . . that is what we seek." It had been done, at least partly. There were noticeable changes—the shift of the *Bulletin* to grand folio format at the beginning of November 1904, and the striking increase in activity within the capital, each election district responsible for sponsoring a rally each month on the day corresponding to its number. There was also the promise in the *Bulletin* of a positive program as well as clever exploitation of the scandal of André and the fiches.[27] The less obvious gains in the provinces combined with these so that Piou and de Mun opened the congress on 15 December at the Société de Géographie with unabashed optimism. When Piou rose to make the keynote address, he stood before 900 delegates from 78 departments, part of the 160,000 members organized in 700 new local committees, assembled to report that the party's unstinting propaganda had joined with the government's policies to swell the ALP ranks in every region. His vibrant speech recalled the goals of the party and how a questionnaire, circulated to each committee prior to the congress, revealed exceptional progress during the previous two years. There was an unmistakable decision to emphasize the party's social program, Piou claiming that "if state socialism is a threat, state abstention is a desertion." Later there were reports from Laya, acting as executive secretary, congratulating the committees on their work but urging them to continue striving to begin the important task of revising the voting lists, the source of much election fraud—votes cast by those long dead and multiple votes by those still resident—

throughout the years, most of it since 1879 against the Right, to maintain regular committee meetings, to expand placement and *secrétariats sociales*, to visit voters personally rather than relying only on colportage, and even to imitate any successful ploy of the Radicals and Socialists. In the evening there were the first of many glorious and rhapsodic speeches by ALP deputies, although de Mun excused himself because of his health. The most impressive was by Xavier Reille, scion of an old royalist family of the Tarn and a former artillery officer turned litterateur. To the ecstatic applause of an audience estimated by the police to be swollen to two thousand, he provided the arresting image of a train unslowed by individual snowflakes but halted totally by a snowbank. The allusion to organization and unity was obvious to everyone.

The mornings and afternoons of the following two days were taken up with work sessions to frame a number of resolutions that could serve as part of the ALP platform. Under the leadership of Gailhard-Bancel, the delegates debated and finally approved, with a hesitation that testified to much doubt, plans for retirement pensions, increased powers for labor unions, and a broad Code de Travail that embodied most of the reforms for which de Mun had spoken during three decades. In sessions chaired by Jean Plichon and Louis Ollivier, important ALP lieutenants in the Chamber, there was more enthusiasm and near unanimity for proposals to reform elections. Provincial delegates were keen to endorse the secret ballot, obligatory voting, and proportional representation through *scrutin de liste* to help overcome the stranglehold of local Radical civil servants. The evenings each day allowed for more passionate oratory and for joint appearances with Progressives like de Marcère and Beauregard. Ever larger crowds each night began to chant in unison calls for Combes's resignation as the scandal of the fiches was waved at them like a bloody flag. Maurice Spronck, a deputy from Paris, elicited a roar when he perorated that the ALP had to defend "not only our liberty but safeguard our flag, our army, even our nationality itself!" But it was Paul Lerolle, always a magnificent platform speaker, who best caught the combative fervor when he challenged that "we must reclaim our place in this land not by humble prayers but, heads high, by a will fiercely affirmed. For defense, patience and tenacity will suffice; for conquest, we require audacity."

For the final day Piou and de Mun had planned a great banquet with seats for twelve hundred. Dressed formally, the delegates were escorted to long tables, and, at a sign, a concealed band struck up the "Marseillaise." Here was the signal for Piou and de Mun to lead an impressively long column of party deputies, senators, municipal councillors, and departmental councillors into the enormous room in a triumphal procession. It seemed that the crucial election of 1906 had already been won. There was great emotion among the delegates and cheers of "Vive Piou!" and "Vive de Mun!" Planning had been so thorough that a table was set aside for the press, and every great Parisian newspaper, whatever its sympathies, was represented to assess the strength of this new political phenomenon. Maximum publicity was assured. When the toasts were offered, Piou saluted the delegates, reiterated the ALP program, and promised victory, but only if a united opposition could be fashioned. His final charge was extreme, but it accurately reflected the spirit of the congress. "I do not ask you to violate the law," he began shrilly, "but you must not be the dupes of a false moderation." And, almost shouting, he finished, "For today the swords are crossed; either we or the sectarians must succumb!"[28]

With the congress a seemingly clear success, Piou and de Mun hoped to march the ALP quickstep toward the 1906 election. They planned to exploit shrewdly the issues raised at the 1904 congress, increase momentum at a second congress near the end of 1905, and finish with a dramatic sweep of the country in the final months before the ballot. Under normal circumstances, with many French voters outraged at the policies of the leftist majority, this strategy would have been sound. The ALP commanded wealth and members and could doubtless manage some form of conservative union made up of all groups to the right of the ARD and perhaps win even a portion of them. But at no time between the beginning of 1905 and the election of 1906 did "normal circumstances" prevail in France.

On 19 January 1905, Combes resigned without ever losing a vote of confidence but rightly convinced that his majority would no longer bear the onus of his system of delation. To replace him Loubet called Maurice Rouvier, an Opportunist recently gone Radical, veteran of both the 1887 experiment in conservative coalition and the Panama Canal scandal. More interested in financial affairs than anticlericalism, the new premier was nevertheless fully aware of the tenor of the majority that supported him, and he felt compelled to complete his predecessor's work of destruction by toppling the last vestige of clericalism, the 1801 Concordat. When he first presented his ministry before the Chamber, the ALP declared itself ready for détente, for an "opening of credit" to the change from Combes. The sentiment quickly reverted to bitter hostility in early February, when Rouvier called on the parliamentary committee studying proposals of Separation to report out a bill as quickly as possible. Reporter Aristide Briand already had a draft near completion and, with a speed unprecedented in these matters, presented it for debate on 21 March.[29]

The provisions of the proposal were as involved and open to interpretation as their author, a Radical who began as a Socialist and would by 1914 trek across the political spectrum almost to the Right, the man of the eternally dangling cigarette, drooping mustache, and *souplesse*, who, as Clemenceau would say, "knew nothing and understood everything," and who believed only in his fitness one day to be premier. The bill he presented to the deputies had the vague quality of the diplomacy in which he would later excel, partially hiding a compromise that might be stringent enough for the anticlericals to accept yet sufficiently conciliatory for the church to live with.[30] By the bill's provisions the state declared that it would no longer recognize an established religion and henceforth pay no salaries to the clergy, although these would be continued in reduced amounts for four years as a transition and some pension rights would be observed. The government thereby would lose its right to nominate the episcopacy, giving the Vatican the latitude to appoint and discipline its own choices. All church property, including the buildings, would belong to the state, with the exception only of what had been acquired wholly through private donation since 1801. It was to be vacated within a year but might be utilized by the church if so-called religious associations were formed in each commune to assume its charge and to regulate all religious activity within the area. In Briand's vague wording, the religious associations seemed to constitute a possible threat to the church because their composition was to be of both clerics and laymen, who might include Jews, Protestants, and, most crucially, nonbelievers, with laymen in the majority. It was possible to imagine communes where, with Catholics in the minority, the religious association could prevent the celebration of the sacraments within its jurisdiction. Briand suspected that Catholics might be wary of countenancing this provision, and to help persuade them, his bill provided a stinger, that wherever the associations were not formed within a year's time, all church property would be subject to confiscation.

The ALP greeted Briand's effort with vehement criticism, but the denunciation was a cover behind which to consider strategy. Rome had offered no opinion on the merits of Separation since its details were yet moot, and the episcopacy was divided, the majority opposed in fear of the unknown and of the menu an anticlerical government was likely to serve, a minority seeing in the end of the Concordat a release from state control and an invigorating freedom. The ALP headquarters in early 1905 mirrored this quandary, with the Abbé Gayraud telling the Chamber that as a cleric he "welcomed" a Separation, while de Mun in *Le Gaulois* called this attitude "blind to the intent of the ministry" and termed the divorce of church and state a denial of French history and tradition. The *Bulletin* reprinted de Mun's editorials, and in speeches Piou denounced "the blow aimed at the heart of the church," but an ambiguity remained. Should the party commit itself to diehard and hopeless resistance to the Separation, a resistance that would be shared by some but by no means all of its potential allies, especially those to the left? Or should it attempt discreetly to temper this bill in favor of the church, an effort that might attract far greater support and even end in success? But this attitude might offend the Vatican, should the pope decide against Separation, and alienate fervent Catholics. It was a contest between dogmatism and pragmatism, one in which Piou's instincts were inevitably for the latter. And for all of his archclericalism, de Mun stood with Piou. Together they conceived a multifaceted strategy. Under the concealment of a blustery campaign of opposition, the ALP would use its influence and money to add carefully drawn amendments. In the countryside immoderate language, Piou's specialty, could galvanize Catholics and provide the climate of demonstration and confrontation that made elections more passionate and less amenable to control by an incumbent majority.[31]

The cover of an irreconcilable opposition was easy to mount since the ALP boasted deputies who could equal any Radical in bombast and vitriol. When debate opened they were eager to launch their diatribes. Henri Groussau, Paul Lerolle, and Gailhard-Bancel lambasted the "atheists" who would convert France into a land that knew "neither God nor master." But a reformed Gayraud outdid them, roaring at the Left in the name of the church, "We have centuries to take our revenge, and history proves that we always do!" Piou traversed the nation to deliver a set speech, damning those who would "hand the church over, bound hand and foot, to the French descendants of Ali-Baba and his forty thieves." Unable to lend his voice but more and more able to capture his eloquence in print, de Mun came close to matching this language in a remarkable series of editorials during March and April. Publishing biweekly in *Le Figaro*, and more occasionally in *Le Gaulois* and *La Croix*, he dissected the "Masonic plot" with its "historic lies" and "official apostasy." More calmly, he tried to force the debate of awkward questions. The salaries paid by the state in accordance with the Concordat were recompense, he felt, for the property of the church expropriated during the Revolution. If they were now to be halted, there seemed obvious reason for the church to insist on a lump-sum restitution. When this contention did not interest even the ALP allies, he posed others, looking, never successfully, to divide the majority for Separation, or at least to provide lucid and cogent justification for the policy of opposition.[32]

In counterpoint to this stout defense of the existing order, Piou initiated delicate negotiations with the ministry. He knew Rouvier to be a man of moderation who might be open to entreaty, especially if it were accompanied by an unsolicited gift. The premier also had close associates who might share this delightful—as Piou at least would have it—flexible morality, among them Ernest Constans, who as minister of the interior in 1889 had pardoned Piou and de Mun their involvement in Boulangism, and Eugène Etienne, an Independent with important investments in the colonial empire of North Africa. Through them in February, Piou proposed that Rouvier sponsor moderating amendments to the Separation bill in return for ALP subsidies and perhaps an election alliance if he could detach the right wing of the Radicals, loosely organized in the Chamber as the Union Démocratique, from their present policy. Through a Byzantine series of responses, Piou was given to understand that the premier's role could be only that of endorsing initiatives with substantial backing in the Chamber, for which the ALP would need the support of every possible ally.[33]

Piou found his issue in the desire to revise Article IV of Briand's bill, rules for constituting the religious associations. As originally drafted, these regulations took no note of the hierarchical organization of the Catholic church and enabled extreme anticlericals to envision quite happily bitter disputes between bishops and the lay-dominated communal associations. Along with the ALP and the Progressives, this prospect was considerably less appealing to many others, among them much of the Union Démocratique and almost all of the ARD and unattached Independents, few of whom made antagonism to the church a fetish. Also unenthusiastic about the anticipation of further religious strife was Jean Jaurès of the Socialists, who had hoped to see in the Separation bill a means of clearing anticlericalism from the French docket, making room for the question of socialism; the Radical-Socialist alliance had been biased totally in favor of the former so far. During debate in late March, Paul Deschanel and Louis Barthou of the ARD raised the fear of possible schism because there was no guarantee of episcopal control, but Briand, hearing no specific amendment and failing to perceive any intense support for change, suggested none. At the beginning of April, however, Piou arranged to collect a political debt from Ribot, whose victory in 1902 had come largely from ALP backing. Respected as a statesman, with impeccable credentials as an Independent although he allied himself with the ALP, Ribot proposed on 3 April that the Chamber add a sentence to Article IV specifying that the religious associations be created "according to the rules of the organization of the faith." Presumably, Rouvier then applied pressure to Briand to accept this revision and to defend it against the criticism of the most vociferous anticlericals. Strongly backed by the ministry, on 22 April the amendment received an overwhelming majority, 485 to 52, carrying along even most of the Radicals. "The Separation is accomplished!" cried Jaurès, thinking that even the Catholics would now accept the rest of the bill. In the corridors afterward, de Mun publicly shook Briand's hand and in *Le Figaro* called the change a "coup de pic."[34]

This victory was only one concession, and it did nothing to attenuate the financial losses of the church. The ARD and Independents did not find priestly poverty as outrageous as the ALP did, and afraid of seeming too solicitous about the table of fat clerics, they refused absolutely to make an issue of the monetary settlement. Piou spread more offers about, but there were few takers. In desperation for new allies, he insinuated himself into very odd councils, even approaching Clemenceau, who had recouped his political fortunes after Panama by winning election to the Senate. Piou suggested that Clemenceau's authority as the most voracious "priest-eater" could persuade deputies, or at least senators, to strike out the entire provision for religious associations and abandon church property to the faithful without hindrance. The shrewd old Radical, exactly de Mun's age, may have been interested but asked too much for the favor. Or he may have been toying with Piou. For whatever reason, his price was too high and the risk of compromise to the ALP too great.[35] Without allies in the Center or secret supporters among the majority, further amendments by the ALP and Progressives were in vain. Because even many of the Independents felt that the revision of Article IV adequately protected the rights of Catholics, the Separation bill passed the Chamber on 3 July without further change. The majority of 341 to 233 contained the votes of many Independents, including that of the relatively conservative Barthou of the ARD. Like the Radicals and Socialists who stood with them, they would all later be excommunicated for their decision, a fiat in pique that would make any possible reconciliation with the ALP impossible in the near term. The decision in the Senate was even easier for the ministry, a 179 to 103 vote after a series of debates so stage-managed that consideration of the bill by the upper house became perfunctory. Loubet then promulgated the bill over his signature three days later, 9 December 1905, writing finis to the 104 years of church-state conflict ironically called the Concordat.

There would be new sharp conflict under the Separation, but that would be short and come only in 1906, a curious coda in a year that began a curious decade very unlike that dating from the beginning of the Méline ministry. In 1905 the Separation proceeded portentously, inexorably, almost as a cathartic finally purging the body politic of the anticlericalism that had halted the normal consideration of new issues. French eyes were so fixed on this one domestic question that the passage even survived unruffled the sensational interruption of the Tangiers incident and the consequent fall of the foreign minister, itself a premature leitmotiv of the coming decade. Following colonial agreements with Great Britain in the Entente Cordiale of 1904, and without the slightest interest of the Chamber or public opinion, the Quai d'Orsay had in February 1905 presented the sultan of Morocco with a program of reforms that, if enacted, would give France a virtual protectorate over the area. Learning of this demarche only in the newspapers, German leaders were highly displeased, feeling somewhat unjustifiably that Delcassé, the molelike and resolutely anti-German foreign minister, had wantonly excluded them from the Moroccan negotiations. To humiliate France and teach Delcassé respect for German prerogatives, the Wilhelmstrasse convinced Wilhelm II to visit Tangiers on 31 March, there to proclaim his empire's intention to preserve Moroccan independence. The kaiser carried out his assignment with panache, and German diplomats then demanded an international conference to settle matters. There was a panic within the French cabinet, and when Delcassé urged resistance to Germany, the fearful Rouvier forced his resignation as a sacrifice to peace.[36]

There was good reason for Rouvier's fear. Calling Germany's bluff would be to play with a very weak hand. Russia had just been humbled by the Japanese and was tottering in revolution. Whatever the attitude of the new Entente partner Britain, the French would have to bear almost alone the brunt of land warfare. For this the army was almost totally unprepared, the damage of a decade's distrust and cleavage multiplied by a new recruitment law enacted far too lightly earlier that year during the most hectic maneuvering of the Separation bill. At stake had been the proposal to reduce required military service from three years to two, originally questioned by some of the opposition during the affair of the fiches when the condition of the army seemed for a time to emerge as a political issue. Because the new system would eliminate the practice of allowing university students to serve only one year, a provision clearly favoring the rich, supporters of the bill crowed that it would enhance the French tradition of *égalité*. Chauvinistically, they also claimed that if the Germans were able to fashion a recruit into a soldier within two years, the French could do as well. Detractors warned that unlike their enemy's army, the French did not have enough long-term noncommissioned officers to complete the training so rapidly and, far more important, that the effect of the law was to reduce by nearly 30 percent the number of men in the nation's standing army. For obscure reasons of parliamentary procedure, the Senate had approved the bill first, and it appeared for the Chamber's consideration in mid-March, at the height of the intrigue about Article IV. No wars were in sight, the measure seemed genuinely popular in the country—especially with those of draft age and their parents—and the deputies were anxious to deal with the religious question. The result was a lopsided vote of 504 to 34 in approval on 17 March. The misgivings of a few of the deputies were easily overlooked, since indeed there had been almost no comment on the bill since the previous fall, and the army itself, still reeling from the fiches, did not strenuously oppose it. Voting their constituents' wishes, and for their own reelection, such ALP deputies as Groussau and Gailhard-Bancel joined the huge majority in favor, and although de Mun personally stood with the tiny minority, he obviously made no effort to impose his views on the rest of the party.[37]

After Delcassé was set adrift on 6 June, de Mun began to question his acquiescence in the weakening of the army. He had no sympathy for Delcassé as an individual since it had been the foreign minister whose policies had led to the break with the Vatican. But in *Le Gaulois* as early as 15 June he worried that in their relief that France had avoided war, his countrymen would fail to see that the crisis and Delcassé's dismissal had revealed French weakness. A capitulation, however disguised, was a capitulation. In subsequent editorials he raised for the first time disturbing questions that should logically have occurred to him during the friction with Germany in 1887 and Great Britain in 1898. He asked whether the nation could be ready to wage war when torn by religious strife, whether Jaurès and the Socialists would carry out their threat to call a general strike in time of mobilization, whether the rivalry of ministers and the rancor of parties had not sapped France until the nation had need to "remake its soul." He recalled the "patriotism of yesterday," the attitude of February 1887, when the Chamber, without debate, voted unanimously for the expensive development of a new artillery piece, the Le Bel gun; in 1905 the "patriotism of today" was the fiches and the reduction in the army. Sensing an issue that might be exploited, the *Bulletin* and the propaganda net started to echo him, beginning by denouncing Delcassé's competence in alienating the Vatican and adopting such a pugnacious attitude when Russia was not available as a counterweight. And, like de Mun, the party publicists soon began a journalistic inquest into the condition of the military, with the conclusions foreordained. Under Rouvier, the war ministry had allowed anarchists and socialists like the inflammatory Gustave Hervé to preach sedition and antimilitarism among the soldiery, and now by the new service law units would be denuded of men. "Are we ready?" the *Bulletin* asked; the reply, not without some justification, was "No!"[38]

In 1905 the intense, even remarkable, preoccupation of the French people with domestic concerns ensured that general public opinion greeted these arguments with indifference. It was bizarre that for the twenty years between 1890 and 1910 Frenchmen and their elected representatives were so inward looking, paying little attention to foreign policy and the possibility of a new war with Germany.[39] Even the saga of Boulanger bore relation only tangentially to European rivalries, and no premier since the unfortunate Ferry in 1883 had fallen because of reverses outside of domestic affairs. Senators and deputies were seemingly content to leave the conduct of state relations to the Quai d'Orsay, so seldom were the ministries of these decades questioned on such issues. The representatives knew that Russia had joined France in a defensive pact against Germany and, after 1904, that Great Britain was a friend. But their lack of interest in the precise engagements made by these allies to France, and by France in return, revealed the legislature's indifference to foreign policy. The committees for foreign affairs for both Chamber and Senate were moribund without effective leadership. Instead, the energies of the two houses were spent in furious internal struggles over the nature of the homeland. The Dreyfus affair had largely obscured the severity of the Fashoda crisis, and the anticlerical disputes quickly diverted attention from the Moroccan question. The Algeciras conference in early 1906 removed any threat of war over the territory, but Frenchmen were, in any event, too busy to fight abroad. By then they were engaged in unexpected riots over the execution of the Separation law.

The riots were unexpected by the government but not entirely by the ALP. In a final denunciation before the Chamber approved the Separation, Paul Lerolle and an aggressive young deputy from the Aveyron, Léonce de Castelnau, warned obliquely of possible violence when the faithful witnessed the expropriation of the churches. The party then set about to stimulate protest if not indeed that violence. It was clearly good politics to excite their followers with appeals to emotion, and agents of the Sûreté had already begun to dispatch cautionary reports to Paris warning of ALP operatives who descended upon the countryside to portray the law as the rape of the church. In *Le Gaulois*, de Mun wrote of the "day of responsibilities" and of how Catholics would settle scores with the 341 deputies who voted the Separation, because "no excuse can cover them." Piou had earlier proclaimed that "when a law outrages conscience, conscience demands the violation of the law." This language was inflammatory, but the ALP leaders were less afraid of raising violence than of simply failing to raise any protest at all. The *Bulletin* thought it necessary constantly to remind party members to petition and poster. Piou revealed his fears frankly when he told audiences that too many Catholics "groaned, looked sad, and remained silent, playing the soldiers who will not fight," "the congregation of folded arms and weeping willows." Most often, however, there was "the speech," variations on which Piou and other ALP orators and stump speakers had delivered at rallies for almost four years: France was a nation clearly divided between "Jacobin sectarians" and "liberal patriots," and the only salvation from the evil of the former was "the formation of a great national and liberal party resolved to respect the traditions that have made France one of the first nations of the world." To help spread this gospel, Piou hastened the expansion of the press network in the provinces, whether in the form of papers owned outright or heavily subsidized, and in Paris by the purchase of *La Presse* and *La Patrie*, evening dailies with a total general circulation of 160,000, and the acquisition of editorial control of *Le Peuple Français*, originally directed by the Christian Democrats but now taken over by the young men of the ACJF.[40]

The gospel did attract more believers, whether their arms were folded in resignation or raised in protest, and it was this baptism of more believers, a secular church-militant, that was absolutely necessary right up to election time if the ALP was to continue its role as the most dangerous threat to the majority. After four years of undiminished, even increased, vitality, the party and its possible victory had become truly credible. Piou could play a French "shadow prime minister" with de Mun as his *éminence grise.* Open attacks in the Chamber by the ministry only reinforced the party's dominant position among the opposition. Other factions were not "honored" by charges, always true and always unsubstantiated, that they accepted illegal contributions from the church and had compiled their own set of fiches on voters in precincts throughout the nation. Bonnet, the perpetually worried executive secretary of the Radicals, repeated his warnings of the previous year, singling out the party's "clever organization" and the dedication of its members, "imbued with the principles of Loyola."[41] Although only the Progressives under Paul Beauregard had never strayed far from the ALP since 1902, the other sections of the opposition would soon, Piou and de Mun thought with satisfaction, be trekking back to do obeisance in hope of receiving representation in Piou's potential cabinet and of dipping deeply into the ALP's campaign chest. As late as the spring of 1905 and the critical votes on the Separation bill, most of the ARD and Independents and even some of the Patrie Française resisted Piou's leadership. By fall the delights of autonomy and of snubbing the powerful had given way to decisions about the elections: to run for the ministry or against it. If the latter, then ALP support, seemingly well organized, with records on many voters, might have to be sought. As each individual deputy or faction made the pilgrimage to the Rue Las Cases, he asked what the ALP required as tribute. To all, Piou replied enigmatically that beyond calling for unspecified revision of the Separation law, any election coalition would draw up a "liberal" platform at the ALP's party congress in December.[42] This deliberate obscurity was a gamble, meant to forestall any movement to establish an alliance purely among centrist groups, including possibly the Union Démocratique of the majority, leaving the ALP with little claim to represent more than a Catholic right wing. Piou schemed to avoid alienating any possible base of support and thus maintain a broad coalition of opposition groups under him. By December, with the election only four months away, those who did finally oppose the ALP's platform might find it too late to make new alliances. Some who broke away would probably return for want of anywhere else to go. But there was also the risk that by December it might be too late for Piou and de Mun to impose any true unity on their coalition partners.

Some of Piou's reticence to make demands was based on the weakness of his personal political situation. However much it had freed him to campaign through the countryside and to oversee the organization of the ALP, his absence from the Chamber was galling to him and left him with the sense, if not the reality, of being in an equivocal and inferior position when dealing with the leaders of other factions. At first after 1902 he had paid little mind to where he might run in the next election except to declare that there had to be an easier seat than at Saint Gaudens against Jean Bepmale. When he did launch inquiries in early 1905 about a possible easy district, he found there were very few. He finally tried to settle in June upon Montfort in Ille-et-Vilaine, but to the horror of local ALP members, he was rebuffed by Catholic leaders who preferred to nominate one of their own rather than have the distinguished, and outsider, Piou forced upon them. Acutely sensitive of his own poor election record since 1892, Piou then briefly gave serious consideration to resigning in disgust and dismay. The organization and alliances he had vaunted were a failure. Only a sudden offer from conservatives in Mende dissuaded him. At that, the constituency, although a "safe seat," was in Lozère, nestled in the most insular and backward region of the country. It hardly seemed brave for the self-proclaimed leader of the opposition to retreat so far into the hinterland to assure himself election, and the majority press caricatured Piou's timidity mercilessly.[43]

De Mun had his own reasons for not making demands. He had decided that the ALP should make a great deal more of its social program than it had in 1902. Expecting the opposition of some possible allies, he planned to spring the issue on them at the party congress and overwhelm them with its potential for new support. Besides his basic commitment to social Catholicism, he continued to believe, and persuaded Piou to believe, that the conservatives might finally take the vote of the working class away from the Left. The record of the Radical-Socialist majority since 1900 on social legislation was barren, and Millerand had left the Combes ministry as soon as he discovered that his scheme for retirement pensions was not to be made an issue of confidence or even of policy. From without he relentlessly pursued a very independent political course and denounced Combes for constructing a policy so "abject" that it could "limit its horizons totally to harrying nuns." Millerand had even found kind words for Gailhard-Bancel's alternative proposal for pensions, admitting that they shared the same goals and sentiments. De Mun felt that if the conservatives could now adopt a realistic and forward program of social reform as part of their election platform, they could win away from the Radicals and Socialists some of the votes of a lower class perhaps disgusted with its supposed friends. He even outdid the Socialists for the ballots of the civil service by editorializing in *Le Gaulois* and *Le Figaro* that in theory public employees should have the right to unionize and even to strike. But aside from his personal efforts for thirty-five years, the conservatives had not distinguished themselves by their social mission. It was vital to de Mun's idea, therefore, that he exploit to the full what examples he had. Henri Bazire's term as president of the ACJF was over, but he had been succeeded by Jean Lerolle, son of the ALP deputy and orator, who was also amenable to suggestion by de Mun. When the ACJF held an impressive four-day conference in May 1905 at Albi on "conditions of work," his influence was everywhere, not least in the decision by *Le Gaulois* and *Le Figaro* to give the meeting wide coverage. By exerting all of his influence, de Mun was also able to win a remarkable concession from the ACJF leadership, a reversal of their long-held refusal to try to rejuvenate the *cercles* by assuming their charge. In February 1905 past president Henry Reverdy and Robert de Roquefeuil, the son of de Mun's deceased colleague Félix de Roquefeuil, became vice-presidents of the Oeuvre des Cercles. Bazire, Joseph Zamanski, Eugène Flornoy, Pierre Gerlier, and Charles Geoffroy de Grandmaison also came from the Jeunesse Catholique to fill important positions. Even de Mun realized that it was far too late to revive the *cercles* or for them to regain even a shadow of their original vitality, but if they could kick up sparks for only the few months before the election, for present political purposes even a dance of death would be sufficient.[44]

De Mun finally tipped his hand in mid-November, about a month before the congress was to convene in Paris, when the ALP administrative staff sent out questionnaires to each committee asking that their representatives come prepared to debate "social institutions" and "professional organization." This hint gained substance on the morning of 14 December, when, along with leading members of allied factions, fourteen hundred delegates from the provincial committees squeezed into the Salle de la Société de Géographie to hear Piou's keynote address set the tone of the congress. "Messieurs," he began, "the Separation law is a declaration of war against Catholics, one that we accept. The gauntlet has been cast down; we have only to pick it up!" But after raising his audience to their feet with such defiance, he reminded them that "as well as a political mission, we pursue at the same time a social work, and it should be perhaps the principal mission of our party, for men of courage and faith." Now the applause was more restrained, but in demanding that the party follow them on the issue of social reform, Piou and de Mun were insisting on their power at the apex of its hierarchy. During the final stages of the campaign, they wanted the confidence of knowing that the party would follow their orders faithfully. This insistence, somewhat in contrast to the ALP's previous emphasis on decentralization, continued in the afternoon, hardly giving the delegates time to digest their long Parisian lunches. Piou presided over the session, while administrators from the headquarters, Laya, Salvetti, and new associate Paul Séverac, sought to demonstrate that the party apparatus in Paris had comprehensive plans for organization and tactics and alone had the capability to choose the best course for the campaign. Local committees were praised for their success in recruiting forty thousand new members and founding five hundred new groups since 1902, raising the vital statistics on total membership and committees to two hundred thousand and twelve hundred, respectively. But the delegates simultaneously suffered through a scolding for failing to send dues payments to Paris promptly or even to keep membership rolls strictly up to date as required by the 1901 Associations law. They were also warned that their traditional tendency to subordinate all other issues to "religious defense" would be fatal—1902 had been the proof—and that a social platform to attract new voters was imperative.

No speeches or sessions were planned for the first evening,

and the provincial representatives returned the following morning somewhat chastened and sobered by their experience the preceding day. Now they were confronted by a long report on unions by Georges Maze-Sencier, a protégé of Gailhard-Bancel and de Mun, and were asked to endorse resolutions from it, specifically approving the spread of unionization among workers, terming such unions possible instruments of education, progress, and social pacification, and calling for owners to engage willingly in collective bargaining with their workers. Some portions of the ALP had never embraced the ideas of de Mun, and now their representatives sputtered at these sweeping goals. Fairly innocuous social resolutions like those of 1902 and even a few unions were acceptable to them as trappings to lure votes, but these sentiments sounded genuine this time and Maze-Sencier a zealot. What would happen to the average owner if he had to face his workers organized in a so-called union, asked industrialist André Bernard of the Nord. All unions were bad, he argued, and although some were better than others, there was no way to prevent them all from becoming socialist. The worker's lot was not to be improved by concessions from his hard-pressed employers; rather it was through the government's cutting taxes and closing infamous cabarets! Before anyone else could speak in such terms, Joseph Zamanski of the ACJF quickly stood up to proclaim that "a great party like the ALP has no future if it deliberately attacks the beneficial work of social reconciliation." This reproval imposed an embarrassed silence, and the resolutions were quickly approved in spite of the abstention of those who had protested.

Piou and de Mun had imposed their will, and the bitter draught administered, they arranged the remainder of the congress to be more palatable to the delegates. After dinner they were treated to the full-blown oratory of Paul Lerolle and a lesser effort by Amédée Reille, the younger of the Reille brothers, both of them deputies. The two produced that hyperbole of condemnation that makes many of the speeches at political conventions both rousing and tedious. Once again the delegates heard that the Radical-Socialist bloc would destroy God, the family, and the nation, and once again they stood and cheered to pledge that they would fight to the death to prevent it. Here was a chance to vent the frustrations they had accumulated since Piou's keynote address, and there was another the following day, when the morning and afternoon were given over to denunciations of the majority's injustices to the Catholic schools. By that evening much of the hard feelings about the social resolutions had disappeared in the freshly exercised hatred of the government, and Piou was able to orchestrate a remarkable series of speeches before them. On the dais to Piou's right sat Denys Cochin, the suave royalist who recently had been the party's foe, to his left, Beauregard, the leader of the Progressives. In turn both rose to endorse the ALP and to pledge the energetic support of his followers. Then Piou took the rostrum and in a few words set his audience aflame with a sense of coming triumph and toppled the sureties of French politics: "It is time, I have said, for union. To the monarchists, to those who have retained the faith of the past, I say: you are our allies, we fight at your side. To proven republicans, whom I see all about me, who have dreamed and hoped for an honest, liberal, and tolerant Republic, I say: if you want our concourse, our devotion, you have it. That is how we see our duty to France. We do not ask whether our allies are stronger or weaker than we are, whether they have more or less to profit from victory. That matters little. What does matter is that France wins!" Even some of the Independents came to their feet and cheered. For through a combination of promises and threats, Piou and de Mun had accomplished the delicate task of bringing into the party the remnant of the royalists from the Comité Catholique, while largely maintaining the alliance with the Progressives and some of the Independents. The appearance together of Cochin and Beauregard was a symbol of the pact in the coming election. Several leading members of the ARD and Independents, even such conservatives as Ribot and, of course, those who had voted for the Separation, refused further close relations with the ALP once there was the scent of Cochin's ilk within; about two-thirds of them left. Piou counted on retaining the other third and almost all of the Progressives. With the voting five months away, there was ample time to adapt these alliances at the national level to fit various local conditions.

The excitement of the evening was carried over undiminished into the following day, when a closing banquet was planned at the mammoth Restaurant Bonvalet. The impressive entrance to the "Marseillaise" was repeated, this time with even more pomp.

Champagne was poured with dessert, and Piou stood to toast his "loyal followers," urging, in his final exhortation, to "grasp a hand to the left and one from the right. Whoever combats the bloc and defends liberty is our ally, whoever he may be, from wherever he may come!" It was an emotional moment, with the delegates standing to cheer, when the sudden sight of de Mun preparing to speak caused a stunned hesitation and then frenzied applause. Cajoling the royalists and planning the alliance in the weeks before the congress had sapped his strength. He had hardly appeared at the sessions, and now he could say only a few words. But at such a moment, he claimed, no one could keep silent, all had to do their duty. He was almost overcome by the acclamation, but when he began to speak the banquet hall was utterly still. He called himself, as so many times before, a "Catholic above all else, resolved to subordinate all political questions to the defense of his faith," a faith sorely tried often in the past by its enemies but never found wanting. It would not fail now. This faith of his was broad; to be a Catholic meant not just the practice of religion but devotion to liberty, patriotism, and social justice. It was, he affirmed, the commitment of the ALP to these virtues that made the party strong. All it lacked was victory, and it should seek that "in the hearts of the small and humble people, where springs forth the inexhaustible source of sacrifice and devotion. There is the root of your strength. There is the supreme hope for tomorrow, toward which today, with the last effort of my voice, I cast the most profound cry of my soul." The impact of his words, his very exertion in addressing them, was overwhelming, and as he sat back down the applause redounded, continuing for many minutes as a standing ovation. No more effective appeal for the social platform could have been devised; no more effective finale to the congress could have been planned.[45] The delegates caught their trains that evening convinced that they would soon make Piou the premier of France and de Mun the conscience of the nation.

By seriously mishandling the initial application of the Separation law in early 1906, the Rouvier ministry almost immediately contributed to the ALP's confidence and, seemingly, to its chances for victory. On 29 December 1905 and 2 January 1906, the ministers of public worship and the interior sent out circulars to the prefects ordering an inventory of the movable property in every one of the many church buildings now belonging to the state. Many Catholics mistrusted the motives of the government, de Mun writing in *Le Figaro* and *L'Univers* that here was the first step in a general confiscation of church goods, but at this point there was no hint of obstruction. De Mun's editorials counseled the faithful not to provoke confrontations, and he wrote Bazire that "a passive attitude is the only practical, prudent, and dignified one." On 11 January, however, *La Croix*, alerted by an informant, confirmed rumors that anticlericals would profane sacred objects by revealing that even the consecrated Host and relics were to be examined by the surveyors. In the following day's *Le Gaulois* de Mun urged Catholics to "fruitful intransigence." The sudden shift in tactics came from a judgment by Piou and de Mun that the maladroit conduct of the government had once more transformed the question of the church from a chronic irritant into an issue of paramount importance. The outrage of the inventories would convert the lethargic to action, and the ALP would be ready, as in 1902, to organize them first into demonstrations and then into loyal voters. Heedless of their own warnings at the congress, they recklessly discarded all other appeals, including the carefully planned social platform, to gamble on the religious. During the next two months, many sections of the country were in chaos as fervent Catholics resisted the inventories; the ALP was the precipitating force.[46]

Serious riots and confrontations broke out first in Paris and set the pattern for the rest of the country. Here demonstrators blocked the entrance of government officials into Saint Pierre de Gros-Caillou and Sainte Clothilde, piling up heaps of chairs before the doors of the sanctuaries. Police had to dismantle the crude barricades, and inevitable scuffling and jostling broke out between them and the demonstrators. Each time, de Mun, Cochin, and Paul Lerolle, who disingenuously claimed merely to be walking in the neighborhood, intervened to prevent serious violence. But Marc Sangnier, working closely with the ALP at least in political matters, and Baroness Reille, mother of the two deputies and leader of the Ligue Patriotique des Françaises, had used inflammatory words to rouse the crowds originally and belied the peacemaking of the ALP. In *Le Figaro* de Mun called the government's policy "religious war." As long as it did not become excessive, minor violence, after all, did seem in the interest of the party since it would create harder feelings toward the ministry, bruised heads to exacerbate bruised sentiments. In the provinces local members of the ALP, ACJF, and even the Sillon played the role of their leaders in Paris, and within a few days Rouvier realized that particularly in conservative parts of the country the government faced almost open rebellion.

Once again the Bretons brandished their harpoons and shotguns, and in many other places the demonstrators carried only slightly less lethal clubs. Almost everywhere the ALP pasted up seditious posters, especially one entitled "Pourquoi Ces Crimes?" turned out by the thousands from Féron-Vrau's presses. In response the premier refused to entertain debate on his conduct of the inventories and told his prefects to take vigorous countermeasures. They called up detachments of troops, used hatchets to break down locked doors, and sentenced active resisters, including young girls, to prison terms. Police began swinging their own clubs with abandon and occasionally firing weapons over the heads of the crowd. Violence begot violence. By mid-February Piou and de Mun had become deeply worried that their plans for resistance had gotten out of hand, but they no longer had control over those they had inflamed. On 6 March at Boeschêpe, a small town in the Nord, a demonstrator fired at the police as they broke through a barricade into the church. They shot him dead with their return fire. Rouvier could no longer avoid a withering attack from all sides for his failure to quiet the country. When his response was weak and insufficient, he badly lost a vote of confidence. Jean Sarrien, a journeyman politician who led a group of moderate Radicals and was neither truly attractive nor truly offensive to any other faction of the majority, replaced him. To mollify the intransigents of the Left and to strengthen his cabinet, the new premier took Clemenceau as his minister of the interior, but the priest-eater disappointed his followers. Instead of pursuing the inventories with even more rigor and repression, he announced their suspension with the sarcastic aside that calculating the value of cathedral chandeliers was not worth the loss of even a drop of French blood.[47]

De Mun was exultant. Here was proof, he wrote in *Le Gaulois*, that "the law of Separation has been checked by the spontaneous resistance of the people." Clemenceau had admitted the impotence of the government. And, matching the valor of the Catholic laity, the pope had finally pronounced an opinion on the Separation, anathematizing it root and branch. In *Vehementer nos*, issued 11 February but published on 18 February, Pius X condemned the unilateral separation of church and state and declared the Separation unacceptable because in spite of the celebrated addition to Article IV—"according to the rules of the organization of the faith,"—there were insufficient guarantees that the religious associations would not provoke schism. By proscribing the associations, Pius dared the government to confiscate all church property in December 1906 when the deadline for their formation would be reached. But in March de Mun felt that the wager was a safe one. Short of calling the Vatican's bluff and converting the churches into meeting halls, an act certain to provoke more of the bloody riots the government was now hoping to avoid, the authorities had no threat to use as a means of enforcing the law against the solid resistance of French Catholics. In late December and January, when the papal decision was still in doubt, the high French episcopacy had tentatively agreed that the "difficulties" with the religious associations could be overcome. Even after *Vehementer nos* twenty-three Catholic Académiciens and intellectuals, the so-called Green Cardinals from the color of their regalia, had delivered a letter to the pope expressing a similar hope. Although the Green Cardinals included Denys Cochin and Ferdinand Brunetière, de Mun had no qualms in replying to them in *La Croix* on 28 March. The intellectuals had clever arguments, he admitted, and in trying to preserve the patrimony of the French church they were well-intentioned. But "the people," he insisted, knew instinctively what could be endured and what could not; they had the "invincible power of simplicity," sure in the conviction that the Separation was wrong and demonstrating that any government trying to enforce it could be stopped.[48] This was an argument, or more accurately a gamble, that seemed to match up to reality, but one de Mun should have realized depended on the victory of the ALP in the elections.

It was a victory de Mun expected and Clemenceau feared. To prevent it the minister of the interior had been willing to grant the ALP an apparent success, the suspension of the inventories, in order to conduct a strategic retreat by the government. From the ministry at the Place Beauvau he had the task of winning the elections for the government, and with the first ballot scheduled for 6 May, the situation was urgent. He considered soberly that if riots and demonstrations still convulsed the nation at the time of the voting, many normally progovernment supporters might accept the ALP's charge that the Radicals and Socialists pursued a religious war. Already opposition posters in garish colors accused them of planning to padlock the churches after 9 December because the pope had forbidden the formation of the religious associations. The implications were listed in frightening language, and the posters concluded with the stern warning that the only way to assure the continuance of the sacraments was to elect a new majority. Clemenceau nullified much of this threat by ordering all enforcement of the Separation law to cease. De Mun's delight in proclaiming the impotence of the ministry aided his task by encouraging local opposition leaders to misjudge the government's strength and determination. But having secured his flank, Clemenceau did not underestimate the potential of the ALP and its allies. Well informed by the Sûreté of the party's development and plans, he was determined to attack and discredit it. He found his chance in the back files of the police reports, in the allegation that in an overly clever attempt further to undermine confidence in the government, Piou had secretly given money to the syndicalist Confédération Générale du Travail (CGT) in January with which to foment strikes and labor unrest in the weeks prior to the elections, particularly on 1 May, Labor Day. Even according to the otherwise unsubstantiated informant, little money changed hands, and the operation could never have amounted to more than a minor harassment. It was uncharacteristic of Piou or de Mun to deal with the extreme Left or to play the game of *agent provocateur* with organized labor, and the government was never able to produce proof of the charge. Clemenceau pretended, however, to have stumbled upon a plot in which ALP and CGT groups around the country were supposed to have planned revolutionary disturbances for May Day, and he dramatically announced his discovery in late April. The government newspapers gave the report banner headlines, and to make his charges seem realistic, Clemenceau called up troops from the provinces to man key points. Housewives in the wealthy districts were terrified and hoarded stores of nonperishable goods in preparation for a siege. This concoction caught the

ALP completely by surprise, coming as it did in the last stages of the campaign. Through the *Bulletin* and the press network Piou and de Mun issued indignant, then desperate, denials, but fear is easier to instill than to dissipate.[49]

Although Briand, elevated to minister of public worship under Sarrien, recalled later that he and the rest of the cabinet opened the first returns from the balloting with much foreboding and trembling of hands, Clemenceau's devious strategy, to halt enforcement of the Separation law and to charge the ALP with revolutionary conspiracy, ended whatever slim possibility there may have been for an opposition triumph. In order to win their self-predicted victory, the ALP and its allies had not only to retain the new voters they had captured in 1902 but also to attract those who supported the Union Démocratique and some of the ARD, those centrists who had moved to the Radical camp. But these Frenchmen would disavow their favorites only if they believed that the government was not just anticlerical but anti-Catholic and that the ALP, as the leading member of the opposition, offered a moderate, sane alternative. Before Clemenceau took charge, the ALP felt that it could win them through its wealth, propaganda, organization, and fervor. Afterward, even the party realized that this hope was illusory. The backers of the moderate Left were reassured by the government's restraint and terrified of what the ALP might have planned.

Even without Clemenceau's machinations, there had been only a slight chance of victory for the opposition. Although the members of the ALP election coalition worked in almost perfect harmony on the local level and provided the maximum gains possible for the opposition, the temper of the country had changed from 1902, when the antiministerial forces had come close to an upset. Appeals to save the nation, church, and private property from godless Socialists and Radicals were not sufficient this time to win elections outside of conservative bastions, even when delivered by parties with exemplary organization. In spite of all the measures taken against it, the church remained in existence and continued to administer the sacraments. The rule of the Radicals in alliance with the Socialists had not brought ruin to the country. Instead, if the problems with the administration of the Separation law could be resolved, it could be hoped that the incumbents might provide a high degree of stability. A victory by the opposition, on the other hand, would mean an effort to reverse all of the changes of the previous six years and cause further intense turmoil. The average French voter in 1906 sought stability and found the ALP, especially with its new burden of royalists, unlikely to provide it. Realizing the obvious danger of remaining in sterile opposition, about two-thirds of the Independents, mostly members of the ARD, deserted the ALP after its incorporation of the royalists, supported candidates against the ALP election coalition in about one hundred constituencies, and cost the opposition fifty-seven deputies, forty-six Independents who would now support the ministry and eleven seats where the presence of a ministerial Independent in the race led to the victory of a Radical or Socialist. The small chance of the ALP and its allies was even exploited by Clemenceau to whip up support among the government's voters and to ensure the solidarity of the Radicals and Socialists. In these circumstances, it is hardly surprising that the ALP coalition suffered a serious reverse, winning only 41 percent of the popular vote and only 190 deputies, 64 from the ALP, 83 Progressives, and 43 Independents. Both the Progressives and the Independents who remained with the ALP generally held their own, winning in their traditional strongholds. The ALP sustained a major setback, dropping fourteen seats. Most of the new royalist members of the party were defeated as the political strength of monarchism reached bottom. The rest of the losses came principally from among the new deputies elected in 1902, largely in sections of the Nord and the North-East, where the strategies of the previous election failed and where the deputy had not had sufficient time to ingratiate himself with the voters. Only the West, the South-West, and some few other sections of the Nord remained solidly in ALP control.[50]

To some extent these losses stemmed from what would become an axiom of the Third Republic, that an opposition party of the Right or Center had but two elections in which to produce a triumph; failure would mean inevitable disintegration. Piou and de Mun came to feel considerable pressure to defeat the Radicals and Socialists by 1906. French Catholics, the main element in the party's following, unreasonably feared that the influence of the church might be totally destroyed if the anticlericals were not quickly removed from power. More important, allies to both flanks,

Progressives and Independents on the Left, the royalists on the Right, could be united with the ALP only briefly and tenuously, and only if victory seemed imminent. Driven to produce an immediate one, Piou and de Mun made errors that became institutionalized as flaws in the party's structure and image. With only four years in which to complete a national organization, there was sometimes insufficient time to allow cadres to develop naturally, and many provincial and regional party committees were artificially stimulated from Paris. The number of committees, twelve hundred by 1906, was impressive, but too often local initiative, imperative during the actual conduct of an election, was lacking. A more serious defect was the popular impression of the ALP as the "Catholic party," since despite the variety of issues in its platform it essentially campaigned on a single one, the defense of the established church. Although it was difficult to develop others at a time when anticlericalism seemed to overshadow all else, de Mun, and to a lesser extent Piou, were aware of this overemphasis and fought to add a social program that would attract broader support. Nevertheless, the party continued to appeal primarily to outraged Catholics, and it was clear that the chief concern of the party's founders was the church and that all other causes were relegated to an inferior status, as was the social platform after resistance to the inventories began. The ALP could readily claim as its own all of those who truly cared for the maintenance of traditional religion, but this group could never be an electoral majority: in Belle Epoque France, anticlericalism was too strong a component of the conception of sociopolitical emancipation. In the circumstances, the party became caught in a basic contradiction, with its platform and claims broad and its real focus and possible base of support narrow.

These flaws decisively influenced the ALP's relationship with its allies, for the election of 1906 destroyed forever the vast hopes of the party. Henceforth its objectives would be much less grandiose than "victory." The bid of de Mun and Piou to make it the nucleus of a great conservative party had to be judged a failure, and there was considerable danger that the election alliance might split permanently into its component parts. In the history of coalition politics in France, an offended member had always broken away to practice a *politique du pire*, and de Mun and Piou constantly feared such a disintegration of their own carefully constructed one. Despite leading the wealthiest, strongest, and best-organized element in the opposition, they did not, therefore, impose their own ideas or even true discipline very often on their allies. By refraining from the dictation of policy, they held it together through the 1906 voting, but this delicate approach showed no promise of preventing fragmentation after the defeat, not having tempered the brittle nature of the coalition relationship. Supported by Pius X, some conservatives might consider that the voting had written finis to the Ralliement. Tired of opposition and hungry to reenter a governing majority, the remaining Independents and the Progressives might eventually compromise their fiscal principles sufficiently to wean the Radicals from the Socialists. These defections would leave the ALP solely a Catholic confessional party, exactly what it had labored to avoid. There was no doubt that de Mun and Piou would have to reconsider their strategy as they attempted to regroup their shattered legions.

7
The New Course: The Search, 1906–1910

The disaster of 1906 proved that the original strategy of the ALP could not lead to victory. Continuous, though responsible, opposition in the Chamber and demagogic appeals in the countryside were not sufficient. Neither was a platform that, although progressive and not purely negative, did little more than assert on each issue the reverse of the Left. The ALP would not be transformed into the great party of the Right, nor Piou into the next premier. To register substantial new gains, the party would have to develop different issues, carry out more imaginative tactics in the legislature, and yet do nothing to jeopardize its relations with coalition partners or alienate its basic bloc of popular support. This would present an insuperable task to de Mun and Piou, and they would never find the means to win a general election. The ALP's dissensions could only increase in the wake of the election debacle, new issues were difficult to create and even more so to exploit, and a bold strategy in the Chamber could bring results only if the Left, so powerfully in command, began to splinter. The present was dismal. The first task for them was to demonstrate that the party and its sixty-four deputies had not lapsed into a defeated silence. The *Bulletin* accused the government of election fraud and blamed all of the party's defeats on these "infamies" and on Clemenceau's trumped-up charge of a plot. It also coordinated the exultation, and relief, at Piou's return to the Chamber, although somewhat less dramatically than he had intended, and announced that Piou himself would undertake an inquiry into the party's unexpectedly poor showing. In quick succession, leading party members kept the ALP name prominent by introducing bills to institute proportional voting in all French elections, establish a supreme court on the American model, grant free medical care to the indigent, and organize labor in corporations. The last proposal, a social Catholic reply to the syndicalist unions of the Socialists, was sponsored by de Mun. Workers and employers would join self-governing occupational groups that would control collective bargaining, arbitration and conciliation, industrial regulations, vocational training, social insurance, and welfare programs within each industry. The bill represented a national, lay, and compulsory version of the social theory de Mun had advocated since founding the *cercles* in 1871. It was the most ambitious social idea of the ALP, a revival and extension of the promises made before the 1906 elections but forgotten in the months of the inventories. In August both de Mun and Piou would defend the party's social programs as a means to recruit new voters.[1] The introduction of such legislation was, however, merely for emphasis. As the Radicals and Socialists had no intention of enacting opposition proposals, all of the ALP bills met a quick death in committee.

Piou was also anxious publicly and finally to refute Clemenceau's accusation that he had plotted with the CGT. On 10 July, almost as soon as his election was validated, he indignantly demanded that the minister of the interior withdraw his charges or bring him to trial. The elections won, Clemenceau had little desire to risk the ministry's reputation on a verdict that would have to lean on meager evidence, principally a single report by an informant. Certain of his majority, he smoothly replied that the government had, in its magnanimity, decided to grant a general amnesty for the "plot" and that the question was henceforth closed. Piou and his supporters argued vainly that an amnesty could apply only to those already found guilty; no one from the party had even been indicted. There would be no way to clear the record. Shut off from further debate in the Chamber, they tried to keep the issue current in the press, but it was quickly overshadowed by the question of the French church's acquiescence to the Separation law.[2]

From 30 May to 1 June 1906, the French bishops had met in Paris in plenary session, an assembly that ironically would have been forbidden by the Organic Articles of the Concordat. Like Pius X they condemned the Separation law in principle, but unlike him, they could not do so with disinterest and asked to be allowed to seek a modus vivendi with the law. His Holiness refused this request on 10 August in the encyclical *Gravissimo*, published four days later, and the bishops, reconvening in early September, acknowledged their submission to his orders. The law required that if the church did not comply with its provisions within a year's time, by 11 December 1907, all church property could be secularized. Trapped by the decision of the pope, the bishops had to make provision for income by imposing the *denier du culte*, a levy on communicants, and prepare to see the state expropriate the cathedrals, parish churches, bishops' palaces, and rectories. Clemenceau, who already exercised the dominant influence in the Sarrien cabinet and would become premier in fact on 25 October, remembered the violence of the inventories and hoped to avoid a new conflict. But his obtuse effort in a speech at La Roche-sur-Yon to separate the bishops from their pope was maladroit. As earlier in the year, French Catholics were determined not to accede to the government's plans. If it wanted to despoil the church, it would have to assume the onus itself. Typically, de Mun was the principal spokesman of the ALP for this grim determination. He applauded *Gravissimo* and the bishops' unanimous adherence to it—this time there was no Talleyrand—and then he assailed Clemenceau, outraged that in his speech this "malevolent Jacobin" should pillory ultramontanes as "mauvais français" and term the pope "a foreign power." Pius had rightly, de Mun claimed, refused to treat with an ultimatum, and no matter what the plans of the Radical ministry, "France and the church have between them a long and mysterious alliance, which, through long travails, has formed the body and fashioned the soul of our nation. That cannot be abolished." He counseled the faithful to remain calm even if the state should close the churches since no power yet had ever triumphed over the church for long, "history being her perpetual revenge over the pride of her enemies."[3]

After Clemenceau replaced Sarrien as premier, he responded to these words with a policy combining sanctions and appeasement, neither of which was effective. He began in early November by suddenly carrying out all of the postponed inventories, always with a show of force, usually mounted guards, to ward off hostile demonstrators. Local ALP leaders rarely revived the protests of the spring, but churchmen, although sullen, did not break. Simultaneously, Clemenceau's supple minister of public worship, Briand, who had guided the Separation bill's passage through the Chamber and whose prestige depended on the law's success, sought to strike a compromise. He begged Catholics to allow the Separation a chance to operate before condemning it. As a gesture of conciliation, he offered to extend by another year the time for the church to form religious associations and to grant priests free use of the churches if they would present a declaration of such intent to commune authorities annually. Piou and de Mun immediately replied to crush his hopes: why forswear the pope to follow Briand? Through Monsignor Carlo Montagnini, who had been assistant to the nuncio and who remained in Paris after his superior's recall, the Vatican informed Cardinal-Archbishop Richard that French priests must no longer admit any state authority over religious services and under no circumstances make any yearly declaration. Richard promptly publicized these instructions in a 7 December circular to the episcopacy. Incensed at his double failure, Clemenceau decided to enforce brutally the letter of the Separation law.[4]

On 11 December 1906, the premier ordered police to break into the nunciature on the Rue de l'Elysée, seize Montagnini's papers, and convey him to the Swiss border forthwith. Before the Chamber that same day he defended this profanation of diplomatic privilege by accusing Montagnini of nefarious but undisclosed plots. During the next week he ordered priests and bishops expelled from their rectories and palaces. This callousness came to a climax in Paris on 17 December, when gendarmes evicted the aged and infirm Richard, who, carried on a litter, was forced to fly from the persecution of 1906 as his uncle, a bishop during the Revolution, had been compelled to flee the Terror of 1793. These provocative acts produced the demonstrations notably absent the previous month and stiffened the resolve of most Catholics to reject the formulas of the government. The resort to force had not succeeded, and Clemenceau, always ready to seek a scapegoat, sent special agents to break into Piou's villa at Saint-Gaudens to look for potentially incriminating evidence linking him to the demonstrations. They found nothing of political value, but perhaps they discovered something else untoward since Piou, who learned of the burglary very quickly, revealed the premier's illegality only in a posthumous memoir.[5]

Despite their antagonistic relationship, Piou provided Clemenceau a possible escape from the impasse. Speaking authoritatively as the leader of the "Catholic party" in denouncing the treatment of Richard, Piou suggested that while the church would continue to insist that the French state regularize its relations with the Vatican by negotiating the terms of the Separation, the clergy and laity could accept a situation in which the government did not single them out in any fashion. At the urging of Briand, Clemenceau seized this opportunity, and in the laws of 2 January and 28 March 1907, enabled priests to become the "unofficial occupants" of the churches. The Vatican agreed to this procedure, and the government in effect remanded permanent custody of the churches to the priests. As de Mun explained it in *Le Gaulois*, instead of a single Concordat for the entire nation, there would now be "thirty-six thousand little concordats concluded by the mayors of all the communes with the priests of all the parishes, the bishop, in the name of the pope, authorizing this, the prefect, in the name of the government, authorizing that." The compromise ended the disputes about the Separation, but it was a victory only for calm and peace. The anticlericals were forced to grant this concession, and the church, stripped of all its property but the church buildings themselves, accepted a nearly ruinous loss. But by their vigor in the crisis, the pope, French Catholics, and the clergy had shown that the church was not moribund and won new respect, although by no means love, from many hostile to it. This response laid the basis for important, even shocking, new conversions during the few years before 1914, Charles Péguy, the ardent Dreyfusard, and Ernest Psichari, the grandson of Joseph Ernest Renan. De Mun saw this revival as early as January 1907, proclaiming in *Le Gaulois* the first success for the united front of Catholicism.[6]

Although few realized it at the time, the settlement of the Separation controversy ended the period of sharpest church-state conflict during the Third Republic. There would soon be more trouble over the schools, and particularly over what Catholic parents would term "ungodly" textbooks, but tempers would not again be so hot nor emotions so ugly as during the previous ten years. Nevertheless, anticlericalism remained a stock item in the vocabulary of the Radicals—the words had become a ritual—and leaders on the Right, including de Mun, would feel compelled to respond in equally harsh terms. Partly because they did not recognize any ebbing of the resentments amidst these verbal pyrotechnics, conservatives saw the Separation as the first victory in an assault on all French tradition. Believing their own rhetoric and that of their opponents, they began to succumb to a paranoia, fearing that they, and by extension, *their* France, were besieged. They found much to encourage this belief. Besides the Separation law, 1905 had brought the Moroccan crisis, which upon reflection revealed just how woefully unprepared France was to wage war in defense of its North African interests. At the same time the militancy of workers and peasants began to seem increasingly dangerous. Many of them were syndicalists, whose incendiary language assailed the bourgeoisie and whose prophet, Georges Sorel in his *Réflexions sur la violence* of 1906, would sanctify the general strike and urge anarchic destruction as a purgative. At a congress in 1906 at Amiens, the CGT, its ranks heavily infiltrated by syndicalists and anarchists, endorsed an antimilitarist resolution, leading many of the middle class to fear that if the workers did not topple the state from within, they would allow it to be crushed from without.[7]

As a concern for the "preservation" of France, a sense of decadence in the country, came to replace the church as the dominant issue in the minds of the conservatives, new splits appeared in their ranks, so recently and tenuously united by the ALP. Some became fey, loudly bemoaning the doom to come and its inevitability. At times the ALP's *Bulletin* and some of the party's deputies joined this chorus of banshees, Piou occasionally among their number. Several others, barely repentant royalists like Denys Cochin, considered that the Ralliement had been proved an utter failure and deserted de Mun and Piou for a new pressure group, the Action Française. Its leader, the deaf and dogmatic intellectual Charles Maurras, concealed behind a doctrine of "integral nationalism" his proposed marriage of reactionary elitist royalism to the popular radical creed of chauvinism. In various tracts, especially *L'Enquête sur la monarchie* of 1900, he claimed that France's tradition was Catholic, military, and agrarian, but that the nation had been diverted from it by the men who had come to power after 1789, Protestants, Jews, and *métèques*—literally foreigners, but Maurras's all-inclusive epithet for those he disliked. Beginning in the spring of 1908, the group published a daily newspaper, *L'Action Française*, and attempted to subvert the Republic by vomiting vitriol on its leaders—Maurras's assistant Léon Daudet was a master practitioner of slander—and issuing calls for hooliganism in the streets, ably carried out by its youth brigade, the Camelots du roi. Although not believers, the leaders of the Action Française tried to capitalize on Catholic sentiment by adopting the traditional royalist pledge that the overthrow of the Republic would bring a revival of church authority and privilege. Maurras and his circle were essentially negative men, their movement hopelessly untimely and futile. Before 1914 its accomplishments were limited to splitting the conservatives and winning the condemnation of both the Vatican—although the censure was not made public until 1926, so little did Pius X and his successor love the enemies that the Action Française attracted—and the pretender, the Duke d'Orleans, whose causes it ostensibly sought to espouse.[8]

The response of de Mun to the same anxieties was not to reject the Ralliement, the labor of fifteen years, but to shift the direction of his efforts. Like Maurras he would devote his energies to leading France back to its traditions, but he would do so within the Republic. For issues he had merely to trace his own career, the continuation of social reform, the revival of the church, and the championing of the army and with it nationalism. These three threads interweave to form the pattern and fabric of de Mun's thought and writing between 1907 and 1910. They were the basis of the new course he sought for the conservatives, and for him they were interdependent. Socialism and antimilitarism raged because France had deserted the church; the churches were empty because Frenchmen no longer upheld the nation's ancient tradition of Catholicism and nationalism. He considered that the disasters of May and June 1907 in the French Midi, long a land of deserted churches and the seedbed of the Radical party, proved the burden of his ideas. Grape growers and their workers, who had barely recovered from the waste of phylloxera, found their product undersold by cheap imports and themselves reduced to penury. They formed violent mobs, and Clemenceau was forced to call out the army. But rather than fire on the insurgents, whole companies, originally recruited from the area, mutinied, laid down their weapons, and joined the demonstrators. De Mun was horrified. His harshest words were for the government, and not merely because it had failed to attenuate the crisis with tariff protection or to prevent the agitation of the syndicalists and some opportunists from the Action Française who had contributed to the trouble. Far worse was that the government had allowed the army to reach such a state.[9]

For more than a decade elements within the public school system had increasingly treated patriotism with the same "neutrality" as religion, declaring it a personal decision and actually encouraging a more universal ideal than allegiance to a single country. The Dreyfus affair had badly tarnished the reputation of the army, and afterward, young state schoolteachers considered the open expression of antimilitarism part of their emancipation from the beliefs of the past. The Radical governments since 1898 had regarded the army as a stepchild but still found it necessary to call out the troops whenever there were violent demonstrations, most often in the case of strikes or mob action as in the Midi. Since it was usually directed against their supporters, the Socialists particularly regarded the army as their foe, and one wing of the party, led by Gustave Hervé, initiated a widespread campaign to undermine discipline among working-class recruits. Between 1907 and 1909 the number of desertions increased from five thousand to seventeen thousand a year. Clearly, de Mun argued, the Radical governments were reaping the harvest they had allowed to be sown. Early in 1907 he publicized the new disclosure that among army recruits from the state schools five years earlier, 36 percent did not know of the war of 1870–71, 42 percent did not know that it had been then that France lost Alsace and Lorraine, 50 percent had not heard of Jeanne d'Arc—who suffered presumably because she was both a religious and a patriotic figure—and an incredible 75 percent could not adequately explain why 14 July was a national holiday. He admitted that the figures entered the realm of the fantastic, but in July 1908, under intense pressure and questioning, the head of France's state primary education system for the previous decade, Ferdinand Buisson, an important Radical and a leading Freemason, acknowledged unhappily that they were clearly possible, that the situation had if anything grown worse, and that illiteracy among recruits had actually increased since the state closed many of the clerical schools and assumed much more of the burden of educating French youth.[10]

De Mun regarded socialism's evolution into a godless, antimilitarist creed as one of the chief seats of the evil, and his basic convictions ensured that he considered part of his task the revival of social Catholicism as an alternative. No one could charge that he had ever forsaken his devotion to his brand of Christian socialism, but his emergence as the dominant politician among the conservatives, the onset of his angina, and the immediate requirements of defending the church from anticlericalism and of constructing the ALP had driven him to neglect it. Without his constant attention, the Oeuvre des Cercles had faltered badly, and by 1905 de Mun had been compelled to ask the ACJF, formed originally to provide the *cercles* with young leaders, to absorb it. He had insisted that the ALP develop a social Catholic program and introduce legislation to implement it, but despite much bravado, the social initiatives had never become the party's great aim. The ideas he had launched seemed to make little headway without his personal direction. He was unwilling to allow social Catholicism to die for the want of his effort, but where and how should that effort be expended? He could no longer speak in the Chamber, the *cercles* were all but dead, the appeal of the ACJF and Sangnier's Sillon was not very broad, and the ALP's platform had not proved an altogether suitable sounding board. But during the preceding five years he had acquired an entirely new constituency, the readership that followed his editorials in *Le Gaulois*, *Le Figaro*, *La Croix*, and, beginning in 1908, *L'Echo de Paris*. His was a famous name, and *L'Echo* alone had a circulation of more than one hundred thousand copies daily.

De Mun launched his new campaign in the press, and by selecting only a few issues for attention, he could force concentration on them, as in his detailed condemnation of the abuses suffered by bakery workers and by the *travailleuses à domicile*, the women who sewed clothes at home for dress designers in a modern putting-out system. Did the Parisian housewife know the human cost of having her *petit pain* fresh each morning, out of the oven less than an hour, of having the latest "creation" from her couturier within twenty-four hours, no matter how demanding the material or the design? He called for more humane treatment of baker apprentices, and he introduced legislation to provide the women in home sweatshops with a minimum wage. It was embarrassing to the government that no one before de Mun had taken up these causes. This embarrassment turned to anger when he continued to support the freedom to strike of state employees and defended the PTT (Postal, Telegraph, and Telephone) civil servants when they did go out on strike for two months beginning in March 1909, creating chaos in communication. Doing so separated him from almost all of the conservatives and even the Independents, but de Mun was consistent, claiming the rights and privileges of unionization and collective action for all. It was the future basis of the nation, he argued, and there was an obligation to determine whether the form it took would be the syndicalism of the CGT or the corporatism implicit in social Catholicism. He counted it a great triumph when the long strike in 1909 of the building trades unions in Paris was settled by a collective contract between all owners and unions.[11]

In late 1908 he published *Ma Vocation sociale*, his memoirs of the founding of the Oeuvre des Cercles, reminding both Left and Right how successful the *cercles* had once been. He dedicated them to the memory of his brother Robert and to La Tour du Pin, who, although firmly allied to Maurras and the Action Française, contributed a touching letter of gratitude, calling the pages "the history of all I have loved the most." Self-consciously, de Mun recalled his own conversion to this faith, "this great movement, both Catholic and social, which thirty-seven years ago caught up many men of my generation and decided their lives." He was immensely pleased when the book proved to be unexpectedly popular, with readers exhausting two press runs of it before the end of the year. In the months immediately before and after, de Mun emphasized to the conservatives who read *Le Figaro* and the masses who bought *L'Echo de Paris* that the reluctance of the bourgeoisie to grant the legitimate demands of the working class had determined the success of the violent syndicalists and Socialists. Surely if the workers were not offered good leadership, they would perforce follow bad. In a mixture of irony and despair, he wondered how, after nearly forty years of social Catholic effort, some conservatives still condemned any government intervention as socialist. At the Paris diocesan congress in 1908 de Mun had formulated a resolution calling for a minimum wage for the *travailleuses à domicile*, and although he had carried his motion, he had been bitterly opposed by Count d'Haussonville, a spokesman for the Orleanist pretender. In an apostrophe to that type, de Mun asked,

"What progress, what general amelioration in the condition of the workers and their families during the past half century has been accomplished by the sole effort of personal charity, by the free exercise of private initiative?" He took his readers on walking tours of working-class districts to prove his point and to claim that as the most energetic of the post-Separation priests advanced boldly into these strongholds of the Socialists, they won conversions and carried effective social Catholic works with them. "What institution, what party," he boasted, "can now offer such a spectacle?"[12]

Le Temps, the lordly bastion of laissez-faire and official anticlericalism, took note and serious offense at de Mun's new campaign for reform through the auspices of the church. Throughout the summer of 1909 it denounced what the editors called his "rousing of popular passions" and repeated the hackneyed charge that Socialists and social Catholics were equally dangerous. It also expressed consternation that in Cologne sixty thousand workers carried both union and religious banners in the midst of a church procession; were not the church and the working class enemies? When, at de Mun's urging, first the ALP and then Archbishop Léon Amette, who replaced Cardinal Richard in Paris upon the latter's death in early 1908, called for an end to night labor in bakeries, the editors termed the action "clerical demagogy," moving de Mun to wonder openly whether *Le Temps* might now actually fear the new influence of the church. Certainly it was taking him more seriously, publishing on the front page in January 1910 an interview he granted to the paper's Joseph Bois and admitting that it could no longer deny the revival of religious influence.[13]

In 1875 de Mun's passionate devotion to social reform had led him to resign his cavalry commission to enter politics. Although he left the army, it remained his second great love, and his speeches to the Chamber on military affairs were always among his most eloquent and stirring. He had poured into the army his entire youth, and from it he had emerged the man he was. Old bonds of kinship and a sense of duty carried over from fifteen years in the officer corps defined his defense of the army during the Dreyfus affair. He saw the army as a bulwark of order and tradition and as the nation's only shield in any possible war. It had to be nurtured, defended, forgiven. The slow improvement in his health and the lessening of the controversy about the church gave de Mun greater opportunity to reflect on the army as well as on social reform. The campaigns of his friend Lyautey in Morocco near Oudjda in 1904 and 1905 and the Tangier crisis awakened his memories of African service. The André scandal and the mutiny in the Midi evoked his outrage. He was deeply disturbed by what he saw as the disorganization of the military and a profound discouragement among the officers. Martial vocations were lacking—"our time has lost the cult of heroes"—and the number of candidates for Saint Cyr dropped from 1,920 in 1897 to 982 in 1907. Almost 50 percent of the graduates of the Ecole Polytechnique were resigning their commissions within three to five years. It was a symptom of decadence, a "symptôme douloureux," that would preoccupy him increasingly.[14]

What later became de Mun's obsession with national defense and a pompous sense of duty to awaken the dormant nationalism within Frenchmen began in the spring of 1907 with a short series of editorials in *Le Gaulois* on France's dealings in Morocco. In the first few he recounted his own experiences in Algeria and compared them to the current Moroccan expeditions of Lyautey and General Albert d'Amade. By the end of the year, when the Chamber also took an interest in North African policy, he adopted a clear position for himself. Along with a vocal and heterogeneous contingent of deputies, many of the conservatives, the "colonial party" of Eugène Etienne from the ARD and Independents, and some of Clemenceau's old foes like Delcassé from the Left, de Mun castigated the government for having acted with such trepidation in Morocco, for failing to deal firmly with the Arabs who menaced commerce from their bases near Oran. Had previous Radical ministries presented Europe with a French protectorate, de Mun argued, rather than the intention of one, Morocco would still be solely a French concern, not a European one. If France must continually bow to the whims of Germany in setting colonial policy, what good were the vaunted Russian alliance and the entente with Great Britain? "We are very proud of them, but for what do they serve if we dare not, with their support, defend our most certain rights?" No one yet called for the outright appropriation of Morocco, but the situation was treacherous there, internal order was dissolving, and as de Mun expressed it, "Conquest! No one wants it: that is understood, but conquest may impose itself as a necessity." Here was the classic argument of the expansionist and militarist, and preoccupied for the first time in his political career with international and colonial affairs, de Mun embraced it easily.[15]

At the same time, he consciously identified nationalism with religion, emotions he called one and the same in France because of the integral role played by the church in the history of the nation. De Mun considered the argument self-evident and expressed it often, but he had another motive, soon revealed in his writing, that induced him to proclaim that God and country could be worshiped at the same altar. He realized that Catholics must not so immerse themselves in the politics of religion—as he himself often had—that they neglect the defense of their homeland and its traditions, all of which for de Mun could be subsumed in the word *patrie*. Instead, Catholics should lead France to a nationalist revival, the success of which would assure not only the survival of the state but a new place of honor for the church and political power for its champions. Once again de Mun had convinced himself that his latest political fascination would be the salvation of French Catholicism. Finally, he would be right. He first linked religion and nationalism in an editorial he wrote for *La Croix* on the funeral of Cardinal Richard, who died at the end of January 1908. The frail archbishop, whom Clemenceau had ordered unceremoniously expelled from his palace, was to be interred in splendor at Notre Dame. His eviction had marked the lowest point for the church in the Separation crisis. The more than fifty thousand who followed his bier showed how much respect the church had regained in little over a year. A witness to the Requiem Mass on 1 February, de Mun saw the crowd as proof that France was returning to its traditions. His words became almost mystical as he described "a high communion of nationalism," language defining a new variety of that secular faith, rendering it spiritual rather than material, adding to it a sense of quest and of the sacred.[16]

In de Mun's hands the defense of the sacred could be a weapon of attack. In March and April he contrasted for his readers the attitudes of clerical and lay schools. At the Ecole de la Rue des Postes, the Jesuits had taught their charges to give France "their strength, their labor, their blood if necessary, and the example of their lives." Yet the state schoolteachers refused to teach the worship of either God or country, and for de Mun, "neutrality on patriotism as on religion is fatal!" Once on the offensive, he found ample opportunity, far too much he believed, to develop his theme. In August 1908, Gaston Thomson, the navy minister, took the unprecedented action of refusing to allow clergy to be present in the funeral procession of several sailors killed in a shipboard accident. In November five young army officers at Laon, considered suspect by the government because they attended gatherings of the local ACJF, were relieved of command for failing to leave a mass during which the celebrant made vaguely critical remarks about ministerial policy. At the funeral of Victor Cardinal Lecot in Bordeaux in December, troops stationed along the route of the procession were ordered to reveal no sign of sympathy or respect. No salute was given the passing coffin. Taken together, these insults seemed a return to the excesses of André and his Masonic spies. For de Mun it was even appropriate that Picquart, rehabilitated along with Dreyfus, promoted to general, and installed as war minister by Clemenceau, should strongly defend the disciplining of the Laon officers. De Mun's harshest words were for Socialist leader Jaurès, who, although less outspoken than Hervé, had been leading his party toward pacifism rather than mobilization in case of a "capitalist war." When he made this position explicit during a speech before the Chamber on Morocco, de Mun called him a traitor, a coward, one who had planted "the poisonous growth of antimilitarism" in French soil. As if to demonstrate what the proper spirit of patriotism should be, he recalled his own years of military service and in poignant lines described his pilgrimage in the fall of 1908 to stalk the battlefields and cemeteries among the stunted mountains of Lorraine and about Metz, "so long the pride and buckler of France, now become her calvary." He returned physically and emotionally exhausted by this tearing experience but with his desire to restore a martial vigor redoubled.[17]

By May 1909 he found his melding of religion and patriotism personified in Jeanne d'Arc and the intimation that Frenchmen might become believers. On 18 April in Saint Peter's, Pius X had beatified the Maid of Orleans before forty thousand French pilgrims, and in Paris thousands more spontaneously laid flowers at her statues. Annoyed, the ministry pettily ordered the flowers removed, but de Mun, sensing that he had public opinion with him this time, warned the Radicals that "from everywhere a revolt begins; all are tired of your tyranny without grandeur, without glory." In an impressive ceremony of medieval splendor at Notre Dame on 8 May, the French clergy repeated the ritual and words of Pius X a month earlier. The crowd of witnesses on the Ile de la Cité was immense, far overflowing the cathedral into the tiny grounds and adjoining streets. They shouted, "Vive la religion!" "Vive la pucelle!" and, above all, "Vive la France!" De Mun felt overcome, never having contemplated such a tableau, never having seen anything "more moving, more poignant for the soul, for the heart, and for the eyes." It was a "delirium of praise that put tears into the eyes of all of us," it was "the great sigh of the national revival!" De Mun's sense that the recovery had begun was premature by at least four years, but if his campaign to revive nationalism had up to now borne only blossoms, it had had an unexpected effect upon de Mun himself. As nationalism replaced the church and social reform as his principal interest, he began to reevaluate his attitude toward many republican leaders. Always the arch-Catholic, de Mun could feel no kinship with the Radicals, the Socialists, or even many of the Independents on religion, since they had all voted for the Separation law. Conversely, while the Socialists were increasingly pacifists to a man, some of the Radicals and many of the Radical-leaning Independents shared de Mun's intense patriotism, although they did not, of course, connect it to the church. Nationalism offered a bridge over the clerical divide that sharply cut all French political life and the Chamber particularly.[18]

By 1908, de Mun was disgusted with many of his colleagues on the Right, seeing them lapse into cynicism and depression or drift away from the ALP to the Action Française. They seemed most capable of the internal broils that traditionally afflicted the conservatives. Jules Delahaye, an antisemite, a royalist, and one of the most hated men in the Chamber, challenged Piou to a duel in May 1908 over a supposed insult. As Piou's seconds, de Mun and Paul Beauregard had to mediate a tactful solution, Delahaye agreeing that Piou had attacked only his views and not his person. At the same time de Mun gained a greater appreciation for his political enemies. Immediately after the 1906 election and particularly after he became premier, de Mun had attacked Clemenceau with unusual fervor. He was a "malevolent Jacobin," whose code of extreme individualism portrayed life as a gladiatorial combat and who ruled as a tyrant contumacious of courtesy and right. De Mun was also supremely scornful of the civil servants who carried out the Radical commands. Jean Cauchy, the prefect in Finistère, he knew would prefer to serve a Méline but did not blush to do the bidding of a Combes or a Clemenceau. Cauchy had closed the school in Roscoff in 1902; he had been touched by the drama, but he remained at his post. As early as 1907, de Mun's attitude was changing, and in May he pointed out that Clemenceau, Briand, and Millerand were all disgusted by the growing pacifism of the Socialists. Although he continued to gore them publicly in his editorials, it was somewhat less fiercely. Twice in the last half of 1908 he rebuked Henri Bazire for attacking Clemenceau and Millerand too vigorously in *Peuple Français*. There was a point beyond which de Mun no longer wanted to go. By the end of 1908 and early 1909 he could even venture grudging praise of Clemenceau in public and go much further than that in private. He saw the premier as another Gambetta, a patriot, who unfortunately divided France religiously, both *homme d'état* and *homme de parti*. He acknowledged that this Jacobin still dreamed of a truly united France, a *France totale*, and that in him he could see "something of the rude nationalism of the Convention; he is able, with his imperious word, to crush the dissolving dreams of Jaurès." Later de Mun would quote approvingly Clemenceau's almost forgotten remark from the 1890s that if all Christians truly practiced their religion, there would be no need for social reform. Then, on 13 May 1909, there occurred in the Chamber an unforgettable and frightening incident. To show his opposition to a military defense proposal, Jaurès, from the tribune, led the Socialist deputies in singing the "Internationale." Standing on their desks, waving their fists, their voices drowning out frantic efforts to restore order, they provoked a suspension of the session. It was an intimation of revolution, a glimpse of what Jaurès might be planning for any mobilization. Many deputies wandered among the desks and about the corridors stunned, shamefaced, and even afraid, Two days later in *Le Gaulois* an overwrought de Mun called Jaurès the *fossoyeur*, the gravedigger, of France and openly rejoiced that Clemenceau, Briand, and Barthou had shared his outrage.[19]

In mid-July, Clemenceau's enemies finally toppled his three-year-old ministry on a minor issue. Delcassé took the particular honor, but the Chamber had long grown tired of the premier's haughty ways. Briand smoothly replaced him, and although he brought about no immediate substantive changes, there was a definite shift in tone and emphasis. Although Briand had begun his career as a presumed syndicalist, he actually had few convictions other than a sincere patriotism and a belief in his own ability to govern. He had proved his suppleness and capacity to compromise while enacting and implementing the Separation, and by 1909 he was ready to try to create a new governing majority, dispensing with the Radicals' dependence on the Socialists, whose pacifism and growing strength in the countryside he had begun to fear. Briand himself had moved almost to the center of the political spectrum and could depend on the votes of all of the Independents. In an obvious effort to reach into the conservatives, his ministerial declaration promised "liberal politics" and a "Republic open to all." These code words for a religious "appeasement" won him the votes of the Progressives and the encouraging abstention of the ALP. De Mun had few illusions about either Clemenceau or Briand, as he made clear to Jesuit Father Louis Trégard, whom de Mun had just chosen to replace the dying du Lac as his spiritual adviser. In a remarkable letter he introduced Trégard to the complex amoral political world. Cynically referring to the present powerlessness of the conservatives no matter who might be premier, he exclaimed: "We shall be 'eaten,' perhaps in a somewhat different, less piquant sauce, but we shall be 'eaten' . . . Briand, Bourgeois, even Poincaré, all of these are only forms of the same regime. . . . But with Briand it is so much easier to discuss matters than with Clemenceau, because he is not insolent and because he is not a doctrinaire Jacobin, a man of the 'Bloc.' In his heart I am sure that Briand would like to arrange an entente with the Vatican about the Separation, but since the agreement would have to be open, he will not dare to do so. Once again it will be Freemasonry that will govern." Clemenceau's ministry had fallen because he had surrendered to arrogance, assuming that he had the votes, "fifty swinging mamelukes," to beat back any challenge, and to the "extraordinary wantonness that had always prevented him from being a statesman."[20]

De Mun did not expect any sudden concessions from Briand. For the present it was sufficient that the premier and Millerand no longer exchanged insults with the conservatives. As de Mun explained it to Mackau in August, "I have not a great deal of confidence . . . but it is after all something to be able to talk and to receive one another socially . . . I have very good relations with our new master. I am almost friendly with Barthou, on good terms with [René] Viviani, on excellent ones with Millerand, and very courteous with [Georges] Cochery, with [René] Renoult, with [Jean] Cruppi, and with [Joseph] Ruau [all important and moderate Radicals]. Little is advanced but the forms, but one does what one can." His friends were less sanguine. Even de Mun was disappointed by the immediate results, admitting that "I was naive enough, at my age, to think that Briand, Millerand, Barthou, and even Cochery wanted to carry out a liberal policy." Yet he wrote to Mackau in September to reemphasize that Briand, dependent as he was on the Radicals for his majority, was compelled to uphold the anticlerical laws. In November he had to ask Bazire to moderate his attacks on the premier. By the beginning of 1910, de Mun found even Piou unwilling to refrain any longer from a complete discounting of Briand's good intentions and ready to attack him bitterly. In a long memorandum of January 1910, de Mun complained to Piou:

> You astonish me by your plans. What good do you see in taking an immediate attitude of hostility and rancor? Are we unable loyally and openly to expose our ideas and situation in the country and the legislature, to declare ourselves ready to collaborate on social, electoral, and administrative reforms? . . . From Briand's ministerial declaration, I can see no reason to oppose him. On the contrary, I see why we should vote for him. Only his language should bother us; his deeds do not. Moreover, the fear of being denounced as appeasers, as Briandistes, should no longer influence us. What is important is to execute our policies, for these are politics of rapprochement, of entente with the Progressives. They will vote for Briand. How long can we separate ourselves from them? We must not become a small group, isolated with the intransigents, but continue to orient our conduct so as to constitute a great party. If Briand, by his language or acts, obliges us to vote against him, there will be time to resolve the problem, but to have in advance the intention of opposing him seems to me to be dangerous.[21]

Piou's reluctance to follow de Mun in gambling on Briand was based on the situation of the ALP between 1906 and 1910.

The party's failure in the 1906 elections destroyed its illusion of being a French "Tory" party. More seriously, it encouraged its most intransigent element to forsake it for the Action Française and to begin with Maurras a guerrilla war against the ALP. De Mun considered that the party should cut its losses by detaching itself from the past and plotting a bold new course. Fearful of more and grievous disasters if he forsook the familiar, Piou wanted instead to defend desperately the ALP's remaining prestige and accomplishments. The assignment was not so very difficult since money from the congregations and rich industrialists still flowed into the ALP coffers, and the membership rolls increased steadily, although more slowly. Some economies were necessary, and in November 1908 the *Bulletin* was reduced to a bimonthly. But, while Piou could still attract the dedicated to pay dues and work on the local political level, he continued to be incapable of luring the votes of the enormous majority of the French electorate, who belonged officially to no party and voted more for the individual deputy than for his program. Many of them were supporters of the deputies who had once constituted the Left-Center and who now formed the right wing of the Radicals. Piou recognized this failing, but he did not know how to remedy it, and some of his proposed solutions smacked of panic or hasty thinking. When Clemenceau's majority forced through a drastic increase in salary for deputies, from nine thousand to fifteen thousand francs a year—at a time when the average French workingman made less than three thousand francs—Piou urged the ALP representatives to donate the additional monies to charity and so shame the Radicals. His colleagues protested that they were not as rich as he, with his two hundred thousand francs a year in *rentes*, and that they preferred to keep the increase for themselves. Piou then suggested that the national office on the Rue Las Cases should work with local committees to delve into the personal life of each Radical candidate to determine whether anything compromising might be found and exploited. With rather more forethought, he also committed the party firmly to proportional representation, so-called "RP." If RP were enacted, voting would be from departmental lists and would tend, most politicians thought, to favor parties like the ALP with a strong local organization and to decide elections more on issues than on personality. There was increasing agitation in the country for RP during the years before 1914, especially after the Socialists endorsed it and Briand adopted it as a "future" reform with which to threaten the Radicals, whose lack of national coherence and reliance on the local spoils system for election would make them suffer the most from the change. Unfortunately for Piou, RP was not enacted until 1919, and although the victory for the conservatives in the 1920 elections implies that RP was a sound approach for the ALP, Piou was placing his hopes on a change in election procedure, the immediate passage of which was remote.[22]

If Piou's judgment was less sure and his strategy occasionally bizarre during these four years, he could claim the distraction of being constantly sniped at by the Action Française. The neoroyalists tried to lure away the ALP's constituency, to subvert Piou's leadership within his own party, and to win from Pius X a disavowal of his predecessor's liberal policies, the Ralliement and social Catholicism, and thus of the ALP. Although nagging and provoking, the first threat held little danger. Despite the boasting and boisterous propaganda of the Action Française, the movement actually drew little response in France prior to World War I. Whenever the Action Française sent its orators into an area, the ALP followed them a few weeks later, invariably drawing much larger and more enthusiastic crowds and collecting far more in contributions. Piou merely had to be more careful and to risk less in word and deed. But he could not afford to treat Maurras and his clique cavalierly since they threatened a *politique du pire*, urging royalists to abstain from voting for ALP candidates and in some closely contested areas depriving them of narrow victories. Henri Bazire would twice be their victim running at Sables d'Olonne.[23]

The attempt to undermine Piou within the ALP was likewise futile. Denys Cochin schemed to obtain control of the party by setting up Léonce de Castelnau, on whom Piou had been counting to assume greater authority, as his straw man. Castelnau challenged Piou by urging a vast decentralization of the ALP in which the national office would lose its control and the party could be attacked in detail. In 1906 and early 1907, Piou was particularly vulnerable. The opposition had been slaughtered in the voting, he had been depicted as the confederate of the CGT, and a parliamentary examination of Montagnini's papers produced documentary proof of his attempt to bribe the church's way to an acceptable Separation bill. There were instant hypocritical denunciations of his conduct as the ministerial majority and the Action Française found rare agreement. Since all of those whom Piou had approached, and especially Clemenceau, adamantly denied any involvement, it was fairly easy for a hostile press to charge that he had merely trousered the church's funds while claiming to buy favors: certainly he had gotten little value for his money. Piou was embarrassed and so sensitive that he ordered all important records removed from the Rue Las Cases and hidden in various secret locations. Although he had acted with the knowledge and implicit approval of Merry del Val, he felt badly discredited by the revelations and by what most conservatives, ignorant of the enormous difficulties of constructing a national party in only five years, considered a mediocre performance by the ALP. As in 1905, he seriously thought of resigning the presidency, but de Mun and most of the rest of the party hierarchy dissuaded him. Despite this vote of confidence, Piou felt that his authority had been shaken, and he never again acted decisively to impose his will. When Castelnau presented the proposal for decentralization, Piou did not dismiss it brutally as a clumsy challenge to his power but rather outmaneuvered him. He gave the impression of granting greater regional autonomy by holding the party congresses of 1906 and 1907 in Lyons and Bordeaux respectively and sponsoring resolutions to study and even implement local control. He always found some reason for delay, however, and when he was forced to name an autonomous committee for Bordeaux, he managed to pack it with members loyal to him. Cochin lost his puppet when Castelnau died prematurely in March 1909, but Piou had already proved that he could survive the threat without undue struggle. The cost was the drift of the party as Piou plotted to do by craft what he had formerly done by fiat. The ALP had ceased to be a credible threat to the Radical majority.[24]

The party's torpor and Piou's weakness were all the more serious because the Action Française did not conceal that it expected Vatican aid in destroying the ALP. The royalists did have to tread gingerly because the creation of Piou and de Mun was the most visible symbol of Leo XIII's Ralliement, which Pius refused explicitly to renounce, however much he and Merry del Val might consider it a failure. Accepting this limitation, curial friends of the Action Française, especially the outrageously antisemitic Assumptionists dispersed in 1899 from their houses in France, did not urge His Holiness to forswear the Ralliement entirely but to call for the creation of a purely confessional party, thus destroying the basis of the ALP. As soon as rumors of this plan reached France in mid-1907, de Mun quickly composed a series of editorials for *Le Figaro*, "La Conquête du peuple," in which he argued forcefully that fervent Catholics were too few, apathetic, and divided ever to form a majority party in France. Only where churchmen were fully agreed on the form of government, as in Belgium and Germany, could such a confessional party be a redoubtable force. In France, as he well remembered from his experience in 1885, the right wing of the church would condemn the party as too "constitutional," the left wing as too "reactionary." To win a majority in the nation, Catholics should continue to defend their rights through the ALP, which could escape the crippling epithet of clericalism and rally all who believed in liberty, whether Catholic or not.[25]

These arguments had no appeal for Pius, but the Action Française was unable to convince him to launch a confessional party from the Holy See. By late 1908 they decided to act alone, with Xavier de Cathelineau and Colonel Prosper Keller, son of the famous Alsatian royalist deputy, as the ostensible organizers. Cathelineau formally requested that Piou include the ALP in a proposed gigantic coalition of fifteen religious and political groups as diverse as the ACJF and the Sillon on the Left and the Action Française and the Ligue Antisémite on the Right. With a different pope and cardinal secretary of state, the threat of the ALP's being engulfed was much more serious than in the case of the Comité Catholique in 1903. Piou and de Mun genuinely feared this threat and in early 1909 rallied considerable support in France against it, particularly within the hierarchy, which was still Leonine, and from *L'Univers*. Archbishops Léon Amette of Paris and Paulin Andrieu of Bordeaux and Bishop Félix Guilibert of Fréjus led the episcopacy in reaffirming their support for the ALP, and, while admitting the theoretical appeal of confessionalism, François Veuillot in *L'Univers* observed that Piou's judgment was sounder. The ALP leaders seemed to have won a great tactical victory when Pius received Piou and Amette in a private audience on 30 April and specifically charged Piou to "create a good government in the Republic." But Merry del Val was pursuing a different program of his own. After Colonel Keller made one last appeal in May for an exclusively Catholic party, Merry del Val announced that the Vatican found that "the most practical and opportune policy was to rally all men of good will onto ground clearly Catholic and religious." The confusion was never satisfactorily resolved, but it was clear that if the ALP had not yet become a stepchild, it was no longer the favored son. Henri Groussau even questioned whether or not he should remain within the party. None of the republican Catholic groups would treat with Cathelineau, and without their money and mass support, he and Keller could not even hold together the royalists and antisemites. Nevertheless, the pressure had baneful effects on the ALP. Piou grasped for outside support so avidly that he arranged an alliance with Paul Déroulède, returned from ten years of exile for his part in the abortive coup d'état at Faure's funeral, whose rabble rousing was more suited to the Action Française. Piou and de Mun had long chafed at the way their enemies at Rome played on the name of the ALP, accusing it of espousing "liberalism," a proposition denounced in the *Syllabus*. To ward off the wholly unmerited charge that the party had become preoccupied with secular issues, they cast about for a new clearly "Catholic" one, finding it in the alleged antireligious bias of public school textbooks. To ensure the Vatican's attention they organized Associations des Pères de Famille and made the question of the schools a significant item in their propaganda. Increasingly, de Mun and Piou were caught in a dilemma: to retain the support of Rome the ALP had to play the role of the "Catholic party," while aware that to do so limited their appeal and might not even be judged sufficient zeal by the curia. De Mun complained circumspectly to Trégard that the Vatican no longer seemed to value his opinions. To Bazire he confessed, "I do not at all understand what Rome would have me do. I no longer write because for more than a year no one has bothered to reply."[26]

De Mun was in disfavor at the Vatican because the Action Française was pursuing one more and very dangerous strategy against the ALP. Soon after his accession, Pius had taken alarm at the theological experiments of the Abbé Alfred Loisy, who taught that the church should accommodate itself to the modern epoch by aligning its dogma more closely to the advances in scientific thought. The nineteenth had been a particularly difficult century for the church in France, and in reaction to the Revolution and its offspring, obscurantism had replaced the previous commendable record of the church in scholarship and research. As Loisy's "modernism" caught hold within a clergy ravenous for intellectual stimulation, Pius bestirred himself to lash out at the modernists in the papal decree of 3 July 1907 *Lamentabili sans exiter* and two months later in the encyclical *Pascendi dominici gregis* of 8 September. He termed their ideas a synthesis of all the heresies and demanded a recantation. When Loisy refused, he was excommunicated in 1908—and for his apostasy appointed by the French government to the professorate at the Collège de France. The pope even permitted the establishment of a modern inquisition, the Sodalitium Pianum, more familiarly known as the Sapinière, to ferret out suspect priests and laity. Pius's anathema was thundering but unfortunately imprecise since the decree and encyclical were so broadly worded that a latitude of interpretation was possible. Already by 1909 the vigilantes who would direct the Sapinière and be called "Integrists"—because of their belief in so-called Integral Catholicism—suggested that the Sillon was guilty of a variant termed "social modernism" for too greatly enlarging the sphere of justice at the expense of charity and for limiting the rights of property. If Sangnier and his followers were condemned, no social Catholics, even de Mun and the ACJF, could feel safe since their ideas were only less stridently expressed than those of the Sillon. The ALP would be in absolute peril because its social program was de Mun's creation and Sangnier was one of the party's most eloquent orators. This significance was not lost on the royalists, who decided to damn the ALP through its links to the Sillon. Piou's reluctance to endorse Briand, about which de Mun complained in January 1910, grew directly out of this threat posed by the Action Française. He feared that to support the premier in the face of his avowed anticlericalism would subject the ALP to harsh attack at the Vatican and might even precipitate a condemnation.[27]

Pressure from the extreme Right also reduced Piou's room for maneuver on the critical economic issue before the Chamber, an income tax bill. In February 1907, Clemenceau's finance minister Joseph Caillaux, a dapper, fast-rising, and arrogant Radical with pretensions to financial wizardry, proposed a progressive tax on income. As a party the ALP had serious reservations about the bill, objecting to its progressivity and the necessity to open private books to government scrutiny and fearing that its administration by a man like Caillaux would lead to favoritism. This opposition did not necessarily extend to the principle of an income tax, and a majority of the party reluctantly accepted the argument that France's system of indirect taxes was no longer sufficient to meet the nation's needs. In November 1907 at the party congress in Bordeaux the delegates strenuously opposed Caillaux's formulation but narrowly approved a resolution calling for a nonprogressive income tax, the provisions of which would include unnamed safeguards against administrative abuse. Piou attempted to act on this mandate early in 1908, when the bill finally emerged from committee for discussion in the Chamber. On 17 February he announced that the ALP would not oppose the discussion of the articles of the proposal and in doing so hoped to obtain some consideration of the ALP's position when the party presented amendments. Although the ALP helped to vote some of the articles, Caillaux offered no concessions, and as his bill neared passage by the deputies, Piou led his party to oppose it adamantly. When the final vote came on 9 March 1909, the ALP stood united, entirely and futilely, on the negative side. Although he concealed it well, Piou actually welcomed the government's intransigence since his cautious endorsement of the income tax had threatened to fracture the battered ALP still further. Jules Roche led a vocal minority against any tax on income, and he attracted wide support among his former Progressive colleagues, who objected particularly to the government's insistence on taxing the *rente française*, the interest on government bonds. Because the ALP had provided the bulk of the money to elect Roche and the Progressives, Piou could well have called them to order, but to do so risked losing some of them. De Mun was preoccupied with social questions and trying to chart the elusive relation of religion to nationalism, and although he opposed Caillaux's bill, he took little interest in this controversy, either in the Chamber or within the party. By himself Piou refused to enforce discipline at further expense to unity.[28]

In February 1908, at a banquet for party committee leaders, Piou assured them that the ALP was full of vitality and then nervously added, "would not only ten have been necessary to save Sodom?" The following December he confessed that it was probably not to be given to his generation of party leaders to see victory over the Radicals. He was tiring physically—he had phonograph records made of his set speeches in order to spare himself some of the rallies—and mentally, succumbing to an entirely valid pessimism about the outcome of the next elections in 1910. Party administrator Louis Laya admitted that "it is vital for the ALP to present the public at least with the impression of an active league that can concentrate the efforts of the entire opposition and have the concourse of numerous senators and deputies." But the party's original expectation of winning through a shrewd combination of money, propaganda, and coalition had been dashed. From the usual sources Piou had a campaign chest of five million francs, and the purchase of newspapers had continued, *Le Peuple Français* with a circulation of over fifty thousand bought and Bazire installed as editor in January 1909. At the party congress of December 1909, Piou repeated his plea that all who loved liberty band together beneath the banner of the ALP, but unlike 1906 the words were hollow. Because its right wing had deserted to the Action Française and its left wing was increasingly bewitched by Briand, the old strategy was a ruin. Briand was confident of his ministry's success, since his conciliatory policy had eliminated the opposition's issues, especially as the Senate held the income tax bill in suspense. On the eve of the voting in late April, the *Bulletin* prepared the party for another debacle by calling elections "only an episode . . . not the essence of our labor at association, organization, political education, and social amelioration." Piou had felt so discouraged that in an effort to rally flagging interest he published a brief history of the party in the popular *Revue Hebdomadaire*. His words defined the crux of the ALP's problem: "Should we lose patience and renounce the struggle because it is long and hard? It would be far easier to cross our arms and retire, having lost the first battles."[29]

The extent of the forthcoming opposition losses was the primary political question before the 1910 elections, but even so, it was surprising that their numbers declined to as few as 166. Somewhat to their own surprise the ALP actually registered modest gains, adding a dozen new seats, but the Progressives lost heavily, dropping to half of their former total. Almost unnoticed in the talk of the opposition were the gains of the Independents and members of the ARD, creating a sizable right wing to the ministerial majority. Assiduously cultivated by Briand, this phenomenon meant the recreation of a Center in the Chamber. Nearly 150 strong, these deputies would follow Briand or a moderate like him. At present the premier chose to stand on a Center-Left majority. During the next four years, the finale and climax of his political career, de Mun would ask why such a moderate could not equally well accept a majority of the Center and Right. The question would be rhetorical unless he could discover the issues on which the Center would desert the Left for the Right. Piou had sent his followers into the election with the cry, "Forward to combat, it is France you will save!" The fallen conservatives were called to recover by words written by de Mun in 1909: "We are at the dawn of combat. Lift high your hearts! And cry to France, weakened by so many wounds yet still standing, drink your blood and return to action!"[30]

8
The New Course: Success, 1910–1913

On 4 January 1914, de Mun wrote to Trégard:

As for me, I consider that practically speaking, we can hope to modify the state of the nation only through a discreet entente with the moderates, this term being expanded to include Briand, Millerand, Barthou, and Poincaré. The latter are able to treat with us only by first abusing us, by beginning with an affirmation of their laicity and anticlericalism. From this necessity, we and they must calculate our public declarations carefully. Piou has instead changed the focus of the ALP, making it the Catholic republican party—and at bottom, through a curious evolution, this transformation is what he wants, while I have come round to the first conception of the party, which is almost that of the Progressives. That is why Piou preoccupies himself so much with the pope and the cardinal [Amette], while I believe that an entente with the moderates, at first secret but made public after its success, could give us diplomatic relations with the Vatican, a Separation negotiated with the pope, one including the congregations, and a return to the education law of 1882, leaving to private schools complete freedom in the choice of instructor. Would that not be a good beginning?[1]

The words allude only slightly to the dramatic success the discreet entente with the moderates had already won for the conservatives and even less to the difficulties with the church of the Integrists that de Mun's strategy had cost himself and his party. It was this ironic transposition of de Mun's reputation, stunningly lower at the Vatican and just as astonishingly higher within the Chamber of Deputies and the Elysée and throughout a France that first prepared for and then withstood a new assault from Germany, that gave the last four and a half years of de Mun's life, from the election of 1910 to the aftermath of the First Marne, a peculiar poignance and triumph.

Those elections of April and May 1910 precipitated his dilemma since de Mun now knew that the conservatives would have to treat with Briand. He was the true victor of the voting, with his policy of appeasement and a revived Center. Most of the conservatives were unsure whether or not the premier was sincere, but he seemed to hint at a political course the ALP and Progressives found desirable, especially battered and disheartened as they were. If they cultivated Briand, he might become a new Méline, an incarnation that would be particularly pleasing since even the conservatives were convinced that they would never come to power without assistance. Now that Briand had increased his strength so markedly, their continued opposition would risk seeing him succeed in guaranteeing religious peace and social order, while basing his ministry on a majority that combined the new moderates with some coalition of the Left. He would have no need to bargain for support on his right flank and could destroy the conservatives politically by appropriating their chief issues.[2] De Mun had considered approaching Briand in 1909, but the exigencies of the ALP's internal disorder and of prosecuting the elections crippled his efforts. Before he could hope to convince Briand to rely on conservative votes, he would have to convert the hesitant and demoralized Piou.

Writing in *Le Gaulois* immediately after the elections, de Mun offered Briand praise for having lowered the political temperature and suggested that under certain conditions, perhaps the preservation of private Catholic schools and the reestablishment of diplomatic relations with the Vatican, Catholics could support the premier. His subjunctive attracted only resistance within the ALP, with Laya writing in the *Bulletin* that the opposition should not "enter the camp of the enemy" and Piou urging that no one forget those who had been accomplices in the spoliation of the church. De Mun carefully replied with a panegyric in *Le Figaro* to "Jacques Piou and his work" in creating a party based on "a sincere care for justice and liberty," code words that were identical to those of Briand in his ministerial declaration a week later. He had turned in these two editorials to subtle public prodding because Piou had remained unconvinced by closely reasoned memoranda.[3] When Piou continued to resist moving the ALP's pessimistic and extremely cautious opposition, de Mun finally indicated his extreme impatience in another memorandum to his colleague and an open threat in *L'Echo de aris*. By claiming that politics had been in flux since the advent of Briand and that it might be best for the younger deputies among the conservatives to assume command during this time when no questions were predetermined and old prejudices could be laid aside, he made a scarcely veiled attack on Piou's leadership: "What harm would come from allowing some of the younger deputies to take charge?"[4] This pressure was at last sufficient, and on 27 June, the day following the appearance of de Mun's "Aux jeunes" in *L'Echo*, Piou very warily questioned Briand about his philosophy of anticlericalism.

Recalling that while the premier had repeated many of the standard Radical formulas and called for the "consolidation of the laic conquests," Piou suggested that in practice the ministry had refrained from harassing the church. While the ALP and its supporters could never, he emphasized, vote to consolidate or even to maintain these "conquests," they could "second with all their strength the government's movement toward the ideas of conciliation, equity, and liberal reform." This formula was close to de Mun's position, but it would have almost no immediate political impact. On the following day left-wing Radicals presented the ministry with a resolution similar to that which defeated Méline in 1898, demanding that Briand limit his majority to deputies "clearly favoring laic reforms," thereby hoping to offend the conservatives and frighten the ministry's Radical supporters by drawing anew the clerical line through the Chamber. Briand had no wish to affront any faction, prudently aware that he might need votes from either extreme to buttress his moderate strategy, and he was evasive in reply. Aynard of the Progressives came to his rescue, pledging their votes despite the excommunication of the resolution. Briand then won a test of confidence by an overwhelming 403 to 110, with the ALP deputies badly divided between opposition and expressing hesitant faith in the premier. The ambiguity of the Radical formulation, but fourteen of the younger ones, seemingly taking de Mun at his word, abstained, ignoring the resolution and expressing hesitant faith in the premier. The ambiguity of the vote and the dilemma it caused had caught even de Mun, and he hastened to explain himself in print, candidly admitting his ambivalence toward Briand and reiterating Piou's promise that the ALP might find agreement with him. This opinion, half a hope, seemed to be given basis in mid-July, when the Chamber created its first standing committees and assigned the ALP leaders to those exercising important roles. Piou took his seat on the Foreign Affairs Committee and the crucial Budget Committee, the first time since 1898 that the opposition had been given representation in the formulation of the budget. De Mun joined Piou at Foreign Affairs and, in rare public recognition of his contribution to social reform by the majority parties, was elected vice-president of the Labor Committee.[5]

Even as de Mun led a wavering ALP in the search for a way to embrace Briand, new complications at the Vatican made any further probing infinitely more delicate and dangerous. In the early summer of 1910 the Integrists among the papal curia convinced Pius X that the Sillon was tainted by modernism. The assault on the work of Leo XIII was beginning in earnest. Nearly a year earlier Father Julien Fontaine, a reactionary Jesuit, had termed the teachings of the Sillon, and even those of the ACJF and the ALP, "social modernism." Emmanuel Bailly, the former Assumptionist editor of *La Croix*, encouraged Pius to believe that the ALP was failing to give French Catholic youth the example of militant faith. At *L'Univers*, François Veuillot, never previously an enemy, denounced de Mun for venturing even an approving word about Briand and lumped the Action Libérale Populaire within the general category of "liberals" condemned by the *Syllabus*. De Mun had protested immediately in *Le Gaulois*, calling his editorial "Réponse nécessaire," but by early August he was very pessimistic, writing Bazire that the Integrists were "damaging the cause of the pope, the Vatican, and all Catholics." Too well aware that his personal influence at Rome had waned, he worried that the papacy had returned to the black reaction of the 1830s and compared his lot to that of Lamennais before Gregory XVI, "remember the Pilgrims of Faith of 1832." When he heard rumors that Pius was composing a condemnation of the Sillon, he sent Georges Piot of the ACJF to plead the case of social Catholicism, and when Piot returned in mid-August, he assured de Mun that only the Sillon would fall under the ban. But when the expected pastoral letter, *Notre charge apostolique*, appeared on 25 August, de Mun found it fulfilling all but his worst fears. Although Pius accused the Sillon of lapsing into the heresy of modernism, he failed utterly to explain how. Instead, he damned Sangnier and his followers for attracting non-Catholics to their ranks, for ignoring the church's hierarchical conception of society when calling for social reform, for engaging actively in politics, and for praising democracy as a form of government superior to any other. As in *Pascendi dominici gregis*, the pope seemed to attack far more than his presumed target. By choice if not by definition, every French social Catholic group was guilty of one or more of the Sillon's so-called errors—none of them definable as modernism—and it was not only the faithful who concluded that the letter would prove to be the prelude to a general condemnation of the entire movement. *Le Temps* dared to ask on its front page the unthinkable, "The condemnation of M. de Mun next?" Many expected it soon.[6]

Even de Mun himself expected it, and he felt overwhelmed, reduced to profound anguish. In a letter startling in its revelation of his despair, he told Trégard:

> When I arrived back here I found the terrible papal letter. I read it through at a sitting, and I found myself greatly moved. As all the others, this one seemed to me to be quite remarkable, profound, and highly researched, and it is perhaps impossible more clearly to analyze the complex and subtle error of the Sillon, more clearly to raise the alarm. But too, as in the other encyclicals, what a smashing blow, striking far beyond those intended, attacking indirectly all who in some form or another have subscribed to Sillonist doctrines, encouraging all of those who, for reasons more or less openly avowed, struggle against the social works and philosophy inaugurated by Leo XIII.
>
> I do not say that this kind of reproof was not called for or that it was not necessary to cut short fatal tendencies in the social and economic realm as the encyclical on modernism has done in the intellectual and doctrinal one. I do believe that the time will come when yet a third hand will reestablish the equilibrium between abusive interpretations of the encyclicals of Leo XIII and the reaction shown in these last two. And I can admire quite sincerely this constant reinterpretation by the church, now bold and stimulating, now prudent and curbing, leading the world through its authority, sure of itself and its times.
>
> But for the present, what trouble, tests, and uncertainty! Assuredly, I do not believe that either my ideas or my work has been rebuked, but I do feel myself profoundly troubled, uncertain of my way, and worried what gain the eternal enemies of Catholic social action will take from this. How many of them have in their hearts if not on their lips the words of *Le Temps*, "the condemnation of M. de Mun next?" You can understand, I have no spirit of revolt, even inwardly, against the encyclical. I understand and recognize the necessity of an act that frightens me. I admire the strength that has enabled it to be completed. But I am sad,

very sad, very affected, almost discouraged. I am sad at the thought of all the abuse that will be hurled at those not condemned by the encyclical but simply part of the social Catholic movement; affected by the thought of the grief and anguish that will fill the hearts of so many young people, especially young priests, working in this movement; discouraged by the thought of all the difficulties that will surge up about me, blocking my way, and that I no longer have the strength nor the time to surmount.

After all the ideas, works, and institutions I have seen crumble, before my death am I also to see the social movement to which I have attached my name founder and die? And this time it will not be by act of the enemies of the church but by her own hand, the hand of the church I have wanted to serve so ardently that I have given myself totally to social Catholicism.

You will help me to escape from this kind of thinking, to read the encyclical fruitfully, to discern exactly what it permits and what it does not. It will be necessary for me to speak about this: I owe as much to my work, to my friends, to all those who have faith in me. I owe it to my past and to the complete obedience to the church that has been the rule of my life. But how can one talk about it without either avowing that one has been condemned or seeming to triumph over the condemnation of the others?[7]

Here was an absolute crisis for de Mun and the ALP, one that required careful resolution. Sangnier submitted totally to the Vatican, and the *Bulletin* took care to praise first the pastoral letter and Sangnier's recantation and then what might be called the complete work of Pius X. But if these forced marches covered the party's exposed flank, they did not clarify the Vatican's attitude toward the ALP and its leaders. Piou and de Mun entrusted Gailhard-Bancel with the delicate mission of sounding the depth of papal support, telling him to threaten the ALP's retirement from the field unless there was a new positive statement in its favor. Pius received Gailhard-Bancel and insisted in his limited French that the ALP "must continue, must persevere," but beyond that he provided little encouragement and no apology for the criticism of the Integrists. Since de Mun and Piou had not actually intended to withdraw, they could interpret Pius's faint praise as a new charge. But Piou was strongly reinforced in his caution, and, particularly after Veuillot in *L'Univers* defined "compromise with the enemies of the church" as a modernist tendency, de Mun could hardly deny Piou's counsels. As a bulwark against Integrist assaults on social Catholicism, de Mun pretended to resurrect the *cercles* to assume the leadership of reform, although they remained under the control of the ACJF, and with the assistance of Bazire he laid plans for a grandiose general convention in Paris for their members during March 1911. Because the Oeuvre des Cercles had been specifically praised for its orthodoxy, not just by Leo XIII but four times by Pius IX, he considered that Integrists would find it embarrassing to attack them, as indeed they would. To spare the ALP further blame for its political tactics, de Mun agreed with Piou to avoid any semblance of a truce with Briand during the next few months.[8]

The premier himself made de Mun's decision easier. Before Gailhard-Bancel's return, Briand had lost some of his support on the Left but picked up more on the Right, including that of the Progressives and the ALP for what seemed a policy of social order and the curbing of labor militancy. He had crushed the strike of the *cheminots*, the railway workers of the Compagnie du Nord, by mobilizing the reserve units of which the workers were members and condemning to court-martial those who resisted, and had claimed that since the railroads were an essential part of national defense, he would have acted illegally if necessary to restore service. Even this vote by the ALP in support of authority was potentially open to denunciation, but Briand was not convinced that he wanted them among his majority. He did not believe that he could depend on the support of the conservatives to remain in office if he were deserted by large numbers of Radicals; the mere introduction of a proposal on public education would be sufficient to split such a bloc. Many of the Radicals were restive at Briand's courting of the conservatives and demanded proof that he was not the prisoner of clericals. To mollify them he reshuffled his cabinet on 2 November, adding Louis Lafferre, sometime master of the Grand Orient, the largest association of French Freemasons, and one of the few defenders of André's system of talebearing. In *Le Gaulois* de Mun called Lafferre's inclusion in the ministry an outrage, and all the more so since as minister of agriculture he would sit in the former archiepiscopal palace secularized in 1906. But although he told Bazire that he was "en pleine bagarre," in an uproar, over Lafferre, he wrote to Trégard that Briand's predicament had required a bow to Freemasonry and that "nothing substantial had happened." What had been altered drastically were the political possibilities open to the ALP, and with Gailhard-Bancel back bearing new warnings, Briand's manipulation "renders any maneuver of détente, of rapprochement impossible." Although the Progressives would feel secure in continuing their support of the ministry, the ALP could not and began to appear increasingly isolated, as de Mun had foreseen in his memorandum the previous January. Ultimately, Briand's cleverness was not sufficient, since in early 1911 the Radicals began to tire of the symbol and demand the substance of new laic conquests. When their harsh attack on his attitude toward the separated church forced him to rely on the Progressives for a 258 to 242 survival, he resigned, convinced of his imminent defeat.[9]

The pures of the Vatican and the Radicals could forbid the ALP leaders and the new moderates undisguised cooperation, but there remained many less formal, more circumspect, even clandestine occasions to circumvent the prohibition. Piou maintained his connections to the *grands avocats* and *bâtonniers* of the Paris legal world, and as president of a party very friendly to business, he could not avoid social contact with Poincaré, the counsel for Saint Gobain, or Millerand, for Le Creusot. Piou had never fully emancipated himself from his heritage of a barrister from Toulouse, revealing it in his failure to overcome the awkwardness of the provincial bourgeoisie as well as in the pedantry of his politics. He was perfect company for the Progressives, for such men as Beauregard and Méline, who shared his staunch respectability if not his clericalism. For the literati and the new lions of Paris society, the suddenly powerful moderates, who had been adopted for their novelty by many of the salons, Piou had to defer completely to de Mun. Of this world by right of birth and facility of voice and pen, de Mun could understand the social and cultural links that allowed him, in the same evening, to debate genteelly with Germain Bapst the strategy of the battle of Rezonville in 1870, receive verses from Georges de Porto-Riche, consult Arthur Meyer of *Le Gaulois*, and then turn to greet Millerand, Briand, and particularly Paul Deschanel, handsome, dashing, empty-headed, the dandy of the moderates. In 1908, when there came open three vacancies within the Académie Française, Poincaré asked his blessing and assistance for his candidacy, knowing that de Mun had wide respect among those who wore the august green regalia and could rally such friends as the critic Count Eugène Melchior de Vogüé. He did so to elect Poincaré in 1909. Besides his polemics, de Mun wrote history and memoirs, and his frequent editorials had recovered for his name much of the notability it had had earlier in his career.[10] His opinions on labor questions were broadcast widely as he forced a hearing in the press and before his committee. He wrote in favor of replacing the standard eleven- or twelve-hour workday with one of ten hours, but only eight before Sundays and other holidays. He also condemned Briand's refusal to force the vindictive Compagnie du Nord to rehire those railway workers who had struck in October. His language in *L'Echo de Paris*, and later at the congress of the *cercles*, was florid enough to irritate moderate newspapers and draw embarrassing tributes from *L'Humanité*, the organ of Jaurès's Socialists. Briand and his labor minister René Viviani did not take offense because during committee meetings de Mun exchanged posturing for accommodation and because from his position as vice-president he initiated proposals the government was willing to endorse, a simple ten-hour workday and the reinstatement of the railway workers who had not committed sabotage, and which even Jules Guesde, the dogmatic Marxist, could deem acceptable to his social conscience.[11] The tone of relations was almost amicable, attitudes softer, and, as de Mun had remarked, that in itself was worth continuing.

But what was possible for the ALP leaders to do individually they could not lead the party to do collectively. It seemingly had to maintain an official antagonism toward all "enemies of the church," and the Holy See had come to define all who did not stand with it as standing against it and thus to include among the reprobate Briand, Millerand, even Poincaré. The addition of this constraint made the defeated party seem old, tired, even feeble. Its futile candidates and campaign aides lightly tossed recriminations and charges of corruption at one another, and the ALP no longer attracted collateral support. When Baroness Reille died in late 1910, the Ligue Patriotique des Françaises retired to good works, withdrawing as the distaff salient of the party. The new president of the ACJF, Pierre Gerlier, succeeding Paul Lerolle's son Jean, similarly, although more slowly, abandoned the ALP. The most crippling defection was by the Progressives, under their new president Joseph Thierry, who announced in November 1910 that his followers were now willing to embrace all of the legislation passed under Radical auspices since 1899, even laws they had combated. It was a blatant effort to escape to the other side of the clerical line, and while the Radicals remained deeply suspicious of them, the old alliance between the Progressives and the ALP, one based upon common fears and ALP subsidies, had come to an abrupt termination. Piou rightly regarded Thierry as a traitor and told Catholic audiences bitterly, "Be intransigent; at this hour your intransigence is your safeguard. To expect serious concessions is folly, . . . for let us be able to say to our adversaries, 'Do not count on us to be either your accomplices or your dupes!' " In language he had hardly used since the Separation, he praised the pope who had stood his ground, the church that had lost its money but maintained its liberty and respect. When he had exhausted his caustic words, there were still decisions to be made about the future of the party. Given the attitude of the Vatican, it appeared that any search for new allies would have to be made on the right flank, among those elements who had favored the grand design of Keller and Cathelineau, toward confessionalism and a more or less avowed royalism. Piou and de Mun together decided to gauge the cost of such support before committing themselves to it and began to meet with prominent royalists who were not allied to the Action Française or were restive within it, including Colonel Keller. Piou spoke vaguely of "the union of all Catholics for the safety of France" and addressed a formally royalist assembly in Bordeaux, but the price included very much more, the xenophobia and antisemitism Maurras preached. De Mun and Piou disdained to touch pitch, but with their tacit approval Laya and Cavalier published editorials in the 15 April *Bulletin* denouncing the increasing naturalization of immigrants—thirteen thousand in 1910—and inciting "the people against the Freemasons and the Jews" in the best tradition of Drumont. And there it ended because de Mun and Piou deemed the price too great. The ALP would hobble alone rather than accept that crutch, although alone the limping would be very painful. De Mun's general congress of the *cercles* in March 1911 for the benefit of the Integrists, specious as it was, had attracted four hundred delegates, and its success was less in its numbers than in the cordial greeting conveyed to it by Merry del Val in an open letter to de Mun. But that only four hundred delegates attended the ALP's first congress since the 1910 elections when Piou called it to order in June 1911 was a humiliation. Here was quantitative proof of the demise of the party's vaunted organization and of how unprepossessing it had become. The sessions were shrill and negative, signs of decline, with even Piou insisting that henceforth the ALP should have "not just a candidate but a simon-pure candidate." The only new proposal was for *répartition proportionnelle scolaire*, a so-called RP *scolaire*, an impossibly complicated scheme to allocate the government's budget for education to all schools, private (that is, Catholic) as well as public, in proportion to the number of students attending each one. The congress seemed proof that the ALP was settling among the extreme reactionaries of the Chamber, but since March the Progressives had also found Briand's successor so unpalatable that they joined the ALP in opposition.[12]

That successor was Ernest Monis, a nonentity, who gave office to three particularly rabid Radicals—Louis Malvy, whose parliamentary question had brought down Briand; Maurice Berteaux, who had championed the cause of the railway workers during the October strike; and Caillaux, who even more than Briand was convinced of his fitness to govern France and who made Monis a figurehead within his own cabinet. Again finance minister, Caillaux wanted to resurrect the old anticlerical majority of Radicals and Socialists by concentrating on the passage of an income tax—the Senate never having approved his original bill that the Chamber had enacted—and new proposals for the "defense of the laic school" from attack by the episcopacy, which condemned many of the textbooks, and Catholic parents, who in consequence sometimes withheld their children from school or even brought formal charges against teachers who were outspoken in their denunciation of religion or country. He could do little more than plan this strategy before a bizarre accident decapitated the government and Morocco again became the focus of French, and European, concentration. By the Algeciras settlement of 1906 and the Franco-German agreement of February 1909, France was declared to have "special political interests" in Morocco and to exercise police powers within its boundaries but forbidden to infringe directly upon the independence and integrity of the country. This language presupposed more stability than the pro-French sultan Moulay Hafid could maintain, since by early 1911 he had provoked a rebellion among his subjects and found himself and the European colony besieged in Fez. The Monis ministry hesitated when beseeched for aid but finally dispatched a column of troops, which relieved the city on 21 May. The subsequent occupation of Fez appeared to be the obvious prelude to the assumption of a protectorate and raised the critical diplomatic question of Germany's response to France's unilateral act. Any French preparations were severely complicated by the serious injury of Monis and the death of war minister Berteaux in a freak crash on 20 May at the Paris Air Show. Caillaux assumed total control of the cabinet and, when it became certain that Monis could not quickly resume his office, was invested as premier on 28 June, the opposition to him remaining the same as that to Monis. On the first of July, Germany ended a month of speculation about its reaction by sending the gunboat *Panther* to the Moroccan Atlantic port of Agadir, thus serving bellicose notice that it proposed to exact a price for France's intended gain.[13]

Caillaux conceived himself a diplomatic as well as a financial genius, and unlike many connected to the Quai d'Orsay, former minister Delcassé, senior official Maurice Paléologue, and ambassadors Georges Louis and Jules and Paul Cambon, he believed that if sufficiently appeased and linked to France through trade and commercial arrangements, Germany might agree to genuine cooperation. After failing to conclude an agreement with the Wilhelmstrasse through normal channels and his foreign minister, Justin de Selves, who assumed an intransigent attitude, Caillaux turned to certain business associates who had contacts in the German diplomatic corps. After a tediously long period, during which Caillaux naturally released no details of his irregular negotiations, he announced in a speech at Saint Calais on 5 November that the French and German governments had signed a convention the previous day by which Germany would acquiesce in the establishment of a French protectorate in Morocco in return for France's cession of part of its Congo territory connecting the German Cameroons to the Congo and Ubangi rivers. The reaction of the nation to these terms, which seemed very like extortion, of what would be called the 4 November convention was deeply felt outrage. It was not a unanimous emotion and it was not chauvinistic; throughout the late summer and early fall the Socialists had held increasingly popular pacifist demonstrations, claiming fifty thousand faithful at the Aero Park of Paris on 24 September. Yet there was everywhere the sense that the dormant rancor of Frenchmen against Germans, the product of five centuries of history, awakened by the warlike dispatching of the *Panther* and nurtured by four months of anxiety, had finally been rubbed raw by this apparent diplomatic defeat. With such nationalists as Clemenceau and Briand from the Left and Center joining those of the Right in arming against him, Caillaux flouted this exasperation at his hazard. For its most immediate result was to raise substantially the prestige of those who had long before counseled a revived nationalism and a strong policy in Morocco. They had the status of prophets, and among them no one had foretold the outcome of French weakness more surely than had de Mun.[14]

He had been the one who had accused the Radicals of forgetting the sacred duty of revanche, of neglecting ever to waken the "sleeping warrior soul" of France, of forming a generation that felt nothing was worth dying for; the true measure of a man, of a nation, he wrote, is what he is willing to die for. It was time for the clarion to sound "to the flag!" that France might not later have to depend on *débrouillage*, muddling through with a French cast, even though "the glories of a people come in their heroic madness." From March to June 1911 de Mun excoriated the Monis cabinet for its failure to act quickly in relieving Fez: "Order and authority are not decreed by protocols but imposed by the ascendancy of arms." The road to Taza from Oudjda was open, and from there Fez was less than a hundred kilometers. The strategy of continuous pressure and offensive could quickly lift the siege if only the government would commit the soldiers. Immediately after the *Panther*'s descent on Agadir, the impatient tone disappeared, and he counseled sang-froid and *garde à vous* even while denying that anyone expected war. He was much more pessimistic in private, and Piou remembered that "before Agadir de Mun wanted war but did not expect it; after, he expected it but did not want it." All three of his sons were reserve officers, and from his position on the Foreign Affairs Committee he knew more than most the cost and chance of victory in any war. During July he considered the possibility of conflict very great, especially after the Germans replaced the relatively weak-gunned *Panther* with the cruiser *Berlin*—"which by a miracle of activity arrived at the same time that the German chancery announced its departure"—and the government's decision not to make the members of de Mun's committee privy to the course of negotiations.[15]

After the first week in July he obeyed his own injunction to suspend comment on Morocco and to trust the ministry, even one he opposed, to uphold the nation's interests. It was a precept he could not keep after hearing rumors in mid-September of what proved to be the ultimate terms of the convention and beginning to fear that Caillaux's conception of the national interest might be greatly at odds with his own. Had the Chamber not been in recess he could have posed his question there or demanded a session of the Foreign Affairs Committee. Under the circumstances he could only protest in his editorials, and because his suspicions were no more than that, he couched his criticism cautiously. He described the unverified reports and reminded all that a French protectorate in Morocco was not Germany's to grant since Spain had claims in the northern sector. "I will not do injury to our government," he concluded, "by believing it capable of accepting this abdication." But his fears grew when neither Caillaux nor de Selves took this transparent opportunity to repudiate the speculation and instead announced the release at the end of September, on schedule, of the army recruit class of 1908 after its two years of active duty rather than its retention in case of potential war. There remained only a single chance to extract information. Piou would have to corner de Selves when he appeared before a special meeting of the Budget Committee in mid-October to ask for an increase in the appropriation to the foreign service. When Piou abandoned the agenda to question the possible cession French territory in the Congo, de Selves replied sharply that committees cannot negotiate treaties. Piou persisted, arguing that the cabinet should "take note of the sentiment of the nation," since a treaty once signed might not be rejected by the legislature without provoking war. The reply of the foreign minister was rigid silence since he was unwilling to admit that Caillaux's personal diplomacy had left him humiliated and impotent even to discuss proposed terms and consequences.[16]

As soon as Caillaux formally announced the signing of the convention, de Mun rallied resistance to it in the Foreign Affairs Committee, which would have to act favorably on the treaty before it could be presented to the Chamber, and in *L'Echo de Paris*, where his editorials and accounts of the committee proceedings dominated the front page of the newspaper with the largest circulation in Paris. He argued heatedly that the only justification for handing over part of the Congo territory to Germany would be an assurance that France would be completely unfettered in Morocco, a guarantee impossible to make until the negotiations with Spain initiated in mid-November were completed. There were three particularly ominous questions about which de Selves and other government representatives seemed deliberately vague. What concessions would France have to make to Spain; would it be a "decapitated Morocco," with the entire Mediterranean coast under Spanish control? Was the compensation to Germany the result of threat; was that why the *Berlin* still lay anchored off Agadir? And why was there such immoderate haste to rush the treaty through the legislature? De Mun proposed instead that any ratification of the convention with Germany await the French understanding with Spain. Advised that de Mun was gaining support among the committee, Caillaux appeared on 22 November to testify that he considered any delay a "very dangerous plan," that Alfred von Kiderlen-Wächter, state secretary of the German Foreign Office, had intimated that French failure to ratify the convention speedily would be considered a casus belli, and that he intended to make any votes on the question of delay, whether in committee or the full Chamber of Deputies, a matter of confidence. This threat was sufficient to ensure the committee's approval on 29 November by a fifteen to two vote, but de Mun led ten others in abstaining, a dramatic measure of the backing he had attracted and a warning, even an affront, to Caillaux. It was also a challenge, because when de Mun recounted the committee action in *L'Echo de Paris*, he pledged to renew in the Chamber the proposal for adjourning consideration of the treaty and to speak from the rostrum himself in its behalf. Except for an occasional riposte from his seat, he had not addressed the deputies formally since October 1902, and it was to general astonishment and the profound concern of his family and friends that he decided to do so now. But what he called the "peril of France," and not the fate of social reform or even the church, finally provoked him to risk a fatal heart seizure from the exertion and emotion of his oratory.[17]

During the almost two weeks before the debate on 14 December, the newspapers argued the significance of the committee vote for Caillaux's political future and tried to forecast the effect of de Mun's return to the tribune at a time when he seemed more popular than at any other point in his long career. When the afternoon session of the Chamber to consider the treaty was called to order, the crush of reporters and the curious and the extraordinarily high attendance of the deputies testified to the importance of the debate. At his desk de Mun waited with Piou, occasionally pacing in the aisles, his face pallid, revealing his nervousness. In the past month he had come to seem the single greatest symbol of a revived nationalism, a man who on this issue at least spoke not for his party but for France. If there were any further doubts of it, they were dispelled when he left his desk to walk across to the tribune. From the surcharged galleries, looking as if they would collapse from the load, came the first cries of "Bravo!" and a kind of frenzied applause, spontaneous and irresistible, which the Chamber had not heard since the partisan debates of the Dreyfus affair. It was quickly picked up by the deputies, who from Right to Center and through much of the Left stood almost in unison to cheer as he faced them from the rostrum. For a moment he was amazed and uncomprehending, but his face suddenly became illumined with a glow of joy, and he remained silent for a moment, paying homage to the new spirit in France. Although he felt certain that he could last through a short speech—because he had tried one in Saint Pol de Léon, near Roscoff, in mid-November—he worried that he would be unable to regain his old mastery, and in the tension his first sentences were stumbling and labored. But within moments the eloquence returned, his phrasing, his gestures, his tone recalling many speeches of his past. The language of this one was as harsh as any he had ever used, and with it he assailed the ministry for requiring the Chamber to ratify a treaty that was ambiguous in motive and consequence. As he had before the Foreign Affairs Committee and in *L'Echo*, he demanded answers to why the *Panther* had been sent to Agadir, whether or not Germany had threatened war to force humiliating concessions from France, whether or not there would be difficulty coming to agreement with Spain, and, above all else, why the urgency to approve the convention so rapidly? As de Mun posed each question he was cheered to the echo, so much so that he was continually forced to wait for the applause to die down in order to continue. This acclamation reached near delirium at the Right and Center when he pointed directly at Caillaux to upbraid, "For a nation, the sentiment of patriotism is the safeguard of its honor, and honor is the first of its interests. You should thank this generous nation that may save you from yourself!"[18]

However much at this one moment de Mun voiced the emotion of the vast majority of deputies, the Chamber could not agree with him to delay ratifying the convention. Many were now willing to overturn Caillaux, but nearly all understood that in the premier's careful reply, the "necessity for détente" with the Germans meant that France, unready for war, could not risk the insult to Germany of repudiating its government's signature. Although the deputies voted to approve the treaty by 393 to 36, with de Mun and 140 others abstaining, they had demonstrated by their reception of the "man of all the reactions," from the wrong side of the clerical line, that they saw it not as a compromise but as a defeat. Nationalism was henceforth a power within the Chamber and in the Senate also; for it had to consider Caillaux's work next, and if the senators could not reject the treaty, they could reject its author. Early in the new year, on 9 January when Caillaux appeared before the Senate's Foreign Affairs Committee, he denied speculation that he had conducted any negotiations outside of official channels. Clemenceau then interrupted to ask de Selves whether or not he could confirm that statement, and the foreign minister, humiliated long enough, declined to answer, the equivalent of a direct condemnation of the premier, and resigned immediately. Caught in a blatant lie and the morale of his cabinet shattered, Caillaux found himself harried out of office two days later. In commenting on his fall, de Mun wrote in *L'Echo de Paris* that in his more than thirty years in politics, he had never seen a more grave government crisis, one created for the first time during the Third Republic by the conduct of foreign relations. Within, the nation had undergone a profound change, the creation of a virile resolution, not warlike but determined to resist further humiliation. For too long "antimilitarism and pacifism had grown like poisonous plants in a fen when suddenly the coup of Agadir struck the torpid hearts of France and in a moment her sons saw in one another's eyes their ancestral heritage. Among them was the cry, running like an electric shock, Enough!" Fine words, but what attracted attention was his remarkable conclusion: "I have no authority now in the councils of government, and I say this not without bitterness, but I call upon France's representatives to find a strong leader. My pen and my words are at his service, and I am resolved to pursue to the end the campaign that I open today."[19]

In 1912, at the age of seventy, when most politicians still active are certain of their way, de Mun was beginning a maneuver as audacious and risky as his conversion to the Ralliement twenty years earlier, this time as a Rallié to the politics of nationalism. With this manifesto he committed himself to the new course, the new strategy he had tried to evolve to replace the failed attempt at a grand conservative coalition. Since 1909, when Briand became premier for the first time, de Mun had been aware that with the divisive issue of the church's relationship to the state largely settled, at least to the satisfaction of the moderates, it was no longer inevitable that the conservatives be automatically excluded from any governing majority. Moderates and conservatives shared many of the same fears, the dissolution of society, lower-class unrest, the income tax, antimilitarism, and the threat of German arms, but the clerical division died hard. All appearances indicated that most French Catholics were satisfied with the constitution of the church separated from what was now definitely a secular state. Without the popular support of the faithful, the church would never regain its former position; any thought of a clerical society, or even of the role of special counsel envisioned by de Mun for the *cercles*, was no longer thinkable. The attitude of Rome intruded into this relative stability, with Pius X and Merry del Val siding with the few intransigents unwilling to recognize that without a rechristianization effort on the scale of foreign missions or some unexpected return to religious fervor, the Catholic church would simply have to accept its reduced position in France and work slowly from within by example and conversion to improve it. Pragmatically, it was political and religious suicide to insist continually on the "respect" due the church or to create such basically ephemeral issues as the "textbook index" since they only encouraged the anticlericals to bind the church more tightly and moderates to contemplate the spectacle of misplaced zeal and to question the reason of those with whom they might otherwise think to ally.

As an alternative de Mun would have the conservatives

turn to Briand or his like to negotiate in secret the best treatment politically possible for the church, pledging their votes in return and permitting him to say whatever he liked, no matter how outrageous, to satisfy the anticlericals, who would inevitably form a portion of the majority but administer according to the prearranged terms. There were few laws in the entirety of French history that remained unbearable under friendly enforcement. Certainly Briand imagined a working relationship of this form in his conception of appeasement, and de Mun had asked Piou to consider seeking such an arrangement in 1909 and 1910. The rub was that the Vatican's anathema of the Sillon and encouragement of the Integrists and the Action Française made it impossible for any Catholic leader to pursue this strategy without risking condemnation. Before Agadir the best that de Mun could have hoped to claim as the product of collaboration would have been some lessening in the harassment of the church, a minimalism bordering on treason any ultra could, and did, claim. After Agadir and the experience with Caillaux, he could add the rationale of nationalism, citing the necessity of national union for patriotism and defense. Even so, this "new course" still represented an exposed position for de Mun because it was impossible that anyone, even the strong leader to whom he had pledged his support, would be designated premier who was further to the right than the new moderates, and none would be willing or politically able to retreat from the letter of the laic conquests. But neither had Méline, and with him the church had learned that it was the spirit that counted the most. De Mun's words in 1892 to embrace the Ralliement had won him the hatred of the royalists; so these in 1912 that of the Integrists. He had suffered severely twenty years before; he expected to do so again. It was not merely expulsion from royalist society he risked now but the profound abasement of a public disavowal by his church and an abrupt end to his public life. He called himself Catholic above all, and social reform long had burned his heart, but in offering himself to a savior of France, as in denouncing Caillaux before the Chamber, de Mun revealed that his highest allegiance was to the nation.

The designation of Caillaux's successor lay with President Armand Fallières, elected in 1906 by the anticlerical majority to follow Loubet and like him a doddering pork-barreler of the Left.

The circumstances of Caillaux's fall indicated even to him that someone less pliant toward Germany might best suit the temper of the legislature, and the choice fell almost automatically on Poincaré. A brilliant and wealthy attorney with an astonishing capacity for industry and attention to detail, a confrere of de Mun in the Académie Française, and a product of the stern patriotism of Lorraine, Poincaré was by choice and action an independent, balancing himself among the critical issues of the past fifteen years so that he emerged with his reputation intact and reasonably acceptable to most factions of the Chamber. Like Abbé Siéyès he had survived; a Dreyfusard but not stridently so, opposed to the Associations law, allied to the ALP only when it was at its broadest, and in favor of the Separation as sufficiently liberal for the church. The cabinet he presented to the Chamber was exceedingly powerful, with Bourgeois, Millerand, and Delcassé heading the ministries of labor, war, and the navy, and with Briand made minister of justice, the ranking minister after the premier, an indication of his stature as chief adviser. The composition had wide appeal, and the new government won approval by a vote of 440 to 6, 14 of the ALP, the younger deputies again, voting for Poincaré's determination that the nation "remain equal to all its duties." De Mun, Piou, and the rest of the delegation took offense at his promise to uphold faithfully all of the anticlerical legislation. But in the midst of the spectacle of the ALP's hopeless disunity and the scoffing at how de Mun honored his pledge, it was also not unnoticed that however distasteful Poincaré's declaration on the laic laws may have been, de Mun and Piou had led their few followers to abstain, not oppose.[20]

Abstention was fence-sitting, peculiarly uncomfortable and unproductive, an exposed position open to attack from the Integrists and unlikely either to attract Poincaré's favorable regard. It is not unusual to experience hesitations at the critical moment in a sea change of policy, but de Mun knew that he had to confront the indecision of his vote. On 18 January, two days after the presentation of the new ministry, he revealed his escape from ambivalence during the induction of Henri de Régnier into the Académie Française. Although the poet-aristocrat had been elected to fill the seat of Melchior de Vogüé, who had died in 1911, the two writers could hardly have been less alike, Régnier the symbolic and melancholy follower of Stéphane Mallarmé, Melchior the analyst of religious and patriotic emotion in his study of the Russian novel. Charged with the welcoming remarks, de Mun dissected these differences courteously but unmistakably to Régnier's disadvantage, accusing him of failing in what he termed a writer's sacred duty to contend with the critical ideas of his time rather than fall into solipsism.[21] The words seemed as much for de Mun, insisting that he pass beyond a sterile preoccupation with the lost cause of Christian France to face the larger issue of the nation in danger. To secure this cast of mind, de Mun needed only an effective excuse to begin open support of Poincaré, and one appeared immediately. On 20 January, the Italian government, at war against the Turks in Tripolitania, ordered the forcible boarding of two French steamers to seize Turkish passengers and suspected contraband. Poincaré's protestations were public and very stiff, causing de Mun to celebrate the "wind blowing from Lorraine, wholesome and invigorating, toward the Quai d'Orsay." Very soon after, the premier executed the distasteful duty of gaining Senate passage of the 4 November convention, calling it a disgrace but requiring that France's signature be honored. Clemenceau added that Caillaux had evidently misunderstood his patriotic duty during the negotiations. De Mun could easily encourage these sentiments even while requesting that chaplains be restored to the army, especially in Morocco, where there was fighting and dying, and joining his name to a project by Piou to constitute a small advisory body of representatives of the Chamber and Senate to assist in negotiating treaties and thus avoid sudden surprises like the latest adventure by Caillaux. For his part, Poincaré was unwilling to bind his own freedom in foreign policy and not at all prepared to make public gestures to religion. De Mun's attitude could still best be described as détente, not entente, when an incident that threatened to demolish the very tentative accord between them served instead to strengthen it measurably.[22]

On 5 March, Poincaré arrived late in the afternoon to testify before the Chamber's Elections Procedure Committee, which was then considering, as it had for the past half decade, projects to institute proportional representation. Poincaré favored the change, and there appeared to be a majority for it within the Chamber, but composed only of the conservatives, the Socialists, and the new moderates of the Center, with most of the Radicals remaining opposed. Poincaré hesitated to make RP ministerial policy since like Briand he feared to lose the votes of the Radicals and knew that he could not depend for his survival on a majority of the extremes. Maintaining RP in suspense was also a political advantage for him since it separated the Radicals from the Socialists and handicapped the emergence of a majority of the Left, as Caillaux had in mind. In his testimony Poincaré insisted that RP be voted by a majority of "republicans," an ambiguity that Charles Benoist, a Progressive closely allied to the ALP and one of the most fervent supporters of RP, sought to resolve by interrupting, "between you and us there is really not so much difference." Perhaps because of fatigue, the premier retorted without reflection, "There is the entire religious question! I have never varied on that!" It was a careless and insensitive remark that deeply offended Catholics and appeared a calculated repudiation of de Mun's praise. *La Croix* called the words "a traitorous blow. . . . Is this Poincaré speaking or Combes?" The reaction was so sharp because so much had been expected of the new premier. When de Mun first heard the story, he rushed to find Benoist and grasped him by the lapels, demanding to know whether or not it was true. Although clearly injured by his champion's callousness, de Mun overcame his indignation and strove valiantly to avoid breaking with him. In the 11 March *L'Echo de Paris* he wrote, "Yes, the religious question separates our souls. That is only too true. But in this grievous separation there remains to unite us, despite all, something so sacred that we must not allow it to be torn by disputes and passions, there remains France." Poincaré was so struck by this reaction that on the following day he arranged an interview with *L'Echo* to praise de Mun and offer in return, "It goes without saying that in all questions of national interest, this difference is effaced by the unanimity of patriotism."[23]

These declarations reveal the profound effect of the Agadir incident and its aftermath on French politics: the reaction would have been unimaginable less than a year earlier. Unlike the previous international crises, this one was not overshadowed by a serious domestic dispute and was all the more intense because of the cumulative effect of Franco-German friction since 1905. The words of Poincaré and de Mun symbolized the feeling of an increasing number in France that all other issues would have to be subordinated to the defense of the nation. They also established an understanding between the two men, de Mun giving more and more proof that he would brave the outrage of Integrists to endorse a patriot who was also a defender of laicism, Poincaré determining to practice the politics of nationalism, which meant an entente with the conservatives, and to court its prophet to plaster over the cracks in French unity caused by a decade of anticlericalism. Nationalism would be the bridge to arch over the clerical line. As a sign of trust and new responsibility, Poincaré immediately assigned de Mun a minor but delicate diplomatic mission. He had long worried at the exposure of Belgium's eastern border to German attack but had been able to discover no means through normal channels of exploring some agreement on common defense with Belgian leaders without seriously compromising that country's status as a neutral. Ironically, in the same mode of personal diplomacy for which both had blamed Caillaux, Poincaré suggested that de Mun approach his relatives and friends among Belgium's ruling Catholic party to see whether or not they would present the topic. On 22 March, de Mun reported that the Belgian government considered neutrality a surer defense than any alliance and could not presume to entertain conversations on the French proposal. Although the result of the mission was a disappointment, the collaboration seemed to seal a compact between the two. De Mun began campaigning openly in favor of conservative support for Poincaré by which the Right would become partners in the government. This alliance might be the sole salvation of France in what he predicted would soon be the supreme test of an inevitable European war. The alternative was a return to the Radicals and the policy of weakness. Writing in *L'Echo de Paris* in late March, de Mun asked his readers to consider with him the tensions in the Balkans—both Russia and Bulgaria coveting Constantinople, Austria preparing to move toward Salonica, Germany urging its ally Turkey to recovery—and to answer whether or not the posture of France permitted "the leisure of internal discords." He became increasingly convinced of his own prophecy of war and wondered why others could not see the future so clearly. Too many of the conservatives still squinted through a glass darkened by the memories of battles long lost; de Mun was well aware of this self-incurred blindness, especially among his ALP colleagues, but considered that enthusiasm for nationalism could lighten the lens by making the grievances of anticlericalism less immediate, less poignant, as his own case proved.[24]

Poincaré's decision to make renewed patriotism and vigilance the basis of his ministry greatly eased de Mun's task of conversion. It had been nearly fifteen years since the conservatives had been able to cheer a premier, and many hardly knew how to react to Poincaré and his ministers. In April and May Poincaré appointed Lyautey, de Mun's personal recommendation, as resident general of Morocco, ensured the election of Deschanel to the presidency of the Chamber over the Radical candidate Georges Cochery, and declared the intention of the government to establish a national holiday in honor of Jeanne d'Arc. During late June and early July he handled Socialist objections to Moroccan policy very firmly by replying that the ministry would prosecute the establishment of a protectorate vigorously and would give Lyautey every support, since "France must never give the natives the impression of weakness or timidity." A month later he left for negotiations with Tsar Nicholas in St. Petersburg as a grand symbol of the continuing alliance. His war minister Millerand had restored the military tattoo to Paris, eliminated the reports by prefects of officers' political opinions, and confirmed Joseph Joffre as generalissimo, a hard-bitten soldier who favored a long-term professional army and who took as his chief of staff General Noël de Curières de Castelnau, the brother of the late ALP deputy Léonce de Castelnau and so clerical that he was known as the "monk in boots." Because these acts and de Mun's support found him warming admiration among the conservatives, Poincaré decided to press for RP, winning its passage in the Chamber 339 to 217 on 10 July. The majority was somewhat larger than expected because many Radicals, aware that there was a better chance to defeat the bill in the Senate, were reluctant to oppose the premier when he seemed so popular and perhaps even willing to isolate them by relying on the Right. They were shaken by the paradox of archclerical de Mun cajoling the hesitant conservatives slowly toward Poincaré, content at first to have them support him only on votes involving the military or RP, where no concessions to their principles had to be made. By mid-fall Emile Combes would conclude that Poincaré had forsaken the Left for the Right.[25]

De Mun would have thought Combes's fears premature, although he would have agreed that Poincaré was more friendly to the conservatives. He had been genuinely overjoyed at the selection of Lyautey, feeling that at last Morocco would be in sure hands. Almost filially, Lyautey addressed him as "Mon Capitaine" and sent him long, frank letters from Morocco full of details for his editorials. With them de Mun composed stirring accounts of the progress in taming the interior tribes that galvanized many not already caught up by nationalism. Day by day in *L'Echo de Paris* he advertised the firm stand of the ministry and warned those who would oppose Poincaré that they placed themselves with Jaurès and the Socialists, who referred to the soldiers in Morocco as "your army" and protested the destruction of "the ages-old civilization" of the desert nomads even after they burned captured French officers alive. His words were picked up and became the subject of speech after speech by moderates as well as conservatives. In the midst of the premier's trip to St. Petersburg, de Mun was not far wrong when he wrote boastfully, "Because I have wanted, during the great national anguish, to exalt patriotic pride, unfamiliar hands, from all directions, have stretched toward me . . . they seek not the writer, not the orator, but the idea, the fecund idea that makes a people great." Yet although the conservatives found themselves supporting the ministry on Morocco and RP and appreciating the gestures toward their sensibilities by Poincaré and Millerand, they remained deterred by the premier's legalistic attitude toward the anticlerical legislation of his predecessors. He was determined to enforce all of these laws and was oblivious to any pleas for special consideration. By the terms of Combes's 1904 law, the last congregational schools run by authorized orders were to be closed as soon as the state public school system could absorb their students. In June de Mun wrote to Poincaré as "cher confrère" to ask that a Catholic school a block up the street from his *hôtel* be spared in order not to disturb "the concord of good Frenchmen so necessary in these difficult hours." Poincaré refused to make exceptions to the law and, along with the one on the Avenue de l'Alma, closed fifty other congregational schools during the summer. He welcomed the votes of the conservatives, whom he considered more steadfast on nationalist issues than any segment of the Radicals, but they would have to accept the lay Republic before he would commit himself to depend on them. He was willing to redraw the clerical line in a different spot, as he made clear in a speech in his home constituency in April 1912, but he would draw it. "There are parties that on the relations of church and state profess opinions that are the negation of republican doctrine," he explained. "Whether one wishes it or not, here is a first frontier. I assign no one a place to the left or right of it. Each is free to settle where he chooses, but he must be on one side or the other. As for us, we are, of course, among those who defend the laicity of the state." This attitude left little room for even token concessions, but de Mun considered that Poincaré might eventually acknowledge the justice of the church's complaint against the lack of "neutrality" in the public schools, especially since it was a question of patriotism as well as religion. Ministerial criticism, or even better, correction, of the teachers would make conservatives and the hierarchy far more ecstatic than they would be about any mere lessening of harassment, since it would effectively constitute an official endorsement of the church's position. It was extremely fortunate for de Mun's campaign that the union of schoolteachers, meeting in Chambéry, voted on 17 August to support the Sou du Soldat, an enterprise inspired by Hervé to spread antimilitarist propaganda among recruits. Receiving the news in the midst of his negotiations with the Tsar, Poincaré was enraged at this desecration of his nationalist policy by government employees, and on his return to France he ordered the dissolution of the union, upsetting the Radicals and rendering the conservatives exultant. After dismissing the leaders of the schoolteachers, Poincaré promised in a speech at Nantes on 27 October not only to make the rest of them paragons of patriotism but to repress sternly their gratuitous criticism of religion.[26]

De Mun had his own party in mind when planning much of his campaign for Poincaré. As individuals, the ALP deputies had what Piou called a *réserve sympathique* for the premier, but the official position of the party was much more critical, a duality that was the result of the almost complete disappearance of internal cohesion. While de Mun believed that the ALP's sole chance for recovery lay in seeking a national leader outside its ranks, Piou pessimistically concluded that Catholics were the only constituency to which he could appeal any longer and began to act increasingly after 1910 as if he directed a confessional party, although one not embracing the extreme Right. The *Bulletin* served as a Catholic spokesman instead of a conservative one, at times seeming a left wing of Integrism. It found nothing to approve in Poincaré and gave him credit only for the "same official brigandage" as occurred under any Radical. Piou sometimes used this language as a screen for the party because, unlike the ultras within the church, he did not believe that his followers could be seriously faulted for joining the majority to support the Moroccan protectorate or the establishment of RP even though *L'Univers* had labeled anything less than complete intransigence to a laic ministry opportunism open to censure. Piou's policy might be marginally acceptable to the Veuillots, but it could never produce what de Mun had planned his strategy to do, win concessions for the church. In what the Integrists would term the supreme opportunism, he was proposing to make the ALP a dependable and necessary portion of a general conservative-moderate majority and then bargain this support for whatever he could get. Piou was in no position to impose his own policy because since the 1910 elections about a quarter of the party's deputies, almost twenty led principally by Colonel Emile Driant and Louis de Chappedelaine, had been attracted to de Mun's more forward strategy, particularly since the fall of Caillaux. Piou had no means of calling de Mun back from operating essentially on his own, and as the party split wide open, his prestige declined at a time when his fatigue and despair made it impossible for him to recover it.

Until the fall of 1912 it was very difficult to tell where the ALP stood, with de Mun almost daily praising Poincaré's foreign policy and at least publicly ignoring his determined laicism, and Laya in the *Bulletin* omitting any reference to the premier's nationalism but concentrating on his words to Benoist and the school controversy. These contradictions were not unusual in a party no longer certain of its identity and afraid for its survival. The ALP emphasized fewer issues because some of its former stands seemed dangerous. Approval of any form of income tax or change in collection was unmentionable because the whole question had become associated with the hated Caillaux. With the departure of the ACJF, social Catholicism also quietly disappeared from the pages of the *Bulletin* since it might recall the fate of the Sillon.

Those few deputies like Gailhard-Bancel who were seriously committed to reform did not waver, and de Mun continued to shape legislation in the Labor Committee, to campaign for it in the press, and even to join in projects with a chastened and chary Sangnier, but about two-thirds of the party took this opportunity to cast off ideas with which they had never been quite comfortable. The deputies felt more secure embracing nationalism, and the ALP had always brandished the flag and the army. After experiencing Caillaux and then vicariously participating in the subjection of Morocco under Lyautey, they were emotionally susceptible to de Mun's appeal for Poincaré, but most shared Piou's caution sufficiently to hesitate until November 1912, when the *Bulletin* openly called for Frenchmen to rally round the premier. By then, of course, he had become much more attractive because of his condemnation of the public schoolteachers and his careful course for France through the crisis of the Balkan War.[27]

Along with his party, de Mun praised Poincaré's "courageous firmness" and "ingenious capability" in directing French policy during the fighting in the Balkans, but once again he was far ahead of the ALP in comprehending the significance of these battles. For him they were the dawn of the apocalypse. In words laden with doom, he wrote that "there are, in the history of a people, decisive hours. We touch one of those hours." "L'Heure décisive" was the title of every one of his editorials in *L'Echo de Paris* analyzing the war that fall. Germany's Balkan policy had failed humiliatingly, its vassal Turkey thoroughly beaten, and the shame all the greater since the Greek armies had been trained by the French, the Turk by the Prussians. With its allies, Greece now threatened to block German plans for a Berlin-to-Baghdad railroad. Austria had the cruel shock of suddenly confronting a greatly strengthened Serbia on its southern border and, in blocking Serbian access to the sea, had permanently antagonized Russia. As de Mun described the heightened tension, the ethnic hatreds, the lethal competition of the Great Powers, he could come to but one conclusion. "No one in Europe wants war," he wrote, "and yet it moves closer and closer, despite intentions, fears, exertions, and resolutions, led by the blind force of situations and events." His prophecy of war had never been so bald or so dire, perhaps because he had never known so well the looming dangers. Poincaré had flattered him at the beginning of the war in October by inviting his views during a private meeting and briefing him on the government's intentions. In December he asked de Mun to evaluate the plenipotentiaries of Greece, Bulgaria, and Serbia by conferring with them as they passed through Paris on their way to the London Peace Conference—called to negotiate an end to the Balkan War—and then to meet with him to discuss his impressions. De Mun's reaction to these unexpected new marks of respect and to the premier's frank and pessimistic assessment of the European situation was an urgent demand that French military preparations be drastically improved, ideally through the extension of required service to three years, and a strengthened conviction that only Poincaré could provide the leadership for a physical rearmament of France to match the spiritual revival begun with his ministry. This response was precisely what the premier had planned and needed because he had decided to seek the presidency of the Republic when Fallières's term expired in January 1913. He felt himself capable of converting the largely ceremonial role into that of a vigorous national leader who would not be handicapped by the hesitations of the legislature. Reckoning the votes very carefully, he concluded that he would need the support of the conservatives to assure the election, and as de Mun was the only one who might be capable of delivering these votes, he would have to offer him the first proofs that the Right would be restored to the councils of state.[28]

This necessity for Poincaré, whose majorities in the Chamber and Senate had been large and stable and whose firm leadership seemed genuinely popular in the nation, to recruit new allies to ensure his election as president was an anomaly of French politics that requires comment. Working against his candidacy was the tradition of the office he sought. Since the resignation of MacMahon, the Chamber and Senate had met at Versailles as the National Assembly seven times to elect a president of the Republic, choosing a series of docile second- or third-rate politicians, men willing to be ceremonial chiefs of state. Casimir-Périer was the only exception, and he had resigned quickly from frustration. It was dogma to the Left that a strong man at the Elysée, no matter what his origins, was a threat to legislative dominance, and Poincaré had proved himself a strong man. Earlier in his career he had also called for strengthening the powers of the president. Opposing Poincaré were powerful enemies, principally Clemenceau and Caillaux, who although personally antagonistic to one another and not overly concerned to see Poincaré serve a stint as premier in which he might be readily deposed, were determined to bar his ascension to the presidency for a septennate during which he would be almost untouchable. Both were also concerned to obstruct the return of Briand, who would be President Poincaré's likely designation as premier. Clemenceau wielded great power in the Senate, and Caillaux still commanded a sizable following among the Radicals despite his conduct of the previous year. Together they considered that their chances of blocking Poincaré were very good. They could probably control a majority of the Left and impose "republican discipline" on most of Poincaré's backers. Despite de Mun's year-long campaign for the premier, they considered it unlikely that he could prevent a large group of the conservatives from proposing their own candidate or engaging in a *politique du pire*. Poincaré would be left with certain support only from the moderates.

To ensure the opposition of the conservatives, the Radical leaders appealed to Catholic prejudice, threatening in mid-December to publish a dossier on Madame Poincaré revealing her illegitimacy, her years as Poincaré's mistress, and the civil character of their marriage. Unable to offer a refutation, Poincaré reacted by calling Henri Simond, editor of *L'Echo de Paris*, Arthur Meyer, and de Mun to a secret meeting just after Christmas. He confessed his inability to marry in the church because his wife was divorced and did not know whether or not her first husband was still alive. After declaring that the three could do what they wished with his admission, he made what they considered an implied promise to submit to a consecration of his marriage as soon as his wife found herself able to do so. De Mun in particular was impressed by Poincaré's candor, and after their departure, he, Simond, and Meyer agreed privately to reassure the Catholic milieux about the state of the Poincaré ménage by hinting at the premier's "promise." It took all of their prestige to calm indignant churchgoers at a time when Queen Mary of Great Britain was ready to breach the Entente Cordiale rather than be included in photographs with Madame Poincaré. De Mun could not fail to realize that the premier would not have sought his aid directly or implied so compromising a break with official laicism had he not determined that the votes of the conservatives were essential to his bid for the presidency. He suspected that Poincaré might be capable of overturning the traditional conception of the chief of state and that, if so, he could certainly be a far more valuable ally elevated to the Elysée than as premier, especially if he owed that increase in dignity to the conservatives. It would not do to dictate terms to the premier, but de Mun concluded that he could require a greater premium than the hint of a religious marriage in return for the support he might rally.[29]

Writing to Poincaré soon after the secret meeting, de Mun strongly suggested that further concessions would be the price for a continuation of his efforts for him among the conservatives.

> You must know that there are grave differences between us. I feared so even as you took power. The experience of this year has confirmed me in that apprehension. We do not understand in the same fashion "religious peace." You have given only a verbal pacification. Proposals for "laic defense" remain a worrisome menace for Catholics. The laws against the congregations are applied with a persevering rigor. The fundamental question of reestablishing diplomatic relations between France and the Holy See has not taken a step. However, and in spite of these disappointments, confident of your patriotism and recognizing the firmness with which you would defend the national interest, I have not hesitated, as you well know, with an abnegation not always rewarded, to give you a support to the limit of my resources, support the utility of which you have often recognized. [Reproduced with permission from Fernand Payen, *Raymond Poincaré: L'Homme, le parlementaire, l'avocat*, copyright by Editions Bernard Grasset.]

Much was left unsaid but clearly understood in these words. Hardly a week earlier de Mun had written another letter to Poincaré, one of very different tenor. He announced formally that in his capacity as chairman of the board of the Ecole de la Rue des Postes, which had remained open but bereft of its Jesuits since 1899, he had to appear during the following week to defend the school against closure in pursuance of the 1904 law. "I ask nothing of you," he had concluded stiffly, "but I place this question before your conscience." Poincaré had refused, as always, to intervene, even to save the Postards to whom de Mun was devoted. But now, the premier's ambition and the threat to it from the Radicals immensely strengthened de Mun's bargaining position. With his new letter as a preamble, de Mun began more secret meetings with Poincaré, proposing that as the price for the votes of the Right to assure him the presidency, the premier assume two obligations, carefully chosen to fit into the general political framework established during the past year by his ministry. As a logical extension of Briand's appeasement, he would temper the enforcement of existing anticlerical laws, while the conservatives in return would tolerate the official proclamation of the laic ideal and not immediately seek the repeal of the Radical legacy. Even more important for de Mun, he would also vow to press for new legislation to strengthen the army, specifically a three-year-service law. Because it would demand concrete sacrifices from Frenchmen and not merely the sentiment of patriotism, this law could well be very unpopular and certainly would be expensive. De Mun was convinced that despite the surge of nationalism that the premier had so commendably abetted, only his presence at the Elysée could guarantee the enactment of this revision. Poincaré did not find these terms difficult to accept. Although each would require caution and careful maneuvering, neither condition was particularly onerous. He had himself come to believe in the necessity for rearmament, and while the pact on the laic laws involved some sacrifice of principle, it was one by both sides that might calm, if not suppress, the conflicts of doctrine. The essence of the terms was less potentially compromising than his clandestine negotiations with the symbol of the Right, and de Mun could threaten to reveal them should he fail to honor his commitments. For Poincaré the risk was worth taking because he saw in it the opportunity to bring the conservatives more completely into a coalition with the moderates and because he felt in absolute need of the votes.[30]

At the beginning of January 1913, during a series of turbulent sessions with other conservative leaders, de Mun set about to fulfill his pledge. There were numerous objections and hesitations, but to all of them de Mun replied bluntly that an accommodation with Poincaré was the best for which they could hope. His laicism was unfortunate, that was true, but no realistic candidate for the presidency was less objectionable in that regard. A haughty abstention, while ideologically pure, or worse a *politique du pire*, would gain nothing for the conservatives, and since Poincaré's defeat would mean the election of another Radical, it might even compromise the question of nationalism to which they had a duty to address themselves. Poincaré had been willing to treat, to make specific and significant promises. He had the potential to render valuable support throughout an entire term of seven years. It would be politically disastrous to reject this first chance in more than a decade to be on the side of the victor. The Progressives required little convincing because since January 1912 they had been voting with the ministry in most instances. Surprisingly, neither did Piou, although he was not completely won over to de Mun's strategy. During the last months of the year he had seen the ALP slip away from his caution, dazzled by Poincaré's foreign policy and stern treatment of the teachers. De Mun's pact with the premier was attractive, the kind of glittering opportunity he had sought previously for the ALP, and he feared that to oppose it would split the party permanently, since a majority were sure to reject his counsel. He, too, wanted to be on the winning side and gave his blessing, taking some comfort in the knowledge that the votes of the National Assembly were not recorded by individual representative and were less conspicuous to those outside. After hearing out de Mun, even the few remaining independents of the extreme Right, such as Denys Cochin of an unresurgent monarchism, conceded an enthusiasm for Poincaré that ranged from tepid to genuine. De Mun concluded that he had rallied almost unanimous support.[31]

During that first week in January, Poincaré's foes were also busy. They had discovered that Millerand had committed the incredible indiscretion of reinstating in his rank as a reserve officer Lieutenant Colonel Mercier du Paty de Clam, who had been required to retire in 1900 because of his role as one of the chief accusers of Dreyfus. The timing was probably not sabotage, since Millerand's loyalty to Poincaré before and after was unquestioned, and it could not have been another bid for conservative support, de Mun himself hurrying to Briand to assure him that "we did not ask this." Instead, it was an amazing lapse of political sensitivity, which Caillaux attempted to exploit in the Chamber on 10 January. If Poincaré defended Millerand, he would likely cause the fall of his ministry and his own discredit on the eve of the presidential election since Paty de Clam was too much a principal of the affair for the Left ever to forgive. The alternative, the sacrifice of Millerand, Caillaux and the premier's other enemies thought, would also be a political disaster for Poincaré since it would offend his new conservative allies, who had applauded the minister of war throughout the year and many of whom considered that Paty de Clam had been poorly treated all along. Because he felt certain of de Mun's support, Poincaré was not confronted by this dilemma and could disown his colleague with confidence. Although de Mun "wrote to him afterward that for himself and for others the team of Poincaré and Millerand had been the double security of national confidence at a formidable hour," he confirmed that the premier's response to the Radical threat had not hurt him among the conservatives. "Your position continues to be very strong . . . I remain today [toward you] what I was before the incident. I would have said so clearly in the editorial I have just sent to *L'Echo* for tomorrow morning, where I denounce, with all of the indignation of my soul, the conspiracy of which you were the victim with Millerand, if I had not feared to compromise your cause." For those who doubted the conservative support, the language of the editorial was clear enough. "[Poincaré] knows with what perseverance I have sustained him in his patriotic task despite our disagreements on other and grave subjects. I am ready to do so again." Piou was much less enthusiastic, claiming that at Versailles the ALP "will have no candidate of our own," but acknowledging publicly that "it is not indifferent to us that the new chief of state come from the Académie Française rather than from the 'stagnant bogs.' "[32]

The last chance for Clemenceau and Caillaux to stop Poincaré was to hold all of the Radicals as a solid voting bloc. On 15 January they convoked what they termed the "republican caucus" of senators and deputies, but excluded from it the conservatives—Progressives and the ALP as well as the extreme Right—and the Socialists, with whom they were quarreling over RP. After two ballots that day and a third the following, the premier's enemies commanded a plurality for Jules Pams, a wealthy manufacturer of cigarette paper whose most impressive political achievement was to have been minister of agriculture in Poincaré's cabinet. Clemenceau's axiom, "I vote for the stupidest!" was never more apt. Then, along with Caillaux and Combes, Clemenceau brazenly stalked to Poincaré's office to demand that he withdraw his candidacy in the face of "republican opposition," because now it was clear that he could be elected only by the votes of the Right. The premier replied that the result of the caucus was meaningless since perfectly good republicans like the Progressives and the ALP had been omitted and that, as he had no intention of being "guillotined by persuasion," he would refuse them. He could afford this defiance because he knew that his votes outside the caucus were certain and that it would be impossible for the Radical leaders to impose discipline on his supporters within as long as he declined to eliminate himself. The victory was now undeniable, and once more the pact with de Mun had provided the guarantee of its success. More Radicals began to join Poincaré's side as the strength of his position became obvious, and the newspapers of the Left admitted so by the virulence of their attacks.[33]

When the National Assembly convened at Versailles on 17 January, the conclusion was foregone, with Poincaré winning election as president of the Republic by the overwhelming margin of 483 to 287 over Pams. The victory belonged not just to the Lorrainer and his gospel of nationalism but to de Mun and his new course. It was his vindication, and although it was indiscreet to say so, *L'Autorité* was hardly exaggerating when it editorialized that "it was the first time since Boulangism that the conservatives had reached for the highest realms of power." De Mun expressed the mood best in an apostrophe to the new president that he meant for himself as well, "You have the power to reorient national life."[34]

9
Playing the Game, 1913–1914

Poincaré's victory gave de Mun such an unjustified sense of political power that he imperiously prescribed the formula for this reorientation of national life, the exclusion of the Radicals from power forever, preventing

> the offensive return of men who for fifteen years have emasculated the nation, destroyed its moral energy, annihilated its material strength, and who, by a criminal maneuver, in the face of an indignant nation, of a consternated army, of a stupefied world, tore from his post the minister [Millerand] whose name appeared to the country as a safeguard; men who, closed in the narrow prison of their sectarian passions, insensitive to the aspiration of all patriotic hearts toward concord and union, intend to perpetuate the divisions and hatreds, by the laws of a discredited legislature and habits of an enslaved administration. The danger to the nation is the return of these men to government.

The elimination of the Radicals would allow the secret engagements to become the basis first of ministerial policy and later of a general conservative revival. Poincaré would designate only thoroughly trustworthy men to be premier, and de Mun would labor to ensure that they always enjoyed a working majority of the moderates and conservatives, who had demonstrated their common interest during the presidential election. Briand, minister of justice for the past year, shrewd and already half-trusted by the Right, was the obvious choice to begin the strategy as premier. He could learn the rules of this new political game more quickly than anyone else and maneuver within them to survive.[1]

Poincaré's conception of his presidential role was not so blatantly partisan. Although he intended to make use of the powers of his office, he would not risk the fate of MacMahon by forcing a manifestly unpopular premier on an unwilling legislature.

Policies meant more to him than personality or party affiliation, and a necessary turn to the Radicals, who, *pace* de Mun in *L'Echo*, were not monolithic, would not be fatal for the program he had traced out. It was convenient, of course, for his relations with de Mun and the conservatives that Briand was clearly the heir to the nationalist majority and could carry on the alliance immediately as premier, while he waited an awkward month for the presidential inauguration. Like de Mun, Poincaré was confident that Briand could carefully tilt toward the Right without arousing an extreme reaction within all sections of the Radical party. He was less certain of the behavior of the conservative deputies, who would have to tolerate language offensive to their religious beliefs and not exult too openly in their new influence. Briand put them to the test when he appeared before the Chamber on 24 January with a ministry composed mostly of moderates but with a few of the less militant Radicals in unimportant posts. In his ministerial declaration he promised to continue Poincaré's nationalism and strong foreign policy, avoid abrupt financial experiments (a reference to the income tax), and press for Senate passage of RP. Taking a breath, he added that "the admirable work of the laic school, going on for the past thirty years, should be finally completed, without provocation and without violence, but with tenacity. The laic school is one of the vibrant strengths of the Republic; to abdicate its defense would be to deny the Republic." On the conservative side there was absolute silence, not a catcall, not a word of protest. Veterans of the Chamber found it uncanny. The ministry then proposed a vote of confidence on its pledge of "national defense, social progress, and laicity, with the concourse and by the action of republicans," winning by 324 to 77. Half of the Radicals preferred to abstain since they recognized Briand as the agent of Poincaré, whom they now despised, but de Mun almost compensated for them by providing the ministry with 86 votes from the conservative seats, where only 30 deputies abstained—including Piou and Groussau to de Mun's regret—and not a single one opposed. Forever afterward the Integrists would refer in horror to this "resolution for laicization" on which de Mun led the conservatives to forsake the paths of righteousness. It would likewise be the criterion by which the moderates would judge de Mun and his followers, proof that they had learned and could play their part.[2]

Briand left unmentioned in his declaration the greatest enticement of conservative support, the plan to strengthen the army immensely by returning to three years of required military service for all adult Frenchmen. The idea of three-year service had been the property of a few conservatives, most notably Driant of the ALP, and of some segments of the army since mid-1912, when it became clear that the enchantment of the high command with the offensive would require more and better-trained troops than static defense, especially in the cavalry and the artillery, where precision of execution was essential. Poincaré may have mentioned three-year service to Nicholas II in August 1912 as an example of how the French might improve their army, but the fear of war inspired by the fighting in the Balkans created a sense of urgency about it among conservatives generally and made de Mun require it as a condition of support in the presidential election. It fell to Poincaré and Briand to discover some politically opportune pretext for honoring this promise, and the German general staff quickly provided one. In early 1913 it decided on the immediate implementation of laws passed during the 1912 Reichstag to increase the German army by 150,000 men over the next four years. The French army of 480,000 was to be confronted suddenly by a German opponent nearly twice as large, with 860,000 effectives. Because of its booming birth rate, Germany could increase its forces merely by drafting more recruits. With its own birth rate stagnant or declining and two years of service already required from all of its male youth, France did not enjoy this option and would have to extend the basic conscription term in order to keep pace. Each September all twenty-one-year-olds, the so-called class, marched off to the training camps, and the change to three-year service would provide three classes in uniform at all times instead of two. There would be an increase of 50 percent in the number of draftees and of approximately 30 percent in the army as a whole, enabling it to face the Germans with roughly 625,000 men, somewhat better odds. The response would be unpopular, taking sons away from families and out of schools for an extra year, but for those who did not believe that an accommodation with Germany was possible, it was a question of national survival. Briand's minister of war Eugène Etienne began drawing up the proposal as soon as the cabinet won its vote of confidence, and on 6 March he presented it to the Chamber.[3]

At the same time, de Mun began a campaign through *L'Echo de Paris* to convert public opinion, particularly after the German increases were announced in mid-February. Claiming that he had "not time for personal animosity" since "the defense of the national soil alone obsessed" him, he argued that the only complete reply to Germany would be a return to three-year service made retroactive for the class of 1911 in order for the army to be at its new strength by 1914. Two-year service, he claimed, had left infantry units and the cavalry so weak that they were mere skeletons. What was the value of any diploma, of any pursuit that an extra year in the army might disrupt, when compared to the safety of the nation? There was always the reserve, some retorted, especially Jaurès, who preferred a *levée en masse* if war broke out instead of a large professional army, but de Mun questioned the value of citizen soldiers, who had grown soft away from the military discipline of body and mind. By the end of February, Jaurès and the Socialists were emerging as the most strenuous opponents of any increase in time under military authority, expounding instead the theory of the "new army"—de Mun called it "the fantasies of Jaurès"—by which the Great Powers would imitate Switzerland in disbanding their expensive armies in favor of local militias. "C'est de la folie!" Jaurès cried, and the Socialist deputies stood on their desks chanting "Réaction! Réaction!" as Etienne tried to read the proposal before the Chamber. In the sessions of the Army Committee, Jaurès and Independent Socialist Victor Augagneur harassed Etienne, foreign minister Charles Jonnart, and even Joffre with detailed and repetitious questions, asking anything in order to delay consideration of the bill. Driant, who also sat on the committee, scornfully called them "a comedy, but tragic for France," causing Jaurès to retort without particular relevance that when the Socialists had taken power everywhere there would be no more wars since disputes would be settled by compulsory arbitration. As a warning to the ministry of their strength, the Socialists held a rally against the bill at the Pré-Saint-Gervais in Paris on 16 March, drawing between 150,000 and 200,000 demonstrators. To confront this determined opposition to three-year service, de Mun quickly dropped his pretense of avoiding polemic and claimed that the battle lines were clearly drawn between a nationalist France and an isolated band of Socialists, antimilitarists, and the dupes of Germany in their ideal of international brotherhood.[4]

De Mun failed to consider that all nationalists were not necessarily Poincaristes, particularly Clemenceau, who like many Radicals was determined to prevent the passage of RP by the Senate, where he dominated debate. He was not friendly to the president, and his anticlerical soul suspected the darkest machinations from the moderates, all of whom he would soon abuse openly as "the protégés of Albert de Mun." Briand, Clemenceau decided, required reminding that the Radical party remained much stronger than the conservatives, and he administered a painful lesson to the premier on 18 March by leading the Senate to reject RP by a 161 to 128 vote. Although Poincaré urged him to reconstitute his ministry, eliminate RP from his program, and return as premier, Briand insisted on resigning. His departure created Poincaré's first cabinet crisis and a loss of confidence by his conservative allies. Immediately after the Senate vote, de Mun wrote him demanding that Briand's resignation be refused in order to demonstrate that "the three-year law is an absolute condition!" When that failed, he published an incautious editorial in *L'Echo* declaring that the president had failed in his duty to his electors and that as a minimum effort at reconciliation he should require the continuation of Etienne and Jonnart at their posts in any new ministry. Poincaré had no intention of abandoning the service law, but he did not believe that Briand was the sole moderate capable of maintaining the alliance with the conservatives. To defy the Senate would have been a symbol, as de Mun had written, but too much of one, an unreasonable antagonism of the Radicals. It was safer to rely on a new ministry under Barthou, Briand's own minister of justice, who promised to retain Etienne but replaced Jonnart with Stéphen Pichon at the Quai d'Orsay. De Mun expected much greater power and intervention from Poincaré as president. It was not enough that he had directed Jonnart's foreign policy for him or that the Briand ministry had hardly moved without coordinating with the Elysée. De Mun did recognize that Briand's defeat was an indirect attack on the president himself, but he had presumed that Poincaré would challenge the theory of legislative dominance over the executive. As he wrote to Etienne, there should be no accommodation with the enemy.[5]

In his recalcitrance de Mun worried what form the pacification of the Radicals might take. He had little confidence in many of the ministers Barthou presented, calling the cabinet a "political pharmacy," containing both dangerous and safe "drugs," and he feared that the new premier would be less skillful than Briand in directing the alliance. Some of this reaction was resentment at Poincaré's refusal to dictate to the chambers, but more originated in the belated understanding that the president's powers were limited and that his special entrée at the Elysée meant only the restoration of political influence to the conservatives and not the overturn of the political tradition built up for forty years. Barthou faced the Chamber on 25 March and made pledges similar to those of Briand, adding the promise of the service law, but now de Mun joined 53 other conservatives to abstain, reducing the ministry's vote of confidence to a perilous 225 to 162, only a plurality of the deputies. De Mun also complained to Etienne of Poincaré's failure to utter "a word about the *vital* question [of the army]" during his official visit to Montpellier on 30 March and to the nation at large of the ministry's allowing the deputies to adjourn for six weeks without having replied to Germany. But regardless of his disappointment, he had the sense to rally to Barthou after venting his pique, especially when, in early April, Jaurès began a series of editorials against three-year service in *L'Humanité*, the circulation of which rivaled that of *L'Echo de Paris*, and dared de Mun, "the great leader of the campaign of 'three years,' " to debate him.[6]

For the next two months they parried in successive editorials, picking at arguments, haggling over numbers of reservists and the speed with which they could be mobilized, each only confirming the other and his followers in their position. De Mun was won from abstention back to open support of the government. Jaurès was now wary of openly challenging the need to provide some new strength to the army, and he was willing to concede a small increase in the amount of service. He kept returning to his ideal of the reserve, envisioning how on mobilization day every Frenchman would take down his rifle from above the mantle and troop to the colors. To de Mun the idea still smacked of absurdity and of danger. His friends in the officer corps convinced him that Germany's troop increases would enable its army to mount a sudden attack, an all-out offensive against France, without waiting to mobilize its reserve. If so, France could depend only on its ready troops, since the decisive actions would be over long before Jaurès's rifle-toters in mufti could be rallied. Many in the high command considered any surprise attack impossible since the Germans would have to cross Belgium to reach France or else slog through the heavily fortified border with Alsace and Lorraine, but the idea frightened de Mun and other conservatives, and it was an effective weapon to use against those who were undecided about three-year service or who preferred to place their faith in the reserve. "Europe has no soul," he wrote to Poincaré, pessimistic as always, "or if it does, that soul is black." War would come, and when it did, nothing less than full rearmament could save France.[7]

De Mun felt that he had to be obdurate about the impracticality of halfway measures since he had divined the strategy by the Socialists and the left-wing Radicals of proposing thirty-month service as an intermediate position between Etienne's bill and no increase at all. In mid-May mutinies at Toul, Macon, Nancy, and Rodez in reaction to the ministry's decision to hold over the class of 1910 if the service law were not enacted by fall forced a final choosing of sides. While preparing to propose "compromises" of thirty months, the Socialists openly condemned the "besotted army, the decided enemy of the Republic," and justified the rebellion of the soldiers as a worthy response to the chauvinists of the government and the press. Poincaré became so disturbed that he called his antagonist Clemenceau to the Elysée and won him to an extraordinary investigation of the CGT and the Sou du Soldat, which he believed responsible for instigating the trouble. Barthou's resolve was stiffened, and deputies who at first had been frightened and might have been willing to accommodate their desire to strengthen the army with something less rigorous than an extra year's service came round to follow him. The clerical line was replaced by another of nationalism, and there were excommunications almost daily from each church. As he dissected and then destroyed the proposals for thirty-month recruits in *L'Echo*, de Mun reflected better than anyone else the hardening of positions, the end of debate, even if it was of the extreme example, himself and Jaurès. "He wants," de Mun wrote, "for France to be no longer a military nation; I want it to be one more than ever. He wants the country to have only a national guard; I want it to have an army. He encourages sedition in the military; I consider that an inexpiable crime." In his new paper, *L'Homme Libre*, Clemenceau contributed his own intransigence, this time for Poincaré and de Mun, warning the deputies that if Frenchmen recoiled before the sacrifice of three-year service, they would have to renounce their independence and go on their knees to Germany. Barthou and Etienne won their last converts and solidified their ranks with one final change in the bill, to avoid the inequality, and danger, of holding over a class already in uniform. The draft age would be lowered to twenty, and in the fall of 1913 both twenty- and twenty-one-year-olds would be inducted simultaneously to get the army up to strength immediately. With the bill in this form, Barthou finally risked its passage in the Chamber on 19 July, winning 358 to 204, a margin all the more impressive in light of his mere plurality on assuming power and the strident voices on the Left denouncing his obvious reliance on the conservatives. With Clemenceau demanding quick action in his bailiwick, the ministry had no trouble in the upper house either, winning an amazing 254 to 37 triumph on 7 August in the Senate, where only five months earlier Briand had been upended.[8]

On 21 July, on the front page of *L'Echo de Paris*, de Mun celebrated "a decisive act of national resolution" led by Barthou, who "by his courage, by his ready eloquence, by his capable and vigorous words, has, almost alone, carried the weight [of this responsibility], has saved a weakening legislature from the furious attacks of Jaurès and his allies." Many Catholics were doubtlessly shocked to read such publicly unrestrained praise from him for the premier who, as his own minister of education, had personally conducted the defense of the laic school. Elation over the Chamber's passage of the service law dictated part of his emotion, but more broadly, by midsummer 1913, de Mun could believe that the bargain he had sealed half a year earlier with Poincaré was fulfilled, that every promise would be sure. Any anger over the president's "desertion" of Briand had disappeared long ago as the wisdom of choosing Barthou became clear. Poincaré had lent his name and prestige to the three-year law and, had it failed in the Chamber, he was prepared to ask the Senate for a dissolution and new legislative elections. From the Elysée he had acted decisively to crush the mutinies in May. His foreign policy meant the freeing of Lyautey from all hobbling restraints in conquering Morocco, and in a year's time, to de Mun's utter delight, the resident general had gloriously carried off Marrakesh and Tadla and placed eight thousand square kilometers of territory under French control. For such an accomplishment there seemed to de Mun to be relatively little loss, 402 dead, 1,532 wounded: "Is that too much for half an empire? Nothing great, nothing lasting, can be done without sacrifice." For de Mun's precarious reputation at the Vatican, the authority of French arms meant little, the honoring of another pledge very much. Soon after the voting at Versailles, Madame Poincaré's picture was recognized by her former sister-in-law, who told her that her first husband had died in the United States in late 1909. This knowledge enabled Poincaré to seek the blessing of the church for his civil marriage, and he asked his friend Monsignor Alfred Baudrillart to officiate, saying nothing of the arrangement with de Mun but admitting that "the head of a Catholic state owes this example to his nation." Fearful of arousing the fiercest criticism from anticlericals and making his personal life a political issue again, he insisted that the celebration, on 5 May 1913, take place in the strictest secrecy, with only his brother Lucien and two friends as witnesses. All were sworn to reveal nothing. The story eventually spread because Poincaré called de Mun to the Elysée to tell him, and as protection against the diatribes of his enemies in Rome, de Mun sent the news to Pius X, writing through Vicenzo Cardinal Vannutelli and emphasizing that, while the church should rejoice, it should not do so publicly.[9]

When Pius revealed the secret to the Integrists of the Sapinière, they reacted with anger and disappointment since once more de Mun seemed to have eluded their efforts to silence him through a papal condemnation. They preferred to regard his relations with Poincaré and the moderates as "criminal folly" and claimed that "under the pretext of the politics of national union he had deliberately kept silent on the demands of Catholics and the immortal rights of the church." There was more truth to this charge than they realized, but it was an exaggeration that did not take account of the understanding on language and deeds reached with Poincaré, and de Mun felt compelled to refute it. In a very detailed letter written 16 March 1913, he explained to Trégard the arrangements he had undertaken, and specifically the dissimulation necessary to safeguard the interest of the church, asking that the Jesuits take up his defense. He took particular care to justify his vote for Briand's "resolution for laicization"—the fate of the three-year-service law was at stake—and his increasing separation from the intransigently clerical Groussau, "a kind of lay nuncio." "We are at the end of the war [of beliefs]," he claimed. "There is a feeling of inevitable peace that will not come all at once but will be prepared by measures of circumstance . . . and end in an accord with the Vatican for the safety of the churches, the religious congregations, and the schools. We must march toward this certain result, and we must aid it with patience, moderation, prudence, and an activity combined with wisdom in acts and words." He concluded very bluntly that "this policy is a truly fruitful and practical one that the successor to Pius X will necessarily adopt and for whom it is imperative to prepare the way." Even more mindful of the danger at Rome, Piou told an audience at Bordeaux in February that the ALP had voted not only for Poincaré's nationalism but for his essential moderation toward the church, for his "hostility to Jacobin violence and sectarian exaggerations: his nomination is a reaction against the spirit of Combism." He also dispatched Duke Xavier de La Rochefoucauld, newly appointed executive secretary of the ALP, to the Vatican in April to meet with Eugenio Cardinal Pacelli, an opponent of the Sapinière, who was in a position to act as a powerful ally. The news of Poincaré's marriage in May, although it had to be kept relatively secret, was a substantial achievement by de Mun to oppose to the criticism of the Integrists.[10]

Yet the very nature of relations between the conservatives and the moderates required Barthou to make strident laic comments before the Chamber and the deputies of the Right not to take serious offense, thus exacerbating the leaders of Catholic Integrism even more. On 11 June, in reply to a question by Groussau, the premier insisted that "for you, to have the schoolteachers instruct students in their duties toward God would constitute respect for neutrality of teaching. I tell you that for my part to do so would be the most certain means of violating that neutrality." Taken aback by this bluntness, Groussau could barely force out, "Nothing so grave has ever been spoken here!" a reference as much to the conservative support of the ministry as to the premier's candor. In midsummer, Barthou and Poincaré also refused to intervene to prevent the closure of the Ecole de la Rue des Postes. But before audiences at Caen and Bordeaux, Piou addressed

Barthou to promise that the ALP "will not allow you to be overthrown unless you render the task impossible for us." The premier belied his harsh language and indifference to Catholic sentiment by ordering shipboard observance of Good Friday in the navy and specifying increased parental influence in the choice of texts for the public schools. Clemenceau understood only too well that there had to be secret arrangements to account for such irregular behavior on both sides. Mercurial as ever, he deserted support of the ministry as soon as the service law was passed and began a series of editorials in his *L'Homme Libre* against the "clerical tendencies" of the premier and the president. Barthou and Poincaré soon felt compelled to deny his rumors of their desire to reestablish diplomatic relations with the Vatican and to vaunt their own reputations as "free-thinkers."[11]

Clemenceau's pen complicated matters by forcing the government to issue its paeans to laicism even more frequently. Every action creates a reaction, and, predictably, the outrage of the Integrists came easily. The pressure on de Mun increased throughout the summer of 1913, with Jacques Rocafort of *L'Univers* mounting increasingly polemical attacks upon him. Since 1910, François Veuillot had made his paper the French spokesman for Integrism, and during the next two and a half years the editorials of *L'Univers* developed the position that what was termed the "politics of Ralliement" were a betrayal of Catholicism by encouraging accommodation to a laic conception of society. Now de Mun became the personal target, singled out for having "committed the liberals to Poincaré, to Briand, to Barthou, to the three-year law, without winning any positive benefits for the church," for having "led them last January to vote in favor of the resolution for laicization, creating a schism extending into the heart of the ALP, placing de Mun against Piou," even for contributing editorials to newspapers "not truly Catholic." Although he continued to be regarded popularly as the most important, with Piou, political spokesman of French Catholicism, de Mun found that his influence within the church had declined as precipitously as his reputation as a nationalist had risen. When Poincaré, worried in the spring of 1913 that the ailing Pius X might die, suggested to Paléologue that de Mun be assigned to maintain contact between the government and the French cardinals, Paléologue dissuaded him, arguing that de Mun was too compromised by his politics to deal with some groups within the hierarchy.[12]

De Mun found his new status as a semioutcast wholly unfair, as he complained to Trégard. Although he now wrote most often about foreign affairs and the military, his critics ignored those editorials, in the same newspapers where he glorified nationalism, in which he called for a resumption of diplomatic relations with the Vatican, for the assignment of chaplains to the armed forces, for a more tolerant attitude toward Catholic schools and the sensibilities of Catholic parents with children in state schools, for the mitigation of laws against the congregations, and for the project of Maurice Barrès to restore the historic churches that since the Separation had been crumbling into disrepair because so little money was available for their upkeep. They ignored them because his language was no longer intransigent enough; the Knight of the *Syllabus* was now too compromising. He had in him too much of Leo XIII and too little of Pius X. At the Vatican his political success with the moderates was poorly understood at best, but even had the view been limpid, these dealings would have been denounced as too tolerant, too minimum a program. Merry del Val resented de Mun's finding quickness in the body of the Ralliement he had pronounced dead; he was likewise indignant that de Mun had managed to preserve, however weakly, a social Catholic movement he had considered condemned. In December 1912, de Mun advised the Vatican that he was forsaking joint unions of workers and employers to endorse separate ones, a logical development in his social thought to which he had been led by his young colleagues of the ACJF. They had managed the details of his social Catholic work since the 1890s, and they now convinced him that it was preferable to organize workers into Catholic unions without their employers than to fail to attract them at all. The cardinal secretary of state replied the following month in an open letter, which on initial reading raised no objection to this shift and offered praise to the Oeuvre des Cercles for continuing to remain "perfectly orthodox." But there was an edge to the language that contained a warning that any deviation from its traditional teaching toward such dangerous ideas as the social equality of all men—which eliminates the need for charity—would be sufficient to place even the *cercles* under the taint of modernism. Merry del Val had already forced Henri Lorin, an occasional collaborator of de Mun and founder of the Semaines Sociales, a yearly study retreat under lay direction, to repudiate the teaching that there was a natural right to join a union, that private property was not inviolable, and that justice bore a greater burden than charity in the solution of social problems.[13]

As anyone would, de Mun looked for vindication. He pointed to the progress of bellicosity among the Germans and quoted Pan-German propagandist Adolf Sommerfeld's proposal that France be divided between Germany and Italy. In the preface of his *L'Heure décisive*, he claimed that "the pages gathered here are not the reckless appeal for a premeditated war but the reflective warning by an attentive patriot of an inevitable one." There would be no French church to defend if the faithful were defeated. But this argument was far too rational and pragmatic for Integrism to accept, and, stated so simply, it could not satisfy even de Mun. His career had always been a quest, a crusade, and the greatest and most memorable of his speeches and editorials had always been distinguished by a species of mysticism, that of social reconciliation, or the inalienable tie between the church and the French state, or the imperative of national honor and the defense of the native soil. He was, at the same time, an incurable optimist who always expected, but rarely received, "victory," and a fatalist who occasionally penetrated the fatuity of the conservatives to comprehend acutely the realities of politics. Without a general condemnation to accompany them, the calculated slights of the Vatican could not silence him, but they were so undeserved and unceasing that they encouraged his anguish and apocalypticism. In early April he visited Paléologue at the Quai d'Orsay and began to talk to him of de Maistre's theory of war as a law on the spiritual plane, an instrument of sovereign justice. "War," he explained, "is indispensable here on earth as the expiation of social crime. . . . It is a punishment that people inflict upon each other for having offended God. . . . To restore the equilibrium of the moral world, periods of hecatombs are necessary. Do you not understand, my dear friend, that France, fallen so low, is able to rehabilitate herself before God only through war? Do you not understand that we should wish this war, taking shape on the horizon, to come inevitably and soon?" Paléologue upbraided him for this manner of speaking, but de Mun left sadly concluding that they could not understand one another.[14]

There was more here than de Mun's usual surety that war stalked implacably after Europe. He seemed almost to wish for its appearance as the proof of his foresight and the harsh but necessary purgative for a France grown fetid in its own excretions. There was a desire to frustrate the criticism of his enemies and former allies, to counter their vituperation with his own, to reverse the irony now afflicting his life. In July 1913, François Veuillot began planning for the celebration later that year of his uncle's centenary. De Mun was the eldest of Louis Veuillot's political associates still living, and etiquette required that he be asked to preside, despite his present feud with the family. To the surprise and resentment of the *L'Univers* staff, he accepted and carried off his role with aplomb and malicious delight the following November, a standing reproach to the paper's editorials against him. For the first time de Mun seemed to relish polemic, not that he had not criticized Jaurès, Combes, and others *vivement*, as he put it. But this abuse had been straightforward, unalloyed by the subtler techniques of humorous sarcasm, faint praise, and calculatedly vague responses to challenge or question. When in August and September, Clemenceau began to plot the "revanche de Versailles," a Radical victory in the 1914 elections, through his columns in *L'Homme Libre*, de Mun took him on in succeeding editorials in *L'Echo de Paris*. It was a contest like that with Jaurès earlier in the year, but this time a fencing match of wit instead of ponderous computations and figures or shrill denunciation. Clemenceau claimed with much precision that the election of Poincaré and the survival of Barthou had been possible only with the complete cooperation of the conservatives and concluded that for these arrangements there must have been clandestine meetings and "antirepublican" alliances for which the moderates would have to be punished. As his nickname *le Tigre* implied, Clemenceau was vicious but also unpredictable, and there was no way to discover whether or not he had come upon certain evidence for his charges. It would be unwise to answer him categorically, and de Mun's reply was a masterpiece of obfuscation. "It costs me nothing to recognize that, at certain times, [Clemenceau] has had, of the national interest, a sense that I would have preferred to see in all of his successors," de Mun began, hedging the salutation of his opponent with all manner of qualification. But for all his good sense, Clemenceau "wants to finish off Premier Barthou by announcing that I have sustained his ministry, when anyone knows that a minister seconded by de Mun is immediately a dead man." As for any secret relations between Poincaré and certain conservatives, sealed in private meetings by "intimates of the Elysée," who enter furtively, de Mun acknowledged that while anything was possible, he "knew nothing about it, not having colloquies on public affairs except in the pages of the newspaper with his readers, not entering the seats of the mighty except by the doors open to everyone, and not having had, for twenty-five years or more, familiarity with power except through the blows with which it has gratified me."[15]

This easy, mocking tone hinted that, while enduring the trials, de Mun relished the power and responsibility his pact with the moderates also brought his way. The passage of the service law greatly increased his confidence in the dependability of the moderates and, pompously but understandably, in his own political judgment. Barthou had patiently learned the rules of his coalition and applied them to work his way cautiously through most of the problems that had seemed overwhelming in March. Only one great difficulty remained to him—where to find the funds for the vast new expenses required by three-year service, but, perhaps from overconfidence, it was on this question that Barthou and his majority stumbled. There was no shortage of plans for raising the money; the problem lay in choosing which one. The decision was as much political as economic, and for three months after the passage of the law Barthou refused to commit the cabinet. His task was not lightened by the general incompetence of his finance minister, Charles Dumont, who rarely managed to keep his figures straight. Piou and de Mun advanced the proposal most generally favored by the conservatives. Opposed both to any income tax and to the government's fiscally dangerous practice of borrowing to cover budgetary deficits, they suggested that the wealthy bear most of the burden through a surtax on their current indirect taxes. The plan would avoid the inquisition of Caillaux's proposals and set a valuable example of sacrifice, especially since a similar tax had been introduced in Germany to pay for the army increases there. Caillaux's Radicals, and later their allies the Socialists, proclaimed their solution at a congress in Pau during mid-October, a general progressive income tax combined with an unspecified "revision" of the three-year law to return to the 1905 spirit in military service. Barthou found both of these ideas too adventuresome and finally proposed the unsatisfactory expedient of raising the funds through a new issue of government bonds, the sales increased by the promise of a permanent exemption for the interest from any future income tax.[16]

A new apportionment in early November 1913 of the seats on the Budget Committee placed both de Mun and Piou among the members. After hearing the testimony of Dumont, Barthou, and Etienne, they agreed to the new loan, but only for the nonrecurring extraordinary expenses, estimated at nine hundred million francs, to implement three-year service and replace outmoded equipment. They insisted that the remainder of the expected deficit, four hundred million francs, be covered by new taxes. De Mun even campaigned for this position in *L'Echo de Paris*, claiming that Frenchmen should be forced to realize, through an increase in exactions, the cost of such Radical programs as the destruction of Catholic schools and the consequently necessary expansion of the state system to incorporate the students. It was the most critical attitude de Mun had taken toward the moderates since the presidential election, but it did not seem likely to be a costly division. When Caillaux announced that he would try to unseat the ministry, the conservatives hurried to declare that they preferred Barthou's continuance in office to the purification of the nation's finances. The crucial votes came on the first two days of December. Although de Mun and Piou voted against borrowing the entire thirteen hundred million francs, this opposition was only a symbolic protest by the conservatives since all of the rest of their votes went for the cabinet to give it a narrow 291 to 270 victory. On the following day the backing of the conservatives became unanimous on the question of exempting the bonds, but this time it was not enough. There were defections from Barthou's support at the left fringe of the moderates, deputies disturbed by Dumont's incoherence in presenting the government's proposals and unwilling to commit any future legislature on a tax issue. The vote was very close, 290 to 265 against the cabinet, and it was at least very probable that those deserting Barthou were unaware that their individual decisions would cost the ministry its majority. Barthou had maneuvered poorly—"C'est un suicide," Poincaré declared—by failing to count his votes more carefully and by forgetting that the Chamber had already passed an income tax once and might object to limiting its application. But the deed was done.[17]

Poincaré now faced his second ministerial crisis. Despite the passage of the three-year-service law, the experiment in moderate-conservative government had gone badly, with his first two choices for premier overturned by Caillaux in less than a year. Despite his personal feelings, Poincaré felt constitutionally constrained to select his third from among the Radicals, although he would avoid calling Caillaux himself. He chose instead Gaston Doumergue, whose allegiance, when it could be ascertained, lay somewhere between the ranks of Barthou and Caillaux. The conservatives remembered him for his anticlericalism and recognized his intention to press for the income tax in the appointment of Caillaux as finance minister. Doumergue was unsure of his attitude toward the service law, not having opposed it in July but subscribing to the platform of the Radicals at Pau in October. After being prodded by Poincaré, he declared that he would not attempt to alter the law before the 1914 elections, five months away in late April. Playing the nationalist again, Clemenceau added his own promise, a threat to the premier that he would not allow Doumergue to betray the army or Caillaux to influence foreign policy. Even so, the conservatives and most of the moderates remained worried. The Socialist Edouard Vaillant had cried, "Down with the three-year law!" as Barthou led his defeated ministry from the Chamber, and this exclamation had goaded Briand to warn Doumergue and his cabinet grimly, "The service law has become an organic instrument in the national defense; it was not voted with the intention of modifying it every six months." Since even de Mun by now had a realistic understanding of the limits of presidential power, no one blamed Poincaré for being unable to dictate to the Chamber, but it was only slowly that the Poincaristes expressed their relief that Doumergue was less dangerous than they had supposed and that his choice, a shrewd gamble, had apparently guaranteed the preservation of the service law at least until after the elections.[18]

The abrupt fall of Barthou and the newly crucial nature of

the elections forced the conservatives and the moderates to look to their organizations and alliances. On 22 December, in a major address at Saint-Etienne, Briand declared political war on Caillaux and the Radicals of the Pau manifesto and formally announced the coalescing of the great majority of the moderates into a single faction, the Fédération des Gauches, whose leadership would include all of the new darlings of the conservatives, Briand himself, Barthou, Millerand, and Etienne. He promised a campaign for RP, the preservation of the service law, a balanced budget, and the blocking of Caillaux's brand of income tax. The slogan the Fédération quickly adopted, "La République, c'est la liberté," revealed a pronounced affinity for the Right and an appeal to Catholic sensibilities. In *L'Echo de Paris* de Mun immediately promised a limited concourse for the elections to these anticlericals turned nationalists. It was all he dared as yet publicly, but he was already prepared to join them and to find some means of mobilizing the Catholic vote behind them. For the first time he would ask not just the deputies but the faithful among the electorate to support men who had enacted the separation of church and state and remained vocal advocates of laicism.[19]

To prepare the Vatican for his decision, de Mun composed a detailed letter to Merry del Val and sent it to Rome by La Rochefoucauld in late December. It would be his last effort to justify his politics before the Holy See, and to a surprising degree he would be successful. The alliance of the conservatives with the moderates, he argued carefully, had contributed to tangible benefits for the church, "in spite of the efforts by a faction of Catholics to discredit and lessen it." This alignment was "the sole force capable of combining those who are able to exercise a real influence, of assembling the indispensable resources for the struggle, and of knotting together an effective coalition." To be elected in the country and heard by the government, it was imperative, he continued, that there be no question of a candidate's allegiance to the Republic or of his desire to restore the power of the church in any fashion that would do more than allow for complete liberty of belief, the meaning of "Libérale" in the ALP's name. Even so, de Mun offered to pledge the party to support without question any "Catholic" candidate if in other constituencies the Vatican would not condemn the ALP's backing of its moderate allies from the legislature, who would otherwise be branded enemies of the church. At the same time, he asked Trégard to enlist the Jesuits for his project, baldly claiming that "we are able to modify the state of the country only through a discreet entente with the moderates." Perhaps because Merry del Val had learned to appreciate political reality as he understood that the aging Pius X would not be occupying the papal throne much longer, or because de Mun's standing had increased since the disclosure of Poincaré's marriage, and certainly because Piou and de Mun had important new support from Cardinal Pacelli, the Vatican, while not endorsing the plan, raised no specific objection. Here was the first hint that the position of the Integrists was open to challenge.[20]

This reaction was not the authorization de Mun had sought, but it was enough that for the first time since 1910 the silence of the Vatican was not ominous for him and the ALP. He and Piou rapidly called provincial representatives of the party together at the end of January 1914 for their first general congress in two and a half years. On 31 January, after careful instruction, the delegates approved a platform nearly identical to that of the Fédération des Gauches, but with the addition of three planks to appeal to Catholic voters, reestablishment of diplomatic relations with the Vatican, RP *scolaire*, and complete freedom of teaching and association, vital to restore the position of the congregations. More important, by approving the election tactics La Rochefoucauld had submitted to Vatican scrutiny, they voted to work closely with the Fédération. The following day at a closing banquet, de Mun stood up at the head table to acknowledge tumultuous applause for his exertions. Exhausted by a year of intricate maneuvering, too weak to remain on his feet, he nevertheless insisted, his voice only a whisper, on raising a toast to the party that, "in spite of all the inventors of heresy, has been faithful to the ideas that brought us together originally, fidelity to the [republican] constitution, demands for all of the liberties necessary for national life, above all else religious liberty, and preservation of the grandeur of France through its military strength." Then in words that went far to heal his quarrel with Piou during the last three years, he praised his long-time colleague without reserve and concluded, "This man deserves that with his friends grouped around him he receive the comfort of their affection, the tribute of their gratitude, and the witness of their faith and trust." In the midst of long hurrahs Piou stood to urge the ALP to its greatest efforts ever and to toast the cooperation with the moderates as the very buttress of French patriotism. Less than a week later, at the request of La Rochefoucauld, Cardinal Pacelli extended a confidential, unofficial, but undeniable blessing on the enterprise.[21]

Even as the conservatives and the moderates made common cause, Caillaux's Radicals completed final arrangements in their alignment with the Socialists. With the alliances for the election set, partisan debate became more acrimonious on the hustings and within the Chamber. The sessions of the Budget Committee seemed always in commotion as Caillaux futilely sought its approval for a plan to finance the deficit, which could succeed only with the adoption of his income tax proposal. He also argued for economies in military appropriations, while a majority of conservatives and moderates pressed for greater expenditures for defense. The discussions were technical, but from them it was clear that Caillaux's sentiment was for France to depend less on its arms than on a reconcilation with Germany. The threat of Caillaux's becoming premier again if the Radicals and Socialists won the elections preoccupied de Mun, making him wonder whether in spite of the "brave deeds" of 1913 the "gangrene was not too deep" in France. The nation had let the "decisive hour" pass; would it now allow the "somber hour" to ring until the last? Caillaux had never been much esteemed for his integrity, and along with his financial and foreign policy schemes this question suddenly became primary on 16 March when his wife shot and killed Gaston Calmette, the conservative editor of *Le Figaro*. Encouraged particularly by Barthou, Calmette's press campaign since the first week in January against the finance minister had been extraordinarily bitter, including the publication of indiscreet letters written by Caillaux to his present wife while married to his first. What had appeared thus far had affected Caillaux's already shaky reputation for political candor, and Calmette had promised further sensational disclosures. Accused by the *Figaro* staff of prompting his wife's act, Caillaux vehemently denied the charge but resigned his ministry. Although the conservatives and moderates believed that the revelation of their chief enemy as a man of plastic morality would be an effective election issue, to a France accustomed to political scandals of much larger proportions these misdeeds were not damning. In July, during the tense days of Austro-Serbian negotiations after the assassination of Franz Ferdinand at Sarajevo, a jury of Frenchmen would find Madame Caillaux's explanation that her gun had "gone off six times by itself" acceptable and gallantly acquit her for defending her husband's honor. During the four months before the trial, neither Caillaux's brand of Radicals nor the Socialists found him a liability, and he continued to lead their coalition into the election struggle. De Mun offered this attitude as evidence of the amorality of the left-wing parties and further proof of Caillaux's unfitness to rule, but it is doubtful that he converted anyone who was not already so convinced.[22]

It was in this state of agitation and defamation that France voted on 26 April and 10 May 1914. The results were, and remain, difficult to interpret. More than usual, candidates compromised their national platforms to cater to local sentiment, and a movement toward the center, from the right by some members of the Fédération des Gauches, from the left by Radicals Caillaux had called his own, produced a blurring pattern impossible to decipher. In general the alliances formed for the election, the Socialists with Caillaux, the conservatives with the moderates, operated fairly smoothly, limited local recalcitrance being the rule as always, but they came into play in many cases only during the *ballottage*. The ALP, for example, considered it necessary, as part of the bargain with the Vatican, to back any "Catholic" candidate, whatever his potential for election, on the first ballot, reserving decisions based on pragmatism for the second. Despite the complications, it was not tactics but the temper of the electorate that produced difficulties for the conservatives and the moderates. As well as de Mun, Poincaré and Briand had convinced themselves that the revival of nationalism meant an end to the domination of elections by the Left since it had been everyone else who had created the nationalist program. They ignored the power of other issues, particularly the income tax, and forgot that quite recently they had been frightened by the rapid growth of the Socialist constituency. Most of the parties and factions returned little changed, but everywhere there were small subtractions to account for the sole true winners in the voting, Jaurès and his followers, who left with 85 seats but returned to claim 102 of them. Numbering the Socialists in three figures produced a hysteria among the conservatives, as if some symbolic barrier had been crossed. Far more important was the threat that if they remained allied to Caillaux and the other 182 Radicals pledged to the program of Pau, it would require the firmest sort of discipline among the remainder of the deputies to keep them out of power. Yet the total of these forces was deceiving. Because almost a third of Caillaux's men hedged their attitude toward the service law, only 235 deputies were clearly in favor of a return to two-year service, a division of the Chamber still not truly in accordance with a general, if grudging, national acceptance of the 1913 law. Likewise, there was no majority for a socialist or collectivist program since Caillaux's economic proposals did not extend beyond the modest redistribution of wealth implicit in a progressive income tax.[23]

"What will Jaurès do?" de Mun asked. "He tells us every morning, and at least thanks to his frankness positions are clear. The great objective is the three-year law. . . . Thus the law is at present the criterion of all politics. Its fall would be the victory of Jaurès with all his program of internal and external disorganization." But the potential for dissension within the Left gave the moderates and conservatives more of a chance than they had earned in the elections to maintain their position. The Chamber and Senate would not reconvene until mid-June, and Doumergue, who had taken his role as a caretaker premier literally, had announced before the elections that he would resign without facing the renewed houses. Poincaré had plenty of time to look for a new moderate candidate for premier, but he discovered considerable reluctance to test the new strength of Caillaux and Jaurès. De Mun called for a statesman to form a government of national defense, claiming that "France awaits this man. If he is ready, let him stand up! Otherwise the reign of Jaurès has begun." Despite this challenge, the chance to form a ministry was declined by Delcassé, Deschanel, and Jean Dupuy, among others, before Ribot finally accepted Poincaré's charge. To command a majority he would have to win back the votes on the left fringe of the moderates, which Barthou had lost half a year earlier, but his opposition to the anticlerical program under Combes and his close ties to de Mun and the ALP in the past made him suspect to the faction he needed most to attract. It appeared to Ribot that other than through the essentially meaningless pledge to press for further laicization, only a clear endorsement of the income tax could mollify them. There were hurried consultations among moderate and conservative leaders, and the public support of de Mun and Briand for Ribot's proposal to stand firm on the service law but to press the Senate for quick passage of some form of income tax revealed which issue was the more important to them. For all that, the pledge proved insufficient, and on 12 June, when Ribot presented his cabinet, he failed to survive even the first vote of confidence, losing 302 to 262. The votes in favor of a moderate ministry were almost identical in June 1914 to those of December 1913 when Barthou had been overturned.[24]

The Chamber's immediate execution of Ribot's ministry was a warning to Poincaré that the experiment of government under moderate-conservative auspices had come to an end. The Left clearly expected, and custom demanded, that Caillaux be called as premier. Poincaré briefly considered asking the Senate to dissolve the Chamber and call for new elections to resolve the stalemate between the Elysée and the deputies, but he was uncertain of his votes among the senators, and the precedent of MacMahon was not comforting. After careful thought, he concluded that the last chance, and the least unpleasant alternative, to block Caillaux was to elevate René Viviani, who had subscribed to the program of Pau but had always displayed a marked independence. More important, he had managed the remarkable feat of remaining friends with Caillaux, Briand, and Poincaré at the same time. Although he had voted against three-year service, he agreed not to press for an immediate change in the law, particularly after Paléologue, at Poincaré's request, took him aside to warn that the Quai d'Orsay considered war imminent. Still, he needed some formula to assure the support of the Left, and he found it in the promise that in return for the passage of a progressive income tax the service law would remain intangible "until European conditions allow a revision." Although excluded from the ministry, Caillaux was content with this declaration and added his Radical followers to the moderates to form Viviani's majority, while Jaurès broke with his ally over what he called an intolerable concession to militarism. Briand and de Mun accepted Viviani reluctantly, but like Poincaré, they gambled that he would defend the service law.

Briand willingly led the moderates to vote for his friend. De Mun, grumbling at the premier's past, preferred a symbolic opposition for himself but convinced most of the rest of the conservatives to abstain. The result of all the maneuvering was the investiture of the cabinet by a vote of 370 to 137, with 93 abstentions.[25]

The success of the new ministry evoked ambivalence in de Mun. It meant a check, perhaps even the defeat, of his determination to tie the moderates to the conservatives, since Viviani had a working majority without the votes de Mun controlled. At the same time, the most important fruits of his policy survived. Poincaré had six more years in the Elysée, and the three-year law was in no immediate danger. He could criticize Viviani's choice of colleagues, especially Augagneur at the ministry of education, who were reportedly determined to prevent the holdover of the class of 1913 for a third year when the time came in 1915, but for now the editorials were not bitter. Even in the Budget Committee, with Caillaux no longer directly in charge of finances, he could work in harmony with the government, even as it planned its expenditures counting on the receipts from an income tax. As so often in de Mun's career since 1910, it is impossible to avoid recognizing the irony. He himself could hardly have been unaware of it. He had restored the position of the Catholic conservatives to a degree considered dangerous by the Left and almost unbelievable by such of his own colleagues as Piou, but his reward had been the wounding attacks of the Integrists and a near repudiation by the pope. And when the Vatican finally did grant, in a tentative manner, its imprimatur to de Mun's endeavor, the Radicals and Socialists were the victors in an election that moderates and conservatives alike had considered would be determined by the nationalism that had seemed so powerful a year earlier. His Oeuvre des Cercles had taken the lead of social Catholicism again, and in a time of Vatican disfavor of the movement, had its orthodoxy reaffirmed by Merry del Val himself, but only because with the Sillon condemned, it was too dangerous for any of the more vibrant lay groups, even the ACJF, to do so. As if to complete the mockery of irony, like most French leaders de Mun failed to grasp the significance of Franz Ferdinand's assassination on 28 June. Having prophesied war since 1911 and identified the Balkans as the site of its outbreak, he suddenly forgot his own warnings. Instead, exhausted by his constant activity of the past three years and by the election, in which he had faced his first serious opponent in a decade and a half, and feeling increasingly old and unwell, he allowed his family to persuade him to leave the Chamber before its summer recess in mid-July. Planning to rest in Roscoff until early fall and then to visit his children and friends, he talked delightedly of traveling in an automobile for the first time. He had even arranged a vacation from his editorials, his first since he began them in 1905, and to take them up again only after the Chamber reconvened in November.[26]

In the midst of the frothy headlines about the trial of Madame Caillaux for the murder of Calmette, the fact of looming war suddenly appeared in French newspapers during the last week of July. From Roscoff on 29 July, de Mun hastily wrote an anguished editorial, "L'Heure, a-t-elle sonné?" sure of war but confident that "no Frenchman is able, would even like, to hesitate [to do his duty]." He added the prayer that divisions cease in time of war, but even as he took the train to Paris two days later, a nationalist fanatic shot Jaurès dead as the Socialist leader, in his noblest campaign, desperately urged the working classes of every nation to halt their government's fall into European war. At this moment, by writing a touching letter of condolence to Madame Jaurès, de Mun took the first step in forming a "sacred union" of all France, even before the casket of the opponent whom he had bitterly fought for so long. On 2 August every major newspaper published a manifesto in the name of the government: "We count on the sang-froid of this noble nation in order that it not fall into an unjustified emotion. We count on the patriotism of all Frenchmen and know that there is not a single one who will not do his duty. At this hour there are no more parties, only France, eternal, pacific, and resolute, the mother country of law and justice, completely united in calm, vigilance, and dignity." The words could have come from one of de Mun's editorials, but he surpassed them on 3 August in *L'Echo de Paris* with a sudden genius for generous sentiment. The followers of Jaurès, numbering in the hundreds of thousands, had passed bareheaded before his bier, but they had produced no riots, not the slightest obstruction of the mobilization that began on 1 August in response to a German ultimatum and the extreme likelihood of war. "France will reply with one heart," de Mun wrote, "as a single people. . . . And we must render homage to those whom I have combated the most, to the Socialists, smitten by the pacifist ideal, who despite the horrible, odious, and absurd assassination of their leader, provide the highest example of obedience to the national voice."[27]

On 4 August, when Poincaré and Viviani faced a hurriedly gathered Chamber to ask for a reply to the German declaration of war the previous day, they were cheered mightily. There was never any doubt about the vote to send France against Germany in a war of revanche about which some had dreamed since 1871. All of the deputies were on their feet, the Chamber emotionally charged by the responsibility of its decision, when in an act the significance of which was lost on no one, de Mun left his desk on the right to walk across the front of the hemicycle to the left and grasp the hand of Edouard Vaillant, Jaurès's lieutenant, a Communard who had never before deigned to speak to the cavalry officer who had taken part in the repression of 1871. Then they had been on different sides of the barricade; now they were on the same. In the corridors afterward, de Mun had another chance to practice these new politics of national union, and to do so in a manner curiously revealing of how much he had changed, and suffered, in the decade since the separation of church and state. Delcassé, who had engineered Loubet's trip to Rome in 1904 and prepared the ultimate rupture of relations between France and the Vatican, was accepting congratulations for the success of his diplomacy, Great Britain fighting beside France, Italy neutral. When he noticed de Mun among the well-wishers, he leaned toward him, and in a voice bereft of any sarcasm, laying bare his most profound fears about the outcome of the war, he asked, "And will God be with us too?" De Mun replied softly in words he meant for more than Delcassé's question, "Yes, you may rest easy. God forgives, and he takes into account the sacrifices of Catholics. He will grant their prayers."[28]

One victory of the anticlerical program had been the elimination of chaplains from the armed forces. Particularly after the outbreak of heavy fighting in Morocco, de Mun had petitioned the government to restore them, but not until Etienne's decree of 5 May 1913 were four chaplains assigned to each army corps. This number was entirely insufficient for the enormous numbers of dead and wounded on the western front, and the troops demanded more. Viviani was reluctant to entangle his ministry in such a disavowal of lay society, but on 11 August he authorized de Mun to recruit two hundred fifty priests for immediate service, without pay, and for an indefinite period. Given an office at the Paris Red Cross and the assistance of a staff officer from the war ministry, de Mun began the project the next day, and two weeks later, on 27 August, the first chaplain corps was completely organized and sent to the front. More than a thousand other volunteer priests were waiting the formation of new units, and all of the expenses had been paid by a public subscription surpassing a hundred thousand francs raised through *L'Echo de Paris*. "Here I am," de Mun had said. "I have only two difficulties: walking for even short distances and stairs. Otherwise . . . I am ready for service." He had now proved it.[29]

By the end of August, Poincaré began to urge Viviani to broaden the base of his ministry and specifically suggested the inclusion of Briand, Millerand, and de Mun, whose energy he had noticed. There was much suspicion among the Radicals that Poincaré was using the unassailable shibboleth of sacred union to bring his friends back to power, but Viviani reshuffled his cabinet to make Millerand his minister of war and include Briand as a minister without portfolio. Further right he would not go immediately, but he raised no objection when Millerand appointed de Mun to oversee the reprovision of troops in the field after the system had functioned poorly during the opening weeks of the fighting. Such an assignment was actually more to de Mun's taste than serving, as would Briand, as a general adviser with no specific responsibility. He genuinely regretted that his age and infirmity made it impossible for him to be recalled to army service, and working in the war ministry gave him the sense of intimacy with the military he craved. He also felt certain enough now of the conservatives' influence in government to be unconcerned by their absence from the ministry. As he wrote Gailhard-Bancel in September, "We need no showy positions or sterile posturing. Our immense, incalculable strength comes from our attitude at the same time ardently patriotic and generously unselfish. We should not lose this benefit to seek the satisfaction of useless pride."[30]

De Mun's relations with Poincaré and assignments at the war ministry were enough to give him the status of an unofficial member of the cabinet, but it was his wartime editorials, now daily in *L'Echo de Paris*, that won him the honor of "minister of public confidence" from the nation at large. Every day after a routine of mass, visits with the wounded at the Red Cross, and consultations with his staff about the chaplains and supplies, he would sit with the most recent communiqués from the front to bring up to date the map, studded with red- and blue-headed pins, on which he followed the course of the fighting. Only then, late in the evening, would he compose his editorial for the next day, full of sang-froid if the reports were bad, as they were throughout August as the Germans stormed through Holland and Belgium into northern France, exultant when the French were victorious in Alsace and Lorraine in early August and at the Marne, where during the first week in September Joffre first blunted, then halted, and finally reversed the German attack on Paris. The war ministry was overwhelmed by letters from soldiers and their families extolling the comfort and confidence that reading de Mun had given them. Anxious to exploit any advantage, the army quickly put together a special newspaper for the troops, the *Bulletin des Armées*, and republished many of de Mun's editorials there to ensure their wide dispersal. Not everyone was as confident of Joffre's ultimate victory as de Mun, and when the German guns came within reach of the capital at the end of August the government took the precaution of moving to Bordeaux. Poincaré insisted that de Mun and his wife accompany him to make certain that he could continue this ministry of inspiration.[31]

What de Mun wrote during the two months left to him from the outbreak of the war until his death in early October defined almost his entire attitude toward life, devotion to God and France, a willingness to sacrifice, an eternal optimism combined with a refusal to acknowledge defeat. "*Mulhouse est prise*! . . . France returns to Alsace! After forty years of mourning and grievous waiting . . . here is the dawn of deliverance, the sacred day of revenge." "Among the allies of France stand God and Jeanne d'Arc." "Once more the soldiers of France fight for civilization and liberty. . . . Be heroes! France expects it of you! The world is watching!" "Be calm and composed." "In the hour of crisis, for soldiers and citizens alike, the only order is that of Wellington at Waterloo, hold, hold to the last man." "No punishment will be too severe for those guilty [of preaching defeat and fear] which will place them where they can do no more harm." "War is a school for the entire nation, causing it to meet responsibility heroically with moral firmness. . . . It is easy to face the enemy in the heat of battles, far harder to be courageous day by day between." "The victory at the Marne is not a solution. It is the first act of a new phase in this terrible war." "Germany has, by its insupportable arrogance, repeated provocation, and increasing outrage, remade the French national soul and will, piece by piece, year by year." "Whether marshal or private, all French soldiers are equal in death; they have given all for France." His titles were a litany in themselves: "Le jour sacré," "Dieu est grand," "L'aurore de victoire," "Offensive," "Dieu avec nous," "Vive la France," "Confiance," "Discipline de fer," "Inébranlable confiance," "Tenir," "Toujours tenir," "Sang-froid," "Qui peut douter?" "Dieu et patrie," "Endurance," "L'union des âmes," "L'effort nécessaire," "Nous ferons le nécessaire," "Vague d'espérance."

What he asked of the nation he asked of himself, and that was clearly too much for a man seventy-three years old with a severe heart condition. He had not had the chance to rest during the summer as he had planned. After the beginning of August his pace was so frantic and his weakness so great that he had to be carried from one office to the next in a light armchair. When he left for Bordeaux, friends remarked how gaunt and austere his face had become, his smile contorted by the constant pain of angina, his voice halting. He had assumed responsibility as if he were a young man, and he felt the personal anguish of constant worry about the fate of his three sons, all reserve officers called to their units at the front. He became so preoccupied that even personal greetings on 3 September from the new pope—Pius X died on 20 August—Giacomo della Chiesa, Benedict XV, an opponent of the Integrists and a friend of Cardinal Pacelli, failed to make much of an impression on him. Amazed at his activity but appalled at its effect on him, his friends and family warned him with increasing concern and vehemence to rest or at least to reduce his work. He brushed them aside, even Simone, aware only that he had so much to do for France, and, he knew himself, so little time. He had survived their fears before. In the last days of September his condition became seriously worse, but he refused to acknowledge it. On

6 October his youngest son Fernand arrived in Bordeaux on assignment, and de Mun celebrated with him the progress of Joffre's counterattacks in the north. Later that evening, after finishing an optimistic editorial for the following day and telegraphing it to Paris, he felt a sudden attack. Simone immediately had him lie down and summoned a priest. When he appeared, de Mun, bemused and finally admitting the pain, murmured, "I did not know that I was so ill." The agony was not long. He died shortly after receiving extreme unction, comforted by Simone and Fernand. As much as any soldier on the battlefield, de Mun had died for France.[32]

Conclusion

Fall is the dreary season for the seacoast cities of the North Atlantic. The water casts off the blue it has worn for the summer and turns a dull green, becoming rougher, presaging the gales that sweep down from the North Sea into the Bay of Biscay and whip white water across the jetties. The sky turns an ashen grey, and pale clouds hide the sun for days on end. The weather mourns the passing of summer, and in the fall of 1914, also of peace. So it was in Bordeaux on 10 October. The wind whirled dead leaves across the face of the city as a funeral procession wended its way through the broad streets. Bordeaux said France's farewell to Albert de Mun.

His funeral provided one more opportunity to seal the nation's sacred union. In Notre Dame de Bordeaux, where Cardinal-Archbishop Paulin Andrieu himself pronounced absolution, the leaders of the nation stood in silent rows. Poincaré, Viviani, Delcassé, Briand, Barthou, Millerand, and Ribot, the presidents of the Chamber and the Senate, and the vast majority of deputies and senators, all broke precedent by attending a religious service. Further back were the ambassadors from France's allies, bearing expressions of condolence from their governments at the death of the French patriot. The casket was borne from the catafalque by an honor guard from the 104th Brigade Infantry, Poincaré himself leading the procession from the cathedral. Outside nearly twenty thousand mourners lined the streets. The burial was at the nearby cemetery of La Chartreuse. Deschanel, president of the Chamber, delivered a eulogy calling de Mun "the immortal honor of France" and evoking his brilliant oratory. As he finished, Poincaré, weeping openly, embraced him. Piou followed with brief remarks that were occasionally choked and inaudible because of the emotion in his voice. De Mun, he reminded the immense crowd, had devoted forty years to the defense of lost causes, social Catholicism, the established church, and nationalism. Only at the last did the country come to appreciate his work. "He spent his life defending the unpopular, but he died the most popular man in France." None could gainsay him.[1]

It is tempting but finally inaccurate to assume that de Mun underwent a profound evolution during the course of his political career, that at least his brush with power after 1911 must have softened the rancor of the outsider and made him more willing to appreciate the qualities of his opponents. To be sure, he was a gentleman to them, and after 1909 he mingled socially with men whom he denounced daily in his editorials. Yet in 1914 as in 1875 he saw his accomplishments not as the victory of a faction or party but as the triumph of principle. He remained a paladin, investing every cause with a sense of quest. Despite the inevitable discouragement that the holy crusade ended so often in failure, he found honor in the attempt and always believed that somehow the next victory would be his. Over forty years he drew his ideas from both the Left and the Right, choosing eventually to stand on the issues of nationalism, social reform, and established Catholicism. In a bizarrely idealistic fashion, he made belief in this political program almost a religious creed by elevating it to the status of dogma. Although this triune canon had the power to win elections in such intensely conservative areas as Brittany, de Mun was sufficiently foolhardy to believe that it was the basis for something between a national movement and a faith for France. The defense of the established church was anachronistic politically after 1870, given the precedents of previous French republics, and particularly so after anticlericalism became the staple program of the Radicals and Opportunists. By insisting on the tie of social reform to the church in this environment, de Mun ensured that social Catholicism and the movement of the *cercles* would be fatally handicapped by their identification with clericalism. The franchise of the Third Republic determined in advance the defeat of these two tenets of the creed because there could never be a majority of Frenchmen for them. In a France preoccupied with domestic strife, nationalism could do no better before 1911. But de Mun refused to acknowledge political reality and quaintly continued to believe that his program could become the basis of government and would revive and renew the nation. This delusion contributed to his failure ever to acquire the politician's easy tolerance for his adversaries. Whether Gambetta and Ferry, Waldeck-Rousseau and Combes, or Caillaux and Jaurès, they were not merely the opposition but traitors to his France. De Mun was not so rigid that he refused to accept allies unless they approved the creed in its entirety. First the royalists, then the Progressives and Independents, and finally the moderates, and even at times Clemenceau, could worship at one altar in de Mun's church while ignoring the rest. There is no denying that de Mun was an opportunist, but he was one who insisted that his conscience be assuaged, or at least allowed it to be befuddled, before he made his pact with the unconverted.

His whole career was born in social Catholicism, but ironically, despite his success in winning the long-sought papal endorsement of *Rerum novarum*, he accomplished very little that was lasting for social reform. As he became drawn into the thicket of royalist intrigues in the late 1870s and early 1880s, he let his attention wander from the *cercles* that had made his reputation. Unless the workers within them were to be committed to such men as Charette and their plans for insurrection, the *cercles* had little appeal to the social reactionaries of royalism or to the church, whose hierarchy would cease its opposition only in 1891 on Leo XIII's orders. Without de Mun's personal guidance the *cercles* quickly degenerated into another tired movement vying for the hand of the working class. De Mun continued to preach their goals with great fervor and felt keenly the injustices suffered by French workers, but he should be remembered only as an eloquent precursor. He found it difficult to convert even his own faction to social Catholicism, and he was compelled to watch with envy as the anticlerical Radical-Socialist coalition, his declared enemy, enacted the reforms he had futilely proposed as much as a decade earlier.

As vindicator of the Catholic church he had even less success. The identification of the church with royalism and the persecution of Dreyfus made it an easy target for politicians of the Left, who argued that it was in league with opponents of the regime. Preoccupation with the position of religion in society allowed many French cabinets to avoid grappling with the nation's more substantive issues, about which there was little agreement, and anticlericalism as a program became a means to evade difficult decisions. By their incredibly obtuse politics, churchmen like de Mun contributed to their own predicament. However much they criticized the France of 1870 as straying from the ideal expressed in the *Syllabus*, the France of 1914 was vastly more secular, and de Mun's best efforts, first intransigence, then compromise, had not prevented it. By the eve of World War I, Catholics had seen their church fall from the privileged position of official religion to being unable, realistically, to expect to be more than a free church in a free state. Integral Catholicism was in part a product of the frustration produced by this decline. It reacted to de Mun's failure by denying him, placing him in the ironic position of being disavowed by those he had labored and was laboring to defend.

As a nationalist de Mun's accomplishments were mixed. In leading the conservatives to defend the army against the Dreyfusards, he ensured that the Radicals and Socialists would appoint a General André to discipline it. His efforts to revive patriotism by recalling France to its traditions, best symbolized in his glorification of Jeanne d'Arc, attracted few followers until the Agadir crisis. Only then did many Frenchmen come to feel that a bellicose Germany threatened their nation's survival and turn to those who had preached nationalism earlier. Governed all of his adult life by the code of the officer corps, de Mun acted instinctively both times, and if he reached the zenith of his prestige through the second, it was only because the arrogance of German foreign policy sustained his direst predictions. But as the prophet of the political sea change taking place, he won a position for the conservatives in the government. Here he did not so much forsake social reform and defense of the church as relegate them to a secondary position from which they might be reprieved when the politics of nationalism had gained them leverage, and for once his political sense was acute. Although the alliance of the conservatives and the moderates was weakened by the result of the 1914 elections and deprived soon after of de Mun's guidance, it was greatly reinforced by the experience of the war years. The German invasion was the final justification of de Mun's patriotic foresight, and the steadfast support of the conservatives for Clemenceau during the most dangerous months of the fighting marked them as the staunchest defenders of the fatherland. As de Mun anticipated, the church and social Catholicism did benefit after the war from the ardor of their patrons during it. In the 1920s France reestablished diplomatic relations with the Vatican, halted the harassment of Catholic private schools, and incorporated social Catholic ideas into reform legislation. De Mun's political influence survived in the policies of the Bloc National, a right-of-center coalition that dominated the elections of 1920 and into which Piou merged the ALP and was rewarded with a place on the steering committee. After 1945 the Mouvement Républicain Populaire evoked the names of de Mun and Sangnier and adopted their program of social Catholicism as its own. The influence of the Integrists broken by the death of Pius X, the Vatican also celebrated him. Benedict XV sent special condolences to Bordeaux for his funeral, and in the late 1940s Cardinal Pacelli, now Pope Pius XII, sent Angelo Cardinal Roncalli, himself the future Pope John XXIII, to consecrate a new church in Lumigny, de Mun's birthplace.[2]

This record of victories and defeats for an extraordinary man assumes magnified importance because for most of his career de Mun was the leader of the French Right. A talent for organization, displayed first in the *cercles* and most prominently later in the ALP, and a gift for oratory set him apart from the other claimants —Keller, Mackau, Cochin, Lamy, Maurras, and even Piou—for this position. But without patience and political sense these blessings are of limited value, and de Mun proved to be a mediocre politician. His timing was egregiously poor. He joined the royalist camp only after its cause was lost and once there tried to convince haughty aristocrats that their political salvation lay in a social movement of the masses. The effort to found a Catholic confessional party in 1885 was inept and opposed even by the church. His subsequent heedless participation in the conspiracy with Boulanger was a rash attempt to raise his stock with some conservative leaders, a childish delight in intrigue, and worst of all, self-delusion about the character of the plot and its chief authors.

Yet de Mun was not insensitive to reality when it buffeted him so sharply. By 1890 royalism had proved moribund, Boulanger a knave, and the ballot box and the lower classes the preserve of the republicans. He concluded that if the conservatives were not to remain an isolated and impotent faction they would have to cease their relentless opposition to the Republic and bargain for support in the legislature on their left flank. They would have, in his words, "to have the courage to sacrifice their intimate thoughts and personal views, to forget their long-held hopes and just demands, to try to bring forth a respectable and decent Republic."[3] When these sentiments, however reluctantly held, finally became the common property of most conservatives, they formed the basis of the Ralliement. Through it in loose alliance with Méline and the Opportunists from 1896 to 1898, de Mun savored his first taste of national influence. Unfortunately, the experience did not teach him moderation. Although he recognized and valued the gains won by the conservatives through the Ralliement, he wagered them all on the guilt of Dreyfus. When he lost his venture, he tried to recoup it through the ALP, by reforming the Ralliement majority around antisocialism and defense of the established church. The election of 1902 was close, that of 1906 not so, and soon thereafter some of the conservatives moved to the neoroyalism of the Action Française. Although the isolation of the Right was now almost as complete as in 1890, de Mun never recanted his allegiance to the Republic, and as the German threat appeared, he became its most vocal patriot. Exploiting this status and the surge of nationalism in France after 1911, de Mun concluded an accommodation with Poincaré and the new group of moderates in the Chamber of Deputies that made the conservatives an honored partner in the government. Because of this compact France entered the war of 1914 immensely better prepared not only militarily, through the three-year-service law of which de Mun was the champion, but politically, since the conservatives were immediately part of the sacred union. In 1939, grown accustomed again to antiparliamentarianism and excluded from the councils of state, the Right would oppose the wartime government and divide the nation.

After 1870, de Mun was the only serious leader to emerge from the *gratin*. Their political power broken by the advent of the Third Republic, its members retreated to their salons and clubs to ridicule republicans and toast the monarchy. They were backward, reactionary in the worst sense. De Mun was a curious anomaly in their ranks. Like them he was a man singularly out of place with his times, probably even more so because of his quixotic ideals and dream of the victory that always eluded him. But the substance of that victory changed to reflect less and less of the outlook of the class to which he belonged. He shared few of their prejudices and almost nothing of their obscurantism. An aristocrat, he was for a time the most advanced social reformer in France. Born and bred to Legitimism, before the disgusting finish of the business with Boulanger he was ready to cut the ties binding the conservatives to royalism. Catholic above all, he could finally come to terms with a laic society and call it his *patrie*, his France. Because his eloquence had very early marked him as a future leader of the Right and because its circles counted few young men of promise, the old aristocracy at first overlooked the odd predilections of its Gambetta. In time it would not. He would not be an outcast except at the height of the resentment against the Ralliement or during the worst phases of Integrism, but he would be considered peculiar, not quite comme il faut. For all his difference from the *gratin* he could hardly expect to find acceptance elsewhere; he was far too untimely. Writing to the young men of the ACJF, de Mun once epitomized his dilemma, his entire career, in a quotation from Louis de Bonald: "There are men who by their sentiments belong to the past and by their ideas to the future. They have a difficult time discovering their place in the present."[4]

Notes

CHAPTER 1 Knight of the *Syllabus*

1. The most complete descriptive genealogy of the house of de Mun is found in Jean Baptiste Julien de Courcelles, *Histoire généalogique et heraldique des pairs de France*, 3:1–16. On Claude Adrien de Mun there is an adulatory biography by his descendant Antonin de Mun, *Claude Adrien de Mun*. Mrs. Augustus Craven (née Pauline de La Ferronnays) provides intimate family details about her sister Eugénie and her courtship with Adrien de Mun in *Récit d'une soeur*. So appealing to French readers was Mrs. Craven's maudlin romanticism about young love and early death that by 1908 the book had gone through fifty-one printings. A eulogy to the second Marquise de Mun was published by Mrs. Craven, "La Marquise de Mun," pp. 923–33. Albert de Mun himself has left the valuable memoir *Ma Vocation sociale*. A number of biographies of de Mun have preceded this one, only one of which escapes the damning category of popular and laudatory. Charles Molette's careful and scholarly *Albert de Mun, 1872–1890* is an excellent account of de Mun's early career in social Catholicism but ignores his political activities. Among the better popular biographies are those by Jacques Piou, a close political ally, *Le Comte Albert de Mun*, Robert Garric, *Albert de Mun*, Victor Giraud, *Un Grand Français, Albert de Mun*, Maurice Lissorgue, *Albert de Mun*, Albert Flory, *Albert de Mun*, and Robert Talmy, *Albert de Mun*.

2. For the early phases of de Mun's life, his service in Algeria, marriage, charity work, and participation in the Franco-Prussian War, see his *Vocation sociale*, pp. 2–55, and his other reflections in *Discours du Comte Albert de Mun*, 1:222; *Combats d'hier et d'aujourd'hui*, 4:169; and "Compte-rendu," p. 762. *Discours* and *Combats* are collections of his speeches and newspaper editorials, the "Compte-rendu" a review of a memoir on the Franco-Prussian War by La Tour du Pin.

3. De Mun, *Vocation sociale*, pp. 12–13. Gustave Gautherot, *Un Demi-Siècle de défense nationale et religieuse*, is the only biography of Keller, whose tract, *L'Encyclique du 8 décembre 1864 et les principes de 1789*, borrows many arguments from the likes of Joseph de Maistre and Count Louis de Bonald. Many propagandists of the Right shared his general assumptions, and a guide to them is the anthology of J. S. McClelland, ed., *The French Right*.

4. De Mun, *Vocation sociale*, pp. 21–22, and testimony by Count De Mung [*sic*], Enquête du 18 mars, 22 December 1871, Annales de l'Assemblée Nationale, 9:598–600, C 2879, Archives Nationales (hereafter cited as AN).

5. De Mun, *Vocation sociale*, pp. 57–62, the quotation from p. 62. On Maignen, see his son's biography, Charles Maignen, *Maurice Maignen, directeur du Cercle Montparnasse*.

6. De Mun, *Vocation sociale*, pp. 62–66, and *Discours*, 1:13–20.

7. De Mun, *Vocation sociale*, pp. 70–82. The nine were Albert de Mun, Robert de Mun, René de La Tour du Pin, Maurice Maignen, Emile Keller, Baron Louis Guiraud (deputy from Léonce), Paul Vrignault (bureau chief at the Quai d'Orsay), Armand Ravalet (at-

torney), and Léon Gautier (professor at the Ecole de Chartres). On Robert de Mun, see Mrs. Augustus Craven, *Robert de Mun*, the only biography. For La Tour du Pin there are Paul Chanson, *Autorité et liberté*, Jean Rivain, *Un programme de restauration sociale*, and Robert Talmy, *René de La Tour du Pin*. La Tour du Pin's writings are collected in *Vers un ordre social*, and *Aphorismes de politique sociale*.

8. Gabriel Le Bras, *Etudes de sociologie religieuse*, 2:490–557, confirms the worst of the fears of Melun and Ozanam. He concludes that by 1850 the urban proletariat had left the church, the bourgeoisie was split between belief and unbelief, and the peasantry had largely fallen away. He attributes this to the identification of the church with reactionary politics and its tendency to serve as the policeman for the upper classes. Monsignor Joseph N. Moody comes to the same conclusions in his "The Dechristianization of the French Working Class," pp. 46–69. Later than this time period but still fascinating is a survey of religious practice taken in 1903 and published by Emile Poulat as "Une enquête anticléricale de pratique religieuse en Seine-et-Marne 1903," pp. 127–48, which indicates that only 2 percent of Catholics in the department regularly practiced their religion. Allowance must be made for the survey's having been taken by an anticlerical government at the height of an antichurch campaign. For Melun, Ozanam, and their immediate successors, there is the excellent *Les Débuts du catholicisme social en France, 1822–1870* by Jean Baptiste Duroselle. For the period after 1870 there are a number of general histories: Henri Rollet, *L'Action sociale des catholiques en France, 1871–1914*, Parker T. Moon, *The Labor Problem and the Social Catholic Movement in France*, and Georges Hoog, *Histoire du catholicisme social en France, 1871–1931*. Biographies of leading social Catholics, such as those of the de Muns, La Tour du Pin, and Maignen, already noted, lend personal detail, as do those of two other figures, Léon Harmel and Marc Sangnier. On Harmel see his own *Manuel d'une corporation chrétienne* and Georges Guitton, *Léon Harmel*. For Sangnier see especially Jeanne Caron, *Le Sillon et la démocratie chrétienne, 1894–1910*. Two other participants have written memoirs: Georges Goyau [Léon Grégoire], *Autour du catholicisme social*, and Robert de Roquefeuil, *L'Histoire de l'Oeuvre des Cercles*. There are also a number of excellent monographs: Richard L. Camp, *The Papal Ideology of Social Reform*, Matthew H. Elbow, *French Corporative Theory, 1789–1948*, and three studies by Robert Talmy, *Aux sources du catholicisme social, Le Syndicalisme chrétien en France, 1871–1930*, and *Une forme hybride du catholicisme social en France*.

9. De Mun, *Vocation sociale*, pp. 94–96.

10. Ibid., p. 113, and *Discours*, 1:21–30.

11. De Mun's constitution was published in 1877 by the central governing committee as *Bases et plan général de l'Oeuvre des Cercles Catholiques d'Ouvriers*. The blessings of Pius IX are discussed in de Mun, *Vocation sociale*, pp. 289–90, and the opposition of Dupanloup and Guibert, pp. 97–98. Jacques Gadille's findings in *La Pensée et l'action politique des évêques français au début de la IIIe République, 1870–1883* support the contention that the episcopacy inevitably fought against all new ideas and especially those that could conceivably reduce their power.

12. Molette, *De Mun*, describes through the correspondence of de Mun and Félix de Roquefeuil the unstinting efforts of de Mun and La Tour du Pin to toe the doctrinal line.

13. Precise membership figures for the Oeuvre des Cercles do not exist. The reports on the *cercles* by the Sûreté Générale found in AN F7 12477 and 12478, Oeuvre des Cercles Catholiques d'Ouvriers and Association Catholique de la Jeunesse Française, never give national figures, using instead the terms "growth" and "decline" except in 1883, when the national total was placed at 582 *cercles* with over 56,000 members. The *procès-verbaux* of the central committee of the Oeuvre des Cercles, found in the Archives Cercle Maurice Maignen (hereafter cited as ACM), suffer from a similar lack of precision. The *procès-verbal*

of May 1875 states that at this date there were 150 *cercles* and 18,000 members. Thereafter, the *procès-verbaux* note only the number of *cercles*, and that only occasionally. The one for March 1878 states that there were then 375 *cercles*, from which it is possible to estimate that there were nearly 40,000 members.

14. De Mun, *Vocation sociale*, pp. 141–50, the quotation p. 178, and de Mun to Veuillot, editor of *L'Univers*, 3 March 1873, Louis Veuillot Papers, 24634, ff. 481–82, Bibliothèque Nationale, Nouvelles acquisitions françaises (hereafter cited as BN Naf). De Mun explained under what conditions he would be delivering a series of speeches, thanked Veuillot for his patronage of the *cercles*, and asked the editor to be present if possible at an address planned for 5 March 1873 in Paris at the Société d'Horticulture. This description, and others that follow, are based on numerous photographs and on the recollections of his children as recounted to Henri Rollet, *Action*, 1:139.

15. For "guardian angel," de Mun to Colonel Louis Léon, April 1873, Archives de l'Ecole Albert de Mun, Nogent sur Marne, cited by Molette, *De Mun*, pp. 146–47. For a vivid description of the pilgrimage, de Mun to Roquefeuil, 17 Aug. 1873, reproduced *in extenso* in *Vocation sociale*, pp. 216–42.

16. For Lyautey, André Maurois, *Lyautey*, pp. 17–19; for Pius IX, Cardinal Prince Chigi to de Mun, 18 April 1873, reproduced *in extenso* in *Vocation sociale*, pp. 184–85. De Mun's relationship with du Lac can be investigated in the letters of the former to the latter conserved in the Archives de la Société de Jésus, Province de Paris (hereafter cited as ASJ). De Mun remained on the board of governors of Sainte Geneviève until 1913, when it was closed in virtue of anticlerical laws passed in 1904.

17. For Charette, reports of 14 and 24 Nov. 1873, B A/401, Agissements Légitimistes, Archives de la Préfecture de Police, Paris (hereafter cited as APP). See also Marvin L. Brown, Jr., "Catholic-Legitimist Militancy in the Early Years of the Third Republic," pp. 233–54. For Veuillot, Veuillot to de Mun, 15 Feb. 1874, cited by Molette, *De Mun*, pp. 149–50, and in general the adulatory biography by Eugène Veuillot, *Louis Veuillot*, and Marvin L. Brown, Jr., *Louis Veuillot*. For de Mun's speeches, *Vocation sociale*, pp. 156–58.

18. Interpellations à la Commission de Permanence, C 2840: ff. 13–14, AN.

19. De Mun, *Vocation sociale*, pp. 156–58.

20. De Mun to Roquefeuil, 28 Oct. 1875, cited by Molette, *De Mun*, p. 164. De Mun's file, identified only as "Dossier Albert de Mun," at the Archives du Ministère des Armées lacks his letter of resignation. The other documents pursuant to his termination of service are present. For his reaction thirty years later, *Vocation sociale*, pp. 282–83.

21. André Siegfried, *Tableau politique de la France de l'ouest sous la Troisième République*, pp. 149–62, a pioneer effort in electoral geography.

22. De Mun, *Vocation sociale*, pp. 156–58, 273–74, 279. The correspondence between de Mun and Chambord is reproduced *in extenso*.

23. De Mun to Veuillot, 28 Jan. 1876, Louis Veuillot Papers, 24232, ff. 464–69, BN Naf. For the circular, *Discours*, 2:2–4.

24. Veuillot to de Mun, 14 Feb. 1876, and Bécel to de Mun, 15 Feb. 1876, reproduced *in extenso* in *Discours*, 2:5–8. De Mun to Veuillot, 19 Feb. 1876, Louis Veuillot Papers, 24634, ff. 501–2, BN Naf.

25. Veuillot to Countess de Mun, 10 March 1876, Louis Veuillot Papers, 24222, ff. 554–55, BN Naf. For election systems, strategy, results, percentages of those voting, and the like, consult, and attempt to reconcile, the following: Emmanuel Berl, *La Politique et les partis*, Alain Bomier-Landowski, "Les Groupes parlementaires à l'Assemblée Nationale et de la Chambre des Députés de 1871 à 1914," Raymond L. Buell, *Contemporary French Politics*, Peter Campbell, *French Electoral Systems and Elections since 1789*, Jean Paul

Charnay, *Les Scrutins politiques en France de 1815 à 1914*, André Daniels [André Le Bon], *L'Année politique*, François Goguel, *Géographie des élections françaises de 1870 à 1951*, and *La Politique des partis sous la IIIe République*, Harold Gosnell, *Why Europe Votes*, André Siegfried, *Tableau des partis en France*, and Roger Soltau, *French Parties and Politics*.

26. *Journal Officiel, Chambre des Députés, Débats Parlementaires* (hereafter cited as *JOC*), 23–24 March 1876.

27. Ibid., 3 June and 3 July 1876.

28. On the *cercles*, see the reports of the Sûreté Générale in 1875 and 1876, F[7] 12477, Oeuvre des Cercles Catholiques d'Ouvriers, AN. De Mun's invalidation came on 13 July 1876, see *JOC*.

29. For the poster, *Discours*, 2:120–21; *JOC*, 15 Dec. 1876.

CHAPTER 2 Gambetta of the Right

1. There are a number of excellent general histories of the Third Republic in which the battle can be followed in detail. Sir Denis W. Brogan's *The Development of Modern France, 1870–1939* is the most satisfactory single-volume account, although it lacks documentation. Alfred Cobban's *A History of Modern France* is briefer but also excellent. In French the multivolume works of Jacques Chastenet, *Histoire de la Troisième République*, and Edouard and Georges Bonnefous, *Histoire politique de la Troisième République*, are superb and encyclopedic. Guy Chapman began an unfortunately never-finished multivolume history of the Republic with *The Third Republic of France*. David Thomson's *Democracy in France* is more political science than history but has many excellent points to make. Many other histories are written from bias, a sampling of which are Jacques Bainville's royalist but almost convincing *La Troisième République, 1870–1935*; Jean C. Bracq's *France under the Republic*, a diatribe against the Catholic church; Albert Auguste Gabriel Hanotaux's *Histoire de la France contemporaine, 1870–1900*, written to glorify himself—although the rest of the work is objective; and Maurice Reclus, *Grandeur de "La Troisième,"* written to amuse.

2. On Chambord, see the biography by Marvin L. Brown, Jr., *The Comte de Chambord*. For the royalists, there are Robert R. Locke, *French Legitimists and the Politics of Moral Order in the Early Third Republic*, and Samuel M. Osgood, *French Royalism under the Third and Fourth Republics*. John Rothney, *Bonapartism after Sedan*, and Karen Marie Stedfeld Offen, "The Political Career of Paul de Cassagnac," treat the Bonapartists.

3. On church schools, there are two valuable monographs, John W. Padberg, S.J., *Colleges in Controversy*, and Marc Oraison, *Amour ou contrainte?* Treating narrower topics are John W. Bush, "Education and Social Status," and John W. Langdon, "New Light on the Influence of the Jesuit Schools." There are a host of histories of the Catholic church in France. Some of the best are: John McManners, *Church and State in France, 1870–1914*, Adrien Dansette, *Histoire religieuse de la France contemporaine*, Edouard Lecanuet, *L'Eglise de France sous la IIIe République*, Charles Stanley Phillips, *The Church in France, 1848–1907*, Philip Herbert Spencer, *The Politics of Belief in Nineteenth-Century France*, John Edward Courtney Bodley, *The Church in France*, and the outspokenly anticlerical Antonin Debidour, *L'Eglise catholique et l'Etat sous la IIIe République*. E. E. Y. Hales, *Pio Nono*, is an apologia for Pius IX. Harry W. Paul explores the intellectual experience of the church in his "In Quest of Kerygma." The growth of a "liberal Catholic" movement to oppose the black reaction of the first half of the nineteenth century is detailed in the work of Georges Jacques Weill, *Histoire du catholicisme libéral en France, 1828–1908*.

4. There is no monograph on the growth of the republican party in France, although Jacques Kayser, *Les Grandes batailles du radicalisme*, is very good on Gambetta's group. Emmanuel Beau de Loménie, *Les Responsabilités des dynasties bourgeoisies* is damning on

the Opportunists; for a more favorable view, see Sanford Elwitt, *The Making of the Third Republic*. On the conception of laicism and the evolution of a "republican" morality to replace that of the church, there are several interesting studies: Georges Jacques Weill, *Histoire de l'idée laïque en France au XIXe siècle*, Louis Capéran, *Histoire contemporaine de la laïcité française*, Pierre Bonnoure, "La Formation historique de l'idée laïque," and Herbert L. Tint, "The Search for a Laic Morality under the French Third Republic." On the derivation of the conception of clericalism and anticlericalism, see Monsignor Joseph N. Moody, "French Anticlericalism."

5. For the dissolution crisis, see Fresnette Pisani-Ferry, *Le Coup d'état manqué du 16 mai 1877*, and Alan Grubb, "The Politics of Pessimism," and "The Duc de Broglie, the Conservative Union, and *Seize Mai*."

6. De Mun to Veuillot, 19 Jan. 1877, Louis Veuillot Papers, 24233, ff. 154–55, BN Naf. *JOC*, 1 and 4 May 1877, de Mun listing the Radical daily *Le Rappel* of 2 May 1877 as an example of anticlerical excess. Gambetta's retort came on 4 May. For de Mun's reaction to Broglie, Jacques Piou, *Le Comte Albert de Mun*, p. 38.

7. Marvin L. Brown, Jr., "Catholic-Legitimist Militancy in the Early Years of the Third French Republic," p. 244; report of 31 May 1877, B A/870, Baron Charette, APP; report of 8 June 1877, B A/402, Agissements Légitimistes, APP; Albert de Mun, *Discours du comte Albert de Mun*, 1:230–53, the source of the quotation.

8. De Mun to Roquefeuil, 23 Aug. 1877, cited by Charles Molette, *Albert de Mun, 1872–1890*, p. 305. De Mun to Veuillot, 17 Sept. 1877, Louis Veuillot Papers, 24233, ff. 158–59, BN Naf. *JOC*, 18 May 1878.

9. Albert de Mun, *Ma Vocation sociale*, p. 285. De Mun wrote to Roquefeuil about the credo before he composed it: De Mun to Roquefeuil, 20 June 1878, cited by Molette, *De Mun*, p. 53.

10. De Mun, *Discours*, 1:292–304.

11. On the Falloux law, see Georges Cogniot, *La Question scolaire en 1848 et la loi Falloux*, and John K. Huckaby, "Roman Catholic Reaction to the Falloux Law." Falloux's remarks came in *Le Correspondant* 113 (25 Oct. 1878): 362–76.

12. *JOC*, 16 Nov. 1878.

13. Chambord to de Mun, 20 Nov. 1878, reproduced *in extenso* in *Vocation sociale*, pp. 306–7, and *Discours*, 2:313–15. For "sterile immobility," de Mun to Roquefeuil, 27 Nov. 1878 and 5 Sept. 1879, cited by Molette, *De Mun*, p. 64. For the personal note, see the document communicated by Bertrand de Mun to Henri Rollet and reproduced *in extenso* in Rollet, *Albert de Mun et le parti catholique*, pp. 31–32.

14. Report of September 1879, comments about de Mun in regard to the progress of the *cercles* while he was out of the Chamber of Deputies, F7 12477, Oeuvre des Cercles Catholiques d'Ouvriers, AN. For his reply to his constituents, *Discours*, 2:316–17.

15. Descriptions based upon photographs of the countess and her ménage.

16. On *clubisme* and the salons of the *gratin*, see the memoirs of Count Paul Vassili [Princess Ekaterina Radziwill (née Rzewuska)], *France from behind the Veil*, Duchess Elizabeth de Clermont-Tonnerre (née de Gramont), *Mémoires*, Princess Maria Dorothea Elisabeth de Radziwill (né de Castellane), *Lettres de la Princesse Radziwill au Genéral de Robilant*, and George Wyndham, *Life and Letters*. The following studies are also helpful: George Duncan Painter, *Marcel Proust*, Pierre Villoteau, *La Vie parisienne à la Belle Epoque*, and Gilbert Guilleminault, ed., *La Belle Epoque*.

17. De Mun corresponded with some of the belles-lettrists he met, and his letters to them are preserved at BN Naf: Germain Bapst Papers, 24536, ff. 463–81; Georges de Porto-Riche Papers, 24967, ff. 54–58; Ferdinand Brunetière Papers, 25045, ff. 464–96; Robert de Montesquiou Papers, 15293, f. 62; and Gaston Paris Papers, 24451, ff. 109–23. For gossip about de Mun, Clermont-Tonnerre, *Mémoires*, 1:59. For a British view of the

aristocracy, Wyndham, *Life and Letters*, 1:480. For the Third Order of St. Francis, Archives Provinciales des Pères Capucins de Paris, dossiers 1 R^2 1 and 19 M^1 23.

18. On Leo XIII, besides the general histories of the Catholic church during the Third Republic, see the authorized biography by Charles de T'Serclaes de Wommerson, *Le Pape Léon XIII*, and Edward T. Gargan, ed., *Leo XIII and the Modern World*.

19. For background, see Evelyn M. Acomb, *The French Laic Laws*.

20. Such feelings engendered a pervasive sense of pessimism, much of which is accurately depicted in Koenraad Wolter Stuart Swart's tantalizing *The Sense of Decadence in Nineteenth-Century France*.

21. For the banquets, Brown, *Chambord*, pp. 155–57, and "Catholic-Legitimist Militancy," pp. 249–50; De Mun, *Gardons nos frères*, and *Discours*, 2:320–82. The remark about the fork is cited by Alan Grubb, "The Dilemma of Liberal Catholics and Conservative Politics in the Early Third Republic," p. 374. For the Cercles Catholiques Militaires, report of 28 Feb. 1880, B A/403, Agissements Légitimistes, APP; for Cassagnac, report of 16 Aug. 1879, B A/1541, Agissements Cléricaux, APP; and reports of 2 June and 20 Nov. 1879, B A/402, Agissements Légitimistes, APP.

22. De Mun, *Vocation sociale*, pp. 210–11.

23. Report of 25 March 1880, B A/1541, Agissements Cléricaux, APP; reports of 28 Dec. 1880 and 5 Oct. 1881, B A/870, Baron Charette, APP. For de Mun's speech, *Dieu et roi*, and *Discours*, 2:387–420. For Chambord's published reply, *Discours*, 2:421–22, an encomium of de Mun.

24. Report of 24 Feb. 1883 by Emile Schnerb to the minister of the interior and of public worship, F^7 12477, Oeuvre des Cercles Catholiques d'Ouvriers, AN. The circular to the central committee of the Oeuvre des Cercles is reproduced *in extenso* by Molette, *De Mun*, p. 198. For the address, *Discours*, 1:350–56; for the letter, de Mun to Roquefeuil, 27 July 1878, reproduced in part by Molette, *De Mun*, pp. 178–79.

25. The size of the Oeuvre des Cercles is an estimate based on figures cited in the 1878 *procès-verbal* of the central committee of the group, ACM, and in the report of Schnerb in February 1883, F^7 12477, AN. For episcopal resistance, Henri Rollet, *L'Action sociale des catholiques en France, 1871–1914*, 1:37, quotes Father Julien Hubin, S.J., senior chaplain to the *cercles*, as saying in 1878, "The most general opposition encountered by us has come from the members of the clergy." Pius IX blessed the *cercles* four times in the 1870s: by his approving letter of January 1872, by his gift of money and award of medals to their founders in April 1873, and by his Brefs de Sa Sainteté of October 1874 and April 1877. See de Mun, *Vocation sociale*, pp. 316–20, 186–90. Also, de Mun to Roquefeuil, 3 and 13 Oct. 1878; 27 June, 14 July, 3 and 29 Aug., 5 and 6 Sept., and 13 Nov. 1879; and 11 Nov. 1880, cited by Molette, *De Mun*, pp. 311–19.

26. Brown, "Catholic-Legitimist Militancy," pp. 251–54.

27. For the Union Générale, see Robert Bigo, *Les Banques français au cours du XIXe siècle*, Jeannine Verdès, "La Presse devant le krach d'une banque catholique," and Jean Bouvier, *Le Krach de l'Union Générale, 1878–1885*. There are several valuable studies on labor unrest in this period: Auguste Chirac, *L'Agiotage sous la Troisième République, 1870–1887*, Robert Brécy, *Le Mouvement syndical en France, 1871–1921*, Val R. Lorwin, *The French Labor Movement*, Leo A. Loubère, "Les Radicaux d'extrême-gauche et les rapports entre patrons et ouvriers, 1871–1900," and Jean Maitron, *Histoire du mouvement anarchiste en France, 1880–1914*.

28. Piou, *De Mun*, p. 51. De Mun published the journal in 1910 as *Les Dernières heures du drapeau blanc*; the quotation is from p. 33, the story of the interview, pp. 134–36. *Le Gaulois*, 13 Sept. 1883. For the speech to the *cercles*, *Discours*, 3:99–101. For Lyautey, André Maurois, *Lyautey*, p. 31. For the decision to place the *cercles* before Orleanism, de Mun to Roquefeuil, 21 Sept. 1883, cited by Molette, *De Mun*, p. 201.

29. For de Mun's response to accusations of fainthearted royalism, *Journal de Paris*, 14 Feb. 1884, and *Discours*, 3:102–3. For the banter with Gallifet, *Drapeau blanc*, p. 153.

30. Formation of the Union des Droites was not announced formally but was revealed by informants: report of 7 Jan. 1882, B A/404, Agissements Légitimistes, APP. See MS memoirs of Baron Mackau, Armand de Mackau Papers, 156 AP I, 66, AN.

31. For example, see the drastic split of conservative deputies on 8 December 1882, when half voted against the budget, half either voted for or abstained. On the colonial question, see Thomas F. Power, *Jules Ferry and the Renaissance of French Imperialism*, Fresnette Pisani-Ferry, *Jules Ferry et le partage du monde*, Henri Brunschwig, *French Colonialism, 1871–1914*, and Agnes Murphy, *The Ideology of French Imperialism, 1871–1881*. For the votes on anticlerical proposals, see Acomb, *Laic Laws*. For the constitutional amendments, see *Journal Officiel, Assemblée Nationale* (hereafter cited as *JOAN*), 1884.

32. *JOAN*, 13 Aug. 1884, for the quotation; *JOC*, 9 Nov. 1881, 24 March 1884, and 7 April 1885.

33. For Leo XIII, Capéran, *Laïcité française*, 3:50–174. For Mackau, his MS memoirs, Armand de Mackau Papers, 156 AP I, 66, AN. For de Mun's interventions, *JOC*, 23 May, 10 July, and 14 Nov. 1882; 3, 17, and 18 March and 10 Dec. 1884; and 10 March 1885. De Mun addressed a crowd of approximately four thousand people on 9 June 1882 at Bordeaux to denounce the school laws.

34. De Mun decried the proceedings: *JOC*, 23 and 28 May 1885. There is a description in purple prose of Hugo's funeral, 1 June, and the night before, in Roger Shattuck, *The Banquet Years*, pp. 4–5. The Pantheon had been secularized earlier, during the Revolution, but returned to the faith under the Empire.

35. See the result of Félix de Roquefeuil's work, *Résumé des principes de l'Oeuvre des Cercles Catholiques d'Ouvriers sur le régime du travail dans l'ordre social chrétien*, and de Mun's addresses to the tenth and twelfth general assemblies of the Oeuvre des Cercles, 7 May 1882 and 7 June 1884, respectively, in *Discours*, 1:358–85, 410–26. For "insipid bourgeois," de Mun to Louis Milcent, dated only 1883, cited by Molette, *De Mun*, p. 200. For the parliamentary debate, *JOC*, 12 and 19 June 1883; 14 and 25 Jan. and 2 Feb. 1884. For the survey, *procès-verbal*, 1883, ACM; for background, Robert Talmy, *Le Syndicalisme chrétien en France, 1871–1930*, pp. 20–23.

36. The attitude of the conservatives can be presumed from their outbursts during de Mun's remarks to the Chamber on 12 June 1883. For de Mun's addresses in Belgium and Switzerland, *Discours*, 1:428–68, and Molette, *De Mun*, p. 109. For the attitude at the Vatican, de Mun to Roquefeuil, 27 April 1884, cited by Molette, *De Mun*, p. 201, and Rollet, *Action*, 1:256, who retails the anecdote, which occurred on 23 February 1885.

CHAPTER 3 The Catholic Party and Boulangism

1. Cited by Maurice J. M. Larkin, "The Church and the French Concordat, 1871 to 1902," p. 728.

2. *JOC*, 24 March 1885. The vote was 402 to 91.

3. *Le Pays*, 3 Sept. 1885, copies also in B A/611, Elections Législatives de 1885, APP. For the common list, report of 17 July 1885, B A/611, Elections Législatives de 1885, APP. Conservative accord proved impossible in four relatively minor departments, Hautes-Alps, Basses-Alps, Alps-Maritimes, and Cantal.

4. See the memoirs of Arthur Meyer, the editor of *Le Gaulois*, *Ce que mes yeux ont vu* and *Ce que je peux dire*. Cassagnac's editorial appeared in *Le Matin*, 9 Oct. 1885. For the fear of the other conservatives, see *Le Figaro*, 13 Oct. 1885, and reports of 17 Oct., B A/1000, Paul Granier de Cassagnac, and B A/611, Elections Législatives de 1885, APP.

5. Henri Rollet, *Albert de Mun et le parti catholique*, is the only detailed account of this maneuver.

6. De Mun to Mackau, 19 July 1885, Armand de Mackau Papers, 156 AP I, 278, AN. The Manifeste des Treize was published in *L'Univers*, 13 Aug. 1885. Its signatories were de Mun, Emile François Gaudin, Louis Adolphe Marie Gouzillon Viscount de Bélizal, Albert Benoist d'Azy, Henri Louis Lucien Brun, Charles Chesnelong, Admiral Albert Auguste Marquis Gicquel des Touches, Charles Louis Henri Kolb-Bernard, Emile Keller, Jean Baptiste Henri Edouard de La Bassetière, Paul Henri Count de Lanjuinais, Anne Frédéric Armand Baron de Mackau, and Marie Raymond Gustave Lacroix Baron de Ravignon. A copy is in de Mun, *Discours du Comte Albert de Mun*, 3:321–24. De Mun's letters appeared in *L'Univers*, 8 and 19 Sept. 1885. Copies are in *Discours*, 3:325–32.

7. *Le Temps*, 17 Sept. 1885. The fourteen adherents to de Mun's Catholic party were Louis de Bélizal, Auguste Marie Boscher-Delangle, Joseph Laurent Marie Hillion, Charles Joseph Larère, Emile Cillart Viscount de Kermenguy, Louis Joseph Marie Count de Kersauson-Pennendreff, Henri Alexandre Joseph Count de Legge, Léon Paul Lorois, Gaston Conen de Saint-Luc, Etienne Pierre Marie Roussain, Henri Marie Jacques Charles Marquis de Vaujuas-de-Langan, Hervé Marie Pierre Marquis de Bernis, Paul Baron de Lamberterie, and Alain Charles Louis de Rohan Chabot Prince de Léon. De Mun was reelected for Morbihan, finishing third on the departmental list with 60,341 votes, just 148 short of the leader. For the session of the central committee of the *cercles*, *procès-verbal*, 1885, ACM.

8. De Mun's last effort was published in *L'Univers*, 3 Nov. 1885; a copy is in *Discours*, 3:333–38. The critical letters: Freppel to de Mun, 30 Oct. 1885; Keller to de Mun, 31 Oct. 1885; Mackau to de Mun, 1 Nov. 1885; and Marquis Adrien de Mun to de Mun, 9 Nov. 1885; all are cited by Rollet, *Parti catholique*, pp. 72–78, who details the papal intervention, pp. 98–111. De Mun's letter of disavowal appeared in *L'Univers*, 9 Nov. 1885; there is a copy in *Discours*, 3:339.

9. For "rude blow," Jacques Piou, *Le Comte Albert de Mun*, p. 95. For the letters of de Mun and Falloux to Mackau, 11 and 18 Nov. 1885, respectively, Armand de Mackau Papers, 156 AP I, 278, AN.

10. For the *cercles*, see the *procès-verbaux*, 1880–90, ACM, and reports of 1880–90, F^7 12478, Association Catholique de la Jeunesse Française, AN. For the ACJF, see Charles Molette, *L'Association Catholique de la Jeunesse Française, 1886–1907*, who provides exhaustive and exhausting coverage.

11. Jean Loesevitz, "La Législation du travail." De Mun's reply came in the next issue: "Lettre." For de Mun's letters to du Lac, see de Mun to du Lac, 11 and 14 May and 23 Sept. 1886, Stanislas du Lac–Louis Trégard Papers, ASJ. For de Mun's speeches, *Discours*, 1:542–84. The details of the trip to the Vatican, his emotions of the past months, and the exciting news of the audiences, 15 and 18 October, are related in de Mun to Roquefeuil, 19 Nov. 1887, cited in Charles Molette, *Albert de Mun, 1872–1890*, p. 213.

12. For the chapel incident, *JOC*, 13 April 1886; for de Mun's remarks on the expulsion, see *JOC*, 10 June 1886. For *Le Figaro*'s comment, see the issue of 16 May 1886.

13. For Raoul-Duval, *JOC*, 6 Nov. 1886. See Cassagnac's editorials in *L'Autorité* for June and August 1886 and *Le Soleil* for August 1886. The September letter of the Count of Paris was leaked to the press in December, appearing in *Le Figaro* on 15 Dec. 1886 and in *L'Autorité* two days later.

14. On Boulanger and subsequent Boulangism, the outstanding work remains Adrien Dansette, *Le Boulangisme, 1886–1890*. It is supplemented by the narrower treatment of Frederic H. Seager, *The Boulanger Affair*. Jacques Néré, *Le Boulangisme et la presse*, and Joseph O. Baylen, "An Unpublished Note on Général Georges Boulanger in Britain, June 1889," treat peripheral topics. Boulanger's memoirs, *Mémoires du Général Boulanger*, are a tissue of lies, but those of his political lieutenants, Mermeix [Gabriel Terrail], *Les Coulisses du boulangisme*, and Albert Verly, *Le Général Boulanger et la conspiration monarchique*, have the ring of truth and, used with care, are valuable sources.

15. MS memoirs, Armand de Mackau Papers, 156 AP I, 66, AN.

16. *JOC*, 11 June 1887.

17. For Mackau's concern, see his letter to Cassagnac, 14 Aug. 1887, cited by Karen Marie Stedfeld Offen, "The Political Career of Paul de Cassagnac," p. 296. Cassagnac's own speculations appeared in *L'Autorité*, 1 Sept. 1886. The pretender's manifesto appeared in *Le Gaulois*, 15 Sept. 1887; a comprehensive review of press reaction to the manifesto was published in *Le Temps*, 19 Sept. 1887.

18. Fascinating details are available in Adrien Dansette, *L'Affaire Wilson et la chute du président Grévy*. See also Mackau's memorandum on the fall of the Rouvier cabinet, dated 10 May 1893, Armand de Mackau Papers, 156 AP I, 101, AN. The balancing act began with *JOC*, 5 Nov. 1887. Pressure from provincial royalists can be traced in reports of 17–19 Nov. 1887, F^7 12439, Agissements Royalistes, AN. Rouvier fell after the debate of *JOC*, 19 Nov. 1887.

19. MS memoirs, Armand de Mackau Papers, 156 AP I, 66; see also the account in Mermeix, *Coulisses*, pp. 62–73. For the presidential election, *JOAN*, 3–5 Dec. 1887.

20. Mermeix, *Coulisses*, pp. 39–50. The seven departments in which Boulanger's agents first acted were Hautes-Alps, Côte d'Or, Loiret, Maine et Loire, Haut Marne, Loire, and Marne.

21. *Le Gaulois*, 13 March 1888. For the conspiracy, MS memoirs, Armand de Mackau Papers, 156 AP I, 66, AN. See also the memoirs of other leading conservative Boulangists: Henry Charles Joseph Le Tonnelier Marquis de Breteuil, "Les Coulisses du boulangisme," and Jacques Piou, "Le Boulangisme."

22. De Mun to Mackau, 1 April 1888, Armand de Mackau Papers, 156 AP I, 278, AN, confirmed the meeting; MS memoirs, Armand de Mackau Papers, 156 AP I, 66, AN, recount the interview. De Mun to Parseval, 2 April 1888, cited by Dansette, *Boulangisme*, p. 166.

23. De Mun to Mackau, 12 April 1888, Armand de Mackau Papers, 156 AP I, 278, AN, confirms the date in London for 16 April. The meeting is recounted in MS memoirs, Armand de Mackau Papers, 156 AP I, 66, and Meyer, *Mes yeux*, p. 81. The pretender's instructions appeared in *Le Gaulois*, 25 April 1888.

24. Report written after 8 Nov. 1888, B A/1496, Boulanger, APP. De Mun to Trémoïl, one of de Mun's assistants on the disbursement committee, 17 Jan. 1889, Charles Louis de Trémoïl Papers, 1 AP 518, AN; MS memoirs, Armand de Mackau Papers, 156 AP I, 66, AN. Mermeix, *Coulisses*, pp. 120, 270. Dansette, *Boulangisme*, pp. 180–93.

25. *JOC*, 4 June and 12 July 1888.

26. De Mun to Mackau, 30 April and 20 July 1888, Armand de Mackau Papers, 156 AP I, 278, AN. De Mun to Parseval, 22 July 1888, cited by Dansette, *Boulangisme*, pp. 150, 167. De Mun to Roquefeuil, 28 April 1888, cited by Molette, *De Mun*, p. 330. Mermeix, *Coulisses*, pp. 131–38.

27. De Mun to Mackau, 23 Aug. 1888, Armand de Mackau Papers, 156 AP I, 278, AN.

28. *JOC*, 22, 24, and 26 March, 17, 22, 24, and 28 May, and 11 June 1888. De Mun to Parseval, 23 March 1888, cited by Dansette, *Boulangisme*, p. 158. Mermeix, *Coulisses*, pp. 25–27.

29. De Mun, *Discours*, 4:83–99, 114–47. Robert Talmy, *Aux sources du catholicisme social*, pp. 219–55. *Compte-rendu et procès-verbaux des Etats Libres du Dauphiné*, cited in Robert Talmy, "L'Ecole de La Tour du Pin et l'encyclique Rerum Novarum," p. 273.

30. Seager, *Boulanger*, pp. 203–10, discusses the origins of this myth and examines the evidence for and against.

31. For the change in election procedure, *JOC*, 11 Feb. 1889. Cassagnac

editorialized in *L'Autorité*, 5–6 April 1889. For the reaction of the conservatives, de Mun to Mackau, 3 and 13 May 1889, Armand de Mackau Papers, 156 AP I, 102, AN; reports of 10 April and 3 May, B A/974, Agissements Boulangistes, APP.

32. *JOC*, 8 June 1889. See also de Mun to Mackau, 5 June 1889, Armand de Mackau Papers, 156 AP I, 102, AN. Report of 17 April 1889, B A/969, Agissements Boulangistes, APP; report of 3 July 1889, B A/971, Agissements Boulangistes, APP.

33. There are twenty-nine letters from de Mun to Mackau during this period, 3 July to 16 September 1889, in the Armand de Mackau Papers, 156 AP I, 102 and 110, AN. Dansette, *Boulangisme*, pp. 330–32. Verly, *Boulanger*, pp. 108–13.

34. Copy of Mackau to the Count of Paris, 24 Sept. 1889, Armand de Mackau Papers, 156 AP I, AN. Cassagnac in *L'Autorité*, 25 Sept. and 8 Oct. 1889. For Piou, Piou to Mackau, 3 Oct. 1889, Armand de Mackau Papers, 156 AP I, 279, AN. *Le Gaulois*, 8 Oct. 1889. The Count of Paris accepted full responsibility: Paris to Cassagnac, 6 Jan. 1891, cited by Offen, "Cassagnac," pp. 345–46.

35. De Mun to Mackau, 1 and 10 Oct. 1889, Armand de Mackau Papers, 156 AP I, 110. *L'Univers*, 13–14 Oct. 1889.

36. Maria Dorothea Elisabeth Radziwill, *Lettres de la Princesse Radziwill au Général de Robilant*, 1:18–19.

37. *Le Gaulois*, 14–18 Oct. 1889; *L'Autorité*, 14–18 Oct. 1889. De Mun to Mackau, 18 Oct. 1889, Armand de Mackau Papers, 156 AP I, 278, AN.

CHAPTER 4 The Ralliement

1. For background, see Alexander Cameron Sedgwick, *The Ralliement in French Politics, 1890–1898*. The degree to which the rightist leadership had been compromised can be measured in Albert Verly, *Le Général Boulanger et la conspiration monarchique*, pp. 293–320, which lists those candidates in the 1889 elections who received the Boulangist imprimatur and money from Boulanger's campaign managers.

2. Copy of Mackau to the Count of Paris, 17 Oct. 1889, Armand de Mackau Papers, 156 AP I, AN. For the meeting, see *L'Autorité*, 25 Jan. 1890. On Piou, see Joseph Denais, *Jacques Piou*, an adulatory biography.

3. *Le Figaro*, 21 March 1890, reported the existence of the Droite Constitutionnelle, and that of 31 March listed the sixteen original members and their program. The sixteen were: Piou, Auguste Prince d'Arenburg, Louis Brincard, Pierre Desjardins, Robert de l'Aigle, Joseph Freschville, Jean Hély d'Oisel, Louis de Moutéty, François de Montsaulin, Léon Morillot, Paul Le Gavrien, Charles Paulmier, Léon Renard, Charles Thellier de Poncheville, Jules Delafosse, and Ernest Desjardins.

4. Copy of Mackau to the Count of Paris, 20 May 1890, Armand de Mackau Papers, 156 AP I, AN. The articles in *Le Figaro*, in reality by Mermeix, the pen name of Gabriel Terrail, editor of the Boulangist *La Cocarde*, a confidante of the general, and elected as a deputy from Paris in the 1889 elections, were published under the same title that year as a book.

5. On Lavigerie, see the works of Xavier de Montclos, *Lavigerie, le Saint-Siège et l'Eglise*, and *Le Toast d'Alger*. These supersede James E. Ward, "The Algiers Toast." See also the older study, Joseph Tournier, *Le Cardinal Lavigerie et son action politique, 1863–1892*, and J. Dean O'Donnell, "Cardinal Charles Lavigerie."

6. For d'Haussonville, *Le Figaro*, 9 Feb. 1891; for Cassagnac, *L'Autorité*, 13 Feb. 1891. For the episcopacy, see a trio of articles by James E. Ward, "The French Cardinals and Leo XIII's Ralliement Policy," "Cardinal Richard versus Cardinal Lavigerie," and "Cardinal Place and Leo XIII's Ralliement Policy." For the Union de la France Chrétienne, Sedgwick, *Ralliement*, pp. 41–43; Denais, *Piou*, pp. 48–49; Cardinal Dominique Ferrata, *Mémoires*, 2:74–75. Ferrata was appointed nuncio to France in July 1891.

7. See the letters of de Mun to Roquefeuil cited by Charles Molette, *Albert de Mun, 1872–1890*, pp. 218–20. *JOC*, 23 Nov. 1889; 5, 7, and 8 July 1890; 27 Jan., 2, 3, and 5 Feb., and 4 and 8 May 1891.

8. *Procès-verbaux*, 1885–90, ACM. The decline in enthusiasm is evident. See also the reports of the late 1880s in F[7] 12478, Association Catholique de la Jeunesse Française, AN. For the dissociation of the journal, see Albert de Mun, "Quelques mots d'explication." For the ACJF, Charles Molette, *L'Association Catholique de la Jeunesse Française, 1886–1907*, pp. 33–107.

9. For the situation surrounding the pilgrimage, Molette, *Jeunesse Française*, pp. 108–36; also Ferrata, *Mémoires*, 2:96–113. *Le Petit Journal*, 17 Feb. 1892, for the interview. For the reaction of diehard royalists, Gustave Gautherot, *Un Demi-Siècle de défense nationale et religieuse*, pp. 302–32; Ferrata, *Mémoires*, 2:242–47; and *L'Autorité*, 11 June 1892. Cassagnac's gloat is cited by John McManners, *Church and State in France, 1870–1914*, p. 78.

10. For de Mun's thoughts of a confessional party, *La Corporation* (Parisian weekly), 30 Jan. 1892. For Clemenceau, *JOC*, 18 Feb. 1892. For de Mun's first speech to the ACJF, Albert de Mun, *Discours du Comte Albert de Mun*, 5:133–36. For Ferrata's warning, see his *Mémoires*, 2:238–41. Henri Rollet, *L'Action sociale des catholiques en France, 1871–1914*, 1:140, retails the anecdote of de Mun and Leo XIII. For the speech rallying to the Republic, Jacques Piou, *Le Comte Albert de Mun*, p. 136.

11. Rollet, *Action*, 1:138–44; Piou, *De Mun*, pp. 132–37; and Molette, *Jeunesse Française*, p. 165, n. 110; p. 207, n. 223.

12. Bourgeois's remark is cited by Guy Chapman, *The Third Republic of France*, p. 297; Ferry's by McManners, *Church and State*, p. 73.

13. Sedgwick, *Ralliement*, pp. 60–62; Sedgwick concentrates on Lamy's work. Etienne Lamy, "Le Devoir des conservateurs." Gaston David to Lamy, 15 June 1892, Etienne Lamy Papers, 333 AP, AN.

14. For the negotiations, Sedgwick, *Ralliement,* pp. 59–62. It is impossible to know just how many adherents there were to any of the three groups. Piou commanded a following of about thirty-five, Lamy and David a few less, and de Mun approximately thirty. De Mun was leader of the social Catholic Ralliés only in the sense that they generally followed his lead and allowed him to speak in their name. For Lamy's speech, see his *Quelques oeuvres et quelques ouvriers*, pp. 67–109. For de Mun's interventions: *JOC*, 20 and 29 Oct., 2 and 3 Nov. 1892. On the legislation, see Theodore Michael Altholtz, "The French Labor Law of November 2, 1892." For de Mun at Saint-Etienne, *Discours*, 5:264–79.

15. For Cassagnac and Mackau, see Cassagnac to Mackau, undated but by context from October 1892, Armand de Mackau Papers, 156 AP I, 272, AN. The best work on the Panama scandal is Adrien Dansette, *Les Affaires de Panama*. The full truth of the matter is bound up in the blackmail payments of financier Jacques de Reinach to Cornelius Herz. These totaled 9,072,175 francs over the 1880–89 period. The explanation may well lie in the papers of the former's nephew, Joseph Reinach, who burned many of his uncle's documents the morning of the elder Reinach's suicide, 19 November 1892. Joseph Reinach left his papers to the Bibliothèque Nationale with the proviso that the first twenty-three bundles might be opened in 1951 but the twenty-fourth only in 2010. Lamy's first address was delivered in Paris at the Salle de la Société de Géographie on 28 January 1893, the second at the Salle des Folies Bergères on 26 February 1893: Lamy, *Quelques oeuvres*, pp. 111–75. For Piou and de Mun, see *JOC*, 16 Feb. and 13 March 1893, respectively.

16. The text of the speeches at Toulouse and Arras was lost, but there are précis in de Mun, *Discours*, 5:320–27. The speech to the *cercles* follows, 5:330–56. For de Mun's changed thinking, Molette, *Jeunesse Française*, pp. 137–208. For the banquet, *Le Figaro*, 22 June 1893; for its mood, Piou, *De Mun*, pp. 148–49.

17. For Depuy, Ferrata, *Mémoires*, 2:269–86. See François Goguel, *Géographie des élections françaises de 1870 à 1951*, pp. 30–31, 58–59, for an excellent analysis of this phenomenon. De Mun was defeated 4,427 to 4,160 by Albert Le Clec'h. Piou lost 6,959 to 6,139 to Jean Bepmale at Saint Gaudens in Haute Garonne. Lamy was beaten 12,494 to 9,398 by Georges Trouillot at Lons-le-Sonier in the Jura. Le Clec'h, Bepmale, and Trouillot were all Opportunists, but, of course, only Trouillot was an incumbent.

18. For Ferrata's opinion on de Mun's defeat, *Mémoires*, 2:300–303. For de Mun's reaction and new speeches: De Mun to Charles Geoffroy de Grandmaison, 30 Aug. 1893, cited by Rollet, *Action*, 1:470, n. 1; *Discours*, 5:358–97.

19. André Siegfried, *Tableau politique de la France de l'ouest sous la Troisième République*, pp. 181–94. De Mun, *Discours*, 5:406–8.

20. On anarchism, see Jean Maitron, *Histoire du mouvement anarchiste en France, 1880–1914*, and the lively popular account in Barbara W. Tuchman, *The Proud Tower*, pp. 72–132. On the explosive growth of socialism, see Aaron Noland, *The Founding of the French Socialist Party, 1893–1905*, and the tedious but full biography of Jaurès, the leader of this expansion, Harvey Goldberg, *The Life of Jean Jaurès*.

21. For Spuller, *JOC*, 3 March 1894. On the strategy of the Ralliés there are several interesting studies. Sedgwick, *Ralliement*, is quite clear and concise, and the same can be said of David Shapiro, "The Ralliement in the Politics of the 1890s," published in *The Right in France, 1890–1919*, pp. 13–48, which he edited. More specialized is Jean Marie Mayeur, "Droites et ralliés à la Chambre des Députés au début de 1894," which acknowledges indebtedness to Shapiro. Maxime Lecomte, a Radical deputy of the time, wrote a very complete but biased history of the political relations between Ralliés and Opportunists, *Les Ralliés*. Jacques Piou, although out of the Chamber from 1893 to 1898, managed to involve himself in the negotiations for the 1898 elections and much else before. He reveals all in his memoirs, *Le Ralliement*.

22. *JOC*, 30 April 1894, for de Mun's speech; 22 May 1894 for the fall of the Casimir-Périer ministry.

23. De Mun described his affliction to Mackau in three letters, de Mun to Mackau, 12 and 24 Oct. 1894 and 15 April 1895, Armand de Mackau Papers, 156 AP I, 278. See also Molette, *Jeunesse Française*, p. 221.

24. *JOAN*, 18 Jan. 1895. On the tactics, or lack of them, followed by the Ralliés, see Edouard Lecanuet, *L'Eglise de France sous la IIIe République*, 4:17–20.

25. *JOC*, 28 Oct. 1895. The tax was passed by the Chamber on 26 March, by the Senate on 12 April. On the ministries of Ribot and his successor, Léon Bourgeois, see Lecanuet, *Eglise de France*, 4:20–87, Martin E. Schmidt, *Alexandre Ribot*, and for the Carmaux strike, Joan Wallach Scott, *The Glassworkers of Carmaux*.

26. For Bourgeois's declaration, *JOC*, 1 Nov. 1895. The interpretation of the moderate and conservative reaction is not merely the conclusion of recent commentators, such as Sedgwick, *Ralliement*, p. 137, but was shared by contemporaries, as any sampling of the press reveals.

27. *JOC*, 30 April 1896. On Méline and his ministry, see the premier's speeches, *Discours aux Progressistes*, and the old, but serviceable, Georges Lachapelle, *Le Ministère Méline*. The segment in Lecanuet, *Eglise de France*, 4:88–112, is quite helpful.

28. For the "Clovis speech," *Discours*, 6:53–68. For de Mun's reply to Guesde, *JOC*, 15 June 1896; for the vote on the income tax, 283 to 254, 7 July 1896.

29. For the Méline ministry's attitude toward the congregations: reports on the congregations to Barthou, 1896–98, F^{7} 12393 B, C, D, Culte Catholique, AN; and reports on the congregations to Rambaud, 1896–98, F^{19} 6440 A, Instructions, AN. Méline survived Radical questions on this issue four times: *JOC*, 30 Nov. 1897; 25 Jan., 2 Feb., and 12 March 1898. For the visit of the Russian royal family, *Le Temps* and *Le Figaro*, 5–9 Oct.

1896. See also Lecanuet, *Eglise de France*, 4:96–98. For the premier's help against the Radicals: *JOC*, 21–22 Jan. 1897, with the vote 243 to 48. For the Turks: De Mun broached the topic in the Chamber on 3 November 1896 and later congratulated the government for its intervention, 6 February 1897. On 2 February 1897, de Mun presided over a committee to protest the treatment of Catholic minorities. It included Anatole and Paul Leroy-Beaulieu, Ernest Lavisse, and Gaston Paris among its luminaries: *Discours*, 6:243–48.

30. For the fire, see the vivid description in Roger Shattuck, *The Banquet Years*, pp. 12–13. A list of the victims connected to the *cercles* is included in Albert de Mun, *Ma Vocation sociale*, p. 301, appendix 7. In a letter to his friend Léon Lavedan, editor of *Le Correspondant*, written the day after the disaster, de Mun described how he rushed desperately about the bazaar grounds for nearly an hour, searching for his wife and daughter, before finding them safe: De Mun to Lavedan, 5 May 1897, Léon Lavedan Papers, 305 AP 8, dossier 3, AN. After the service in Notre Dame, *JOC*, 29 May 1897, the government defeated a Radical-sponsored resolution of no confidence by a 274 to 259 vote before passing a resolution of confidence 296 to 231. The vote on the income tax bill came on 16 July 1897, 282 to 249.

31. *JOC*, 28 Oct. 1897.

32. For de Mun's speech to the *cercles*, *Discours*, 6:225–35. For Deschanel's letter: De Mun to Deschanel, 6 Jan. 1897, Paul Deschanel Papers, 151 AP 35, AN. For the vote to sustain Méline, *JOC*, 14 June 1898.

33. The literature on the Dreyfus affair is long, often tedious, and contentious. Joseph Reinach, *Histoire de l'Affaire Dreyfus*, written in the midst of the battle by a passionate Dreyfusard, remains the most encyclopedic source, but it is heavily biased against the army and the church. An example of the kind of rabidly anticlerical writing that the affair produced is that by an Oxford professor, Frederick C. Conybeare [Frederick Cornwallis], *The Dreyfus Case*. There are two excellent objective modern studies, Guy Chapman, *The Dreyfus Case*, and Douglas W. Johnson, *France and the Dreyfus Affair*. Monsignor Joseph N. Moody's "Dreyfus and After" is a hidden gem, an excellent but rarely read discussion of the effect of these years in France. Patrice Boussel, *L'Affaire Dreyfus et la presse*, studies the large role played by the press in the agitation about the affair.

34. Lecanuet, *Eglise de France*, 4:175, the visit of Dreyfus coming on 10 May 1897.

35. *JOC*, 4 Dec. 1897, for Méline's words and those of de Mun and army minister Billot to follow.

36. Reinach, *Dreyfus*, 3:139–42.

37. *JOC*, 13 Jan. 1898, for de Mun's exclamation and the speeches by him and the premier following. See Reinach, *Dreyfus*, 3:231–35.

38. De Mun to Paris, 19 Feb. 1898, Gaston Paris Papers, 24451, ff. 119–20, BN Naf.

39. De Mun to Paris, 13 Dec. 1896, Gaston Paris Papers, 24451, ff. 117–18, BN Naf, and de Mun to Brunetière, 17 Dec. 1896, Ferdinand Brunetière Papers, 25045, f. 466, BN Naf, reveal part of the campaign for de Mun. For his speech, *Discours*, 6:361–94. For Méline's remark, *JOC*, 12 March 1898.

40. The evidence for de Mun's negotiations with Méline is from Jacques Piou, who tells the same story in three different books, the latter two his own memoirs: *De Mun*, p. 176, *Ralliement*, pp. 65–78, and *D'une guerre à l'autre, 1871–1914*, pp. 159–64.

41. Jacques Piou, "Les Conservateurs et la démocratie," forms a stark contrast to Emile Keller, "Les Elections de 1898."

42. On Lamy's selection and plans, see Sedgwick, *Ralliement*, pp. 92–114, and Lecanuet, *Eglise de France*, 4:112–26.

43. On the relations between Piou and Lamy, see the correspondence of two Assumptionist monks, Fathers François Picard and Emmanuel Bailly, April 1896, both very active in clerical politics, cited by Molette, *Jeunesse Française*, p. 221, and further com-

ments on the ACJF by Molette, pp. 218–30. For the Union Nationale and the Justice-Egalité, see F^7 12480 and 12481, by those titles, respectively, AN. For the Christian Democrats: Jean Marie Mayeur, "Les Congrès nationaux de la 'Démocratie chrétienne' à Lyon, 1896–1897–1898," Robert F. Byrnes, "The French Christian Democrats in the 1890s," and, most important, Jean Marie Mayeur, *Un Prêtre démocrate*. For the Fédération: Sedgwick, *Ralliement*, pp. 108–9, Molette, *Jeunesse Française*, p. 230, and Lecanuet, *Eglise de France*, 4:120–22.

44. For the reaction of those outside: Picard to Bailly, 2 Feb. 1898, cited by Molette, *Jeunesse Française*, p. 237, and de Mun to Lamy, 11 April 1898, Etienne Lamy Papers, 333 AP, AN. For de Mun's dislike of the Christian Democrats, see his letter to Abbé Paul Six, likewise an opponent of them, undated but by context from early 1897, cited by Rollet, *Action*, 1:424–25. His public condemnations came in remarks to the *cercle* in Belleville on 4 April 1897 and in an open letter of 3 May 1897, *Discours*, 6:274–81 and 283–90, respectively. For Lamy's optimism, see Lamy to Monsignor Charles Mourey, a papal adviser at the Vatican, 19 April 1897, Etienne Lamy Papers, 333 AP, AN.

45. For Lamy's meeting with Méline: Piou, *D'une guerre*, pp. 139–64, and *Ralliement*, pp. 73–78, Sedgwick, *Ralliement*, pp. 113–14, and Lecanuet, *Eglise de France*, 4:122–26. For Lamy's speech: *Les Catholiques et la situation présente*, with the quotation from p. 31. For de Mun's remark, Piou, *Ralliement*, p. 75. For Méline's speech, see *La République Française*, 19 April 1898, a paper he controlled; for Hanotaux's mission, Piou, *De Mun*, pp. 173–74. For Barthou's reluctance, see the prefectoral circulars, January to May 1898, F^{19} 6440 A, Instructions, AN. For the inability of de Mun and Piou to overcome local resistance: Lecanuet, *Eglise de France*, 4:122–29, Mayeur, *Prêtre démocrate*, p. 247, and Sedgwick, *Ralliement*, p. 159.

46. For the disavowal of Lamy: Molette, *Jeunesse Française*, pp. 274–76. For the new negotiations with Méline: Piou, *Ralliement*, pp. 73–78. De Mun was elected unopposed at Morlaix. Piou gained revenge on Jean Bepmale for 1893 by defeating him at Haute Garonne 7,319 to 6,495. Election analysis identifies at least 57 seats that would probably have been won by the incumbent ministry but for the *politique du pire* of the royalists and Justice-Egalité. See Goguel, *Géographie des élections*, pp. 32–33, 60–61.

47. *JOC*, 13–14 June 1898. Piou reports Méline's remark in *Ralliement*, p. 79.

CHAPTER 5 In Opposition

1. Brisson had already decided on this action; Dupuy merely confirmed it. The Cour de Cassation is not a court of appeal in the Anglo-Saxon sense, but one that can literally "break" the decision of another court, requiring the case to be retried.

2. On *La Croix* and the Assumptionists, see Pierre Sorlin, *"La Croix" et les juifs, 1880–1899*, and Judson Mather, "The Assumptionist Response to Secularization, 1870–1900." For the Henry memorial, see Pierre Quillard, *Le Monument Henry*.

3. On the congregations and the entire question of the relationship of church and state, see Herbert L. Tint, "The Search for a Laic Morality under the French Third Republic," which is the source of the quotation, Adrien Dansette, *Histoire religieuse de la France contemporaine*, Antonin Debidour, *L'Eglise catholique et l'Etat sous la IIIe République*, and Alec Mellor, *Histoire de l'anticléricalisme français*.

4. For the charge against the Postards, see Albert de Mun, *Nouvelle réponse à une vieille accusation renouvelée contre l'Ecole Sainte Geneviève*. For de Mun's hastening of Brisson's departure: *JOC*, 25 Oct. 1898. It is a near impossibility to discover the names of all the members of a parliamentary committee formed before 1902. At that date the committees became permanent standing ones. Previously, they were ad hoc, each formed to consider *one* bill, or occasionally several bills on *one* issue. The members were chosen by the

bureaus method: the deputies were divided by lot into eleven bureaus, from which one, or in the case of important committees, two members were elected to sit on each parliamentary committee. When the committee finished its work on the bill it had been formed to consider, it disbanded, often without keeping proper minutes. Its life span might be as long as the four-year mandate of the Chamber or as short as one hour. Because the bureaus from which the members were elected were chosen by lot, the committees were often highly unrepresentative of the composition of the Chamber. If, for example, the two hundred Radicals of the 1898 Chamber had by some fluke been concentrated into two bureaus and spread very thinly among the other nine, despite having nearly 35 percent of the seats in the Chamber, they would probably never have more than two seats on any committee of eleven. For more details, see Robert Kent Gooch, *The French Parliamentary Committee System*. The papers of Henri Bazire are held by his children in Paris, but they are not currently open to scholars. I am grateful to the Abbé Charles Molette, who, having had access to the correspondence of Henri Bazire at an earlier time, loaned me his copious notes on it. For this round of letters, I cite de Mun to Bazire, 29 Nov. and 2 and 7 Dec. 1898, Henri Bazire Papers.

5. De Mun's letter to the *Times* was also printed in Albert de Mun, *Discours du Comte Albert de Mun*, 6:419–30. For de Mun's contribution to the Henry memorial, see Quillard, *Monument Henry*, p. 130. For the suggestion to Bazire, de Mun to Bazire, 15 Jan. 1899, Henri Bazire Papers. See also Charles Molette, *L'Association Catholique de la Jeunesse Française, 1886–1907*, p. 266.

6. For aristocratic antisemitism, see Robert F. Byrnes, *Antisemitism in Modern France*, and sections passim on the Salon Loynes in Arthur Meyer, *Ce que je peux dire*. For La Tour du Pin's article, see his "La Question juive et la révolution sociale." For the reply of de Mun to Lord Russell, see *Discours*, 7:1–12.

7. This nonsense can best be followed in the police reports, F^7 12449–51, Ligue des Patriotes, 1882–1907, AN.

8. De Mun to Bazire, 6 May 1899, Henri Bazire Papers; Molette, *Jeunesse Française*, pp. 272–79; De Mun, *Discours*, 7:13–39. De Mun even asked Lamy to join, see de Mun to Lamy, 31 May 1899, Etienne Lamy Papers, 333 AP, AN.

9. *JOC*, 15 June 1899.

10. For more details about this breakup of the Center, see R. A. Winnacker, "The Bloc and the Délégation des Gauches." A letter from Poincaré to Méline, 20 May 1899, explaining why he refused to join the Progressives is cited *in extenso* in Fernand Payen, *Raymond Poincaré*, pp. 426–29, appendix 2. For the new premier, see Malcolm Overstreet Partin, *Waldeck-Rousseau, Combes and the Church*, and the brilliant Pierre Sorlin, *Waldeck-Rousseau*.

11. *JOC*, 23 June 1899, and Partin, *Waldeck-Rousseau*, pp. 3–15. See also Leslie Derfler, "Le Cas Millerand," pp. 81–91.

12. Edouard Lecanuet, *L'Eglise de France sous la IIIe République*, 4:206–7. The injunction to let Dreyfus rot came from Georges Berry in *Le Gaulois*, 27 June 1899, and de Mun congratulated Brunetière's speeches for the Patrie Française in de Mun to Brunetière, 28 Oct. 1899, Ferdinand Brunetière Papers, 25045, f. 471, BN Naf.

13. Waldeck-Rousseau's original proposal was inscribed as *projet* 1184, *Journal Officiel, Chambre des Députés, Documents Parlementaires* (hereafter cited as *JOCD*), 14 Nov. 1899. It was sent to an ad hoc committee for consideration and emerged more than a year later, with Georges Trouillot as its reporter. It is difficult to estimate the number of monks and nuns in France because the congregations did not send reports to the government, and attempts by the prefects to tabulate them were handicapped because members constantly moved from one establishment to another. The prefectoral reports to Barthou as minister of the interior, 1896–98, F^7 12393, B, C, D, Culte Catholique, AN, indicate between 75,000 and 80,000 nuns.

14. De Mun to Bazire, 30 Nov. 1899, Henri Bazire Papers. De Mun made the arrangements for his essays with the editor of *Le Correspondant*, Léon Lavedan, by letters of 23 and 29 Nov. 1899: Léon Lavedan Papers, 305 AP 8, dossier 3, AN. De Mun's work was published in four consecutive issues of *Le Correspondant* 197 (10 Dec. 1899): 853–74; 197 (25 Dec. 1899): 1077–1105; 198 (10 Jan. 1900): 3–38; 198 (25 Jan. 1900): 221–59. The four appeared in book form in March 1900 as *La Loi des suspects*.

15. For de Marcère, see Lecanuet, *Eglise de France*, 4:234–36, which cites correspondence between de Mun and de Marcère, and de Mun to Brunetière, who helped to arrange the alliance, 23 Dec. 1899, Ferdinand Brunetière Papers, 25045, f. 472, BN Naf. For Brunetière himself, de Mun to Brunetière, 27 Dec. 1899 and 23 Jan. 1900, Ferdinand Brunetière Papers, 25045, ff. 473–75, BN Naf. For Deschanel, de Mun to Deschanel, 29 Jan. and 2 Feb. 1900, Paul Deschanel Papers, 151 AP 35, AN. The recruits from the Ligue des Patriotes can be investigated in the reports of 1900–1901 in F^7 12451, Ligue des Patriotes, AN. For reports on crowds, see *Le Gaulois*, 19 March and 20 May 1900. For Lamy, the invitation came in de Ludre to Lamy, 27 Jan. 1900, Etienne Lamy Papers, 333 AP, AN. Lamy responded on 22 July 1900, at Sorèze, and the speech is published in his *Quelques oeuvres et quelques ouvriers*, pp. 221–33.

16. Lecanuet, *Eglise de France*, 4:208–15, 229–30, recounts both indignities. De Mun replied to Lanessan in a vigorous letter, published in *Discours*, 7:88–91. For the premier's speech, *Le Gaulois*, 29 Oct. 1900.

17. *JOC*, 15, 17, 21, 24, 28, and 29 Jan. 1901. The rebuke to Lemire came on 28 January.

18. *JOC*, 11, 14, 18, 19, 20, 21, 26, and 29 March 1901. Aynard spoke on 20 March, de Mun on 21 March. Praise for the debates came from Joseph Paul-Boncour, a close associate of Waldeck-Rousseau, in *Entre deux guerres*, 1:122. A detailed discussion of the debates in the Chamber and Senate can be found in Partin, *Waldeck-Rousseau*, pp. 28–44.

19. For Méline and Poincaré, see *La République Française*, 29 April 1901, and *Le Temps*, 13 May 1901, respectively. Piou spoke twice, reported in *Le Figaro*, 31 May and 7 June 1901, before the Société d'Economie sociale et des Unions pour la Paix sociale. Both speeches were published in his *Questions religieuses et sociales*, pp. 59–71, 75–80.

20. For the response of the Progressives and Independents to the offer of de Mun and Piou, see the report of 21 June 1901, F^7 12719, Action Libérale Populaire, AN. The cartons F^7 12719 and 12878, AN, contain voluminous reports to the Sûreté Générale on the Action Libérale, subsequently the Action Libérale Populaire (ALP). The disclosures are occasionally so revealing that one or more members of the party may have been an informant. These police records amply document de Mun's and Piou's understanding of the need for, and the intention to form, a broad democratic party with extensive local membership, the germ of a mass party. In particular, reports of 18 and 21 June 1901, F^7 12719, ALP, AN, bear out such an interpretation. The Stanislas du Lac-Louis Trégard Papers, ASJ, contain letters from de Mun to Trégard, who replaced du Lac as de Mun's spiritual adviser in mid-1909 as du Lac was on his deathbed, in which de Mun claims to have planned from the very beginning that the ALP should be a mass party: see especially the letters of 25 Nov. 1910 and 4 Jan. 1914. See my "The Creation of the Action Libérale Populaire," pp. 660–64. De Mun and Piou had approached the Progressives and Independents in early April about an alliance.

21. Reports of 18 and 21 June 1901, F^7 12719, ALP, AN, on the efforts of de Mun and Piou among the Ralliés and the attitude of the new party. See also de Mun's search for support within the ACJF, de Mun to Bazire, 14 April 1901, Henri Bazire Papers. The announcement of the name was reported in *Le Figaro*, 12 June 1901, and the paper covered Piou's speech, 6 July 1901. The address was also published by Piou as *Les Elections de 1902*.

22. For de Mun's angina: Jacques Piou, *Le Comte Albert de Mun*, pp. 199–200, and de Mun to Bazire, 14 April 1901, and much later, although about the situation in 1901, 24 Feb. 1903, Henri Bazire Papers. For the first report of secret funding, see F^7 12719, ALP, AN.

23. For the recruitment drive see, for example, de Mun to Rambaud, formerly Méline's minister of public worship, 7 Nov. 1901, Alfred Rambaud Papers, 81 AP 4, AN, and Piou to Mackau, an early member, 8 July 1901, Armand de Mackau Papers, 156 AP I, 279, AN. For the Patrie Française, reports of 1901–2, F^7 12451, Ligue des Patriotes, AN. A view of a true intransigent is Keller's "La Revanche des francs-maçons." For the ACJF, de Mun to Bazire, 5 Dec. 1901, Henri Bazire Papers. For Brunetière, de Mun to Brunetière, 19 Nov. 1901, and Bazire to Brunetière, 5 Dec. 1901, Ferdinand Brunetière Papers, 25045, f. 478, and 25030, ff. 153–54, respectively, BN Naf. Leo's reaction is recounted in Lecanuet, *Eglise de France*, 4:317. An almost complete file of the *Bulletin Action Libérale*, subsequently the *Bulletin Action Libérale Populaire* (hereafter cited as *Bulletin*), exists, and it can be consulted at the Bibliothèque Nationale. Féron-Vrau had been a member of the Justice-Egalité but left when it became antirepublican in the latter half of 1900. He brought with him Louis Laya, a clever and efficient writer, who eventually became one of the editors of the *Bulletin*: see report of 13 Dec. 1900, F^7 12481, Justice-Egalité, AN.

24. For de Mun's "captive" speech, *JOC*, 28 June 1901. See the reports of the campaigning in the *Bulletin*, 20 Nov. 1901 to 30 April 1902. The speech at Lille was reported in the first issue of the *Bulletin* and was published by Piou as *L'Organisation pour la lutte électorale*, and in his *Questions religieuses*, pp. 95–108. For a vivid description of the rally, see Pierre Dabry, *Les Catholiques républicains*, pp. 695–700.

25. For the rallies, the *Bulletin* fairly overflows with references, such as Bazire at Troyes in the 31 December issue, industrialist Armand Viel at Bordeaux in that of 18 December, Gailhard-Bancel in Paris in that of 25 December, Paul Lerolle at Besançon in that of 19 February, de Mun and Piou in Paris in that of 15 March. Any number of citations could be offered. Gailhard-Bancel presented the views he had come to share with de Mun to the Chamber: *JOC*, 2 and 17 July 1901, and eventually published them, *Les Retraites ouvrières*. The attitude toward Millerand was very negative; see *Bulletin*, 12 Feb. 1902, as an example. De Mun had consulted with Millerand previously on labor legislation and had no real fear of him as a revolutionary, as Piou, *De Mun*, pp. 194–95, later admitted. For Dabry, see *Catholiques républicains*, p. 696; for Coubé, Lecanuet, *Eglise de France*, 4:313–15.

26. Reports of 6 and 27 Jan., 11 and 19 Feb. 1902, F^7 12719, ALP, AN. *Bulletin*, 9 April 1902.

27. For the allies, see, for example, the reports of their campaigning in *Le Temps*, 15 Jan., 5 and 10 March, and 1 April 1902. In particular, state schoolteachers were encouraged to break up opposition rallies, civil servants told that their jobs depended on the outcome of the election, and the clergy accused of unlawfully pressuring parishioners. Reports from the trials arising out of the 1902 elections, BB^{18} 2209–10, Procès: Elections 1902, AN, tend to substantiate the government's use of pressure and to exculpate the clergy, who generally, and wisely, remained aloof from politics during this election, leaving the burden of defending the church to the Action Libérale. This last is borne out by the reports in F^{19} 5622, Culte Catholique: Elections de 1902, AN, revealing that only thirty-five departments reported any clerical interference at all and that in nearly every case this was limited to preaching against the ministerial candidate. Waldeck-Rousseau spoke at Saint-Etienne on 12 January 1902, his only major speech of the campaign: *Le Temps*, 14 Jan. 1902. Combes spoke at Nantes on 29 January 1902: *Le Temps*, 30 Jan. 1902. The election analysis presented here generally supports the conclusion of François Goguel in *Géographie des elections françaises de 1870 à 1951*, p. 35: "The union of all the adversaries of Waldeck-

Rousseau in the elections of 1902, tightly allied from the monarchists through the Progressives, did not suffice to overcome the premier's coalition, itself perfectly homogeneous, of all tendencies of the Left."

28. For the varying appeals of the Action Libérale candidates, see the *Bulletin* for January to April 1902.

29. Paul-Boncour, *Entre deux guerres*, 1:140–50, and Partin, *Waldeck-Rousseau*, pp. 130–34. By mid-1902, Waldeck-Rousseau had already begun to feel the effects of the disease that would kill him two years later and perhaps thought himself unable to continue in office. It is possible that this resolve was strengthened by the painful injuries he suffered in March 1902 when his carriage was struck by a tram. See Sorlin, *Waldeck-Rousseau*, p. 484.

30. Report of 22 May 1902, F^7 12719, ALP, AN, discusses the attitude of the various segments of the opposition. Piou lost to Jean Bepmale, the Opportunist turned Radical who had defeated him in 1893, the vote 7,803 to 5,973. By contrast, de Mun defeated Georges Victor, another Radical, by the ludicrous 13,433 to 54 vote. For the "absence of organization," see *Bulletin*, 30 April 1902.

31. For the platform in a name, see Eugène Flornoy, *La Lutte par l'association*, pp. 38–61. The Sûreté report is contained in F^7 12719, ALP, AN.

CHAPTER 6 Organizing the Opposition

1. For Combes, there are the two shamelessly adulatory biographies: Yvon Lapiquillerie, *Emile Combes ou le surprenant roman d'un honnête homme*, and Georges Alquier, *Le Président Emile Combes*, as well as the more balanced Gérard Baal, "Combes et la 'République des Comités.' "

2. Prefectoral circulars, 27 and 30 June 1902, F^{19} 6440 A, Instructions, AN. *JOC*, 11 July 1902.

3. For the ALP, report of 21 July 1902, F^7 12719, ALP, AN. For reports from the prefects of Gard, Ille et Vilaine, Vaucluze, Seine Inférieure, Doubs, Haute Garonne, Pas de Calais, Calvados, Finistère, Eure, Côte du Nord, and Morbihan, F^{19} 6076–87, Les Décrets de Juillet 1902, AN. For the *Bulletin*, 23 July 1902.

4. For the march, *Le Figaro* and *Le Gaulois*, 26–28 July 1902. The text of the letter, dated 25 July, can be found in Edouard Lecanuet, *L'Eglise de France sous la IIIe République*, 4:345, n. 1. For the rally, *Le Figaro* and *Le Gaulois*, 29 July 1902, and *Bulletin*, 30 July 1902. De Mun's letter-speech is printed in his *Combats d'hier et d'aujourd'hui*, 1:14–16. There is also a report by the Sûreté, 29 July 1902, F^7 12719, ALP, AN.

5. Mackau's remark came in *Le Figaro*, 29 July 1902. Reports of 28–31 July 1902 on activity in the provinces can be found in F^{19} 6076–87, Les Décrets de Juillet 1902, AN. See also the report of 29 July 1902, F^7 12719, ALP, AN. For the tense month of August, see particularly the report of 7 Aug. 1902 (F^{19} 6077); reports of 30 July and 12 Aug., and intercepted telegrams, Senator de Chamaillard to Deputy Hippolyte Gayraud, de Mun to Gayraud, both 31 July, and de Mun to his wife, 11 Aug. (F^{19} 6079); and the report of 6 Aug. 1902 (F^{19} 6084). The news reports were also intercepted: M. Mauviel to the *Petit Parisien* and an unidentified reporter to the Agence Fournier, both 12 Aug. 1902 (F^{19} 6079).

6. The shift can be seen in the *Bulletin*, 13, 20, and 27 Aug., the issue for 20 August carrying a précis of de Mun's speech, that of 27 August carrying the complete text of Piou's. See also the prefectoral report, 19 Aug. 1902, of de Mun's appearance, F^{19} 6079, Les Décrets de Juillet 1902, AN. The same précis of de Mun's address is found in his *Combats*, 1:34–36; Piou's was published in his *Questions religieuses et sociales*, pp. 111–20. See also Piou to Brunetière, 1 Oct. 1902, Ferdinand Brunetière Papers, 25047, f. 323, BN Naf. De Mun's accounts appeared 28 Sept. and 5 Oct. 1902 and also as *Action Libérale Populaire*. See *JOC*, 14 Oct. 1902, for de Mun's speech to the deputies.

7. Personal testimony from Piou and Countess de Mun on this period can be found in Jacques Piou, *Le Comte Albert de Mun*, p. 220, and Robert Garric, *Albert de Mun*, pp. 171–200.

8. Evidence for these revelations comes from the private papers of Duke Xavier de La Rochefoucauld, who was treasurer and executive secretary of the ALP after June 1912, 142 AP 14 and 15, AN. La Rochefoucauld was asked by Piou to succeed the Marquis Régis de L'Estourbeillon as treasurer, and as a conscientious man, he obtained from Piou and Coutts as much information as possible about the party funds. 142 AP 14, dossier 1, contains a twelve-page list of 262 contributors during the crisis of 1902. For the money from the congregations, he acquired a letter, contained in 142 AP 14, dossier 2, dated 12 June 1912, signed by both Piou and de Mun, empowering Coutts to add La Rochefoucauld's name to the accounts. In communicating a copy of this letter to Coutts, La Rochefoucauld asked for, and subsequently received, a list of the securities bought with the secret funds since 1903, their current value because the capital had frequently been reduced as well as increased, and the means by which the interest would be communicated to him. The value of the securities in midsummer 1912 was 5,777,000 francs; withdrawals were to be accomplished through a complicated process, a very simple example of which, from 142 AP 14, dossier 5, was the following: on 10 October 1913, La Rochefoucauld wrote Coutts requesting that he send 1,500 francs to M. René Dallé, 4 Rue Chauveau Lagarde, Paris, deducting the money from one of the three accounts the party held; that same day he wrote Dallé informing him that he would receive this amount of money and should deposit it to the ALP; on 13 October confirming letters arrived from Coutts and Dallé. Sûreté suspicions can be noted in the report of 12 March 1903, F^7 12393 B, Culte Catholique, and the report of 29 July 1903, F^7 12719, ALP, both AN.

9. Report of 19 Feb. 1903, F^7 12719, ALP, AN. The fourteen were: *Le Nouvelliste de Bretagne, du Maine, et de Normandie*, *La Liberté de Sud-Ouest*, *L'Eclair de l'Est*, *L'Echo de la Loire*, *La République de l'Isère et du Sud-Est*, *Le Télégramme des Vosges*, *L'Eclair Comtois*, *Le Journal d'Amiens*, *Le Courrier du Pas de Calais*, *Le Nouvelliste de la Haute Saône*, *La Chronique Picard*, *La Voix des Familles*, *La Presse Lyonnaise du Sud-Est*, and *La Société Nouvelle du Télégramme de Toulouse*.

10. Cavalier was a veteran of Breton politics, recommended by de Mun, see 142 AP 15, dossier 3, Xavier de La Rochefoucauld Papers; Laya had worked for Lamy's Fédération Electorale in 1898, see F^7 12481, Justice-Egalité; and Salvetti came from Déroulède's Ligue des Patriotes, see F^7 12451, Ligue des Patriotes, all AN. For the editorials, see *Bulletin*, for example, for 15 and 22 Oct. and 26 Nov. 1902, and 14 Jan. 1903. Amédée Reille, who took over for de Mun in the legislature during the latter's illness, coined a bon mot in the 22 October issue: "It has been written that every Rousseau, whether named Jean-Jacques or Waldeck, should give birth to an immortal Emile."

11. The assertions about the deputies are verifiable in René Samuel and Georges Bonet-Maury, eds., *Les Parlementaires français, 1901–1914*. For the statutes of the ALP, see Eugène Flornoy, *La Lutte par l'association*, pp. 99–101, 168–69. The 1904 membership figures are cited in the ALP's *Compte-rendu du Congrès général de 1904*, pp. 20–24, and confirmed by the Sûreté, reports of 17–18 Dec. 1904, F^7 12719, ALP, and the report of 25 Jan. 1905, F^7 12878, ALP, both AN. See also the Sûreté file on the Ligue Patriotique des Françaises, F^7 13215. For comparative figures for other parties, see Léon Ernest Jacques, *Les Partis politiques sous la IIIe République*, pp. 262, 309, estimating the membership of the Radical party at approximately 250,000 in 1911, and that of the Socialist party at approximately 35,000 in 1905 and 63,000 in 1911.

12. The five male orders spared were the Frères de St. Jean de Dieu, Pères Blancs, Missions Africains de Lyon, Trappistes de Cîteaux, and Cisterciens de Lérens. *JOC*: the teaching orders were expelled 300 to 251 on 18 March; the preaching orders 304 to 245 on

24 March; the Chartreux 338 to 231 on 26 March; and the women's congregations 285 to 269 on 26 June 1903. For Gayraud's remark, 19 May 1903.

13. Gustave Gautherot, *Un Demi-Siècle de défense nationale et religieuse*, pp. 354–60, offers what rationale there was to Keller's scheme. For the speech, on 9 November 1902, see Jacques Piou, *Action Libérale Populaire*, and *Bulletin*, 12 Nov. 1902. For the article, see Piou, "L'Action Libérale Populaire," *Le Correspondant*. For Barrès, *Bulletin*, 23 April 1903. For the posters, report of April 1903, F^7 12393 E, Culte Catholique, AN.

14. For de Mun's reaction, de Mun to Piou, cited *in extenso* by Joseph Denais, *Jacques Piou*, p. 118. Piou's reply to Keller is recounted by Gautherot, *Demi-Siècle de défense*, p. 358. For de Mun's statement, de Mun to Brunetière, 30 April 1903, Ferdinand Brunetière Papers, 25045, ff. 283–84, BN Naf; De Mun to Bazire, 30 April 1903, Henri Bazire Papers; De Mun to Mackau, 1 May 1903, Armand de Mackau Papers, 156 AP I, 278, AN.

15. De Mun to Brunetière, 22 Sept. 1903, Ferdinand Brunetière Papers, 25045, ff. 487–88, BN Naf.

16. For the congress, see the ALP's *Congrès social de Pau*, and *Bulletin*, 15 Oct. 1903. See also Gailhard-Bancel before the Chamber: *JOC*, 27 and 30 May and 4 June 1903. For the May conference at Châlons, see Charles Molette, *L'Association Catholique de la Jeunesse Française, 1886–1907*, pp. 346–66, and for the June speeches, pp. 300–307, and de Mun to Bazire, 29 June 1903, Henri Bazire Papers. For the reluctance, de Mun to Bazire, 2 Dec. 1903, Henri Bazire Papers. For de Mun's speech at Besançon, see his *Combats*, 1:439–75. For Piou's, see his *Questions religieuses*, pp. 175–82, also published as *Le Rôle du patron*, and in *Bulletin*, 17 Dec. 1903.

17. On the Sillon, see Jeanne Caron, *Le Sillon et la démocratie chrétienne, 1894–1910*, and Michel Launay, "La Crise du Sillon dans l'été 1905." See also the earlier work by Charles Breunig, "The *Sillon* of Marc Sangnier," and "The Condemnation of the Sillon." For de Mun's proposal, de Mun to Bazire, 2 Dec. 1903, Henri Bazire Papers. The weekly *Le Sillon*, 15 Dec. 1903, pp. 452–55, published a similar letter from de Mun to Sangnier. The final split is described in de Mun to Bazire, 30 Jan. 1904, Henri Bazire Papers. See also de Mun to Piou, 8 Feb. 1904, cited *in extenso* by Denais, *Piou*, p. 139, and de Mun to Monsignor Dubillard, 23 Jan. 1904, cited *in extenso* by Caron, *Le Sillon*, p. 300, n. 67.

18. For Combes's remarks, see his *Une Campagne laïque, 1902–1903*, pp. 312–87, and at Saintes, on 23 August 1903, reprinted in *Bulletin*, 3 Sept. 1903. Piou responded at Puteaux on 27 June, published as *La Lutte pour la liberté*. *Le Radical*, 4 Oct. 1903, carried Bonnet's warning, and the *Bulletin* reprinted it 13 Oct. 1904. For the economic power of the ALP, see the reports of 28 Nov. and 5 Dec. 1903, and 14 and 28 Jan. 1904, F^7 12719, ALP, AN.

19. For the new recruits, reports of 27 Feb., 5 March, 18 and 26 May, and 8 and 12 Dec. 1912, F^7 12719, ALP, AN. Roche and his Ligue des Contribuables were attracted by the ALP's opposition to new taxes; Motte, whose election machine controlled much of the Nord, needed money. Waldeck-Rousseau addressed the Senate on 27 June 1903 and was applauded by the Progressives and Independents. For the immediate ALP reaction, see de Mun to Bazire, 2 July 1903, Henri Bazire Papers, and the report of 21 July 1903, F^7 12393 E, Culte Catholique, AN. For obituaries, see de Mun, in *Le Gaulois*, 31 Aug. 1904, and the editorial in *Bulletin*, 18 Aug. 1904. On 29 July 1904, Combes broke diplomatic relations with the Vatican, and the papal nuncio departed for Rome, leaving behind as an unofficial observer his assistant, Monsignor Carlo Montagnini. For the next year and a half, Montagnini, who delighted in schemes of his own or others' making, kept the Vatican informed of political intrigue in France, as filtered through his prejudices. In December 1906, Clemenceau, as premier, ordered Montagnini's deportation and seized his papers and archives, which were first turned over to a parliamentary committee and now rest in the Archives

Nationales, C 7376–86. The situation of the ALP and the rest of the opposition is described well in a letter of Montagnini to Merry del Val, 6 Dec. 1904, C 7377, slip 7, piece 61.

20. *Bulletin*, 31 March 1904, for de Ludre. For de Mun's "shocking" conviction, see John McManners, *Church and State in France, 1870–1914*, pp. 81–103, and de Mun to Piou, 29 May 1904, cited *in extenso* by Denais, *Piou*, p. 137. For the pilgrims, see Molette, *Jeunesse Française*, p. 470.

21. See de Mun to Piou, 18 Jan. 1904, cited *in extenso* by Denais, *Piou*, pp. 136–37, and *Bulletin*, 14 Jan. 1904, for tactics. For the Piou-Beauregard show, see the regional ALP papers, *L'Action Libérale Populaire de la Gironde*, 6 March 1904, and *L'Action Libérale Populaire de Saint-Brieuc*, 8 May 1904. For the local elections, see *Bulletin*, 5 May and 4 Aug. 1904. Montagnini's remark came in Montagnini to Merry del Val, 30 Nov. 1904, Archives Montagnini, C 7378, slip 14, piece 3, AN. See reports of 2 Dec. 1904 and 27 Oct. 1905, F^7 12451, Ligue des Patriotes, AN; report of 5 Dec. 1903, F^7 12719, ALP, AN; and reports of 3 Dec. 1904 and 28 June and 28 July 1905, F^7 12878, ALP, AN.

22. See *JOC*, 4 March 1904, for Ribot's remark; the votes came 28 March in the Chamber and 5 July in the Senate. The major debates in the Chamber took place 3–4, 14, 17–18, 21–23, and 28 March; in the Senate, 23 and 26 June and 7 July. For de Mun's editorials, *Le Gaulois*, 19 Feb. and 9 March 1904; *Le Correspondant* 214 (25 March 1904): 989–1008; and *The National Review* 141 (1 April 1904): 199–233. It is at this point that de Mun's journalistic career truly began. He would write for four major dailies during the next ten years, *Le Figaro*, *Le Gaulois*, *La Croix*, and *L'Echo de Paris*. The first two appealed to a cosmopolitan, conservative constituency, with *Le Figaro* a bit more "smart." Each had a circulation of between thirty and fifty thousand at this time. *La Croix* and *L'Echo de Paris* both claimed over one hundred thousand daily sales but emphasized different issues. *La Croix* was a mouthpiece for the ALP but stressed religious matters. *L'Echo*, to which de Mun moved only in 1908, was the great exponent of nationalism. Circulation figures can be only approximate, but they are the best available: see Raymond Manévy, *La Presse de la IIIe République*, pp. 143–44.

23. De Mun discussed his plans for the trip in letters to Brunetière and Mackau: de Mun to Brunetière, 29 March 1904, Ferdinand Brunetière Papers, 25045, ff. 490–91, BN Naf; and de Mun to Mackau, 2 April 1904, Armand de Mackau Papers, 156 AP I, 278, AN. The question perplexing the Vatican is admirably elucidated in Maurice J. M. Larkin, "Loubet's Visit to Rome and the Question of Papal Prestige," pp. 97–103. De Mun's conclusion from his trip can be inferred from de Mun to Bazire, 16 July 1904, Henri Bazire Papers. The Sûreté came to the same conclusion in a report of 15 June 1904, F^7 12878, ALP, AN.

24. Maurice J. M. Larkin tells the story quite well in his *Church and State after the Dreyfus Affair*, pp. 130–36. For the ALP justification, see *La Croix*, 20 and 30 May and 3 Aug. 1904, the last the source of the quotation; *Le Gaulois*, 2 April and 4 May 1904. De Mun informed Bazire of the blessng in de Mun to Bazire, 28 July 1904, Henri Bazire Papers.

25. See de Mun's editorial, *Le Gaulois*, 31 Oct. 1904, and the Sûreté reports on the fiches, F^7 12476, Délation dans l'Armée, AN.

26. For a common opposition sentiment, see de Mun's editorial, *Le Gaulois*, 30 Nov. 1904. The quotation is from de Mun to Bazire, 17 Jan. 1906, Henri Bazire Papers, written much later than the fiche controversy but in reference to its effect. Premonition of the trouble can be found in Ferri de Ludre's attack on two-year service, *Bulletin*, 25 Feb. 1904, and de Mun's comment, *Le Gaulois*, 10 June 1904.

27. For the early plans, de Mun to Piou, Jan. 1904, cited *in extenso* by Denais, *Piou*, p. 151. See Piou's "Comment se défendre?" The format change in the *Bulletin* came 3

November 1904; for the policy in Paris, see report of 27 Oct. 1904, F7 12878, ALP, AN; for promises of a positive program, see *Bulletin*, 27 Oct. and 3 Nov. 1904; for denunciation of the fiches, see *Bulletin*, 3, 17, and 24 Nov. 1904, and report of 11 Nov. 1904, F7 12476, Délation dans l'Armée, AN.

28. On the congress, the ALP's *Compte-rendu, 1904*, is a verbatim record conveniently annotated. For Piou's keynote, pp. 13–17; Laya, pp. 18–47; Reille, pp. 64–68; Gailhard-Bancel, pp. 87–135; Plichon and Ollivier, pp. 173–93; Spronck, pp. 165–71; Lerolle, pp. 232–43; for the banquet, pp. 243–63. Police reports of 17–18 Dec. 1904, F7 12555, Rapports, Paris, AN, confirm crowd estimates, as do reports of 17–18 Dec. 1904, F7 12719, ALP, AN. A look at any Parisian newspaper will reveal reports on the congress.

29. For initial hope, see *Bulletin*, 26 Jan. and 2 Feb. 1905, and de Mun in *La Croix* and *Le Gaulois*, 27 Jan. and 2 Feb., respectively. For the disillusionment, *Bulletin*, 9 and 16 Feb. 1905. The Separation proposal of Briand, *JOCD* 2302 of 4 March 1905, was accompanied by his essay of 145 pages describing the debilitating effects of clericalism in France and the conflicts between church and state. He often committed absurd errors in this history, confusing the Carolingian dynasty with the Capetian, having Philip the Fair assaulting Innocent III instead of Boniface VIII, and bishops frequenting the Tuileries a century before the palace was constructed.

30. For Briand's career and personal life, as seen by a biographer who suspected conspiracies everywhere, see Georges Suarez, *Briand*, the relevant volume being the second, rightly entitled *Le Faiseur de calme, 1904–1914*.

31. For de Mun, *Le Gaulois*, 1 Jan. and 2 Feb. 1905, and *La Croix* 12 Feb. 1905; for Gayraud, *JOC*, 10 Feb. 1905. See also *Bulletin*, 5 Jan. 1905, and for Piou, *ALP de la Gironde*, Feb. 1905.

32. *JOC*, 27 March, 3 and 12 April 1905, for Groussau, Gailhard-Bancel, and Lerolle, respectively, and 21 March 1905 for Gayraud. For Piou, see *Bulletin*, 23 Feb. 1905, reporting Piou's speech at Roubaix to five thousand people. See also *Bulletin* for 16, 23, and 30 March and 20 April 1905, detailing speeches to large crowds throughout France. In a letter to Etienne Lamy, who succeeded Lavedan in 1904 as editor of *Le Correspondant*, de Mun explained that he chose *Le Figaro* because of its cosmopolitan readership: de Mun to Lamy, 7 March 1905, Etienne Lamy Papers, 333 AP, AN. See *Le Figaro*, 6, 13, 16, 20, 23, 27, and 31 March, and 3, 8, 14, 25, and 28 April 1905. See *Le Gaulois*, 7 March, 10 April, and 8 May 1905, and *La Croix*, 25 April 1905.

33. For the initial negotiations, see Montagnini to Merry del Val, 23 and 25 Feb. 1905, Archives Montagnini, C 7377, slip 7, pieces 135–37, AN.

34. *JOC*, 23 and 28 March 1905, for Deschanel and Barthou, respectively. For final negotiations with Rouvier, see Montagnini to Merry del Val, 24 March 1905, Archives Montagnini, C 7376, slip 4, piece 119, AN. De Mun's editorial appeared in *La Croix*, 25 April 1905.

35. For the approach to Clemenceau, see Montagnini to Merry del Val, 9 and 17 April 1905, Archives Montagnini, C 7377, slip 7, pieces 180, 190, AN.

36. On Delcassé and the Tangier crisis, see the notable contributions of Christopher Andrew, especially his *Théophile Delcassé and the Making of the Entente Cordiale*, and Pierre Guillen, *L'Allemagne et le Maroc, 1870–1905*.

37. *JOC*, 17 March 1905.

38. For de Mun's editorials, see *Le Gaulois*, 15 June, 20 Aug., 21 Sept., which contains the recollection of 1887, and 3 Oct. 1905, which asks to "remake the French soul." See also *Le Figaro*, 1 Sept. 1905. For "pugnacious attitude," see *ALP de la Gironde*, June 1905. For reflections in the *Bulletin*, 8, 15, and 29 June, 17 and 24 Aug., and 5 Oct. 1905.

39. On French indifference to foreign policy during this period, see: Berta Leaman, "The Influence of Domestic Policy on Foreign Affairs in France, 1898–1905," John C.

Cairns, "Politics and Foreign Policy," and Eber Malcolm Carroll, *French Public Opinion and Foreign Affairs, 1870–1914*.

40. *JOC*, 3 July 1905, for Lerolle and Castelnau. For stimulation of local feeling: reports dating from 10 Feb. to 20 July 1905, F^7 12395, Culte Catholique, AN. For de Mun's editorial, *Le Gaulois*, 12 July 1905; for Piou's charge, report of 20 Feb. 1905, F^7 12878, ALP, AN. There are many examples of encouragement from the *Bulletin*, for example, "Pétitionnons!" in 11 May 1905. For Piou's prodding, *Bulletin*, 30 March and 26 Oct. 1905. For an example of "the speech" see Piou at Lille, 6 November 1905, published as *Les Elections de 1906*. For the press network, reports throughout Aug. and 6 and 11 Dec. 1905, F^7 12715, Résistance aux Inventaires, AN; reports of 26 Aug. 1905 and 4 Jan. 1906, F^7 12719, ALP, AN; reports of 20 May, 16 Sept., 20 and 31 Oct., and 8 Nov. 1905, F^7 12878, ALP, AN; Montagnini to Merry del Val, 23 Nov. 1905, Archives Montagnini, C 7378, slip 14, piece 41, AN.

41. Paul Lerolle denied charges that the ALP received money from the dispersed congregations or compiled fiches: *JOC*, 7 April 1905, as did *Bulletin*, 6 and 13 April 1905. But the Sûreté had proof of the latter: report of 6 June 1905, F^7 12878, ALP, AN; and various reports of 1905 in F^7 12476, Délation dans l'Armée, AN. For Bonnet, see the newspaper *Action*, 7 July 1905, quoted in *Bulletin*, 13 July 1905.

42. Reports of 4 April, 8 July, 5 and 21 Aug., 6 Nov., and 19 Dec. 1905, F^7 12878, ALP, AN.

43. Montagnini to Merry del Val, 30 June, 24 July, and 15 and 19 Aug. 1905, Merry del Val to Montagnini, 5 July 1905, Archives Montagnini, respectively C 7378, slip 14, piece 13A, C 7378, slip 14, piece 27, C 7377, slip 7, pieces 246–47, C 7378, slip 14, piece 26, C 7378, slip 14, piece 16, AN.

44. For de Mun's strategy: reports of 5 April and 15, 16, and 19 Dec. 1905, F^7 12878, ALP, AN; report of 5 Aug. 1905, F^7 12719, ALP, AN. For Millerand's remarks on Combes, *JOC*, 17 March and 9 Dec. 1904; for his support of Gailhard-Bancel, 10 July and 5 and 14 Nov. 1905, and see *Bulletin*, 28 Sept. 1905. For de Mun and the civil servants: *Le Gaulois*, 12 Nov. 1905, and *Le Figaro*, 14 Nov. 1905. For the conference at Albi, 25–28 May, see Molette, *Jeunesse Française*, pp. 394–406; De Mun, *Combats*, 1:550–51; and *Le Figaro* and *Le Gaulois*, 28 May 1905. On the *cercles*, see Molette, *Jeunesse Française*, pp. 391–94; De Mun, *Combats*, 1:516–21, and *procès-verbal*, Jan. and Feb. 1905, ACM.

45. For the congress, see the ALP's *Compte-rendu du Congrès général de 1905*, a verbatim record, and reports of the large newspapers. For the questionnaires, pp. 1–7; for the keynote, pp. 11–15; for the administrative session, pp. 16–68; for Maze-Sencier and the session on social ideas, pp. 70–136; for Lerolle and Reille, pp. 137–41, 147–54; for the session on schools, pp. 155–217; for Piou's dramatic presentation of Beauregard and Cochin, pp. 224–34; for the banquet and de Mun's speech, pp. 237–50.

46. Copies of the government's circulars are in F^7 12399, Culte Catholique, and F^{19} 6440 A, B, Instructions, both AN. De Mun wrote in *Le Figaro* and *L'Univers*, 8 and 10 Jan. 1906, respectively, to urge calm. His letter, de Mun to Bazire, 7 Jan. 1906, Henri Bazire Papers, was similar in tone. For "fruitful intransigence," see *Le Gaulois*, 12 Jan. 1906. For the de Mun–Piou decision, see: reports of 2–20 Feb. 1906, F^7 12715, Résistance aux Inventaires, AN; reports from January to mid-February 1906, F^7 12401–3, Culte Catholique, AN; report of 12 Feb. 1906, F^7 12719, ALP, AN; reports of 9, 14, and 16 Feb. 1906, ALP, AN.

47. For the early inventories, see the reports cited above in n. 46. De Mun wrote in *Le Figaro*, 4 Feb. 1906. The poster can be found in F^7 12401, Culte Catholique, AN. For later inventories and the worries of de Mun and Piou, see: report of 22 Feb. 1906, F^7 12878, ALP, AN; reports of mid-February to March 1906, F^7 12401–3, Culte Catholique, AN. Jean Marie Mayeur, *La Séparation de l'Eglise et de l'Etat*, appendix, provides a valuable

chart revealing clearly the extent and incidence of violent resistance to the inventories. For the fall of Rouvier, see *JOC*, 7 March 1906. Clemenceau's remark came before the Senate on 20 March.

48. For de Mun's exultancy, see *Le Gaulois*, 21 March 1906. For his reaction to the encyclical, *La Croix*, 20 Feb. 1906. For the bishops and Green Cardinals, see McManners, *Church and State*, pp. 158–62, Mayeur, *Séparation*, pp. 148–53; Larkin, *Church and State after Dreyfus*, pp. 197–98. The letter of the Green Cardinals appeared in *Le Figaro* on 26 March 1906.

49. For the opposition posters, see the reports of March and April 1906, F^7 12395, Culte Catholique, AN. De Mun's editorial appeared in *Le Figaro*, 17 April 1906. For the report Clemenceau used, see that of 15 Jan. 1906, F^7 12878, ALP, AN. See *Le Radical* and *Le Temps*, 25 April to 1 May 1906, for examples of the government press. See *Bulletin*, 3 May 1906, and *La Croix*, 27 April to 3 May 1906, for the ALP response.

50. See the reports on the elections, F^7 12544–45, Elections Législatives, 1906, AN. There was now an immense majority on the Left: Socialists 75, Radicals 265, and Radical-leaning Independents 57.

CHAPTER 7 The New Course: The Search, 1906–1910

1. *JOCD*, 12 June 1906, no. 22, Jules Dansette's bill for proportional representation in municipal elections; 14 June 1906, no. 104, Joseph Massabuau's bill for proportional representation in national elections; 15 June 1906, no. 111, Léonce de Castelnau's bill for a supreme court; 24 June 1906, no. 2933, Jean Plichon's bill for free medical care to the indigent; 6 July 1906, no. 217, Albert de Mun's bill for professional organization; 12 July 1906, no. 283, Jacques Piou's proposal to establish a French bill of rights. The defense of the social program came in *La Croix*, 8 Aug. for de Mun, 21 Aug. for Piou.

2. *JOC*, 10 July 1906; *Bulletin*, 12 and 19 July and 2 Aug. 1906.

3. For the bishops, Jean Marie Mayeur, *La Séparation de l'Eglise et de l'Etat*, pp. 160–73. For Clemenceau, *Le Temps*, 2 Oct. 1906. For the response of de Mun, see *Le Gaulois*, 20 Aug., 21 Sept., and 8 Oct. 1906; *Le Figaro*, 3 Sept. and 9 Oct. 1906; *La Croix*, 11 Sept. 1906. The *Bulletin* republished each of them while editorializing itself. The quotations are from *Le Gaulois*, 20 Aug., and *Le Figaro*, 9 Oct.

4. For the new inventories, see: reports of Nov.–Dec. 1906, F^7 12396–12400, Culte Catholique, and BB^{18} 2309^2–2309^8, Procés: Résistance aux Inventaires, both AN. For Briand, *JOC* 10 Nov. 1906. For Piou's speech in reply, 12 Nov. 1906, and for de Mun's reply: *Le Gaulois*, 15 Nov. 1906, and *La Croix*, 13 Nov. 1906. For Clemenceau's reaction: F^{19} 6440 B, Instructions, AN.

5. For more of Clemenceau's brutality: *JOC*, 11 Dec. 1906. For Piou, see his *Le Ralliement*, pp. 145–46.

6. For the uneasy accord see: Piou, *JOC*, 21 Dec. 1906; the government, F^{19} 6440 C, Instructions, AN; De Mun, *Le Gaulois*, 25 Feb. 1907. Maurice J. M. Larkin, "The Vatican, French Catholics, and the Associations cultuelles," p. 298, cites a report by the Senate that by refusing to comply with the Separation law, the church abandoned property valued at 411,745,387 francs. For de Mun's sense of a revival, see *Le Gaulois*, 7 and 23 Jan. and 4 and 25 Feb. 1907.

7. Sorel published *Réflexions sur la violence* in 1906 in a series of essays in *Mouvement Socialiste*; it appeared in book form in 1908. On the CGT and syndicalism, see Peter N. Stearns, *Revolutionary Syndicalism and French Labor*, and F. F. Ridley, *Revolutionary Syndicalism in France*. Ridley believes that the CGT was much more dangerous than does Stearns, but both agree that its language terrified the bourgeoisie.

8. For the reaction of the ALP to "doom," see, for example, *Bulletin*, 20 Sept. 1906; 14 March, 25 April, 11 and 23 May, 13 and 20 June, and 3 Aug. 1907; as well as Maurice

Spronck, " 'L'Esprit nouveau' des revolutionnaires," and "Le ler mai et l'état-major de la CGT." The outstanding work on the Action Française is by Eugen Weber, *The Action Française*. Edward R. Tannenbaum, *The Action Française*, is marred by the author's intense antipathy to his subject. There is an excellent biographical sketch of Maurras in Samuel M. Osgood, *French Royalism under the Third and Fourth Republics*, pp. 56–68. The studies by William C. Buthman, *The Rise of Integral Nationalism in France*, and Michael Curtis, *Three against the Third Republic*, are valuable.

9. *Le Figaro*, 6 May 1907; *Le Gaulois*, 12 June 1907. See Gordon Wright, *Rural Revolution in France*, and Michel Augé-Laribé, *La Politique agricole de la France de 1800 à 1940*.

10. See Emile Bocquillon, *La Crise du patriotisme à l'école*, which began rightist criticism of the schools on this issue. See also David B. Ralston, *The Army of the Republic*, pp. 259–60, 283–84. For de Mun: *Le Figaro*, 3 Feb. 1907; for Buisson: *Le Gaulois*, 29 July 1908. France's *Annuaire Statistique*, 1900–1908, bears out Buisson's admissions in its figures on degree of instruction of recruits. The evidence Eugen Weber amasses in his *Peasants into Frenchmen* seems to indicate that many rural Frenchmen learned almost nothing at all through formal education.

11. For the bakery workers, see *Le Gaulois*, 7 March 1908, and *L'Echo de Paris*, 15 June, 5 July, and 23 Aug. 1907, and 8 March 1908. For the *travailleuses à domicile*, see *Le Figaro*, 16 Feb. 1909 and 4 March 1910, and *L'Echo de Paris*, 6 March 1909 and 1 March 1910. See also *JOCD*, 2 April 1909, no. 2453. For the PTT and collectivism: *Bulletin*, 8 Aug. 1907; *L'Echo de Paris*, 26 March 1908; *Le Gaulois*, 19 and 30 March and 19 May 1909; *Le Figaro*, 6 May 1907, and 6 and 28 April 1908; *Le Peuple Français*, 28 May and 21 Sept. 1909.

12. See the prefatory material to *Ma Vocation sociale* and de Mun to Bazire, 24 Dec. 1908, Henri Bazire Papers. For de Mun's pleas for social concern: *L'Echo de Paris*, 28 July, 20 Aug., 17 Sept., 3 Oct., and 21 Nov. 1908, 4 Jan. and 12 Feb. 1909; "Nos illusions législatives," pp. 16–17; *Le Figaro*, 12 July 1909. The quotations come from the last two, respectively.

13. For *Le Temps*, especially 10 Aug. and 2 Dec. 1909, and 5 Jan. 1910. See de Mun in *Le Gaulois*, 29 June, 17 and 31 Aug. 1909, and 10 Jan. 1910; *Le Figaro*, 12 July 1909; *L'Echo de Paris*, 8 Dec. 1909; *Le Peuple Français*, 24 July, 11 and 22 Aug. and 18 Dec. 1909; De Mun to Bazire, 4 Jan. 1910, Henri Bazire Papers.

14. Some of de Mun's sentiments can be caught in Koenrad Wolter Stuart Swart, *The Sense of Decadence in Nineteenth-Century France*, passim. See Raoul Girardet, *La Société militaire dans la France contemporaine, 1815–1939*, p. 74, for statistics. For de Mun's expressions, *Le Figaro*, 2 June 1909. See also Jacques Piou, *Le Comte Albert de Mun*, pp. 235–36, 273–77.

15. *Le Gaulois*, 2 April, 5 June, 30 Aug., and 10 Dec. 1907, and 23 and 28 Jan., and 12 Sept. 1908; *Le Figaro*, 7 Aug. 1908. The quotations come from *Le Gaulois*, 12 Sept. 1908 and 10 Dec. 1907, respectively.

16. *La Croix*, 5 Feb. 1908.

17. For the Postards and the state schoolteachers, *Le Gaulois*, 24 March and 27 April 1907, respectively. The *Manuel Général* of 28 September 1909, by Ferdinand Buisson, directed schoolmasters to teach French schoolchildren Kantian ethics in order that they might make up their minds about religion and patriotism, cited in Ferdinand Buisson and E. E. Farrington, *French Educational Ideals To-Day*, pp. 128–37. For Thomson: *Le Gaulois* and *La Croix*, 20 Aug. 1908. For Laon: *Le Gaulois*, 10 Dec. 1908 and 5 Feb. 1909. For the Lecot funeral: *Le Gaulois*, 16 Jan. 1909. For Jaurès: *JOC*, 18 Jan. 1909; de Mun replied: *L'Echo de Paris*, 25 Jan. 1909. For de Mun's return to Lorraine: *Le Figaro*, 7 Aug. 1908; *Le Gaulois*, 15 Aug., 12 Sept., 17 Oct., and 23 Dec. 1908; *L'Echo de Paris*, 5 Dec. 1908. The quotation is from Piou, *De Mun*, p. 275.

18. *L'Echo de Paris*, 25 April 1909, for the reply to the ministry; *Le Gaulois*, 18 May 1909, for the ceremony at Notre Dame. See de Mun's other editorials in *Le Gaulois*, 18 April 1909, and *Le Peuple Français*, 10 May 1909.

19. *Bulletin*, 28 May and 11 June 1908, for the Jury of Honor. *Le Gaulois*, 25 June and 28 July 1906, for sample attacks on Clemenceau by de Mun at this time; compare to *Bulletin*, 25 Oct. 1908. For Cauchy, see de Mun to Mackau, 25 Sept. 1904, Armand de Mackau Papers, 156 AP I, 278, AN. For the change in attitude, *Le Gaulois*, 16 May 1907. For sample attacks later, see *Le Gaulois*, 17 June 1908, and *L'Echo de Paris*, 19 Dec. 1909. De Mun's rebuke to Bazire came in de Mun to Bazire, 2 Sept. and 16 Nov. 1908, Henri Bazire Papers, about editorials published under Bazire's by-line in *Le Peuple Français*, 29 Aug. and 14 Nov. 1908, respectively. For the Gambetta reference: *Le Gaulois*, 30 April 1909; for France "totale": *L'Echo de Paris*, 19 Dec. 1908; for "rude nationalism": *L'Echo de Paris*, 8 May 1909. For the Chamber incident: *JOC*, 13 May 1909, and de Mun in *Le Gaulois*, 15 May 1909.

20. For Briand: *JOC*, 27 July 1909. De Mun to Trégard, 23 July 1909, Stanislas du Lac–Louis Trégard Papers, ASJ. Du Lac died 29 August 1909, and a touching eulogy of him by de Mun appeared 8 Sept. 1909 in *Le Gaulois*.

21. De Mun to Mackau, 13 Aug. and 29 Sept. 1909, Armand de Mackau Papers, 156 AP I, 278, AN. De Mun to Bazire, 15 Nov. 1909, Henri Bazire Papers, de Mun objecting to editorials published under Bazire's by-line 5 and 9 Nov. 1909 in *Le Peuple Français*. De Mun to Piou, 11 Jan. 1910, cited *in extenso* by Joseph Denais, *Jacque Piou*, pp. 214–15.

22. Sûreté reports indicate that money came in regularly: reports of 8 and 26 July and 15 Nov. 1907, 28 Jan. 1908, 23 Jan. and (no date) Feb. 1909, and 5 March 1910, F^7 12878, ALP, AN. Membership figures for a party collecting dues can be trusted, especially as those cited by the ALP were verified by the Sûreté. By late 1906 it counted 232,000 members and 1,560 local committees; by late 1907, 257,000 and 1,800; by late 1908, 275,000 and 2,200; and by late 1909, 290,000 and 2,500. These figures are cited from the ALP's *Compte-rendu du Congrès général de 1906*, p. 10; *Compte-rendu du Congrès général de 1907*, p. 33; *Compte-rendu du Congrès gènéral de 1908*, p. 21; *Compte-rendu du Congrès général de 1909*, p. 37. Verification by the Sûreté of the 1906–8 figures can be found in the reports of 13 March 1907, 28 Jan. 1908, and 6 April 1909, F^7 12878, ALP, AN. For the plan for contributions: report of 30 Sept. 1907, F^7 12719, ALP, AN. For investigating the Radicals: report of 22 Nov. 1907, F^7 12878, ALP, AN. For RP: reports of 13 and 23 March 1907, 4 and 13 March 1908, 24 Nov. 1909, and 12 Jan. 1910, F^7 12878, ALP, AN. David E. Sumler, "Domestic Influences on the Nationalist Revival in France, 1909–1914," and "Polarization in French Politics, 1909–1914," develop the issue of RP and propose that the debates surrounding its fate in the Chamber were vital in determining political alignments after 1910.

23. Reports of 16 Nov. 1907, 4, 12, and 14 June 1909, F^7 12719, ALP, AN. Reports of 4 May and 15 Nov. 1907; 27 Jan., 1 and 3 Feb., 11, 17, and 28 March, 19 May, and 20 July 1908; 23 Jan., 9 Feb., 10 March, 13 July, and 28 Nov. 1909; 17 and 22 March 1910, F^7 12878, ALP, AN. Reports of 1 and 8 April 1908 and 31 May 1910, F^7 13215, Ligue Patriotique des Françaises, AN.

24. On the Montagnini revelations and Piou's reactions: *La Croix*, 6 April 1907; *Bulletin*, 11 and 18 April 1907; report of 16 April 1907, F^7 12861, Action Française, AN; reports of 17 July and 22 Aug. 1907, 29 Feb. and 16 March 1908, and 22 April 1909, F^7 12719, ALP, AN; reports of 5, 19, and 20 April, 12 and 15 June, 14 and 18 Aug., and 30 Dec. 1907, and 27 Jan. 1908, F^7 12878, ALP, AN. For Piou's maneuvering: reports of 8 Dec. 1906, 8 and 23 Feb., 6 May, 24, 28, and 29 June, and 3 Aug. 1907, F^7 12719, ALP, AN; reports of 11 Jan., 22 May, and 15 June 1907, F^7 12878, ALP, AN.

25. Reports of 9 and 22 Nov. 1907, F^7 12719, ALP, AN; reports of 8 June, 5 July, 7 and 29 Aug. 1907, 29 and 31 Jan. and 3 Feb. 1908, F^7 12878, ALP, AN. De Mun's editorials appeared in *Le Figaro*, 15 and 29 Oct., 13 and 30 Nov., 17 and 23 Dec. 1907. These six and a conclusion were published under the same title in 1908 in book form.

26. For the Action Française and Merry del Val: report of 26 Dec. 1908, F^7 12719, ALP, AN; report of 13 July 1909, F^7 12878, ALP, AN; report of 30 April 1909, F^7 12861, Action Francaise, AN. For the ALP at the Vatican: reports of 8 January, 24 April, and 14 May 1909, F^7 12719, ALP, AN; reports of 2, 25, and 27 May and 14 June 1909, F^7 12878, ALP, AN. See also John McManners, *Church and State in France, 1870–1914*, pp. 171–72, and Maurice J. M. Larkin, *Church and State after the Dreyfus Affair*, pp. 215–16. For Déroulède: report of 12 June 1909, F^7 12719, ALP, AN; report of 14 June 1909, F^7 12878, ALP, AN. For the school issue: reports of 11, 24, and 25 Nov. 1909 and 17 March 1910, F^7 12878, ALP, AN. For de Mun's complaint: De Mun to Trégard, 6 Sept. 1909, Stanislas du Lac–Louis Trégard Papers, ASJ; and de Mun to Bazire, 26 Aug. 1909, Henri Bazire Papers.

27. On the Sapinière, see Emile Poulat, *Intégrisme et catholicisme intégral*. On modernism, there are a number of good studies, the best also by Emile Poulat, *Histoire, dogme et critique dans la crise moderniste*. For the peril of the ALP: report of 8 April 1908, F^7 12878, ALP, AN; McManners, *Church and State*, p. 170. Typical of Integrist criticism of the Sillon are the diatribes of the Abbé Emmanuel Barbier, *Les Erreurs du Sillon, Les Idées du Sillon, Le Progrès du libéralisme catholique en France sous le pape Léon XIII, Les Démocrates chrétiens et le modernisme*, and *La Décadence du Sillon*. Barbier had already blasted the ALP in *Rome et l'Action Libérale Populaire*.

28. For the successive positions, see ALP, *Compte-rendu, 1907*, pp. 51–63; *JOC*, 17 Feb. 1908, the position announced in the *Bulletin*, 13 Feb. 1908; *JOC*, 2 Feb. and 9 March 1909, the final vote 407 to 166. See Roche's series of ten articles in *La République Française*, Feb.–March 1907, and speeches by Aynard, *JOC*, 17 Feb. 1908, and by Ribot and Georges Bouctot, 25 May 1908. Roche himself made twenty-five interventions during the debate. See Malcolm Anderson, "The Right and the Social Question in Parliament, 1905–1919," published in *The Right in France, 1890–1919*, ed. David Shapiro, pp. 85–134, particularly 110–14.

29. For the February banquet, reports of 24–25 Feb. 1908, F^7 12557, Rapports, Paris, AN. For December, *Compte-rendu, 1908*, pp. 51–53. For the phonograph records, report of 8 Jan. 1909, F^7 12719, ALP, AN. For Laya's statement, report of 17 July 1907, F^7 12719, ALP, AN. For *Le Peuple Français*, report of 9 Jan. 1909, F^7 12878, ALP, AN. For the campaign chest, reports of 8 July and 15 Nov. 1907, 28 Jan. 1908, 23 Jan., 19 Feb., 25 Nov., and 2 Dec. 1909, 5 March 1910, F^7 12878, ALP, AN. Piou's declaration is recorded in *Compte-rendu, 1909*, pp. 81–83. For the *Bulletin*'s admission, see 15 April 1910. For Piou's admission, see "L'Action Libérale Populaire," *Revue Hebdomadaire*.

30. The new Chamber breaks down as follows: ALP 76 (up 12); Progressives 40 (down 43); Independents of all variety, including the ARD 120 (up 20); Radicals 266 (up 1); Socialists 85 (up 10). The new "Center" of 150 seats was composed of the 120 Independents and about 30 right-wing Radicals. Piou's cry came in *Compte-rendu, 1909*, p. 94; De Mun's in *La Croix*, 27 Aug. 1909, written to encourage the revival of the church.

CHAPTER 8 The New Course: Success, 1910–1913

1. De Mun to Trégard, 4 Jan. 1914, Stanislas du Lac–Louis Trégard Papers, ASJ.

2. François Goguel, *Géographie des élections françaises de 1870 à 1951*, pp. 38–39.

3. For de Mun, *Le Gaulois*, 14 May 1910, and *Le Figaro*, 1 June 1910, the latter subsequently included as the preface to Piou's *Questions religieuses et sociales*. For Laya, *Bulletin*, 1 June 1910. For Piou, *La Croix*, 31 May 1910.

4. The memorandum is cited *in extenso* by Joseph Denais, *Jacques Piou*, pp. 219–20. De Mun's editorial appeared in *L'Echo de Paris*, 26 June 1910.

5. *JOC*, 27–28 June 1910, for the debate. For the committees, C 7424, Commission du Budget, Exercise 1911, C 7435, Commission des Affaires Extérieures, and C 7486, Commission du Travail, all AN.

6. For Fontaine, Charles Molette, *L'Association Catholique de la Jeunesse Française, 1886–1907*, p. 347, and John McManners, *Church and State in France, 1870–1914*, p. 170. For Bailly, Maurice J. M. Larkin, *Church and State after the Dreyfus Affair*, pp. 215–16, n. 17. For Veuillot, *L'Univers*, 22 and 24 July and 13 Aug. 1910; De Mun's reply came in *Le Gaulois*, 2 Aug. 1910. For de Mun's letters, de Mun to Bazire, 16 and 28 July and 5 and 11 Aug. 1910, Henri Bazire Papers. The comment of *Le Temps* came 30 Aug. 1910.

7. De Mun to Trégard, 31 Aug. 1910, Stanislas du Lac–Louis Trégard Papers, ASJ. See also my "A Letter of Albert de Mun on the Papal Condemnation of the Sillon."

8. For the "forced marches," de Mun to Trégard, 1 Sept. 1910, Stanislas du Lac–Louis Trégard Papers, ASJ, and *Bulletin*, 1 and 15 Sept. 1910. For Gailhard-Bancel's mission, Jacques Piou, *Le Ralliement*, pp. 155–83, and *D'une guerre à l'autre, 1871–1914*, pp. 262–63. Veuillot's comment came in *L'Univers*, 27 Oct. 1910.

9. For the debate on the railroad vote, see *JOC*, 28–30 Oct. 1910, and for Briand's thinking, Georges Suarez, *Briand*, 2:294–98. De Mun's various reactions came in *Le Gaulois*, 8 Nov. 1910; de Mun to Bazire, 11 Nov. 1910, Henri Bazire Papers; and de Mun to Trégard, 4 Nov. 1910, Stanislas du Lac–Louis Trégard Papers, ASJ. See *JOC*, 9 Nov. 1910, for the ALP-Progressive split, and 23–24 Feb. 1911 for Briand's final two days.

10. See, for example, de Mun to Bapst, 8 Feb. and 19 April 1909; 29 April, 2 and 4 May, and 30 Aug. 1911; 15, 17, 25, and 26 Nov. 1912, Germain Bapst Papers, 24536, ff. 469–81, BN Naf; de Mun to Porto-Riche, 23 June 1908 and 17 March 1909, Georges de Porto-Riche Papers, 24967, ff. 54–55, BN Naf; de Mun to Deschanel, 25 Nov. and 2 Dec. 1905, Paul Deschanel Papers, 151 AP 35, AN. For de Mun, the Académie Française, and Poincaré, see Fernand Payen, *Raymond Poincaré*, pp. 324–35, and *Le Gaulois*, 31 March 1910. For de Mun's history, a sampling would include writing on the French Revolution, *Le Gaulois*, 29 July 1909, and on the Franco-Prussian War, *L'Echo de Paris*, 23 Aug. 1911, and *Le Figaro*, 26 Aug. 1911.

11. See *L'Echo de Paris*, 25 Oct., 8 Nov., 7, 14, and 23 Dec. 1910; 20 and 31 Jan., and 17 Feb. 1911; also *Le Figaro*, 7 Feb. 1911. For the Labor Committee, minutes of 23 and 30 Nov., 7, 14, and 21 Dec. 1910; 8 Feb. and 5 April 1911, C 7486, Commission du Travail, AN. See de Mun's proposal: *JOCD*, 16 March 1911, no. 668. For the congress, see the accounts in *La Croix*, 18–21 March 1911. See also de Mun's ironic comments in de Mun to Trégard, 11 Dec. 1910, Stanislas du Lac–Louis Trégard Papers, ASJ.

12. For the condition of the party, see reports of 10 and 30 June, 5 and 10 Sept., and 14 Dec. 1910; 4 Jan., 25 Feb., 21 March, 10 and 22 April, 10 and 14 June, and particularly 28 July 1911, F^7 12878, ALP, AN. See also *Bulletin*, 1 and 15 Oct. 1910; 1 and 15 April, 1 and 15 May, and 1 June 1911. For a reaction to Thierry, see de Mun to Trégard, 25 Nov. 1910, Stanislas du Lac–Louis Trégard Papers, ASJ; and Piou quoted in *La Croix*, 13 and 17 Dec. 1910. For the congress, see ALP, *Compte-rendu du Congrès général de 1911*, and for Piou's remark, p. 64.

13. Joseph Caillaux's *Mes Mémoires* are self-adulatory and fatuous but generally accurate as to events. They are fascinating, revealing how profoundly Caillaux deluded himself as to his ability. For examples of the legislation to "defend the laic school," see that introduced by Ferdinand Buisson and Jules Steeg, on 6 and 29 March 1911: *JOCD*, nos. 798 and 989, respectively. The details of the second Moroccan crisis and its diplomatic aftermath are the common property of any number of general histories, especially of the origins of World War I.

14. Eugen Weber, *The Nationalist Revival in France, 1905–1914*, pp. 94–99. Herein lies the thesis of Weber's work. For an opposite view, see Herbert L. Tint, *The Decline of French Patriotism, 1870–1940*.

15. For the editorials before March 1911: *Le Gaulois*, 31 May, 9 June, 19 Sept., 10, 16, and 23 Dec. 1910; *L'Echo de Paris*, 23 May and 29 Aug. 1910. For March–June 1911: *Le Gaulois*, 4 March, 30 April, 7 and 17 May, and 20 June 1911; *L'Echo de Paris*, 13 and 28 March, 12 April, 5 May, and 12 June 1911; *Le Figaro*, 22 April and 10 May 1911. For July 1911: *Le Gaulois*, 3 July 1911; *L'Echo de Paris*, 6 July 1911; *Le Figaro*, 7 July 1911, with the quip about the *Berlin* from the last. Piou's observation comes in his *Le Comte Albert de Mun*, p. 298.

16. For September 1911: *Le Gaulois*, 21 Sept. 1911; *L'Echo de Paris*, 23 Sept. 1911; *Le Figaro*, 23 Sept. 1911. For the Budget Committee, minutes of 11–12 Oct. 1911, C 7425, Commission du Budget, Exercise 1912, AN; and *La Croix*, 14 Oct. 1911.

17. For the committee meetings, see minutes of 11, 14, 16–18, 21–22, 25, and 29 Nov. 1911, C 7435, Commission des Affaires Extérieures, AN. For the editorials: *L'Echo de Paris*, 7, 11, 16, 20, 23, and 25 Nov. and 2 Dec. 1911; *Le Gaulois*, 9, 14, and 19 Nov. 1911.

18. The account is based on notations about the applause in *JOC*, 14 Dec. 1911, as well as on Piou, *De Mun* , pp. 299–301, and *Le Figaro*, *Le Gaulois*, *L'Echo de Paris*, and *L'Humanité*, 15 Dec. 1911. De Mun's effort at Saint Pol de Léon was reported in *Bulletin*, 15 Nov. 1911.

19. For Caillaux's reply and the vote: *JOC*, 14 and 20 Dec. 1911. For the scene in the Senate committee room, Edouard Bonnefous and Georges Bonnefous, *Histoire politique de la Troisième République*, 1:270. De Mun's editorial, "La Chute du ministére Caillaux," appeared 12 Jan. 1912.

20. *JOC*, 16 Jan. 1912. On Poincaré there are four biographies, each concentrating on a different facet of his career: Payen, *Poincaré*, the fullest for this period, Jacques Chastenet, *Raymond Poincaré*, Pierre Miquel, *Poincaré*, and Gordon Wright, *Raymond Poincaré and the French Presidency*.

21. *Le Gaulois*, 19 Jan. 1912, printed the speech verbatim. Poincaré mentioned the incident in his memoirs: *Au Service de la France*, 1:46.

22. De Mun's praise came in *L'Echo de Paris*, 23 Jan. 1912, and was continued 3, 12, and 24 Feb. and 1 March 1912. The debate in the Senate took place between 5 and 12 February, the final vote 212 to 42. De Mun's call for chaplains came in *Le Gaulois*, 11 Feb. 1912, and he joined his name to Piou's project, *JOCD*, 23 Feb. 1912, no. 1691, which came up for debate on 1 March 1912, and was rejected by Poincaré.

23. For the incident, minutes of 25 March 1912, C 7447, Commission des Elections, AN, and Charles Benoist, *Souvenirs*, 3:179–81. See also Payen, *Poincaré*, pp. 370–71. *La Croix* reacted 7 March 1912. The patriotic statements of de Mun and Poincaré appeared in *L'Echo de Paris*, 11–12 March 1912.

24. For de Mun's mission to Belgium, Poincaré, *Au Service*, 1:227–28. See also Jonathon Helmreich, "Belgian Concern over Neutrality and British Intentions, 1906–1914." De Mun's analysis came in *L'Echo de Paris*, 26 March 1912.

25. For de Mun's role in the selection of Lyautey, see de Mun to Poincaré, 27 April 1912, Raymond Poincaré Papers, 16010, f. 322, BN Naf, and his editorials praising Lyautey, *L'Echo de Paris*, 24 April and 11 May 1912. For Deschanel's election and the proposal for the holiday: *JOC*, 24 May 1912, and de Mun's praise in *Le Gaulois*, 18 May 1912, *L'Echo de Paris*, 1 June 1912, and the preface to his collected editorials for the previous twelve months, *Pour la Patrie*, dated 1 June 1912. For the Moroccan debates: *JOC*, 14, 21, and 28 June, and 1–2 July 1912, Poincaré's statement coming on the last day. For the trip to Russia, Poincaré, *Au Service*, 2:130–45. For Millerand, David B. Ralston, *The Army*

of the Republic, pp. 324, 331–37, and de Mun's comment, *L'Echo de Paris*, 5 April 1912. For RP: *JOC*, 10 July 1912, and for the reaction of the Radicals, David Edmund Sumler, "Polarization in French Politics, 1909–1914," pp. 152–53. For Combes, Georges Alquier, *Le Président Emile Combes*, p. 180, his letter 16 Oct. 1912 to his principal private secretary, Emmanuel Lafon.

26. For de Mun and Lyautey, Robert Garric, *Albert de Mun*, pp. 215–20, and André Maurois, *Lyautey*, pp. 156–58. For de Mun's articles on Morocco, see *L'Echo de Paris*, 1, 7, 21, and 26 June, and 1, 3, and 22 July 1912. For his boast, *L'Echo de Paris*, 11 Aug. 1912. For the correspondence with Poincaré about the schools: de Mun to Poincaré, 23 June and 4 July 1912, Raymond Poincaré Papers, 16010, ff. 323–26, BN Naf. For Poincaré's speech, 16 April 1912, at Bar-le-Duc, see *La Croix*, 17 April 1912. For Poincaré's reaction to the schoolteachers, see Payen, *Poincaré*, p. 372, and for the speech at Nantes, *La Croix*, 29 Oct. 1912.

27. For Piou's phrase "réserve sympathique," see his *Ralliement*, p. 262. For the condition of the party and Piou's turn toward confessionalism, see reports of 15 June, 2 July, and 6 Dec. 1912, F^{7} 12878, ALP, AN; and report of 8 Nov. 1911, F^{7} 12880, Association Catholique de la Jeunesse Française, AN. Any analysis of the *Bulletin*'s contents after 1910 will reveal the change to a preoccupation with church interests, and particularly anti-Poincaré articles are to be found in the issues of 15 January, 15 March, 15 April, 1 May, and 1 June 1912. Driant and Chappedelaine, who emerged as the leaders of the younger ALP deputies, were joined in late 1912 by Jean Lerolle, who won a by-election to fill the seat vacated by the death of his father Paul on 28 October 1912. The ALP did not formally abandon social Catholicism; it merely ceased to mention it. For de Mun's role in the Labor Committee since Briand's fall: minutes of 7 and 12 June and 11 Nov. 1911; 17 and 31 Jan. and 20 Nov. 1912, C 7486, Commission du Travail, AN, along with his bill to institute the revised workweek: *JOCD*, 11 Nov. 1911, no. 1323. De Mun published numerous editorials on social topics: *Le Gaulois*, 20 April, 12 July, 9 Aug., 9 and 24 Dec. 1911; 25 and 30 March, and 12 April 1912; *L'Echo de Paris*, 23 and 29 April, 16 and 30 May, 28 June, and 5 Aug. 1911; 16 and 20 April 1912. De Mun helped celebrate the silver anniversary of the ACJF on 19 May 1911: see *La Croix*, 21 May 1911, and reports of 20–22 May 1911, F^{7} 12880, Association Catholique de la Jeunesse Française, AN. On 30 May 1911 he became honorary president of Sangnier's Congrès du Pain de Jour, to found a bakery that would avoid night work for its employees: see *La Croix*, 31 May 1911. The *Bulletin* endorsed Poincaré on 15 November 1912, after an important speech in his favor by ALP Senator Emmanuel de Las Cases on 10 November.

28. The quotations from de Mun's editorials are from *L'Echo de Paris*, 4 Nov. and 4 Dec. 1912. The editorials as a series appeared in *L'Echo de Paris*, 27 Sept., 4, 12, 16, 20, and 25 Nov., 4, 9, 14, 17, and 23 Dec. 1912. See Piou's comment in *De Mun*, pp. 306–9. For the appointments with Poincaré to discuss European problems and the French response: De Mun to Poincaré, 17 Oct., 12 and 20 Dec. 1912, Raymond Poincaré Papers, 16010, ff. 329, 332, 335–36, BN Naf. The plenipotentiaries were Eleutherios Venizelos of Greece, Stoyan Novakovic of Serbia, and Stoyan Danev of Bulgaria. These letters reveal de Mun's reaction, as the editorials do likewise. For Poincaré's intentions toward the presidency: Poincaré, *Au Service*, 3:33–39, Payen, *Poincaré*, pp. 380–88, Wright, *Poincaré*, pp. 33–40, Suarez, *Briand*, 2:395, Emmanuel Beau de Loménie, *Les Responsabilités des dynasties bourgeoisies*, 2:448.

29. For the threat of Caillaux and Clemenceau: report of 23 Dec. 1912, F^{7} 12821, Election de Poincaré, 1912–13: Manoeuvres, AN; and Caillaux, *Mémoires*, 3:31. For the secret meeting, Payen, *Poincaré*, p. 389, and Miquel, *Poincaré*, pp. 300–304.

30. For the preamble letter, de Mun to Poincaré, dated only December 1912 but

clearly after the first meeting, cited *in extenso* by Payen, *Poincaré*, pp. 389–90. For the letter about Sainte Geneviève, de Mun to Poincaré, 19 Dec. 1912, Raymond Poincaré Papers, 16010, ff. 333–34, BN Naf. The new secret meetings were long suspected but without proof. De Mun revealed them in de Mun to Trégard, 16 March 1913, Stanislas du Lac–Louis Trégard Papers, ASJ. Caillaux felt sure that Poincaré had made compromises on laic legislation, but he caught wind of the agreement on the three-year-service law only on the basis of an indiscreet remark by Piou in 1916: Caillaux, *Mémoires*, 3:24–25, 34. See also reports of 30 Dec. 1912 and 4 Jan. 1913, F7 12821, Election de Poincaré, 1912–13: Manoeuvres, AN.

31. For de Mun's persuasion of the conservatives: Piou, *De Mun*, p. 313; Caillaux, *Mémoires*, 3:33; report of 30 Dec. 1912, F7 12821, Election de Poincaré, 1912–13: Manoeuvres, AN.

32. There is an excellent analysis of the Paty de Clam affair in Wright, *Poincaré*, pp. 41–43. For de Mun's remark to Briand, see Suarez, *Briand*, 2:402. For de Mun's letters to Poincaré: de Mun to Poincaré, 12 Jan. 1913, Raymond Poincaré Papers, 16010, f. 338; de Mun to Poincaré, 13 Jan. 1913, cited *in extenso* by Payen, *Poincaré*, pp. 391–92. The editorial to which de Mun referred appeared in *L'Echo de Paris*, 14 Jan. 1913. Piou's remarks came in a speech in Paris on 15 January 1913 and were reported in *Bulletin*, 1 Feb. 1913.

33. For the caucus and its aftermath, see Bonnefous and Bonnefous, *Histoire politique*, 1:318–19, and Wright, *Poincaré*, pp. 43–48. For the press reaction, see the report of press opinion on the 1913 presidential election, 17 Jan. 1913, F7 12540, Election de Raymond Poincaré, Président de la République, AN.

34. For the election: *JOAN*, 17 Jan. 1913. See *L'Autorité*, 18 Jan. 1913 and de Mun's "A M. Raymond Poincaré" in *L'Echo de Paris*, 18 Jan. 1913.

CHAPTER 9 Playing the Game, 1913–1914

1. De Mun in *L'Echo de Paris*, 18 Jan. 1913. See also de Mun to Poincaré, 21 Jan. 1913, Raymond Poincaré Papers, 16010, f. 339, BN Naf.

2. *JOC*, 24 Jan. 1913, for the crucial vote.

3. On France's birth rate, see John C. Hunter, "The Strength of France on the Eve of World War I," and "The Problem of the French Birth Rate on the Eve of World War I." On the three-year law, see David B. Ralston, *The Army of the Republic*, pp. 345–66; the severely distorted Georges Michon, *La Préparation à la guerre*; and the memoirs of Maurice Paléologue, one of Poincaré's intimates at the Quai d'Orsay, "Comment fut rétabli le service de trois ans," and *Au Quai d'Orsay à la veille de la tourmente*, pp. 59–174. For Driant: *JOC*, 18 June 1912, and minutes of 20 June 1912, C 7421, Commission de l'Armée, AN. Poincaré discussed the origin of the law in *Au Service de la France*, 2:78–82, 138, 144–57.

4. For de Mun's campaign, see *L'Echo de Paris*, 27 and 29 Jan., 3, 7, 12, 15, 19, 22, and 26 Feb., 3, 7, 13, and 18 March 1913; *Le Gaulois*, 28 Feb. 1913. See *JOC*, 6 March 1913, for the performance of the Socialists, and also minutes of 11, 13–14, 18, 20, and 27 March 1913, C 7421, Commission de l'Armée, AN.

5. For Briand's defeat in the Senate on 18 March 1913, see Georges Suarez, *Briand*, 2:405–30. Poincaré's attempt to make his premier try again is recounted in *Au Service*, 3:155. De Mun's protests came in de Mun to Poincaré, 18 March 1913, Raymond Poincaré Papers, 16010, f. 340, BN Naf; and de Mun to Etienne, 18 March 1913, Eugène Etienne Papers, 24327, ff. 267–68, BN Naf. See de Mun's editorial in *L'Echo de Paris*, 20 March 1913.

6. De Mun's initial reaction to the Barthou ministry came in *L'Echo de Paris*, 25 March and 2 April 1913; in *Le Gaulois*, 31 March 1913; in *JOC*, 25 March 1913; and in de Mun to Etienne, 1 April 1913, Eugène Etienne Papers, 24327, ff. 269–70, BN Naf.

7. For the "debate": *L'Echo de Paris*, 2, 5, 9, 12, 15, 18, and 26 April, 6, 8, 14, 22, 24, and 28 May 1913; *L'Humanité*, 4, 6–7, 9, 11–12, 14, 16–18 April, 3–4, 7, 9–10, 11–14 May 1913. For a discussion of the "sudden attack," Ralston, *Army of the Republic*, pp. 353–66, and Paléologue, "Comment fut rétabli," p. 316. For the letter to Poincaré, de Mun to Poincaré, 16 May 1913, Raymond Poincaré Papers, 16010, ff. 341–44, BN Naf.

8. For the mutinies, Poincaré, and Clemenceau, see Poincaré, *Au Service*, 3:211, and David Edmund Sumler, "Polarization in French Politics, 1909–1914," p. 178. For the Socialist comments: *JOC*, 2 June 1913. For de Mun: *L'Echo de Paris*, 2, 4, 9, 16, and 25 June and 3 July 1913, the quotation from 2 June. For the most serious thirty-month proposal, see Joseph Paul-Boncour, *Entre deux guerres*, 1:229–33, and *JOC*, 30 June-1 July 1913. For *L'Homme Libre*, 8 June 1913. For the vote on the bill, *JOC*, 19 July 1913. The vote in the Senate came 7 August 1913.

9. For de Mun's praise of Barthou, *L'Echo de Paris*, 21 July 1913. For Poincaré's determination to carry through the law, Paléologue, "Comment fut rétabli," pp. 318–19. For Lyautey, *L'Echo de Paris*, 24 June 1913. For Poincaré's marriage, Fernand Payen, *Raymond Poincaré*, pp. 406–7.

10. For the Integrists, Emile Poulat, *Intégrisme et Catholicisme intégral*, pp. 370–71, 516. For Trégard, de Mun to Trégard, 16 March 1913, Stanislas du Lac–Louis Trégard Papers, ASJ. For Piou: *Bulletin*, 1 March 1913; and for La Rochefoucauld, Piou to La Rochefoucauld, 1 and 24 April 1913, Xavier de La Rochefoucauld Papers, 142 AP 14, dossier 1, AN.

11. For the Barthou-Groussau exchange: *JOC*, 11 June 1913. For the decision on Sainte Geneviève, *La Croix*, 1 July 1913. For Piou: *La Croix*, 10 June 1913; *Bulletin*, 15 June and 1 July 1913. For Barthou's concessions, see *La Croix*, 9 and 14 Aug. 1913. For the declarations of laic faith by Poincaré and Barthou, see *La Croix*, 19 and 26–27 Sept. 1913. For Clemenceau, *L'Homme Libre*, 14 Aug.–2 Sept. 1913.

12. For the Integrist position in *L'Univers*: 27 Oct. 1910, 22–23 March, 17 June, 11 Nov. 1911; 3 Jan., 21 Aug., 5, 13, 19, and 26 Sept., 3 and 24 Oct. 1912; 1 March, 20 April, 9 and 17 May, 12 and 23 July, 17 and 20 Sept., 18, 25, 29, and 31 Oct., 22–23 and 29 Nov., 6 Dec. 1913; 7–8 Feb., 7, 22, and 30 May 1914. De Mun was singled out for vicious personal criticism, 20 July, 20 Sept., and 18 Oct. 1913. For Paléologue's comment, see his *Au Quai*, pp. 103–4, 116–17.

13. For examples of de Mun's editorials on these topics: *L'Echo de Paris*, 20 March 1911, 1 March 1912; *Le Gaulois*, 1 and 5 June, 20 Aug. 1911; 7 July, 7 Oct., 11 and 29 Nov., 2 and 31 Dec. 1912; 30 April 1913. For de Mun's shift on the unions and Merry del Val's reply: *La Croix*, 7 Jan. 1913; John McManners, *Church and State in France, 1870–1914*, p. 170; and the very detailed G. Desbuquois, "La Lettre du Cardinal Merry del Val au Comte de Mun."

14. For de Mun on Sommerfeld, *L'Echo de Paris*, 13 Aug. 1913. For the visit to Paléologue, see *Au Quai*, pp. 83–84, 89–91, 118–19, 155.

15. For the dealings with the Veuillot centenary: De Mun to Veuillot, 5 July, 22 Sept., and 24 Nov. 1913, François Veuillot Papers, 24621, ff. 34–37, BN Naf. See also *L'Echo de Paris*, 27 Nov. 1913. For Clemenceau and de Mun: *L'Homme Libre*, 2, 6, 11, 14–15 Sept. 1913; *L'Echo de Paris*, 1, 15, 19, and 25 Sept. 1913, with de Mun's words from *L'Echo de Paris*, 15 Sept.

16. For the problem, and the conservative answer, minutes of 16 July 1913, C 7426, Commission du Budget, Exercise 1913, AN. For the Pau congress, *Le Radical*, 17–20 Oct. 1913. For Barthou's decision, minutes of 17 Nov. 1913, C 7427, Commission du Budget, Exercise 1914, AN.

17. For de Mun and Piou: minutes of 18–21 and 24 Nov. 1913, C 7427, Commis-

sion du Budget, Exercise 1914, AN; *L'Echo de Paris*, 12, 18, 21, and 24 Nov., and 1 Dec. 1913. For the votes, *JOC*, 1–2 Dec. 1913. For Poincaré's comment, *Au Service*, 3:339.

18. On the ministerial crisis: Gordon Wright, *Raymond Poincaré and the French Presidency*, p. 100; Suarez, *Briand*, 2:443–44; Poincaré, *Au Service*, 3:339–40. For Clemenceau, *L'Homme Libre*, 10 Dec. 1913. The exclamation of Vaillant came 2 December, the reply of Briand, 11 December 1913. For de Mun's attitude, *L'Echo de Paris*, 5, 11, 15, and 20 Dec. 1913.

19. For the Fédération des Gauches and Briand's speech at Saint-Etienne, *Le Temps*, 23 Dec. 1913, and Sumler, "Polarization," p. 205. For de Mun's reply, *L'Echo de Paris*, 26 Dec. 1913.

20. For the mission of La Rochefoucauld: De Mun to La Rochefoucauld, 18 Dec. 1913, enclosing de Mun to Merry del Val, 17 Dec. 1913; also draft working papers in La Rochefoucauld's hand, Xavier de La Rochefoucauld Papers, 142 AP 14, dossier 1, AN. For Trégard, de Mun to Trégard, 4 and 6 Jan. 1914, Stanislas du Lac–Louis Trégard Papers, ASJ.

21. The outbreak of the war prevented publication of the *compte-rendu* of the congress. There are full accounts in *La Croix*, *L'Echo de Paris*, and *Le Gaulois*, 31 Jan.–3 Feb. 1914. The *Bulletin*, 15 Feb. 1914, carries a verbatim record of some sessions, and Jacques Piou, *Le Ralliement*, pp. 193–98, quotes his and de Mun's toasts. For the reply of the Vatican, see the unsigned letter in the hand of Eugenio Cardinal Pacelli to La Rochefoucauld, 8 Feb. 1914, written in reply to La Rochefoucauld to Pacelli, 4 Feb. 1914, Xavier de La Rochefoucauld Papers, 142 AP 14, dossier 1, AN.

22. For the committee sessions: minutes of 12–17, 19–24, and 26–31 Jan., 2–6, 11–13, 19, 23, and 25 Feb., 4, 6–7, 10, 14 March 1914, C 7427, Commission du Budget, Exercise 1914, AN. For de Mun's published opinions: *L'Echo de Paris*, 5, 9, 13, 19, 21, 26, and 30 Jan., 11, 16, and 25 Feb., 2, 9, and 12 March 1914. *Le Figaro* of March–April and July 1914 is the best source of information on the Caillaux-Calmette affair. De Mun commented in *L'Echo de Paris*, 19 and 30 March 1914.

23. For the election, see the reports of Jan.–May 1914, F^7 12822, Elections Législatives, 1914, AN, for the way in which the alliances operated. See also François Goguel, *Géographie des élections françaises de 1870 à 1951*, pp. 40–41, 64–65. See the opinion of Poincaré, *Au Service*, 4:120, and Alexandre Ribot, *Lettres à un ami*, pp. 1–4. De Mun commented in *L'Echo de Paris*, 5 May 1914. The new Chamber breaks down as follows: ALP 73 (down 3); Progressives 54 (up 14); "moderates," including the Fédération des Gauches 175 (down 31); Caillaux's Radicals 183 (up 3); Socialists 102 (up 17). The drop among the "moderates" is illusory since some merged with the Progressives.

24. De Mun's quotation is from *L'Echo de Paris*, 14 May 1914, his challenge, 5 May. He discussed alternatives in *L'Echo de Paris*, 17, 21, 25, and 27 May 1914 before endorsing Ribot on 12 June 1914. For Poincaré's thoughts, *Au Service*, 4:120–33; for Ribot's, *Journal d'Alexandre Ribot et correspondances inédits, 1914–1922*, p. 10. Briand claims to have recommended Ribot: Suarez, *Briand*, 2:502–4, and did endorse him in *La Petite République*, 24–25 May 1914. Piou claims to have influenced Briand, Piou to La Rochefoucauld, 16 May 1914, Xavier de La Rochefoucauld Papers, 142 AP 14, dossier 1, AN. The vote came *JOC*, 12 June 1914.

25. For Poincaré, see Wright, *Poincaré*, pp. 119–20, and *Au Service*, 4:148. For the vote of confidence, see *JOC*, 17 June 1914.

26. De Mun's ambivalence is seen best in his editorials in *L'Echo de Paris*, 16, 18, 23, and 26 June, 6 and 9 July 1914. For the sessions of the Budget Committee, see minutes of 18, 23, and 30 June, 2 and 9 July 1914, C 7427, Commission du Budget, Exercise 1914, AN. De Mun received another commendation from Merry del Val for the Oeuvre des Cer-

cles on 12 January 1914, reported in *La Croix*, 13 Jan. 1914, and the *cercles* held general assemblies in April 1913 and June 1914, but according to de Mun in de Mun to Trégard, May 1914, Stanislas du Lac–Louis Trégard Papers, ASJ, the *cercles* were not very alive. See *La Croix*, 22–24 April 1913, 6–9 June 1914. The election campaign was harder than usual, with de Mun winning over Yves Caill 9,547 to 7,166. De Mun had had to have photographs of himself printed up for the first time in years, see de Mun to the famous photographers Paul and Félix Nadar, 23 March 1914, Paul and Félix Nadar Papers, 24279, f. 321, BN Naf. For de Mun's plans to rest, see Jacques Piou, *Le Comte Albert de Mun*, pp. 334–35, and Robert Garric, *Albert de Mun*, pp. 183–93. De Mun's only mention of Sarajevo was a brief one in *L'Echo de Paris*, 6 July 1914.

27. De Mun's editorial was published in *L'Echo de Paris*, 30 July 1914. Piou reports his letter to Madame Jaurès, *De Mun*, p. 337. De Mun's editorial in *L'Echo de Paris*, 3 Aug. 1914, was dramatic trust in the Socialists.

28. There are many descriptions of the 4 August session but none more concisely moving than Poincaré's, *Au Service*, 4:544. Gailhard-Bancel recorded the conversation with Delcassé, *Quatorze années de défense religieuse à la Chambre des Députés, 1901–1914*, pp. 96–97. De Mun himself wrote of the session in *L'Echo de Paris*, 5 Aug. 1914.

29. De Mun had particularly complained about the lack of chaplains in *Le Gaulois*, 5 June 1911 and 21 Dec. 1912. His work on supplying them is detailed in Charles Geoffroy de Grandmaison, "La Dernière oeuvre du Comte Albert de Mun," which also describes his work later for Millerand at the war ministry. The quotation is from p. 658.

30. Poincaré's suggestion to broaden the cabinet is recalled in *Au Service*, 5:259–60. De Mun's letter is quoted by Piou, *De Mun*, p. 344. Wright, *Poincaré*, pp. 144–46, discusses the suspicions of the Left.

31. There were sixty-five editorials by de Mun in *L'Echo de Paris*, 30 July–7 Oct. 1914, all republished in de Mun, *La Guerre de 1914*. Geoffroy de Grandmaison sketches de Mun's daily activities and the reaction to his writing in "Dernière oeuvre," pp. 664–65. Poincaré, in *Au Service*, 5:227–28, discusses de Mun's contribution to confidence. Piou, *De Mun*, p. 341, tells how Poincaré persuaded de Mun to leave for Bordeaux.

32. De Mun's last days are recounted by Piou, *De Mun*, pp. 345–47. Geoffroy de Grandmaison describes the greeting from Benedict XV, "Dernière oeuvre," p. 666.

CONCLUSION

1. See the newspaper reports, *L'Echo de Paris* and *Le Figaro*, 11 Oct. 1914. Poincaré's own testament is moving, *Au Service de la France*, 5:370–71.

2. Jacques Piou, *Le Ralliement*, pp. 213–26. For some of de Mun's most personal expressions of obedience to the church, see Joseph Rumeau, *M. le Comte Albert de Mun*, p. 6, which quotes de Mun's will: "I charge Bertrand, after my death, to send to the feet of the pope the ardent homage of my absolute devotion to the church, Catholic, apostolic, and Roman; to make known my entire obedience to its teachings promulgated by the infallible word of its head and my love for the pope and my unlimited attachment to his cause."

3. *L'Echo de Paris*, 3 Oct. 1908.

4. De Mun to the editor of the *Annales de la Jeunesse Catholique*, 16 Dec. 1905, published *in extenso* in de Mun, *Combats d'hier et d'aujourd'hui*, 1:604–9.

Bibliography

I. MANUSCRIPT SOURCES

A. Personal Papers

1. Stanislas du Lac-Louis Trégard Papers, Archives de la Société de Jésus, Province de Paris (Chantilly): Letters from Albert de Mun to his two confessors, du Lac and Trégard. Because these letters often concern "matters of conscience," they are not normally open to scholars. Copies of the original correspondence were provided me.

2. De Mun Files, Archives Provinciales des Pères Capucins de Paris (Paris): the records of the decision of Albert de Mun and his wife to take the vows of the Third Order of St. Francis.

3. Comptes-Rendus du Comité de l'Oeuvre des Cercles Catholiques d'Ouvriers, Archives du Cercle Maurice Maignen (Paris): the collection of the records of the executive committee of the *cercles* is not complete, running from 1871 only to 1905.

4. Action Libérale Populaire Records, Archives de l'Action Populaire (Vanves): although numerous records were deposited here when the ALP dissolved in 1920, many of them were destroyed during World War II when Vanves became a center of French resistance. Nevertheless, these are the only complete collection of the party's congresses, pamphlets, brochures, and posters.

5. Collections not open to scholars:

a. Henri Bazire Papers, held by his children (Paris): I have consulted the copious notes of the Abbé Charles Molette, who had access to these papers at an earlier time. The collection contains 185 letters from Albert de Mun to Henri Bazire during the period 1897 to 1914 and is of particular value for the years 1898 to 1905.

b. Louis Milcent Papers, current disposition unknown: the few letters of Albert de Mun to Louis Milcent are occasionally valuable to gauge de Mun's mood on social questions; fortunately, most of the correspondence was published in *La Revue Universelle* (éditée en zone Sud), 25 March–10 April 1941.

c. Félix de Roquefeuil Papers, held by Madame Robert de Roquefeuil (Paris): Abbé Charles Molette also had access to this collection of 570 letters, from the period 1872 to 1890, between Albert de Mun and Félix de Roquefeuil. I have cited freely from Molette's work on de Mun and the ACJF.

d. Hyacinthe de Gailhard-Bancel Papers, held by the Gailhard-Bancel-Widerspach family in its ancestral home at La Tour, Allex: there are a few letters from Albert de Mun to Hyacinthe de Gailhard-Bancel in this collection, and Henri Rollet had access to them in the late 1940s. The family now finds it impossible to spare the time to allow scholars to visit.

e. Charles Geoffroy de Grandmaison Papers, current disposition unknown: more than six hundred letters were addressed by Albert de Mun to his young friend Charles Geoffroy de Grandmaison, who kept them carefully. After his death, and that of his wife, these letters were sold at auction and cannot be traced. Few would have been of great importance.

f. Joseph Denais–Jacques Piou Papers, current disposition unknown: Joseph Denais, a longtime associate of Jacques Piou and a deputy for the ALP, saved several letters from Albert de Mun to Piou and published them in his biography of Piou. After the death of Denais in 1958, these letters disappeared, and several efforts to locate them have been unsuccessful.

B. Official Archives

1. Archives Nationales, Section Archives Privées

a. 1 AP 518, Charles Louis de Trémoïl Papers: one letter from Albert de Mun to Trémoïl and two from Piou, all from 1889.

b. 81 AP 4, dossier 12, Alfred Rambaud Papers: one letter from Albert de Mun to Rambaud, 7 November 1901.

c. 87 AP 18, Jules Simon Papers: one letter from de Mun to Simon, 5 February 1880.

d. 142 AP 14, 15, Xavier de La Rochefoucauld Papers: financial records of the ALP and important letters from Albert de Mun and Jacques Piou to La Rochefoucauld for his missions to the Vatican.

e. 151 AP 35, Paul Deschanel Papers: seventeen letters from Albert de Mun to Deschanel from 1896 to 1912. They are of only minor interest.

f. 156 AP I, Armand de Mackau Papers: an important collection of material dealing with Albert de Mun and Boulangism. There are 171 letters from de Mun to Mackau during the period 1876 to 1914, some of great importance. There are also eleven letters from Jacques Piou to Mackau.

g. 305 AP 8, dossier 3, Léon Lavedan Papers: eight letters from Albert de Mun to Lavedan, editor of *Le Correspondant* from 1875 to 1902. The letters cover only the period 1899 to 1903 and are of but passing interest. There are also two letters from Jacques Piou to Lavedan in 1903.

h. 333 AP, Etienne Lamy Papers: of great interest for the study of the Ralliement, this collection contains only five letters from Albert de Mun to Lamy and adds litle to de Mun's biography.

2. Bibliothèque Nationale, Nouvelles Acquisitions Françaises

a. 13669, ff. 95–102; 13671, f. 7; 13672, f. 19, Albert Choquet Papers: letters from Albert de Mun to Choquet; of only minor interest.

b. 14630, f. 198, Marius Sepet Papers: a letter from Albert de Mun to Sepet; of very minor interest.

c. 15293, f. 62, Robert de Montesquiou Papers: a letter from Albert de Mun to Montesquiou; of interest for social activities.

d. 16010, ff. 322–46, Raymond Poincaré Papers: letters from Albert de Mun to Poincaré; a collection of major importance.

e. 24232, ff. 464–69; 24233, ff. 154–63; 24634, ff. 481–82, 501–2, Louis Veuillot Papers: letters from Albert de Mun to Veuillot; an important collection.

f. 24279, ff. 318–22, Paul and Félix Nadar Papers: letters from Albert de Mun to the Nadar brothers; of only minor interest.

g. 24327, ff. 267–71, Eugène Etienne Papers: letters from Albert de Mun to Etienne; important for 1913.

h. 24328, ff. 354–55: a letter from Albert de Mun to an unidentified cardinal; of very minor interest.

i. 24451, ff. 109–23, Gaston Paris Papers: letters from Albert de Mun to Paris; important for social activities and attitudes.

j. 24536, ff. 463–81, Germain Bapst Papers: letters from Albert de Mun to Bapst; important for social activities.

k. 24621, ff. 34–37, François Veuillot Papers: letters from Albert de Mun to Veuillot; of only minor interest.

l. 24882, ff. 531–33, Joseph Reinach Papers: letters from Albert de Mun to Reinach; of only minor interest.

m. 24967, ff. 54–58, Georges de Porto-Riche Papers: letters from Albert de Mun to Porto-Riche; important for social activities.

n. 25045, ff. 464–96, Ferdinand Brunetière Papers: letters from Albert de Mun to Brunetière; a collection of major importance.

II. GOVERNMENT DOCUMENTS

A. Archives Nationales, Series C, Procès-Verbaux des Assemblées Nationales, Versements de la Chambre des Députés

1. Assemblée Nationale, 1871–75

a. 2840 Interpellations à la Commission de Permanence, 1874
b. 2879 Enquête du 18 mars

2. 8e Législature, 1902–6

a. 7300 Commission de Séparation des Eglises et de l'Etat
b. 7305 Enquête de l'Election de Roscoat
c. 7306 Enquête de l'Election de Guilloteaux
d. 7338 Commission du Travail

3. 9e Législature, 1906–10

a. 7375 Commission des Elections
b. 7376–86 Archives Montagnini
c. 7414 Commission du Travail

4. 10e Législature, 1910–14

a. 7421 Commission de l'Armée
b. 7424–27 Commission du Budget, Exercise 1911–14
c. 7435 Commission des Affaires Extérieures
d. 7439 Défense Nationale: Compte Spécial
e. 7447 Commission des Elections
f. 7475 Livre Jaune: Accord Franco-Allemand 5–XI–1911
g. 7486–87 Commission du Travail

B. Archives Nationales, Series F, Administration Générale de la France, Sub-Series F^7, Police Générale

1. 12386 Associations des Pères de Famille, 1870–1912
2. 12393 B-E Culte Catholique: Préparation et Exécution de la Loi du ler Juillet 1901 sur les Congrégations, 1901–6
3. 12394–98 Culte Catholique: Préparation et Exécution des Lois de Séparation, 1897–1909
4. 12399–12404 Culte Catholique: Inventaires, 1905–9
5. 12431–44 Agissements Royalistes, 1875–1908
6. 12445–48 Agissements Boulangistes, 1889–91
7. 12449–51 Ligue des Patriotes, 1882–1907
8. 12464–73 Affaire Dreyfus, 1895–1906
9. 12476 Délation dans l'Armée: Fiches et Contre-Fiches, 1904–7

10. 12477 Oeuvre des Cercles Catholiques d'Ouvriers
11. 12478 Association Catholique de la Jeunesse Française
12. 12480 Union Nationale
13. 12481 Justice-Egalité
14. 12540 Election de Raymond Poincaré, Président de la République
15. 12541–45 Elections Législatives, 1902–6
16. 12554–59 Rapports, Paris, 1904–13
17. 12715 Résistance aux Inventaires, 1905–6; Agitation Cléricale, 1908–13
18. 12716 *La Croix*, 1883–1908
19. 12719 Action Libérale Populaire
20. 12821 Election de Poincaré, 1912–13: Manoeuvres
21. 12822 Elections Législatives, 1914
22. 12861–64 Action Française
23. 12878 Action Libérale Populaire
24. 12880 Association Catholique de la Jeunesse Française
25. 13215 Ligue Patriotique des Françaises
26. 13335–48 Agitation contre la Loi des Trois Ans

C. Archives Nationales, Series F, Administration Générale de la France, Sub-Series F^{19}, Cultes

1. 1944 Rapports entre la France et le Saint Siège, 1891–1906
2. 1961–62 Affaire Geay et Le Nordez
3. 1973 A–C Inventaires des Eglises
4. 1974 A–B Séparation des Eglises et de l'Etat
5. 1983 Affaire Montagnini
6. 5621–22 Culte Catholique: Elections de 1902
7. 5623–24 Atteintes contre l'Ecole Laïque
8. 5642 Action Libérale Populaire
9. 6078–87 Les Décrets de Juillet 1902
10. 6268 Lois et Décrets: Congrégations, 1901–5
11. 6274 Lois et Décrets contre l'Enseignement Congréganiste
12. 6440 A–E Instructions, 1897–1911

D. Archives Nationales, Series BB, Versements du Ministère de la Justice, Sub-Series BB^{18}, Correspondance Générale de la Division Criminelle

1. 2080–81 Procès: Elections 1898
2. 2209–10 Procès: Elections 1902
3. 2212–13 Procès: Calomnie, 1902
4. $2301–9^{1}$ Procès: Loi de Séparation des Eglises et de l'Etat
5. $2309^{2}–2309^{8}$ Procès: Résistance aux Inventaires

E. Archives de la Préfecture de Police, Paris, Series B A

1. 401–4 Agissements Légitimistes
2. 611–16 Elections Législatives de 1885
3. 870 Baron Charette
4. 969–74 Agissements Boulangistes
5. 1000 Paul Granier de Cassagnac
6. 1496 Boulanger
7. 1541 Agissements Cléricaux

F. Archives du Ministère des Armées

Dossier Albert de Mun

III. NEWSPAPERS

Because Albert de Mun wrote for several Parisian newspapers and because the ALP conducted propaganda in many of them, it is necessary to consult a large number of dailies. The most important source for the ALP is its organ, the *Bulletin Action Libérale Populaire*. The Bibliothèque Nationale has an almost complete collection of its issues, but from 1940 to 1972 it misclassified nearly half of them. There are also a number of issues of ephemeral local journals published by provincial committees of the ALP.

Bulletin Action Libérale Populaire, 10 November 1901–1 August 1914 (weekly until November 1908, biweekly thereafter)

ALP Haute Marne, July 1902

ALP de la Haute Garonne, 16 February–18 May 1902 (weekly)

ALP de Quimper, 1903–6 (biweekly)

ALP de Castelsarrasin, 1903 (monthly)

ALP du Comité de Bourg, December 1902–November 1903 (monthly)

ALP du Comité de Clermont-Ferrand, March–December 1907 (monthly)

ALP du Comité Régional et des Comités de la Région du Rhône, scattered issues from 1904 to 1914 (monthly)

ALP de Nevers, November 1904 and December 1905

ALP du Comité de Saint-Quentin de Baron, January 1908–June 1909 (irregular)

ALP de Haute Vienne, 23 March 1903

ALP de Saint Brieuc, April–July 1904; April–May 1906 (irregular)

ALP de la Gironde, 2 May 1903–18 June 1905 (weekly)

De Mun's own editorials from 1902 to 1914 are collected in *Combats d'hier et d'aujourd'hui*, 6 vols., *Pour la Patrie*, *L'Heure décisive*, and *La Guerre de 1914*. All four suffer from a common failing: the date of the column's appearance is provided but not the newspaper in which it appeared. To determine the latter has required the laborious checking of four or more dailies and journals. Occasionally, the date of appearance is incorrect, and there are seventy-seven editorials by de Mun published from 1912 to 1914 in *L'Echo de Paris* that are not to be found in the collections.

The following newspapers, all Parisian dailies, have been consulted:

L'Action, Radical-Socialist bias

L'Aurore, originally Clemenceau's paper, Radical bias

L'Autorité, Bonapartist until the 1890s, right-wing thereafter

La Bataille Syndicaliste, left-wing bias

La Croix, an ALP organ; de Mun was a columnist

L'Echo de Paris, right-of-center bias; de Mun was a columnist

Le Figaro, royalist until the 1890s, right-wing and appealing to the educated elite thereafter; de Mun was a columnist

Le Gaulois, royalist until the 1890s, right-wing and appealing to the snobbish elite thereafter; de Mun was a columnist

L'Homme Libre, Clemenceau's new paper, founded in May 1913, Radical and nationalist bias

L'Humanité, spokesman for the Socialist party

La Lanterne, left-wing bias

La Petite République, Briand's paper, centrist bias

Le Peuple Français, purchased by the leaders of the ACJF in July 1908 and fused with *La Libre Parole* on 10 September 1910 as the latter lost its anti-Semitic bias; de Mun contributed about one column a year to it after 1908

Le Radical, spokesman for the Radical party

La République Française, Méline's paper, spokesman for the Progressive party

Le Temps, probably the most prestigious newspaper in France, centrist or just left-of-center bias, anticlerical and in favor of laissez-faire

L'Univers, ultramontane bias, somewhat more conservative than Leo XIII and more reactionary than Pius X; the bulwark of French Integrists

IV. BOOKS, ARTICLES, AND DISSERTATIONS

Acomb, Evelyn M. *The French Laic Laws: The First Anti-Clerical Campaign of the Third French Republic*. New York, 1941.

Action Libérale Populaire. *Compte-rendu du Congrès général de 1904*. Paris, 1905.

______. *Compte-rendu du Congrès général de 1905*. Paris, 1906.

______. *Compte-rendu du Congrès général de 1906*. Paris, 1907.

______. *Compte-rendu du Congrès général de 1907*. Paris, 1908.

______. *Compte-rendu du Congrès général de 1908*. Paris, 1909.

______. *Compte-rendu du Congrès général de 1909*. Paris, 1910.

______. *Compte-rendu du Congrès général de 1911*. Paris, 1911.

______. *Congrès social de Pau: 11, 12, et 13 octobre 1903, sous la présidence de M. de Gailhard-Bancel, député, compte-rendu, contenant les rapports, les discussions, et les discours*. Pau, 1903.

Alquier, Georges. *Le Président Emile Combes*. Castres, 1962.

Altholz, Theodore Michael. "The French Labor Law of November 2, 1892: A Manifestation of the Declining Influence of Laissez-Faire Liberal Economics in France." Master's thesis, University of North Carolina at Chapel Hill, 1972.

Anderson, Eugene N. *The First Moroccan Crisis, 1904–1906*. Chicago, 1930.

André, Louis. *Cinq ans de ministère*. Paris, 1907.

Andrew, Christopher. *Théophile Delcassé and the Making of the Entente Cordiale: A Reappraisal of French Foreign Policy, 1898–1905*. New York, 1968.

Augé-Laribé, Michel. *La Politique agricole de la France de 1800 à 1940*. Paris, 1960.

Ball, Gérard. "Combes et la 'République des Comités.' " *Revue d'Histoire Moderne et Contemporaine* 24 (April–June 1977): 260–85.

Bainville, Jacques. *La Troisième République, 1870–1935*. Paris, 1935.

Barbier, Emmanuel. *La Décadence du Sillon: Histoire documentaire*. 2d ed. Nancy, 1908.

______. *Les Démocrates chrétiens et le modernisme: Histoire documentaire*. Paris, 1908.

______. *Les Erreurs du Sillon: Histoire documentaire*. Poitiers, 1906.

______. *Les Idées du Sillon: Etude critique*. 3d ed. Poitiers, 1905.

______. *Le Progrès du libéralisme catholique en France sous le pape Léon XIII*. 2 vols. Paris, 1907.

______. *Rome et l'Action Libérale Populaire*. Poitiers, 1906.

Baylen, Joseph O. "An Unpublished Note on Général Georges Boulanger in Britain, June 1889." *French Historical Studies* 4 (Spring 1966): 344–47.

Beau de Loménie, Emmanuel. *Les Responsabilités des dynasties bourgeoisies*. 4 vols. Paris, 1954–73.

Benoist, Charles. *Souvenirs*. 3 vols. Paris, 1932–34.

Berl, Emmanuel. *La Politique et les partis*. 3d ed. Paris, 1932.

Bigo, Robert. *Les Banques français au cours du XIXe siècle*. Paris, 1947.

Binion, Rudolph. *Defeated Leaders: The Political Fate of Caillaux, Jouvenal, and Tardieu*. New York, 1960.

Blanchemain, Paul. *Robert de Mun*. Bar le Duc, 1888.

Bocquillon, Emile. *La Crise du patriotisme à l'école*. Paris, 1905.

Bodley, John Edward Courtney. *The Church in France*. New York, 1906.

———. *France*. 2 vols. New York, 1898.

Bomier-Landowski, Alain. "Les Groupes parlementaires à l'Assemblée Nationale et de la Chambre des Députés de 1871 à 1914." In *Sociologie Electorale*, edited by François Goguel and Georges Dupeux, pp. 75–88. Paris, 1953.

Bonnefous, Edouard, and Bonnefous, Georges. *Histoire politique de la Troisième République*. 5 vols. Paris, 1956–62.

Bonnoure, Pierre. "La Formation historique de l'idée laïque." *Europe, Revue Mensuelle*, October 1959, pp. 5–20.

Boulanger, Georges. *Mémoires du Général Boulanger*. Paris, 1890.

Boussel, Patrice. *L'Affaire Dreyfus et la presse*. Paris, 1960.

Bouvier, Jean. *Le Krach de l'Union Générale, 1878–1885*. Paris, 1960.

Bracq, Jean C. *France under the Republic*. New York, 1910.

Brécy, Robert. *Le Mouvement syndical en France, 1871–1921: Essai bibliographique*. The Hague, 1963.

Breteuil, Henry Charles Joseph Le Tonnelier, Marquis de. "Les Coulisses du Boulangisme." *Revue des Deux Mondes*, 1 June 1969, pp. 467–93.

Breunig, Charles. "The Condemnation of the Sillon." *Church History* 26 (September 1957): 227–44.

———. "The *Sillon* of Marc Sangnier: Christian Democracy in France, 1894–1910." Ph.D. dissertation, Harvard University, 1953.

Brogan, Sir Denis W. *The Development of Modern France, 1870–1939*. London, 1940.

Brown, Marvin L., Jr. "Catholic-Legitimist Militancy in the Early Years of the Third French Republic." *Catholic Historical Review* 60 (July 1974): 233–54.

———. *The Comte de Chambord: The Third Republic's Uncompromising King*. Durham, 1967.

———. *Louis Veuillot: French Ultramontane Catholic Journalist and Layman, 1813–1883*. Durham, 1977.

Brunschwig, Henri. *French Colonialism, 1871–1914: Myths and Realities*. New York, 1966.

Buell, Raymond Leslie. *Contemporary French Politics*. New York, 1920.

Buisson, Ferdinand, and Farrington, E. E. *French Educational Ideals To-Day*. London, 1920.

Bush, John W. "Education and Social Status: The Jesuit *Collège* in the Early Third Republic." *French Historical Studies* 9 (Spring 1975): 125–40.

Buthman, William C. *The Rise of Integral Nationalism in France: With Special Reference to the Ideas and Activities of Charles Maurras*. New York, 1939.

Byrnes, Robert F. *Antisemitism in Modern France: The Prologue to the Dreyfus Affair*. New Brunswick, 1950.

———. "The French Christian Democrats in the 1890s: Their Appearance and Their Failure." *Catholic Historical Review* 36 (October 1950): 286–306.

Caillaux, Joseph Marie Auguste. *Mes Mémoires*. 3 vols. Paris, 1942–47.

Cairns, John C. "International Politics and the Military Mind: The Case of the French Republic, 1911–1914." *Journal of Modern History* 26 (September 1953): 273–85.

———. "Politics and Foreign Policy: The French Parliament, 1911–1914." *Canadian Historical Review* 34 (September 1953): 245–76.

Camp, Richard L. *The Papal Ideology of Social Reform: A Study in Historical Development, 1878–1967*. Leiden, 1969.

Campbell, Peter. *French Electoral Systems and Elections since 1789*. 2d ed. London, 1965.

Capéran, Louis. *Histoire contemporaine de la laïcité française*. 3 vols. Paris, 1957–61.

———. *L'Invasion laïque de l'avènement de Combes au vote de la Séparation*. Paris, 1935.

Caron, Jeanne. *Le Sillon et la démocratie chrétienne, 1894–1910*. Paris, 1967.

Carroll, Eber Malcolm. *French Public Opinion and Foreign Affairs, 1870–1914*. New York, 1931.

Chanson, Paul. *Autorité et liberté: Constitution de la France selon La Tour du Pin*. Paris, 1942.

Chapman, Guy. *The Dreyfus Case: A Reassessment*. New York, 1956.

———. *The Third Republic of France: The First Phase, 1871–1894*. New York, 1962.

Charnay, Jean Paul. *Les Scrutins politiques en France de 1815 à 1914: Contestations et invalidations*. Paris, 1964.

Chastenet, Jacques. *Histoire de la Troisième République*. 7 vols. Paris, 1952–63.

———. *Raymond Poincaré*. Paris, 1948.

Chirac, Auguste. *L'Agiotage sous la Troisième République, 1870–1887.* 2 vols. Paris, 1889.

Clermont-Tonnerre, Elizabeth (née de Gramont), Duchess de. *Mémoires.* 4 vols. Paris, 1929–44.

Cobban, Alfred. *A History of Modern France.* Rev. ed. New York, 1965.

Cogniot, Georges. *La Question scolaire en 1848 et la loi Falloux.* Paris, 1948.

Combes, Emile. *Mon Ministère: Mémoires, 1902–1905.* Paris, 1956.

———. *Une Campagne laïque, 1902–1903.* Paris, 1904.

———. *Une Deuxième campagne laïque: Vers la Séparation.* Paris, 1905.

Conybeare, Frederick C. [Frederick Cornwallis]. *The Dreyfus Case.* London, 1898.

Cooke, James J. *New French Imperialism, 1880–1890: The Third Republic and Colonial Expansion.* Hamden, Conn., 1973.

Courcelles, Jean Baptiste Pierre Julien dit le Chevalier de Courcelles. *Histoire généalogique et heraldique des pairs de France.* 12 vols. Paris, 1822–24.

Craven, Mrs. Augustus (née Pauline Marie Armande Aglaé Ferron de La Ferronnays). "La Marquise de Mun." *Le Correspondant* 108 (10 September 1877): 923–33.

———. *Récit d'une soeur: Souvenirs de famille.* 2 vols. 16th ed. Paris, 1868.

———. *Robert de Mun.* Paris, 1887.

Curtis, Michael. *Three against the Third Republic: Sorel, Barrès, Maurras.* Princeton, 1959.

Dabry, Abbé Pierre. *Les Catholiques républicains: Histoire et souvenirs, 1890–1903.* Paris, 1905.

Daniels, André [André Lebon]. *L'Année politique.* 32 vols. Paris, 1874–1906.

Dansette, Adrien. *L'Affaire Wilson et la chute du président Grévy.* Paris, 1936.

———. *Les Affaires de Panama.* Paris, 1934.

———. *Le Boulangisme, 1886–1890.* Paris, 1938.

———. *Histoire religieuse de la France contemporaine.* Rev. ed. Paris, 1965.

Debidour, Antonin. *L'Eglise catholique et l'Etat sous la IIIe République.* 2 vols. Paris, 1906–9.

Denais, Joseph. *Jacques Piou: Un apôtre de la liberté.* Paris, 1958.

Derfler, Leslie. "Le Cas Millerand: Une nouvelle interpretation." *Revue d'Histoire Moderne et Contemporaine* 10 (April–June 1963): 81–104.

Desbuquois, G. "La Lettre du Cardinal Merry del Val au Comte de

Mun." *L'Association Catholique–Le Mouvement Social* 75 (February 1913): 138–46.

Ducattillon, J. V. "Church in the Third Republic." *Review of Politics* 6 (January 1944): 74–93.

Duroselle, Jean Baptiste. *Les Débuts du catholicisme social en France, 1822–1870*. Paris, 1951.

Edwards, E. W. "The Franco-German Agreement on Morocco, 1909." *English Historical Review* 78 (July 1963): 483–513.

Elbow, Matthew H. *French Corporative Theory, 1789–1948*. New York, 1948.

Elwitt, Sanford. *The Making of the Third Republic: Class and Politics in France, 1868–1884*. Baton Rouge, 1975.

Ferrata, Cardinal Dominique. *Mémoires*. 3 vols. Rome, 1920.

Flornoy, Eugène. *La Lutte par l'association: L'Action Libérale Populaire*. Paris, 1907.

Flory, Albert. *Albert de Mun*. Paris, 1941.

Gadille, Jacques. *La Pensée et l'action politique des évêques français au début de la IIIe République, 1870–1883*. 2 vols. Paris, 1967.

Gailhard-Bancel, Hyacinthe de. *Quatorze années de défense religieuse à la Chambre des Députés, 1901–1914*. Paris, 1928.

———. *Les Retraites ouvrières: L'Assistance aux vieillards et aux infirmes*. Paris, 1906.

Gargan, Edward T., ed. *Leo XIII and the Modern World*. New York, 1961.

Garric, Robert. *Albert de Mun*. Paris, 1935.

Gautherot, Gustave. *Un Demi-Siècle de défense nationale et religieuse: Emile Keller, 1828–1909*. Paris, 1922.

Geoffroy de Grandmaison, Charles. "La Dernière oeuvre du comte Albert de Mun: Les Aumôniers militaires volontaires." *Le Correspondant* 262 (10 December 1914): 657–80.

Girardet, Raoul. *La Société militaire dans la France contemporaine, 1815–1939*. Paris, 1953.

Giraud, Victor. *Un Grand Français, Albert de Mun*. Paris, 1918.

Goguel, François. *Géographie des élections françaises de 1870 à 1951*. Paris, 1951.

———. *La Politique des partis sous la IIIe République*. 3d ed. Paris, 1958.

Goldberg, Harvey. *The Life of Jean Jaurès*. Madison, 1962.

Gooch, Robert Kent. *The French Parliamentary Committee System*. New York, 1935.

Gosnell, Harold F. *Why Europe Votes*. Chicago, 1930.

Goyau, Georges [Léon Grégoire]. *Autour du catholicisme social*. 5 vols. Paris, 1897–1912.

Grubb, Alan. "The Dilemma of Liberal Catholics and Conservative Politics in the Early Third Republic." *Proceedings of the Western Society for French History* 4 (1977): 368–77.

———. "The Duc de Broglie, the Conservative Union, and *Seize Mai*." *Third Republic/Troisième République*, forthcoming.

———. "The Politics of Pessimism: A Political Biography of Duc Albert de Broglie during the Early Third Republic, 1871–1875." Ph.D. dissertation, Columbia University, 1969.

Guilleminault, Gilbert, ed. *La Belle Epoque*. 4 vols. Paris, 1956–57.

Guillen, Pierre. *L'Allemagne et le Maroc, 1870–1905*. Paris, 1967.

Guitton, Georges. *Léon Harmel*. 2 vols. Paris, 1927.

Hales, E. E. Y. *Pio Nono: A Study in European Politics and Religion in the Nineteenth Century*. London, 1954.

Hanotaux, Albert Auguste Gabriel. *Histoire de la France contemporaine, 1870–1900*. 4 vols. Paris, 1903–8.

Harmel, Léon. *Manuel d'une corporation chrétienne*. Tours, 1876.

Helmreich, Jonathon. "Belgian Concern over Neutrality and British Intentions, 1906–1914." *Journal of Modern History* 36 (December 1964): 416–27.

Hoog, Georges. *Histoire du catholicisme social en France, 1871–1931*. Paris, 1946.

Huckaby, John K. "Roman Catholic Reaction to the Falloux Law." *French Historical Studies* 4 (Fall 1965): 203–13.

Hunter, John C. "The Problem of the French Birth Rate on the Eve of World War I." *French Historical Studies* 2 (Fall 1962): 490–503.

———. "The Strength of France on the Eve of World War I: A Study of French Self-Confidence as Evidenced in the Parliamentary Debate on the Three-Year Service Law of 1913." Ph.D. dissertation, Harvard University, 1959.

Jacques, Léon Ernest. *Les Partis politiques sous la IIIe République*. Paris, 1913.

Johnson, Douglas W. *France and the Dreyfus Affair*. London, 1966.

Jolly, Jean, ed. *Dictionnaire des parlementaires français: Notices biographiques sur les ministres, députés, et sénateurs français de 1889 à 1940*. 7 vols. to date. Paris, 1960–.

Kayser, Jacques. *Les Grandes batailles du radicalisme*. Paris, 1961.

Keller, Emile. "Les Elections de 1898." *Le Correspondant* 189 (10 October 1897): 3–15.

———. *L'Encyclique du 8 décembre 1864 et les principes de 1789: Ou l'Eglise, l'Etat et la liberté*. Paris, 1865.

———. "La Revanche des francs-maçons." *Le Correspondant* 203 (10 April 1901): 12–21.

Lachapelle, Georges. *Le Ministère Méline*. Paris, 1928.

Lamy, Etienne Marie Victor. *Les Catholiques et la situation présente*. Paris, 1898.

———. "Le Devoir des conservateurs." *Revue des Deux Mondes* 111 (1 June 1892): 512–36.

———. *Quelques oeuvres et quelques ouvriers*. Paris, 1911.

Landes, David S. "Recent Work in the Economic History of Modern France." *French Historical Studies* 1 (1958): 73–94.

Langdon, John W. "New Light on the Influence of the Jesuit Schools: The Graduates of the Ecole Sainte-Geneviève, Paris, 1854–1913." *Third Republic/Troisième République* 1 (Spring 1976): 132–51.

Lapiquillerie, Yvon. *Emile Combes ou le surprenant roman d'un honnête homme*. Paris, 1929.

Larkin, Maurice J. M. "The Church and the French Concordat, 1871 to 1902." *English Historical Review* 81 (October 1966): 717–39.

———. *Church and State after the Dreyfus Affair: The Separation Issue in France*. New York, 1974.

———. "Loubet's Visit to Rome and the Question of Papal Prestige." *Historical Journal* 4 (1961): 97–103.

———. "The Vatican, French Catholics, and the Associations cultuelles." *Journal of Modern History* 36 (September 1964): 298–317.

La Tour du Pin Chambly de la Charce, Charles Humbert René, Marquis de. *Aphorismes de politique sociale*. Paris, 1909.

———. *L'Armée française à Metz*. Paris, 1871.

———. "La Question juive et la révolution sociale." *L'Association Catholique* 61 (15 December 1898): 23–59.

———. *Vers un ordre social: Jalons de route, 1882–1907*. Paris, 1907.

Launay, Michel. "La Crise du Sillon dans l'été 1905." *Revue Historique* 498 (April–June 1971): 393–426.

Leaman, Berta. "The Influence of Domestic Policy on Foreign Affairs in France, 1898–1905." *Journal of Modern History* 14 (December 1942): 449–79.

Le Bras, Gabriel. *Etudes de sociologie religieuse*. 2 vols. Paris, 1956.

Lecanuet, Edouard. *L'Eglise de France sous la IIIe République*. 4 vols. Paris, 1910–31.

Lecomte, Maxime. *Les Ralliés: Histoire d'un parti, 1886–1898*. Paris, [1898].

Lissorgue, Maurice. *Albert de Mun*. Paris, 1928.

Locke, Robert R. *French Legitimists and the Politics of Moral Order in the Early Third Republic*. Princeton, 1974.

Loesevitz, Jean. "La Législation du travail." *L'Association Catholique* 21 (15 February 1886): 119–41.

Lorwin, Val R. *The French Labor Movement*. Cambridge, Mass., 1954.

Loubère, Leo A. "Les Radicaux d'extrême-gauche et les rapports entre patrons et ouvriers, 1871–1900." *Revue d'Histoire Economique et Sociale* 42 (1964): 89–103.

Lynch, Miriam. *The Organized Social Apostolate of Albert de Mun*. Washington, D.C., 1952.

McClelland, J. S., ed. *The French Right: From De Maistre to Maurras*. New York, 1970.

McManners, John. *Church and State in France, 1870–1914*. London, 1972.

Maignen, Charles. *Maurice Maignen, directeur du Cercle Montparnasse: Et les origines du mouvement social catholique en France, 1822–1890*. 2 vols. Luçon, 1927.

Maitron, Jean. *Histoire du mouvement anarchiste en France, 1880–1914*. Paris, 1951.

Manévy, Raymond. *La Presse de la IIIe République*. Paris, 1955.

Martin, Benjamin Franklin. "The Creation of the Action Libérale Populaire: An Example of Party Formation in Third Republic France." *French Historical Studies* 9 (Fall 1976): 660–89.

———. "A Letter of Albert de Mun on the Papal Condemnation of the Sillon." *Catholic Historical Review* 64 (January 1978): 47–50.

Mather, Judson. "The Assumptionist Response to Secularization, 1870–1900." In *Modern European Social History*, edited by Robert J. Bezucha, pp. 59–93. Lexington, Mass., 1972.

Maurois, André. *Lyautey*. Translated by Hamish Miles. London, 1931.

Mayeur, Jean Marie. "Les Congrès nationaux de la 'Démocratie chrétienne' à Lyon, 1896–1897–1898." *Revue d'Histoire Moderne et Contemporaine* 9 (July–September 1962): 171–206.

———. "Droites et ralliés à la Chambre des Députés au début de 1894." *Revue d'Histoire Moderne et Contemporaine* 13 (April–June 1966): 117–35.

———. *Un Prêtre démocrate: L'Abbé Lemire, 1853–1928*. Paris, 1968.

———. *La Séparation de l'Eglise et de l'Etat*. Paris, 1966.

Méline, Jules. *Discours aux Progressistes*. Paris, 1899.

Mellor, Alec. *Histoire de l'anticléricalisme français*. Tours, 1966.

Mermeix [Gabriel Terrail]. *Les Coulisses du boulangisme*. Paris, 1890.

Meyer, Arthur. *Ce que je peux dire*. Paris, 1912.

———. *Ce que mes yeux ont vu*. Paris, 1911.

Michon, Georges. *La Préparation à la guerre: La Loi de trois ans, 1910–1913*. Paris, 1935.

Miquel, Pierre. *Poincaré*. Paris, 1961.

Molette, Charles. *Albert de Mun, 1872–1890: Exigence doctrinale et préoccupations sociales chez un laic catholique*. Paris, 1970.

———. *L'Association Catholique de la Jeunesse Française, 1886–1907: Une prise de conscience du laïcat catholique*. Paris, 1968.

Montclos, Xavier de. *Lavigerie, le Saint-Siège et l'Eglise: De l'avènement de Pie IX à l'avènement de Léon XIII, 1846–1878*. Paris, 1965.

———. *Le Toast d'Alger: Documents, 1890–1891*. Paris, 1967.

Moody, Monsignor Joseph N. "The Dechristianization of the French Working Class." *Review of Politics* 20 (January 1958): 46–69.

———. "Dreyfus and After." *Bridge* 2 (1956): 160–87.

———. "French Anticlericalism: Image and Reality." *Catholic Historical Review* 61 (January 1971): 630–48.

Moon, Parker T. *The Labor Problem and the Social Catholic Movement in France*. New York, 1921.

Mun, Adrien Albert Marie, Count de. *Action Libérale Populaire: Que Faire? Lettres de Roscoff*. Paris, 1902.

———. *Associations et congrégations*. Paris, 1901.

———. *Combats d'hier et d'aujourd'hui*. 6 vols. Paris, 1906–16.

———. "Compte-rendu." *Le Correspondant* 84 (25 August 1871): 762.

———. *Les Dernières heures du drapeau blanc*. Paris, 1910.

———. *Dieu et roi*. Paris, 1881.

———. *Discours du Comte Albert de Mun*. 7 vols. Paris, 1888–1904.

———. *Gardons nos frères*. Paris, 1879.

———. *La Guerre de 1914: Derniers articles d'Albert de Mun, 28 juillet à 5 octobre 1914*. Paris, 1914.

———. *L'Heure décisive*. Paris, 1913.

———. *La Loi des suspects: Lettres adressées à M. Waldeck-Rousseau, président du conseil des ministres, par le comte Albert de Mun*. Paris, 1900.

———. "Lettre." *L'Association Catholique* 21 (15 March 1886): 241–53.

———. *Ma Vocation sociale: Souvenirs de la fondation de l'Oeuvre des Cercles Catholiques d'Ouvriers, 1871–1875*. Paris, 1908.

———. "Nos illusions législatives." *L'Association Catholique–Le Mouvement Social* 78 (January–February 1909): 9–20.

———. *Nouvelle réponse à une vieille accusation renouvelée contre l'Ecole Sainte Geneviève*. Paris, 1899.

———. *Pour la Patrie*. Paris, 1912.

———. "Quelques mots d'explication." *L'Association Catholique* 29 (15 January 1891): brochure attached to the issue.

Mun, Antonin de. *Claude Adrien de Mun: Sa vie et son temps d'après sa correspondance avec le Baron Mounier, pair de France*. Paris, 1962.

Murphy, Agnes. *The Ideology of French Imperialism, 1871–1881*. Washington, D.C., 1948.

Néré, Jacques. *Le Boulangisme et la presse*. Paris, 1964.
Noland, Aaron. *The Founding of the French Socialist Party, 1893–1905*. Cambridge, Mass., 1956.
O'Donnell, J. Dean. "Cardinal Charles Lavigerie: The Politics of Getting a Red Hat." *Catholic Historical Review* 63 (April 1977): 185–203.
Oeuvre des Cercles Catholiques d'Ouvriers. *Assemblée générale de l'Oeuvre des Cercles Catholiques d'Ouvriers: Tenu à Paris les 25, 26, 27 janvier 1912 sous la présidence de M. le Comte Albert de Mun*. Paris, 1912.
———. *Bases et plan général de l'Oeuvre des Cercles Catholiques d'Ouvriers*. Paris, 1877.
———. *Règlement général des Cercles Catholiques d'Ouvriers de Paris*. Paris, 1875.
Offen, Karen Marie Stedfeld. "The Political Career of Paul de Cassagnac." Ph.D. dissertation, Stanford University, 1970.
Oraison, Marc. *Amour ou contrainte? Quelques aspects psychologiques de l'éducation religieuse*. Paris, 1957.
Osgood, Samuel M. *French Royalism under the Third and Fourth Republics*. The Hague, 1960.
Ozouf, Mona. *L'Ecole, l'Eglise et la République, 1871–1914*. Paris, 1963.
Padburg, John W., S.J. *Colleges in Controversy: The Jesuit Schools in France from Revival to Suppression, 1815–1880*. Cambridge, Mass., 1969.
Painter, George Duncan. *Marcel Proust: A Biography*. 2 vols. London, 1959–65.
Paléologue, Maurice. *Au Quai d'Orsay à la veille de la tourmente: Journal, 1913–1914*. Paris, 1947.
———. "Comment fut rétabli le service de trois ans." *Revue des Deux Mondes*, 8th period, 27 (1 May 1935): 67–94; (15 May 1935): 307–44.
Partin, Malcolm Overstreet. *Waldeck-Rousseau, Combes and the Church: The Politics of Anti-Clericalism, 1899–1905*. Durham, 1969.
Paul, Harry W. "In Quest of Kerygma: Catholic Intellectual Life in Nineteenth-Century France." *American Historical Review* 75 (December 1967): 387–423.
Paul-Boncour, Joseph. *Entre deux guerres: Souvenirs sur la IIIe République*. 3 vols. Paris, 1945–46.
Payen, Fernand. *Raymond Poincaré: L'Homme, le parlementaire, l'avocat*. 6th ed. Paris, 1936.
Phillips, Charles Stanley. *The Church in France, 1848–1907*. London, 1936.

Piou, Jacques. *Action Libérale Populaire*. Paris, 1902.

———. "L'Action Libérale Populaire." *Le Correspondant* 210 (25 March 1903): 1029–40.

———. "L'Action Libérale Populaire." *Revue Hebdomadaire* 22 (February 1910): 476–92.

———. "Le Boulangisme." *Revue de Paris*, 15 March 1932, pp. 301–20.

———. "Comment se défendre?" *Le Correspondant* 217 (10 October 1904): 3–19.

———. *Le Comte Albert de Mun: Sa vie publique*. Paris, [1925].

———. "Les Conservateurs et la démocratie." *Revue des Deux Mondes* 141 (15 June 1897): 787–806.

———. *D'une guerre à l'autre, 1871–1914*. Paris, 1932.

———. *Discours parlementaires, 1885–1909*. Paris, 1909.

———. *Les Elections de 1902*. Paris, 1902.

———. *Les Elections de 1906*. Paris, 1906.

———. *La Lutte pour la liberté*. Paris, 1903.

———. *L'Organisation pour la lutte électorale*. Paris, 1901.

———. *Questions religieuses et sociales*. Paris, 1910.

———. *Le Ralliement: Son histoire*. Paris, 1928.

———. *Le Rôle du patron*. Paris, 1903.

Pisani-Ferry, Fresnette. *Le Coup d'état manqué du 16 mai 1877*. Paris, 1965.

———. *Jules Ferry et le partage du monde*. Paris, 1962.

Poincaré, Raymond. *Au Service de la France: Neuf années de souvenirs*. 10 vols. Paris, 1926–33.

Poulat, Emile. *Histoire, dogme et critique dans la crise moderniste*. Paris, 1962.

———. *Intégrisme et catholicisme intégral: Un réseau secret international antimoderniste, la "Sapinière," 1909–1921*. Paris, 1969.

———. "Une enquête anticléricale de pratique religieuse en Seine-et-Marne 1903." *Archives de la Sociologie des Religions* 6 (July–December 1958): 127–48.

Power, Thomas F. *Jules Ferry and the Renaissance of French Imperialism*. New ed. New York, 1966.

Quillard, Pierre. *Le Monument Henry: Listes des souscripteurs*. Paris, 1899.

Radziwill, Maria Dorothea Elisabeth (née de Castellane). *Lettres de la Princesse Radziwill au Général de Robilant*. 4 vols. Bologna, 1933–34.

Ralston, David B. *The Army of the Republic: The Place of the Military in the Political Evolution of France, 1871–1914*. Cambridge, Mass., 1967.

Reclus, Maurice. *Grandeur de "La Troisième": De Gambetta à Poincaré.* Paris, 1948.

Reinach, Joseph. *Histoire de l'Affaire Dreyfus.* 7 vols. Paris, 1901–11.

Rémond, René. *La Droite en France: De la première restauration à la Ve République.* 2d ed. Paris, 1963.

Ribot, Alexandre. *Journal d'Alexandre Ribot et correspondances inédits, 1914–1922.* Paris, 1936.

———. *Lettres à un ami: Souvenirs de ma vie politique.* 7th ed. Paris, 1924.

Ridley, F. F. *Revolutionary Syndicalism in France: The Direct Action of Its Time.* New York, 1970.

Rivain, Jean. *Un programme de restauration sociale: La Tour du Pin.* Paris, 1926.

Rollet, Henri. *L'Action sociale des catholiques en France, 1871–1914.* 2 vols. Paris, 1947–58.

———. *Albert de Mun et le parti catholique.* Paris, 1949.

Roquefeuil, Félix de. *Résumé des principes de l'Oeuvre des Cercles Catholiques d'Ouvriers sur le régime du travail dans l'ordre social chrétien.* Paris, 1883.

Roquefeuil, Robert de. *L'Histoire de l'Oeuvre des Cercles.* Paris, n.d.

Rothney, John. *Bonapartism after Sedan.* Ithaca, 1969.

Rumeau, Monsigneur Joseph. *M. le Comte Albert de Mun: Allocution prononcée par Mgr. Rumeau, évêque d'Angers, dans l'église Saint-Joseph, le dimanche 15 novembre, à une messe célébrée par les soins du Comité des Cercles Catholiques d'Ouvriers.* Angers, 1914.

Rummel, Leo L. "The Anti-Clerical Program as a Disruptive Factor in the Solidarity of the Late French Republics." *Catholic Historical Review* 53 (April 1957): 126–37.

Samuel, René, and Bonet-Maury, Georges, eds. *Les Parlementaires français, 1901–1914.* Paris, 1914.

Schmidt, Martin E. *Alexandre Ribot: Odyssey of a Liberal in the Third Republic.* The Hague, 1974.

Scott, Joan Wallach. *The Glassworkers of Carmaux: French Craftsmen and Political Action in a Nineteenth-Century City.* Cambridge, Mass., 1974.

Seager, Frederic H. *The Boulanger Affair: Political Crossroad of France, 1886–1889.* Ithaca, 1969.

Sedgwick, Alexander Cameron. *The Ralliement in French Politics, 1890–1898.* Cambridge, Mass., 1965.

Shapiro, David, ed. *The Right in France, 1890–1919: Three Studies.* St. Anthony's Papers, vol. 13. London, 1962.

Shattuck, Roger. *The Banquet Years: The Origins of the Avant-Garde in France, 1885 to World War I.* Rev. ed. New York, 1968.

Siegfried, André. *Tableau des partis en France*. Paris, 1930.

———. *Tableau politique de la France de l'ouest sous la Troisième République*. Paris, 1913.

Soltau, Roger Henry. *French Parties and Politics*. London, 1930.

Sorel, Georges. *Réflexions sur la violence*. Paris, 1908.

Sorlin, Pierre. *"La Croix" et les juifs, 1880–1899: Contribution à l'histoire de l'antisémitisme contemporain*. Paris, 1967.

———. *Waldeck-Rousseau*. Paris, 1966.

Spencer, Philip Herbert. *The Politics of Belief in Nineteenth-Century France: Lacordaire, Michon, Veuillot*. New York, 1954.

Spronck, Maurice. " 'L'Esprit nouveau' des révolutionnaires: Un théoricien du syndicalisme, M. Georges Sorel." *Le Correspondant* 234 (10 January 1909): 35–64.

———. "Le ler mai et l'état-major de la CGT." *Le Correspondant* 243 (10 May 1911): 417–45.

Stearns, Peter N. *Revolutionary Syndicalism and French Labor: A Cause without Rebels*. New Brunswick, 1971.

Suarez, Georges. *Briand: Sa vie, son oeuvre, avec son journal et de nombreux documents inédits*. 6 vols. Paris, 1938–52.

Sumler, David Edmund. "Domestic Influences on the Nationalist Revival in France, 1909–1914." *French Historical Studies* 6 (Fall 1970): 517–37.

———. "Polarization in French Politics, 1909–1914." Ph.D. dissertation, Princeton University, 1969.

Swart, Koenraad Wolter Stuart. *The Sense of Decadence in Nineteenth-Century France*. The Hague, 1964.

Talmy, Robert. *Albert de Mun*. Paris, 1965.

———. *Aux sources du catholicisme social: L'Ecole de La Tour du Pin*. Tournai, 1963.

———. "L'Ecole de La Tour du Pin et l'encyclique Rerum Novarum." Principal Thesis, Doctorat en théologie, Institut Catholique de Lille, 1953.

———. *René de La Tour du Pin*. Paris, 1964.

———. *Le Syndicalisme chrétien en France, 1871–1930: Difficultés et controverses*. Paris, 1966.

———. *Une forme hybride du catholicisme social en France: L'Association Catholique des Patrons du Nord, 1884–1895*. Lille, 1962.

Tannenbaum, Edward R. *The Action Française: Die-Hard Reactionaries in Twentieth-Century France*. New York, 1962.

Thomson, David. *Democracy in France: The Third Republic*. New York, 1946.

Tint, Herbert L. *The Decline of French Patriotism, 1870–1940*. London, 1966.

———. "The Search for a Laic Morality under the French Third Republic: Renouvier and the *Critique Philosophique*." *Sociological Review*, New Series 5 (July 1957): 5–26.

Tournier, Joseph. *Le Cardinal Lavigerie et son action politique, 1863–1892*. Paris, 1913.

T'Serclaes de Wommerson, Charles de. *Le Pape Léon XIII: Sa vie, son action religieuse, politique, et sociale*. 2 vols. Lille, 1894.

Tuchman, Barbara W. *The Proud Tower: A Portrait of the World before the War, 1890–1914*. New York, 1966.

Vassili, Count Paul [Ekaterina Radziwill (née Rzewuska)]. *France from behind the Veil: Fifty Years of Social and Political Life*. New York, 1915.

Verdès, Jeannine. "La Presse devant le krach d'une banque catholique: L'Union Générale." *Archives de la Sociologie des Religions* 19 (January–June 1965): 125–56.

Verly, Albert. *Le Général Boulanger et la conspiration monarchique*. Paris, 1893.

Veuillot, Eugène. *Louis Veuillot*. 4 vols. Paris, 1901–13.

Villoteau, Pierre. *La Vie parisienne à la Belle Epoque*. Paris, 1968.

Ward, James E. "The Algiers Toast: Lavigerie's Work or Leo XIII's?" *Catholic Historical Review* 51 (July 1965): 173–91.

———. "Cardinal Place and Leo XIII's Ralliement Policy." *Catholic Historical Review* 57 (January 1972): 606–28.

———. "Cardinal Richard versus Cardinal Lavigerie: Episcopal Resistance to the Ralliement." *Catholic Historical Review* 53 (October 1967): 346–71.

———. "The French Cardinals and Leo XIII's Ralliement Policy." *Church History* 33 (March 1964): 60–73.

Watson, David Robin. *Georges Clemenceau: A Political Biography*. London, 1974.

Weber, Eugen. *The Action Française: Royalism and Reaction in Twentieth-Century France*. Stanford, 1962.

———. "Inheritance and Dilettantism: The Politics of Maurice Barrès." *Historical Reflections* 2 (Summer 1975): 109–31.

———. "Nationalism, Socialism, and National-Socialism in France." *French Historical Studies* 2 (Spring 1962): 273–307.

———. *The Nationalist Revival in France, 1905–1914*. Berkeley and Los Angeles, 1959.

———. *Peasants into Frenchmen: The Modernization of Rural France, 1870–1914*. Stanford, 1976.

———. "Le Renouveau nationaliste en France et le glissement vers le droit, 1905–1914." *Revue d'Histoire Moderne et Contemporaine* 5 (January–March 1958): 114–28.

———. "The Right in France: A Working Hypothesis." *American Historical Review* 65 (April 1960): 554–68.

———. "Some Comments on the Nature of the Nationalist Revival in France before 1914." *International Review of Social History* 3 (1958): 220–38.

———. "Un demi-siècle de glissement à droite." *International Review of Social History* 5 (1960): 165–201.

Weill, Georges Jacques. *Histoire de l'idée laïque en France au XIXe siècle*. New ed. Paris, 1929.

———. *Histoire du catholicisme libéral en France, 1828–1908*. Paris, 1909.

———. *Histoire du mouvement social en France, 1852–1902*. Paris, 1904.

Williamson, Samuel Ruthven. *The Politics of Grand Strategy: Britain and France Prepare for War, 1904–1914*. Cambridge, Mass., 1969.

Winnacker, R. A. "The Bloc and the Délégation des Gauches." Ph.D. dissertation, Harvard University, 1933.

———. "The Délégation des Gauches." *Journal of Modern History* 9 (December 1937): 449–70.

Wright, Gordon. *Raymond Poincaré and the French Presidency*. Stanford, 1942.

———. *Rural Revolution in France: The Peasantry in the Twentieth Century*. Stanford, 1964.

Wyndham, George. *Life and Letters*. Edited by J. W. MacNeil and Guy Wyndham. 2 vols. London, n.d.

Zeldin, Theodore, ed. *Conflicts in French Society: Anticlericalism, Education, and Morals in the Nineteenth Century*. St. Anthony's Papers, vol. 1. London, 1970.

———. *France, 1848–1945*. 2 vols. Oxford, 1973–77.

Ziebura, Gilbert. *Die deutsche Frage in der öffentlichen Meinung Frankreichs von 1911–1914*. Berlin, 1955.

Index

P

R

THE AUTHOR

Benjamin F. Martin is assistant professor of history at West Virginia Wesleyan College.

THE BOOK

Typeface: Sabon

Design and composition: The University of North Carolina Press

Paper: #60 Warren's Olde Style by S. D. Warren

Binding cloth: Roxite B 51544 Vellum
by The Holliston Mills, Inc.

Printer and binder: Vail-Ballou Press

Published by The University of North Carolina Press